POWER OVER THE BODY,
EQUALITY IN THE FAMILY

EMORY UNIVERSITY STUDIES IN LAW AND RELIGION

John Witte Jr., General Editor

BOOKS IN THE SERIES

POWER OVER THE BODY, EQUALITY IN THE FAMILY

Rights and Domestic Relations in Medieval Canon Law

Charles J. Reid Jr.

William B. Eerdmans Publishing Company
Grand Rapids, Michigan / Cambridge, U.K.

Wm. B. Eerdmans Publishing Co.
255 Jefferson Ave. S.E., Grand Rapids, Michigan 49503 /
P.O. Box 163, Cambridge CB3 9PU U.K.

Printed in the United States of America

09 08 07 06 05 04   7 6 5 4 3 2 1

ISBN 0-8028-2211-8

www.eerdmans.com

This volume is dedicated with love
to the memory of my parents,
Victoria Wozniak Reid
and
Charles J. Reid Sr.

Contents

Acknowledgments

This book was inspired by graduate work I undertook with Professor Brian Tierney of the Cornell University Department of History and my earlier undergraduate studies with Professor James A. Brundage, now of the University of Kansas but formerly of the University of Wisconsin-Milwaukee. It was Professor Tierney who interested me in the medieval, canonistic origins of the western rights tradition. And it was Dr. Brundage who first interested me in the history of medieval marriage. This work, a synthesis of my early training with both men, owes much to their lessons. I express my thanks to both of them.

I must also thank colleagues of mine at the two universities where I have taught since completing graduate study at Cornell University. Harold Berman of the Emory University School of Law has been a helpful and guiding presence in my academic life. His penetrating way of asking questions has been another influence on my own work. And John Witte, also of Emory Law School, took an early and enthusiastic interest in this project. John's work on marriage law and his curiosity about the substructure of the medieval canonistic synthesis are major reasons for this book bearing the imprint of William B. Eerdmans Publishing Company. To Hal and to John, I give my heartfelt thanks. I must also thank my other friends and colleagues at Emory University, especially the members of the Law and Religion Program. Martha Duncan and Rich Freer were also the source of many stimulating conversations.

I must also acknowledge a great debt to my friends and colleagues at the University of St. Thomas School of Law, where I presently teach. My thanks, of course, first of all, to those responsible for opening a new law school in Minneapolis–St. Paul, dedicated to an understanding of the law as essentially moral and religious in character. My thanks also to Tom Mengler, dean of the University of St. Thomas School of Law, and to Patrick Schiltz and Neil Hamilton, who have provided much support in their capacity as associate deans. My colleagues on the faculty have provided me with enormous stimulation and friendship. Space does not allow me to name each of them individually — but I have gratitude toward them all. My students, also, have been a source of intellectual stimulation with their many questions.

Library resources are essential to a project of this sort. I must acknowledge in a special way the services I have received from four libraries. Johns Hopkins University's Milton Eisenhower Library, and the Eisenhower Library's resident guru about all things medieval, Thomas Izbicki, provided important resources at a crucial stage of the project. The University of Minnesota School of Law Rare Books Room was also helpful. Emory University Law School Library also provided invaluable services — my thanks to Robin Mills, Pam Deemer, and Will Haines of the Emory Library.

But one must truly single out for service above and beyond the call of duty the staff of the University of St. Thomas Law Library. Ed Edmonds, Director of the Library, has been invariably prompt and helpful in answering questions. And the rest of the staff has been outstanding. Rick Goheen, Becky Iserman, Tricia Kemp, Mary Wells, Margie Axtmann, Jason Gravink, and others have provided truly yeoman help. Becky and Tricia, who invariably met my insatiable demands for interlibrary loan material with good humor, must be especially thanked. Paddy Satzer, also of the St. Thomas Law Library staff, has prepared the index and the bibliography that are found in this volume.

I have also received outstanding academic and administrative support. Nora Fitzpatrick invariably smiles and greets me warmly whenever I knock on her door to ask whether I might trouble her yet again with another question. Margaret McDowell, my administrative assistant, has provided me with the organizational support that makes the difference between success and failure. Barbara Sauer and Luann Hudson also pitched in where necessary. Nancy Knaak of the Emory University Law School also provided valuable academic support, as did Merita Sapp Craddock and Cynthia Jordan at various times. My student research assistant, Christopher R. Pavlak, also provided assistance in collecting references for the bibliography.

A portion of chapter three was presented at the fall, 2002, gathering of the Medieval Academy of the Midwest, at St. Norbert's University in Green Bay, Wisconsin. My thanks to my old Cornell classmate, Dr. Bill

Hyland, for organizing this conference, and for the insights I gleaned from discussion with other medievalists. Earlier versions of portions of several chapters have appeared in several different venues. These include: "So It Will Be Found That the Rights of Women in Many Cases Are of Diminished Condition: Rights and the Legal Equality of Men and Women in Twelfth- and Thirteenth-Century Canon Law," *Loyola (Los Angeles) Law Review* 35 (2002): 471-512; "Thirteenth-Century Canon Law and Rights: The Word *Ius* and Its Range of Subjective Meanings," *Studia Canonica* 30 (1996): 295-342; and "The Canonistic Contribution to the Western Rights Tradition: An Historical Inquiry," *Boston College Law Review* 33 (1991): 37-92. I acknowledge the permission of the copyright holders and thank them.

By academic custom, thanks to one's family members are always reserved for last. I must especially thank my wife, Cheryl Lynn Thorgaard Reid, for her quiet but strong support. Caroline Victoria Reid, our five-year-old daughter, has been a light at the end of many long days. And I must also acknowledge the formative role of my parents, to whom this book is dedicated: my mother, Victoria Wozniak Reid, a daughter of Polish immigrants, inculcated in me a love of the Church, which remains with me to this day; and my father, Charles J. Reid Sr., a self-taught man and a voracious reader of all things historical, gave me a deep and abiding love for the study of the events and ideas of the past.

Introduction

Marriage in Modern Legal Parlance

This book is about marriage. But it focuses on what might seem a very odd way of thinking about marriage. Those who view marriage from a secular viewpoint, and even many who appreciate the sacral and religious dimensions of marriage, are accustomed to seeing it as grounded and governed exclusively by the love of the parties. Love, of course, is a good thing. But modern secular law also sees such love as a fleeting thing, a transitory phenomenon that can die, or be betrayed, or otherwise lost. Where love dies, the modern view holds, the marriage itself may well be dead. Love is whimsical, it is light-hearted, it is oriented toward self-fulfillment. Less often is love thought of as sacrificial, or as requiring conscious self-denial.

The proposition that the continuing free consent of both parties to the marital relationship is what makes the marriage is perhaps the best expression of the modern viewpoint. The idea that one or another of the parties might have enduring rights in such a relationship is incompatible with a vision of marriage that depends upon the continuing ratification of both parties for its viability. The marriage contract has thus become in contemporary legal analysis terminable at the will of either party, thus reducing it to a lesser status than any other type of contract.[1] The widespread availability and acceptance of no-fault divorce have only cemented in the popular imagination the proposition that marriages are temporary arrangements, terminable when one or the other party decides, for whatever reason, that the union is beyond repair.

The belief that marriage is ultimately a matter for the continuing free consent of the parties is powerfully reflected in modern legal conceptions of the family. The Supreme Court's 1972 decision declaring distinctions

- 1 -

drawn between married and unmarried persons in the area of human reproduction to be constitutionally infirm under the Equal Protection Clause
typifies the lack of special status accorded the marital contract.[2] There is
very little room on this analysis to see marriage as a distinctive community
worthy of protection in its own right.[3] Indeed, if one wishes to frame this
problem in terms of rights, what we have witnessed is the triumph of a notion of individual rights at the expense of a deeper sense of marital rights
that were conceived of as reflecting basic social goods and that embodied as
well continuing obligations toward other members of the family unit.

The modern secular view of marriage as resting principally on the
continuing affection and consent of both parties is a particular manifestation of a kind of philosophical liberalism that sees in the marital relationship merely an aggregation of individual interests. These interests might
sometimes be expressed in terms of rights. Thus a landmark Hawaiian case
ruling on equal protection grounds in favor of gay couples seeking the right
to marry one another defined the marital relationship primarily in terms of
the economic rights accruing to married parties. Marriage was, according
to the Court, a pooling of financial resources and individual initiative and
conferred on those enjoying marital status considerable economic benefit.[4]

Not only courts, but scholars, too, have argued on behalf of individual rights and against a traditional understanding of marriage and the family. Writing in 1981, Lenore Weitzman thus denounced "the traditional
marriage contract" as a socially oppressive institution.[5] This contract was
patriarchal in its demands and served "as the legal instrument for the subjugation of women."[6] Weitzman proposed abandonment of the traditional
understanding in favor of a broad-based contractual approach that "would
facilitate the freedom of married and unmarried couples to order their personal relationships as they wish and to devise a structure appropriate for
their individual needs and values."[7]

Commentators on domestic relationships have also challenged the
primacy of parents in the upbringing and education of children, often sub-
stituting for parental norms the proceduralist values of the liberal state or,
again, a contractarian model.[8] Bruce Ackerman has maintained that a central purpose of liberal education is to equip children with the means of
questioning parental legitimacy and allowing them "to define [their] own
objectives in the light of the universal culture defined by all humankind."[9]
Patricia White has argued for the banishment of religious values from education as anti-democratic in principle.[10] Yet another commentator has proposed that governance of the household should be subjected to a

"contractarian approach" along the lines of "a democratic governance model."[11] Such a model "is highly compatible with our current tendency to view the family as a fluid set of relationships based on voluntary association as well as on status."[12]

This secularized, highly individualistic view of marriage and the family and the rights of parties within those relationships has had an enormous impact on the shape that the American law of domestic relations has assumed over the last several decades.[13] It nevertheless clashes with some other strongly held popular beliefs about marital relationships. It clashes particularly with our instinctive sense that marriage should be about community formation: the parties to a marriage should not be pursuing purely egoistic interests, but should be engaged in meeting one another's needs and providing for the upbringing of their offspring. Some modern critics have appreciated the dimensions of this problem. Writing from a secular perspective, Judith Younger has decried the quest for autonomy and self-gratification within personal relationships which puts at risk the relationships' more vulnerable members.[14]

But must it be one extreme or the other: a traditional life of "subjugation," on the one hand, or a life of liberation defined only by the limits of one's imagination and appetites and given content by the freedom to make and unmake personal relationships at will? Does the marital relationship itself, the union of two persons for better or worse, possess rights? How are the vulnerable members of the family unit to be protected?

Recent Catholic writers have sought to address these theoretical issues by calling renewed attention to the obligations attendant upon the marital relationship. A publication of the Pontifical Council of the Family has taught the indispensability of self-sacrifice to a successful marriage: all Christians are called to living the Love of the Paschal mystery in their own lives. Reflecting on this document, Rodolfo and María Valdes have written:

> [A]nd [if] love is self-giving, then we do not grow in life or in love without sacrifice and without painfully shattering our selfishness. This is the meaning of the Paschal mystery in married life: Christ calls us to a life that is love, self-giving, and there is no love or giving without overcoming the sin which keeps us prisoners in ourselves. There is no growth in love without that pain.[15]

Nor is this publication alone in its teaching. John Kippley stresses the importance of "covenant" to marriage: "With their minds and with their wills, [spouses] have irrevocably committed themselves to each other in marriage."[16] This unity leads to assumption of a variety of responsibilities toward the other partner and with respect to the demands of the natural law.[17] Cormac Burke has written in a similar vein: "[E]arth is not heaven. Love on earth is seldom easy; and if it is easy for a time, the easiness does not tend to last."[18] A work of pastoral advice similarly admonishes married couples that:

> Practically speaking, being partners in Christian identity means that when your spouse asks for more from you, you are obliged to give it, not necessarily because your spouse deserves such generosity (we so seldom deserve to be loved), but because you have a responsibility to God to demonstrate that generosity.[19]

One of the most important examples of this recent body of scholarship is Donald Asci's *The Conjugal Act as a Personal Act*.[20] Asci stresses that "[t]he physical union of husband and wife in the conjugal act symbolizes the personal union they achieve through 'a total personal self-giving, in which the whole person, including the temporal dimension, is present.'"[21] Asci, however, also stresses the importance of "freedom as theonomy" — the obligation freely to choose to follow the dictates of God's law as inscribed in man's heart.[22] "Human freedom," Asci makes clear:

> is the ability to undertake the existential development of one's identity, the ability to be the source of one's growth in maturity by responding to vocation to love. . . . [F]reedom gives man the ability to accept his identity in his actions under the guidance of God's law.[23]

This renewed focus on marital obligation is a most welcome antidote to some threatening trends in popular as well as legal culture.[24] It is not our purpose to criticize it. Indeed, when wedded to a commitment to a properly defined notion of human freedom, as articulated by a writer like Asci, it comes very close to the medieval synthesis that is described in this volume.

There is a risk, however, that by focusing on obligation alone, an important traditional Catholic mode of viewing marriage might come to be overlooked. It is important to realize that Catholic writers, as early as the twelfth century and as recently as the rotal judges of the last two decades, have described marriage in terms of explicitly enumerated rights and duties incumbent upon all those who entered matrimony. This notion of marital rights, it must be stressed, did not presuppose the kind of individualism taken for granted in modern secular society but, rather, reflected a sacramental, community-minded notion of marriage. It reflected the proper exercise of human freedom, within the constraints of the natural law. Marriage, in the classic formulation, exists for the good of the spouses and the procreation and upbringing of children and no canonist ever thought to question that formulation.

In *Arcanum Divinae Sapientiae*, "The Secret of Divine Wisdom," an encyclical widely taken as the starting point of modern papal analysis of the sacrament of marriage, Pope Leo XIII (reigned 1878-1903) explained that the marital right *(ius matrimonii)* itself comprised a bundle of interlocking rights and duties. Man and woman, Leo noted, have certain rights which are fundamentally equal *(aequabile)* among all persons. These rights were established, Leo claimed, for the sake of mutual benevolence and the protection of the dignity of women.[25]

The father, Leo observed, remained the chief of his family and, literally, the "head" *(caput)* of his wife, but this was not an authority to be used abusively. After all, husband and wife have become one flesh, and so husband and wife should be united as "associates" *(sociae),* not as master and subordinate.[26] A husband was thus forbidden to commit adultery or otherwise violate the faith he had pledged.[27] Indeed, Christian marriage differed fundamentally from pagan marriage, in which the mutual rights and duties of the spouses were greatly disturbed and men came with impunity to dominate their wives.[28]

Children, furthermore, while subject to parental authority, were also to be treated with love and educated in the path of the virtues.[29] However great paternal power happened to be, Leo declared on behalf of the Church, it should be limited to ensure that the "just liberty" of sons and daughters not be diminished.[30] Christian revelation, as explicated by the Church, decisively repudiated the potential for parental abuse, and even the paternal power of life and death over one's children that one sometimes saw in ancient pagan societies.

The protection of rights and liberties, Leo continued, was not only important within marriage but also in the process of marital formation. Offspring possessed the liberty *(libertas)* to choose a marital partner, a right that the Church safeguarded with rules such as its prohibition on the use of force and fear in the process of marital formation.[31]

Leo returned to the theme of marital rights in his subsequent encyclical *Rerum Novarum*, which was addressed to the pressing economic disparities of the time and was intended to set out the rights of labor. Fearing the rise of totalitarian claims upon the human person, Leo proclaimed that all persons enjoy certain fundamental rights, in virtue of their personhood and independent of state authority. Among these rights was "the natural and primeval right of marriage," which was conferred by God upon all persons and is prior to the state.[32] The family thus created constituted its own "true society," more ancient than the state, to which certain further rights and duties pertained, such as the right of its members to own property, and the right as well as the duty of the head of household — the *paterfamilias* — to provide for his children.[33]

Leo has recently been taken to task for his use of rights language in *Rerum Novarum*,[34] but he was far from alone among nineteenth- and early twentieth-century canonists and theologians in relying on rights language to describe the marital relationship. Pietro Gasparri, architect of the 1917 Code of Canon Law, proposed that the formal object of the matrimonial contract was the establishment of a common way of life (*consuetudo vitae*), which has at its heart the mutual right of intercourse (*ius coeundi mutuum*).[35] This right, Gasparri noted, was perpetual, exclusive, and ordered to the procreation and education of children.[36] Not surprisingly, the 1917 Code, the edifice Gasparri built, reiterated this idea, declaring that from the very beginning of the marital relationship husband and wife enjoyed the equal right and duty to engage in acts proper to the conjugal life, by which was meant sexual intercourse.[37]

Classic commentaries on the 1917 Code echoed this understanding of marital rights. Wernz and Vidal organized their treatment of "The Effects Arising from Marriage" into sections on the rights and duties spouses have toward each other and toward their children. Marriage itself was defined as a mutual handing over of the right to the body of each other for purposes of generation.[38] This handing over in turn gave rise to the equal right of each party to claim the conjugal debt, which correlated exactly with an obligation "in strict justice" to render it unless excused for a just cause.[39]

Felix Capello, writing after World War II, elaborated on this general idea, proposing that the formal object of the marital contract was "an individuated way of life, or mutual, perpetual, and exclusive right to the body."[40] This form of reasoning was continued in the *Dictionary of Moral Theology*, issued under the direction of Francesco Cardinal Roberti on the eve of the Second Vatican Council. "Marriage," the dictionary taught, "is a bilateral contract by which a man and a woman give and reciprocally receive a perpetual and exclusive right to each other's body for the perfor-

mance of those actions which, of their very nature, are directed to the procreation of children."[41]

The idea of a marital right has remained alive and well until very recent times in rotal jurisprudence. In the years immediately after the Second
Vatican Council, the Holy Roman Rota — a kind of Roman "Supreme
Court" which serves as the final authority on the substantive issues of marriage law — proposed expanding the content of the rights exchanged at the
marriage ceremony to include not only a right to the body of one's marital
partner, but also "a right and obligation to an intimate community of
life."[42] Imported into this expanded sense of mutual rights was an evolving
notion of conjugal love that took account of the psychic and spiritual needs
of the parties, in addition to the traditional understanding of the marital
contract as looking chiefly to the exchange of rights "to the body."[43]

Canonists made productive use of this concept throughout the 1970s
and 1980s.[44] The notion of a right to a community of life became a part of
the draft version of what would become the revised 1983 Code of Canon
Law, although this terminology was omitted from the final product.[45] In a
sense, the rotal judges of the time were attempting to give juridic force to a
very old concept drawn from Roman law — the idea that marriage itself
was a *consortium omnis vitae* — a "companionship of one's entire life."[46]

Rotal decisions of the 1970s and 1980s employed this ancient language and grafted it on to the traditional rights vocabulary used by canonists to describe the marital relationship. In the process, they reversed the
traditional tendency to equate a common way of life solely with the right to
sexual intercourse. Marriage, the rotal judges declared, involved a right by
the parties to a true *consortium omnis vitae*. Thus the decision *coram
Serrano*, May 9, 1980, declared that the formal object of the matrimonial
contract included not only a right to acts appropriate to procreation, but
also embraced a legally cognizable right to a consortium or community of
life that included correlative rights and obligations of intimacy and togetherness by which the parties sought to perfect each other and to provide for
the upbringing of their children.[47] In this way, a very medieval way of
thinking about marriage which explained matrimony as a series of interlocking rights and duties was employed to give legal effect to recent psychological and theological insights about the nature of marital affection.

This religiously grounded vision of marriage as an institution derived
in some way from natural law and oriented to social goods as well as the
good of the parties is also reflected in American legal opinions and legal
commentaries until the early twentieth century. At the dawn of the Ameri-

can legal tradition, Chancellor James Kent of New York, one of the most important founders of American jurisprudence, declared with respect to the fundamental elements of marriage law that "[t]he principles of canonical jurisprudence, and the rules of the common law, are the same. . . ."[48]

The natural law governed matrimonial relationships, Kent declared, and "by the law of nature, I understand those fit and just rules of conduct which the Creator has prescribed to man, as a dependent and social being; and which are to be ascertained from the deductions of right reason, though they may be more precisely known, and more explicitly declared by divine revelation."[49] The mere fact that in America marriage disputes fell to courts of temporal jurisdiction to decide did not mean that a judge was free to disregard the Christian understanding of marriage: "Are the principles of natural law, and of Christian duty, to be left unheeded, and inoperative, because we have no ecclesiastical courts recognized by law, as specially charged with the cognizance of such matters?"[50]

This view of marriage as originating in the dimension of the natural and the sacred is found as well in judicial decisions from throughout the nineteenth century. The United States Supreme Court, writing in 1890, declared: "Marriage, while from its very nature a sacred obligation is, nevertheless, in most civilized countries a civil contract, and usually regulated by law. Upon it society may be said to be built, and out of its fruits spring social relations and social obligations and duties. . . ."[51] "Marriage," the High Court declared in 1888, was responsible for "creating the most important relation in life . . . having more to do with the morals and civilization of a people than any other institution. . . ."[52]

Not only the Supreme Court, but courts of the various states taught much the same doctrine with respect to the transcendent importance of marriage. In the year 1900, the Maryland Court of Appeals wrote: "The rights and obligations of [marriage] are fixed by society in accordance with principles of natural law, and are beyond and above the parties themselves."[53] Indeed, the institution of marriage itself, the Maryland Court reiterated: "has its origin in the natural law and is the foundation of society."[54] The Alabama Supreme Court wrote in 1869:

> Marriage is a divine institution and, although in some respects it may partake of the nature and character of ordinary contracts, it has, with few exceptions, always been considered as standing upon higher and holier grounds than any secular contracts. By a large portion of the Christian world it is believed, and held, to be a sacrament, and is rever-

enced and treated as such. Our Blessed Savior says, "a man shall leave his father and mother and cleave to his wife, and the twain shall be one flesh."[55]

Commentators on the law of marriage expressed similar sentiments regarding marriage's sacred character. Joseph Story (1779-1845), Supreme Court justice and early expounder on the principles of American law, wrote regarding marriage:

> Marriage is treated by all civilized nations as a peculiar and favored contract. It is in its origin a contract of natural law. It may exist between two individuals of different sexes, although no third person existed in the world, as happened in the case of the common ancestors of mankind. It is the parent and not the child of society; *principium urbis et quasi seminarium reipublicae.* . . . In most civilized countries, acting under a sense of the force of sacred obligations, it has had the sanctions of religion superadded. It then becomes a religious, as well as a natural, and civil contract. . . .[56]

Ninety years later, in 1921, in the sixth edition of Schouler's treatise on domestic relations law, one finds a similar sentiment reiterated:

> It has been frequently said in the courts of this country that marriage is nothing more than a civil contract. That it is a contract is doubtless true to a certain extent. . . . But this agreement differs essentially from all others. The rights and obligations of that status are fixed by society in accordance with principles of natural law, and are beyond and above the parties themselves.[57]

The matrimonial relationship, furthermore, served to promote clearly defined ends, or goals. Quoting from an English case, Joel Prentiss Bishop, an important systematizer and commentator on American law,[58] wrote: "[T]he law recognizes these two as its 'principal ends': namely, 'a lawful indulgence of the passions to prevent licentiousness, and the procreation of children, according to the evident design of Divine Providence.'"[59]

Indeed, nineteenth-century courts and commentators continued to conceptualize marriage in the framework St. Augustine first established in the waning days of the Roman empire. Marriage, the case law makes clear, sought to conserve three great goods — the procreation and education of offspring, fidelity between the parties, and lifelong unity. Courts rarely, if ever, cited St. Augustine directly. Rather, they operated in a mental universe shaped by the medieval lawyers who reduced St. Augustine's theology to juridic form and by the early modern Anglican canonists, who transmitted these ideas to modern Anglo-American law.[60]

Nineteenth-century lawyers and judges not only conceived of marriage as originating in naturalistic premises and serving ends defined by the natural law,[61] they also spoke of rights and duties derivable from such premises of which the parties could not divest themselves. Writing of the relationship brought into being by marriage, the Rhode Island Supreme Court announced: "In strictness though formed by contract, [marriage] signifies the relation of husband and wife, deriving both its rights and duties from a source higher than any contract of which the parties are capable. . . ."[62]

These rights and duties were labeled by the lawyers and judges as "conjugal." They were "rights [that] have always been recognized in civilized society."[63] Conjugal rights involved principally the right to the sexual act. These rights endured so long as the marriage itself endured, even "though the husband by his fault is living apart from his wife, and leading a dissolute life."[64] In England, early American courts acknowledged, such desertion by the husband would open the door to "a suit for a restitution of conjugal rights."[65] Because of the absence of ecclesiastical courts in America, however, some courts concluded that the more appropriate remedy for such abandonment was statutory divorce.[66] Because courts conceptualized conjugal rights as valuable property, they were also willing to entertain suits for alienation of affection that sought to recover monetary damages from third parties who insinuated themselves into the marital relationship.[67]

Indeed, abandonment of one's spouse and other forms of marital misconduct were the typical venues in which conjugal rights were asserted.[68] Efforts to seduce women were considered crimes against marital rights. In an opinion that justified a husband's failed attempt to shoot his wife's seducer, the Court flamboyantly pronounced: "The wife cannot surrender herself to another. It is treason against the conjugal rights. Dirty dollars will not compensate for a breach of the nuptial vow."[69]

Conjugal rights, however, were also held to encompass more than a mere right to the body of the other spouse. Explicating the foundation of suits for alienation of marital affection, the Missouri Supreme Court wrote that "[A]t common law the wife certainly had the right to the affection, comfort, and society of her husband."[70] Where a husband "refuses to love and cherish his wife, and excludes her from his heart, and gives his love to another woman,"[71] he thereby deprives her "of every substantial conjugal right."[72]

Perhaps surprisingly, this approach to marriage and domestic relations, redolent of natural law and canonistic categories of thought, retains some vitality even today. A vocabulary of natural rights and natural law continues to color at least one area of modern domestic relations law — the right of offspring to seek support and sustenance from their parents. The relationship of parent and child has been described as deriving its force from natural law.[73] As recently as 2002, William Blackstone was quoted by the Maryland Court of Appeals in support of the contention that "'the duty of parents to provide for the maintenance of their children, is a principle of natural law; an obligation [. . .] laid on them not only by nature herself, but by their own proper act, in bringing them into the world.'"[74] In 1998, the California Supreme Court, in rejecting an argument that a work requirement imposed on a parent violated the Thirteenth Amendment, wrote:

> The obligation of a parent to support a child, and to become employed if that is necessary to meet the obligation, is in no way comparable or akin to peonage or slavery. It is among the most fundamental obligations recognized by modern society. The duty is not simply one imposed by statute, but "rests on fundamental natural laws and has always been recognized by the courts in the absence of any statute declaring it."[75]

The purpose of this volume is to explore the historical foundations of this way of thinking and speaking about the marital relationship. American lawyers and judges were hardly the first to speak in a vocabulary of conjugal rights or duties arising from natural obligations. This vocabulary has deep roots in Western notions of marital relations. This volume explores how a language of rights came to be grafted, at a very early date in Western history, onto the idea of marriage.

The ancient world, for the most part, did not think of marriage in terms of legally enforceable rights and duties. To focus for the moment on the legal system that made significant contributions to the shaping of canon law: Roman law certainly grounded marriage on the requirement that parties give consent, but this idea of consent did not correlate with any belief in the right to select one's spouse free of outside interference. Similarly, the notion of a right to conjugal relations — a dominant mode of thinking in medieval juristic writings — seems to have been unknown to the Roman world. Roman law, to be sure, recognized the existence of some marital rights. Fathers in the Roman Republic, for instance, had a nearly unlimited legal power over their children, but it was the canonists who developed the idea of a *ius patriapotestatis* — "a right of paternal power" — in new and sophisticated ways.

To understand how the juristic world of the high Middle Ages transformed ancient ways of thinking and speaking about marriage, however, one must appreciate the new significance conferred on the notion of individual rights in the jurisprudence of the twelfth and thirteenth centuries. This new significance will be taken up in the third part of this Introduction. First, however, the question must be answered: Why focus on the twelfth and thirteenth centuries?

Origins and Development of Medieval Canon Law

The twelfth and thirteenth centuries have not been selected arbitrarily. Rather they have been singled out because of their fundamental contributions to the shape of the entire Western legal tradition.

The late eleventh century was a time of revolutionary significance.[76] The revolution that shook the last quarter of this century, led by churchmen such as Pope Gregory VII, was opposed to the lay dominance of the Catholic Church, and gave birth to a new, systematic approach to legal issues, both inside and outside the boundaries of the ecclesiastical order. The emergence of an authoritative or normative body of canon law beginning in the twelfth century was a product of these developments.[77]

This "scientific" or systematic form of canon law can be said to have emerged in about the year 1140 with the appearance of a work formally entitled *The Concord of Discordant Canons* (*Concordia Discordantium Canonum*), but typically called the *Decretum* ("The Decree").[78] This work was produced by a lawyer named Gratian, an obscure figure about whom little is known with any certainty.[79]

Canon law, as Gratian inherited it, was a tangled mass of sometimes contradictory, sometimes overlapping sources and ideas. Excerpts from patristic writers such as St. Augustine and St. Jerome, canons from a variety of church councils, penitential texts, and papal decretal letters (both real and spurious) were all considered normative prior to the issuance of the *Decretum*.

Gratian set for himself the task of organizing this material. Recent scholarship on Gratian's project has been concerned with examining the exact nature of his achievement and the extent to which the *Decretum,* as it has been received by later generations of canonists, can be attributed to Gratian's original genius.[80] An effort to address these issues has been offered most comprehensively by Anders Winroth in his doctoral dissertation written at Columbia University under the guidance of Robert Somerville and the late Rudolf Weigand and published in revised and expanded form by Cambridge University Press.[81] Winroth has persuasively argued that the *Decretum* was assembled in two distinct recensions, and that it is even possible that two persons, perhaps more, were involved in this process. Winroth's work has helped resolve many questions concerning the composition of the *Decretum,* although he acknowledges that it has provoked new questions as well.[82] His thesis has also generated a lively scholarly debate.[83]

The *Decretum* itself, whatever the precise details of its composition, is in its final form a massive work in three parts. Part I, consisting of 101 *distinctiones,* is concerned largely with internal ecclesiastical order. Part II, comprising 36 *causae,* or "cases," covers a wide variety of topics. Each of these *causae* opens with a hypothetical fact pattern followed by questions probing the legal implications of the fact patterns. Most of what Gratian has to say about marriage and sexuality is found in this middle section. Part III, the *De Consecratione* ("Treatise on Consecration"), briefly treats issues in liturgical and sacramental law.[84]

While the *Decretum* may or may not have been assembled in stages, and may or may not be entirely attributable to Gratian, it is this tripartate structure that was handed down to canonists, and this text that was glossed and relied upon by subsequent generations of canon lawyers. When we speak of "Gratian," or the *"Decretum,"* in the course of this work we refer to this finished product.

Common to most of the *Decretum* is an emphasis on dialectical reasoning. Contradictory texts are arranged in patterns that make obvious their contradictions. Gratian attempted, through systematic analysis, to resolve the problems posed by the opposing texts. He set out his reasoning in *dicta,* "comments," that followed or preceded particular textual excerpts. Gratian's *dicta* would prove highly useful to his readership. As James Brundage notes, "[e]ven at his most inept moments, Gratian provided twelfth-century canonists with points of departure for alternative and sometimes more successful interpretations of the canonical texts."[85]

Gratian's *Decretum* was quickly disseminated throughout western Europe and struck a chord with Church lawyers. Its publication coincided with the emergence of a learned legal culture in many European centers: it was quickly adopted and utilized as a teaching text by law professors at Bologna, Paris, the Rhineland, Oxford, and elsewhere, and served as a focus for learned commentary.[86]

Legal commentators who worked on the *Decretum* became known as the "decretists." Although commentaries on the *Decretum* continued to be produced well into the thirteenth century and even later, decretist commentary flourished particularly between the years 1140 and 1190. The decretists were concerned both with resolving explicit and tacit inconsistencies in Gratian's texts and with filling in the gaps Gratian had left open.[87] Although their contributions often remain unacknowledged except by experts in the history of canon law, several of these scholars were enormously creative and influential figures who have left an indelible mark on Western legal tradition.

Popes began to issue increasing numbers of decretal letters commencing in the mid-twelfth century. From a contemporary American legal viewpoint, these letters had some features one might associate with case law, and others one might associate with statutory law. Typically, decretal letters were issued to resolve particular cases and controversies and were therefore fact-dependent. At the same time, they also frequently contained rather detailed legislative prescriptions. Some of the more elaborate decretals of popes like Alexander III or Innocent III nearly parallel in structure such judicial opinions as *Miranda v. Arizona* and *Henningsen v. Bloomfield Motors.*[88]

By the end of the twelfth century, however, a problem had become apparent. Decretals issued to resolve particular controversies were scattered throughout Europe. No effort had been made to draw these decretals together into larger collections. This problem began to be addressed in the late 1180s and into the early years of the thirteenth century as legal scholars and practitioners began to assemble collections of decretals. The first collections were private efforts by individual lawyers. Pope Innocent III, however, published an official collection of his decretal letters, as did Pope Honorius III. Altogether, five collections, known as the *Quinque Compilationes Antiquae* — "The Five Old Collections" — gained wide circulation prior to the year 1234.[89]

The *Liber Extra*, the most important canonistic collection after Gratian's *Decretum*, was promulgated by Pope Gregory IX in the year 1234. Pope Gregory had commissioned the compilation to serve as a comprehensive, definitive law book to take the place of the five older compilations. Edited by the Dominican friar Raymond of Peñafort, who carefully excised material not relevant to the legal issues for which *Liber Extra* was being compiled, *Liber Extra* contained a large number of decretal letters issued in the ninety years that had elapsed from the appearance of the *Decretum,* as well as some older material.[90] *Liber Extra* was meant to be binding law. It remained in effect as the duly-enacted positive law of the Catholic Church until the promulgation of the first Code of Canon Law in 1917, and still remains an important source of interpretive guidance for contemporary canonists.[91]

Over the next two-and-a-half centuries, several smaller collections of papal decretals were drawn together in order to supplement the *Liber Extra.* At the end of the Middle Ages, in the year 1501, several of these smaller collections were printed together with the *Liber Extra* and Gratian's *Decretum.* This collection has been known to subsequent generations of scholars as the *Corpus Iuris Canonici* — "The Body of Canon Law."[92]

Already in the closing years of the twelfth century, commentators had been at work analyzing the contents of the various decretal letters. These commentaries reached a new sophistication with the promulgation of the *Liber Extra.* The commentators' method was a close analysis of texts. They would look for inconsistencies within particular letters, or between different letters. They also attempted to reconcile the older material found in the *Decretum* with the *Liber Extra.*[93] Three commentators in particular stand out.

The first of these, Bernard of Parma, was born around 1200. Bernard spent most of his legal career in the academy. A professor of law at Bologna, Bernard authored the *Glossa ordinaria* — "The Ordinary Gloss" — the standard commentary to the decretals of Gregory IX, which was routinely copied with the text of *Liber Extra,* and which was used as the standard teaching text in the schools. Bernard of Parma died in 1266.[94]

Innocent IV (Sinibaldo de Fieschi), born between 1200 and 1207, was a well-trained and active canonist. He studied civil and canon law at Bologna from some of the masters, including the Romanist Accursius and the canonists Laurentius Hispanus, Vincentius Hispanus, and Johannes Teutonicus.[95] Innocent in turn taught briefly at Bologna, and then commenced a curial career, beginning with the position of "auditor," or judge of the *Audientia litterarum contradictarum,* one of the papal courts.[96] Innocent was made a cardinal as a young man, and was elected pope in 1243. He contributed to the development of canon law both with his legislative pronouncements and with his commentary on the law of Pope Gregory IX. He wrote his *Apparatus* to the *Liber Extra* in his spare moments while serving as pope. The work was published in his private capacity, not as official ecclesiastical teaching. Innocent died in 1254.[97]

Hostiensis (Henry of Susa), like Innocent IV, made a career largely in ecclesiastical administration, teaching only briefly at the University of Paris. He was born around the year 1200 and was elected successively bishop of Sisteron, archbishop of Embrun, and cardinal-bishop of Ostia (hence the name Hostiensis). He served on a number of papal diplomatic missions, spending considerable time in England. He composed a *Summa*, published around 1253, and a short commentary on the letters of Pope Innocent IV, also published around 1253. His *Lectura* ("Reading") of *Liber Extra*, a massive work of synthesis only completed at the time of his death in 1271, fills two large, dense volumes in its modern printed edition. Had he not taken ill at the conclave of 1270, he stood a good chance of being elected pope.[98]

These three men were not the only canonists active in the thirteenth century. The contributions of others will also be discussed in the course of this work. But an analysis of the work of these three canonists will form the core of this volume's treatment of marriage law.

The system of commentaries did not disappear with the death of Hostiensis. There were also important fourteenth- and fifteenth-century commentators, such as Johannes Andreae, Antonio de Butrio, and Panormitanus. As synthesizers of the tradition that had preceded them, and as mirrors on the thought-world of the later Middle Ages, their works will also be consulted when the occasion demands.

The emergence of the systematic study of canon law took place against the background of a rising legal culture that dates back to the rediscovery of Justinian's legal compilations at the end of the eleventh and beginning of the twelfth centuries.[99] For a period of several hundred years, from the rise of the Germanic kingdoms in western Europe in the sixth and seventh centuries, to the closing years of the eleventh century, knowledge of the law of ancient Rome was fragmentary at best.[100] Some Roman ideas found their way into the Germanic law codes.[101] But it is now well-agreed among scholars that a "Roman-law tradition of some standing" simply did not exist between roughly the years 600 and 1050.[102]

This circumstance changed with remarkable abruptness in the later eleventh century with the gradual reemergence of Justinian's sixth-century texts. "All of the *Institutes* and at least the first nine books of the *Code* seem to have been the first to reappear and attract scholarly attention."[103] Pepo, the enterprising but obscure Pavian who began to teach the Roman law — "with authority," if the testimony of Odofredus is to be believed[104] — may have passed his knowledge and enthusiasm for the subject to the more famous Irnerius near the end of the eleventh century. While much remains obscure about these early years, it is clear that by the beginning of the twelfth century an active legal culture could be discerned at Bologna and a few other places in northern Italy, dedicated to the study of the texts of Roman law.[105]

This new learning quickly spread throughout western Europe. By the middle of the twelfth century instruction in the Roman-law texts might be had in the south of France and in England.[106] Thence, education in Roman law reached still further abroad, spreading by the end of the twelfth century to Catalonia on the Iberian peninsula and its commercial centers of Barcelona, Valencia, and Terragona.[107] This body of ancient law, revitalized through its application to contemporary social problems, came to influence the development of canon law in important ways. Property ownership, contractual obligations, procedure, and the law of marriage and divorce were among the canonistic categories influenced by exposure to Romanist texts and ideas.[108]

The civilian students of Roman law, like the canonist students of Gratian and the *Liber Extra,* were the authors of extensive commentaries. Placentinus (d. 1192), Azo of Bologna (d. 1220-1230?), Accursius (fl. 1230-1260), and Odofredus were among the most important of the twelfth and thirteenth centuries.[109]

The commentaries generated by the writers on Roman law will also be consulted in the course of this volume. They will not be the main focus of analysis[110] — that place is reserved to the medieval canonists. But the Romanist — or "civilian" writers, as they are frequently called, because of their efforts to explicate the "civil law" — provide a vital source of comparison and contrast, especially on such issues as the right of children to support and the right of offspring to inherit a portion of the paternal estate. By the later Middle Ages, furthermore, the work of Romanists and canonists, taken collectively, comprised the *ius commune,* a transnational body of legal principles expounded upon by the jurists and utilized by the Church and by the secular polities of Europe alike in their law-making activity.[111]

Finally, the medieval scholastic tradition will also be consulted for the light it sheds on marriage and its relationship to rights. Indeed, the separation of canon law from theology was a gradual process.[112] The decretist Rufinus identified himself as writing for theologians, not for civil lawyers.[113]

"The movement to singular usage *(ius canonicum)* from the plural *(ius/iura canonum)*, only completed later in the Middle Ages, itself reflected the slowly consolidating position and discipline of the canonists."[114] Only in the mid-thirteenth century, with the establishment of separate universities for theology, philosophy, and law, with the fixing of authoritative books (the *Sentences* of Peter Lombard for theology and Gratian's *Decretum* and the *Liber Extra* of Gregory IX for canon law), with the adoption of distinctive patterns of reasoning, did canonists fully differentiate themselves from their brethren the schoolmen.[115]

Scholastic philosophy and theology, furthermore, were born in the same matrix that gave rise to the civilian and canonistic legal culture of the twelfth and thirteenth centuries. It was a culture and a context that placed greater emphasis on human freedom than was possible in the early Middle Ages. People experienced a greater range of possibilities — to get married, to enter cloistered religious life, to join the new mendicant orders, to go to law school or medical school, to enter commerce or trade or manufacture — than their forebears enjoyed, and the thought-world of the age recognized these possibilities.[116] In the realm of the scholastic writers, one thus sees in response the emergence of sustained reflection on such issues as what it means to be human and what it means to enjoy and exercise human freedom.[117]

This work does not attempt to provide an exhaustive study of the scholastic treatment of marriage and rights, which would be a vast undertaking in its own right. But scholastic writers remain valuable for at least two reasons: first, where medieval domestic relations law is concerned, they address many of the same issues the canonists address, albeit from the standpoint not of lawyers, but of philosophers seeking to understand the natural order of given behaviors or of theologians seeking to explicate the demands of moral or sacramental teaching. Second, because of their somewhat distinct yet complementary vantage point, their works provide helpful points of comparison and contrast with respect to juristic sources.

Individual Rights in Twelfth- and Thirteenth-Century Jurisprudence

Historians of rights have expressed numerous opinions concerning the origin of the Western rights tradition. In the Anglo-American world, scholars have commonly viewed the seventeenth century as a radical departure from an older tradition that had emphasized the existence of an objectively just order in which individual rights were a theoretical impossibility.[118] On the Continent, by contrast, scholars have tended to view the fourteenth century as decisive for the formation of individual rights: it was then that William of Ockham, the brilliant English logician, succeeded in dissolving the thirteenth-century synthesis of Thomas Aquinas in an acid bath of nominalistic analysis, reducing Thomas's conception of ordered justice to the competing interests and claims of individuals.[119] Both schools of thought tend to view the creation of rights-based legal structures as an aberrant development, either decidedly harmful to society or, at best, something of rather dubious benefit.

Beginning around 1980, first in a series of articles, then in a remarkable book-length synthesis, Brian Tierney challenged this regnant view.[120] Tierney focused his investigation on the shifting meaning of the Latin word *ius*. The primary meaning of this term — in the writings of the Roman jurists, in the writings of early medieval ecclesiastics — is "law," or "right order." Beginning, however, with Gratian's *Decretum* canon lawyers began to use the word *ius* to signify as well the claims of individuals.[121]

The canonists and scholastics of the late twelfth century would come to develop a natural-law basis for this new preoccupation with rights. In the process they would conjure into being a powerful natural-rights vocabulary that continues to resonate to our own day.

In a pair of important articles focused on the emergence specifically of *natural* rights, Brian Tierney has established that by about the year 1160 the decretists were proposing definitions of *ius* that were verging on the subjective.[122] One of the most important definitions was proposed by Rufinus:

> Natural *ius* is a certain force instilled in every human creature by nature to do good and avoid the opposite. *Ius* consists in three things, commands, prohibitions, and demonstrations. . . . It cannot be detracted from at all as regards the commands and prohibitions . . . but it can be as regards the demonstrations, which nature does not command or forbid, but shows to be good, and this is especially so as regards the liberty of all. . . .[123]

Tierney further demonstrates that, unlike a philosopher like Aquinas, who adopted an objective starting point ("What is just?"), Rufinus adopted an inherently subjective starting point, the structure of the human personality ("*ius* is a certain force instilled in every human creature") for his discussion of *ius naturale*.[124] From such a starting point it was a short step to propose an unambiguously subjective definition of *ius*. Tierney indicates that Rufinus himself went part of the way with his assertion that *ius* consisted not only of commands and prohibitions, but also of "demonstrations," by which was meant "an area of allowed conduct where the laws neither commanded nor prohibited."[125]

Rufinus's successors, Tierney continues, developed his insight in two complementary directions. The decretists focused attention, first, on what might loosely be called the "personalist" side of Rufinus's definition. Thus the *Summa In nomine* states: "Natural *ius* is a certain ability by which man is able to discern between good and evil, and in this sense natural *ius* is a faculty — and this is free will."[126] This definition equated *ius* with *facultas* ("faculty") and defined both expressions in terms of free will.

Huguccio, at the end of the twelfth century, developed this aspect of Rufinus's thought most fully. Huguccio proposed that *ius naturale* should have as its first and proper definition the force of reason implanted in the soul by which one distinguishes between good and evil. Secondarily (*secondario*), *ius naturale* was the objective law and the moral teaching one derived from the use of one's reason.[127]

The scope of the thirteenth-century decretalists' subjective understanding of *ius* has also recently been investigated.[128] In this study it was shown that the decretalists routinely used the word as a synonym for such inherently subjective terms as *facultas* ("faculty"), *potestas* ("power"), *libertas* ("liberty"), and *immunitas* ("immunity").[129] The thirteenth-century decretalists, it is clear, were interested in building a structure of rights with implications for many areas of the law.[130]

The decretalists surrounded the possession and free exercise of rights with a high level of legal protection. A maxim of canon law provided that "no one was to be deprived of one's right without fault" (*nemo iure suo privari debet sine culpa*).[131] Canonists noted that sometimes this maxim failed in practice. In a verse that combined cynicism and legal realism, Bernard of Parma noted: "Poverty, Hatred, Vice, Favor, Crime, and Rank, these deprive persons and places of their right."[132] Bernard's verse, in its own way, calls attention to the high regard in which the decretists held the possession of rights, and illustrated the usefulness of rights language for social criticism. Innocent parties were not normally to be disturbed in the enjoyment of their rights and liberties; where they were, some sort of legal remedy might be sought.[133]

The area of the law we are concerned with in this volume is marriage and the family. The subject under investigation is the impact canonistic rights thought had on the structure of domestic relations law as found in the twelfth- and thirteenth-century decretists and decretalists. The twelfth-century canonists had inherited a way of thinking about marriage that placed relatively little freedom in the hands of the parties: parents made decisions for their children and children were expected to obey. Marriage was presumed to be an indissoluble union ordered to the good of the spouses and the procreation of children, but the implications of these teachings for the freedom of the parties to contract marriage, or to allocate responsibilities within the marital union, had not been thought out. The task of reworking and revising this early medieval vision fell to the canonists of the period between roughly 1140 and 1300, who created a formidable synthesis of natural law and rights-based thought to justify the free choice of partners in marriage; the decision to have or refrain from intercourse; and a number of related concerns.

Medieval marriage, in law and in practice, has been the subject of enormous scholarly interest over the last several decades. The present book is indebted to, but has a focus different from, several leading works on medieval marriage. It covers some of the same ground as James Brundage in his magisterial *Sex, Law, and Christian Society in Medieval Europe*.[134] Brundage's concern is to provide a painstaking reconstruction of the major areas of canonistic thought on human sexuality — both within and outside formal marriage bonds. His work thus covers not only issues such as marriage, separation, and divorce, but also addresses non-marital sexual activity, homosexuality, and related issues such as masturbation. The present study, on the other hand, has a narrower focus: a close consideration of the use of rights language in the formation and living out of the marital relationship.

This work, similarly, has some affinities with the important body of scholarship produced by the Honorable John T. Noonan Jr. In *Contraception,* Judge Noonan plumbed the medieval scholastic and canonistic traditions to conclude that the historic magisterium of the Church could support some forms of birth control within marriage.[135] And in *Power to Dissolve,* Judge Noonan explored the development and application of the Church's power over marriage to consider circumstances where it might be appropriate for the Church to dissolve the marital bond.[136]

The present book employs a methodology and a set of assumptions not dissimilar to those found in Noonan's works. It engages in a close analysis of canonistic and scholastic arguments in order to identify the dimensions of the rights-based synthesis of marriage law that came into being in the twelfth and thirteenth centuries. It also employs, particularly in the chapter on the freedom of parties to contract marriage, a case-study methodology, examining in detail the cases of Margery Paston and the Fair Maid of Kent to sketch the scope of the right of women to select their marital partners. Like Noonan's work, the present volume takes for granted the continuity and the self-evident importance of the medieval tradition for the life of the Catholic Church.

The debt of this book to the scholarship of Richard Helmholz must also be acknowledged. Unlike Richard Helmholz's writings on marriage and the family, the present work is not primarily concerned with the application of canonistic theory as revealed in the records of the ecclesiastical courts.[137] Nevertheless, at various points the findings of Helmholz and others are utilized to illustrate the impact a canonistic focus on marital rights had on the life of the Church.

Finally, one must take account of John Witte's recent panoramic study of Western marriage, *From Sacrament to Contract.*[138] In this volume, Witte traces the trajectory of Western ideas of marriage from the formulations of canonistic and scholastic writers to those of contemporary contractarians. Stressing indissolubility, the canonists forbade the right of remarriage following divorce but developed liberal rules governing the potential annulment of marriages; stressing the naturalness of the marital relationship, they forbade acts that were inimical to the natural law — incest, homosexuality, bestiality.[139] Portions of this model were subsequently attacked by the generations of church reformers who followed the Lutheran and Calvinist revolutionaries of the sixteenth century, and by the secular reformers who followed in the train of the "enlightened" thought of the eighteenth century.[140]

The present book, while taking the sacramental model of the Church as basic, is concerned not with its latter-day critics but rather with the survival of various elements of the medieval synthesis — particularly those aspects having to do with rights to and within marriage. These elements have, it will be clear, enjoyed a sturdy second life long after the waning of the Middle Ages.

This book is arranged into four large chapters, exploring the relationship of rights to different aspects of the marital relationship. It begins with the right of persons to contract marriage for themselves, even in the face of familial opposition. This recognition, given definitive shape by the precocious but mysterious Gratian in the twelfth century, had been denied by previous generations of lawyers. Roman law allowed for the possibility of coerced consent making a marriage; Germanic law saw the involvement of parents as an affirmative good necessary to marital formation. The canonists broke with these traditions. The implications of this break are explored in Chapter One.

Chapter Two, then, explores the issue of paternal governance. Biblical teaching proclaimed the husband to be the head of his wife. Roman law taught that fathers might even have the right of life and death over their offspring. The canonists of the twelfth and thirteenth centuries employed rights language to describe paternal power — it was the *ius patriapotestatis* — the "right of paternal power." This was not, however, a right that could be used arbitrarily or capriciously. It was a right that had to be exercised for the building up, not the tearing down, of the family unit. Paternal discipline must be moderate. The needs of children for sustenance and support must be satisfied.

Chapter Three deals with a set of rights that could be characterized by the term "right of women" *(ius mulierum)*. Women, too, were not without rights in the marital relationship. Conjugal rights represented an area of equality between men and women — sometimes merely a formal equality that masked harsh treatment, as in the case of the forcible consummation of marriage; but in other circumstances, such as when a spouse contracted leprosy, the conjugal right was a legal device that could be used to call parties to keep truly heroic standards.

Chapter Four, finally, addresses yet another aspect of the medieval marital relationship: the right of offspring to inherit. The medieval canonists, contrary to popular misconceptions, certainly believed in testamentary freedom. But this was a testamentary freedom circumscribed by the requirement that the natural rights of offspring be protected. The right of children to claim a portion of the parental estate was denominated as the "claim owing by nature." The nature and extent of this claim is sketched in Chapter Four.

At the close of the volume, it is hoped, a new picture of the law governing the medieval marital relationship will have emerged. At least as the lawyers conceptualized it, marriage was not a relationship that featured harsh or arbitrary treatment. It was a relationship that had a certain natural structure that neither the parties themselves nor even the popes were free to alter. Marriage was ordered to the good of the spouses and the procreation and upbringing of children. Within this ordered structure the canonists recognized the existence of certain rights and obligations in order to ensure that the basic goods and goals of marriage were fulfilled. The tradition of rights language of which Leo XIII, Pietro Gasparri, and the contemporary Roman Rota partake is very ancient. Indeed, it is older, deeper, and richer than even they may have realized.

The Right and Freedom to Contract Marriage

The Story of Christina of Markyate

It is not likely that Gratian ever heard of the story of the early-twelfth-century mystic and recluse Christina of Markyate. Born at the end of the eleventh century to an Anglo-Saxon noble family,[1] Christina was attracted to a monastic vocation at an early age. Her various struggles to realize this calling foreshadow many of the issues discussed in the pages of this volume. Christina's life makes one appreciate that the dense legal theory the canonists constructed around the freedom to marry, the proper scope and limit of paternal power, and the nature of the conjugal relationship itself, had real-life consequences.

Christina's hagiographer describes her as an intensely religious young girl. She resolved to follow a monastic calling upon visiting the religious house of St. Albans at about the age of twelve or fourteen. Moved by the piety she witnessed there, Christina took a private vow of virginity, a vow she later confirmed in the presence of a certain Sueno, canon of Huntingdon.[2]

Christina's chosen path was far from easy. She had first to surmount the advances of Ralph, who was both a family friend and the lecherous bishop of Durham. One night, while staying with Christina's parents, Ralph was overcome with lust for the young Christina. He arranged to have Christina come to his bedroom, where he tried to force her to perform an "unspeakable act" (nephanda re). Christina only managed to escape his clutches by a clever subterfuge.[3]

Ralph tried to win the young girl's affections with expensive gifts. When that did not work, he decided to try to ruin the one thing Christina held dear: her vow of virginity. He put it into the head of a young nobleman named Burthred to seek Christina's hand in marriage.[4]

Christina's parents learned of Burthred's interest and approved the match. But they realized they also needed to obtain Christina's consent to the union. They set their minds to obtaining it by fair means or foul. They ridiculed Christina's professed vow of virginity. They made "sweet promises" (blanditi). They heaped on threats (minas addiderunt). They enlisted a friend of Christina's to "sweet-talk" (aures sedulo demulceret lenociniis) her into agreeing to the union.[5]

For a year, Christina held out against these efforts to bribe and berate her into a union she did not desire. One day, however, when they were all gathered in church, the whole lot of them "attacked" (agressi sunt) the young girl suddenly and in concert. Overcome by pressure, Christina agreed to the match, at least outwardly. That day, she became Burthred's bride.[6]

Christina, however, would not take the next step. She fiercely resisted consummating her union to Burthred. Her parents' pressure became even more overt. They prevented her from having "conversation with any religious and God-fearing man."[7] They kept her from visiting the monastery or its chapel. They tried to entice her by getting her drunk, hoping that wine would loosen her inhibitions.[8] Having failed at these efforts, her parents resorted to a blunter mechanism: they invited Burthred to enter her bedroom while she was asleep in the hope that he might catch Christina unawares and consummate the union. Christina, however, "moved by providence," was awake, alert, and dressed when Burthred entered the room.[9]

Christina exhorted Burthred to follow the example of saintly couples from the past who had maintained chaste marriages: St. Cecilia and her husband Valerian, were rewarded with immortality for the chaste way in which they conducted themselves. They could be like the saints of old, Christina assured the young man. Burthred, apparently either convinced by Christina or simply worn down by her defenses, eventually withdrew from the bedroom. Christina's parents and others met him and denounced him as "a cowardly and useless boy" (ignavum ac nullius usus iuvenem conclamant).[10]

Bullied by his putative in-laws, Burthred resolved to enter the bedroom once again on another night. They tried to rouse his courage by scolding him, warning him not to fall for her tricks and telling him that he must not play the part of the woman (ne . . . effeminetur).[11] If he had to, they told him, he was free to use force (vi). That night, Christina hid herself and Burthred was unable to find her. When Burthred tried to enter her room on a third night, Christina was able to escape.[12]

Christina remained with her parents after this night. Although they made a few more attempts to see the union consummated, these efforts were inevitably frustrated. Eventually, her parents turned to the Church, hoping that ecclesiastical power might be brought to bear on Christina's obstinacy. Her father, Autti, visited the local prior, a man named Fredebert. Parental authority (*nostra authoritate*), her father informed Fredebert, must be preserved. It cannot be seen to be publicly mocked. Could the reverend Fredebert ensure that she follow through on the consent she gave and consummate her union?[13]

It was Fredebert's turn to convince the young girl. He lectured her on the nature of marriage. It was through marriage that man and woman became one flesh. St. Paul taught Christians that a woman has no power over her body. Her husband has this power. Man and woman owe one another the conjugal debt (*debitum*). By marriage they are joined together; divorce is forbidden. And furthermore, Fredebert observed, shifting the terms of his entreaties, children owe their parents obedience and must defer to them. Christina should now respect her parents and go through with the marriage that they have arranged.

Christina responded by defending her freedom to choose whether to marry or to follow a religious vocation. Her parents acted against her will (*contra voluntatem meam*).[14] "I have never been a wife," Christina continued. "I have never thought of it. You must know that from my infancy I have chosen to be chaste and vowed to Christ that I would remain a virgin."[15] To force her into an unwilling marriage in violation of the vow she has taken would be to "defraud Christ."[16] Christina, too, knew how to quote Scripture. All those who leave family and friends and surrender all they have to follow Christ, she reminded prior Fredebert, are promised an eternal reward. The marriage she desired was nobler and richer than any fleshly union: marriage to Christ himself.[17]

Fredebert, now sympathetic to Christina's professions, conveyed Christina's response to her father Autti. He was still reluctant to hear this news and thought to appeal to the local bishop, not the lecherous man who had tried to seduce Christina, but the bishop of Lincoln, a certain Robert. His hope was that the bishop would order Christina to submit to the authority (*dominium*) of her husband Burthred.[18] Bishop Robert, however, initially took Christina's side.

Autti made one last attempt to compel her to consummate the union. He offered the bishop a large sum of money to change his mind. Burthred, meanwhile, clearly fatigued by the struggle, decided to release Christina from the matrimonial vow.[19] Autti responded by insisting that Burthred lacked the authority to absolve his bride from her marital commitment, and once again appealed to the bishop. Robert, his palms suitably greased, now sided with Autti.[20]

The bishop did not have the last word. Despite the obstacles put in her way, Christina persevered in her commitment to Christ. She prized her vow more than she valued the wealth and fame her parents might confer on her and more than she valued life as Burthred's wife. Christina finally achieved her calling by escaping her family and openly enrolling in a convent. The marriage was ultimately dissolved by the archbishop of York and Christina became abbess of Markyate Abbey.

Christina's story stands at the beginning of this volume almost like a *causa* in Gratian's *Decretum*. It epitomizes most of the major themes of this book: when and how did the parties to a marriage acquire the right and freedom to contract marriage themselves? What pressure, if any, might be brought to bear against their will? What was the nature and extent of paternal power? What was the nature of the conjugal debt? Might a marriage ever be forcibly consummated? What if the parties chose to withdraw from marriage in order to enter religious life? In what ways were husband and wife equal in their marital rights? In what ways was the wife subordinate to her husband? What did it mean for a child to treat his or her parents with respect? What claims might children make on parents in return for the respect and obedience they showed them? What role did the Church have in enforcing this system of rights and obligations? On what larger theory of human relations was this system of thought grounded? These are among the questions that will be considered in the course of this volume.

The first and most obvious issue highlighted in the Christina of Markyate narrative is the subject of this first chapter, the right and freedom to marry or to refrain from marriage.

Today it is taken for granted that the freely exchanged consent of the parties makes a marriage. This essential human freedom is typically described as a right. These observations are true whether one speaks of contemporary canon law or of contemporary secular legal systems, such as the American domestic relations law.

Marriage, the 1983 Code of Canon Law teaches, is made by the consent of parties legally capable of manifesting consent.[21] This consent is an act of the will by which man and woman bind each other in an irrevocable covenant.[22] All are able to contract marriage who are not prohibited by law.[23] Commenting on this provision of the law, the *New Commentary on the Code of Canon Law* states that "[e]very person enjoys the natural right to marry. This fundamental right is rooted in the social nature of the human person and is recognized by Catholic social teaching."[24]

In so pronouncing marriage a basic right, the *Commentary* was itself following the declaration of Pope John XXIII in *Pacem in Terris* that marriage was among the natural rights of man *(iura hominis).*[25] There are, John pronounced, certain rights grounded in the dignity of the human person by virtue of our status as creatures of God.[26] These rights include the right of life, the right of bodily integrity, the right to have the means by which to earn one's daily bread.[27] But these rights also included the right to choose one's state in life, which included the right "to begin a family, in which a man and wife are able to enjoy equal rights and duties."[28]

American constitutional law has also recognized the fundamental character of the right to marriage. *Loving v. Virginia* presented the case of an interracial couple who married one another in violation of the Virginia anti-miscegenation statute.[29] In holding the statute unconstitutional, the Supreme Court acknowledged that "[t]he freedom to marry has long been recognized as one of the vital personal rights essential to the orderly pursuit of happiness by free men."[30] Quoting earlier precedent, the Court continued: "Marriage is one of the 'basic civil rights of man', fundamental to our very existence and survival."[31] Laws restricting the exercise of this right were thus subjected to the highest form of constitutional scrutiny and where, as in the case of the Virginia anti-miscegenation statute, they failed to serve a compelling governmental interest, they were and are liable to be struck down as constitutionally infirm.

The fundamental character of this freedom is taken as basic. The idea that a family might arrange the marriages of its children, the suggestion that a child might be compelled into an unwanted marriage or that he or she could not afterward object to the force that was employed to obtain coerced consent are notions that are alien to our way of thought. But our own presuppositions have a relatively brief history, extending back only eight hundred or so years. That the freedom to enter a marriage should be considered a basic right would have been familiar to canonists active around the year 1200, but not much before that time. Roman lawyers, as well as the theologians and canonists of the early Middle Ages, adhered to a very different system, one that gave enormous authority to the family in matrimonial decision-making.[32]

To be sure, the canonists of the twelfth and thirteenth centuries did not share our conception of marriage as belonging primarily to the parties themselves to arrange. It would be wrong to imply that they thought of marriage in the exact terms conceived by the modern Code of Canon Law or by the United States Supreme Court. Most marital decisions in twelfth- and thirteenth-century Europe continued to be influenced, above all else, by dynastic and familial considerations. But what is significant is that the canonists put into the legal literature of their time the notion that there was such a right. They were willing as well to establish a structure of law that conserved the right and allowed its free exercise where the parties did, in fact, choose to claim it, even in the face of familial and social opposition. Seen in this light, the canonists stand at the beginning of a line of development that continues to influence the contemporary world.

Part I: The Ancient Requirement of Parental Consent

The Roman-Law Background

That the freely-exchanged consent of the parties is essential to the formation of a marriage is assumed today, but this assumption, like the freedom to select one's place of burial, like other basic rights considered in this volume, originated in the matrix of twelfth-century legal writing, particularly the work of Gratian. Law and social expectations prior to the twelfth century were, in fact, very different.

Roman law followed a set of rules regarding the consent of the parties that differed in some significant ways from the system the canonists put in place. The process of marital formation, at least for those upper class households about whom we have the most evidence, typically began with betrothal.[33] Roman law on the subject of betrothals blended together differing requirements of consent — the consent of the parties to the future marriage, to be sure, but also the consent of the heads of the households whose negotiations were the usual precursor to engagement.

According to Julianus, engagements (*sponsalia*) were made with the consent of the future bride and groom. And so, Julianus concluded, even a daughter within the power of her father should (*oportet*) consent to a betrothal as much as she would be expected to consent to the actual marriage.[34] But where a daughter did not "fight" (*repugnat*) her father's arrangements, Ulpian added, she was deemed to consent.[35] And, Ulpian went on, she might only resist where her prospective husband was "unworthy in his conduct or foul."[36]

A more lenient view, expressed in a decree of the Emperors Diocletian and Maximian, provided that a betrothed woman is not to be prohibited from renouncing that arrangement and moving on to a new betrothal.[37] It seems likely, however, that the two emperors were contemplating the engagement of an adult woman, a mistress of her own affairs (*sui iuris*), whereas Ulpian referred to a daughter (*filia*) under her father's control.[38]

The rules regarding males were less developed, if only perhaps because they were presumed to enjoy a greater range of freedom with respect to betrothals than young females. Regarding sons, Paulus declared that betrothal was impossible where a son "dissented" from his father's choice.[39] Because of the requirement of consent, furthermore, betrothal could not occur prior to the parties' seventh birthday.[40] While such consent might occur in the absence of the parties — "this happens daily," recorded Ulpian[41] — the knowledge of and subsequent ratification by the absent parties were also requirements.[42]

The Roman lawyers also stressed, however, that the consent of the children was not the only factor that mattered in a betrothal — the consent of the heads of household was also required for betrothal, at least where those to be betrothed were still under paternal power.[43] Indeed, the father of a daughter engaged to be married might revoke his consent, thereby invalidating the engagement.[44] Where a daughter was under the care of a guardian, and a disagreement arose between the guardian, on the one hand, and the daughter's mother and relatives, on the other, it belonged to the provincial governor to resolve the question of whom she should marry.[45] The idea that the resolution of such a disagreement might belong to the daughter seems never to have occurred to the lawyers. An emancipated daughter, on the other hand, freed of the normal familial constraints, might still marry, even in the absence of parental approval.[46]

Susan Treggiari has shown that such betrothals occurred for a variety of complex and complementary reasons. In the late Republic and early Empire, intermarriage among noble and equestrian families was, it seems, commonplace.[47] "Political connection is sometimes explicitly attested as the main motive for a particular marriage."[48] Other motives also drove the matrimonial arrangements made by fathers on behalf of their children. "[W]ealth," Treggiari adds, "might compensate for lack of birth,"[49] although moralists such as Cicero were quick to condemn marriages entered into merely for the sake of lucre.[50] A successful military command might also attract marital interest.[51] In short, there were many reasons — political, monetary, dynastic, and other — that drove families to arrange betrothals among themselves.

If betrothals were arranged and consented to by the heads of households acting out of a rich variety of motives, marriages themselves also required the consent not only of the bride and groom but of other interested parties, such as the head of household or guardian. "Marriage," Paulus wrote, "cannot come into being unless everyone consents, namely the parties and those whose power they are under."[52] Julianus affirmed much the same principle.[53]

This principle was extended to apply to a large range of possibilities. What of a son still under parental control but serving in the army? He may not marry "without the will of his father."[54] What of a grandson who remains within the power of his grandfather? Suppose that the grandfather has become "insane" (furente)? If the grandfather has truly become insane, then the grandson's father might substitute his consent, but such consent, Ulpian stressed, remained "necessary" (necessaria).[55]

Similarly, where a father has gone mad and is unable to consent to the marriage of his son, the grandfather's consent might be substituted, if the older man's reasoning remained sound.[56] What of a father who has disappeared, or who had been captured by the enemy? Where three years have elapsed and the fate of the father remains "very obviously unknown," his children, Paulus wrote, should not be prevented from marriage.[57] But Julianus qualified Paulus's statement by adding that such a marriage should only occur where the prospective spouse clearly belonged to a social status which the father would not have repudiated.[58]

The Roman lawyers admonished that the consent of the offspring ought to be freely given even where parents had the ultimate say in marital arrangements. A decree of the Emperors Diocletian and Maximian preserved in the Codex provided that no one was to be compelled to contract marriage or to reconcile following a separation.[59] The power of contracting and separating, furthermore, the emperors labeled a "free faculty" (liberam facultatem).[60]

The jurists whose works comprise the Digest echoed this sentiment. "A son of the family is not to be compelled to take a wife," wrote Terentius Clemens.[61] But this principle was not without limits. A teaching of Celsus, known as Si patre cogente, declared that a son who, at his father's compulsion, took a bride he would not have otherwise married but raised no complaints prior to marriage, could not subsequently challenge the marriage because of compulsion. He would be deemed "to have preferred this [marriage]," Celsus asserted.[62] No specific provision of the Roman law referred to the woman's ability to deny her consent to marriage, although Ulpian had permitted a daughter to resist a betrothal where the prospective husband, as noted above, was "unworthy in morals or foul."[63]

The conclusion one draws from this extended analysis of Roman betrothal and marital formation is that marital consent did not operate in the kind of straightforward fashion we might expect today. The classical and post-classical Roman lawyers made consent to a marriage central, but simultaneously conditioned that consent on a variety of factors. The parties alone, while they were still under the power of their parents, were not free to consent to a marriage of which their parents disapproved, although under some circumstances they might at least reject unsuitable matches made for them by their parents. Where parties to a marriage had been emancipated or otherwise reached maturity, a different standard applied. Clearly, the decision to marry, and the choice of marriage partner, particularly for the upper classes or those aspiring to join their ranks, involved complex calculations and the law took full account of such needs. The exchange of consent was a complex social action that had implications for a variety of dynastic and other interests.

Early Christian Teaching

Strong patristic authority similarly endorsed the importance of parental consent in the formation of a marriage. St. Jerome had been asked by a certain priest named Amandus about a woman whose husband had committed the crimes of adultery and sodomy. Might the woman lawfully move to a new marriage?[64] Jerome rejected the suggestion with an outburst of his famous vituperation: "The Apostle defined it clearly, thereby cutting off all excuses," Jerome began. "A woman is an adulteress if she takes another as her husband while her husband is still alive." Indeed, Jerome emphasized, no excuse could surmount this prohibition. Pressure to marry the man chosen for the girl by the family thus could not invalidate the marriage: "Do not tell me about the violence of a rapist, payment by her mother, the authority of her father, the whole gang of relatives."[65] The Apostle, meaning St. Paul, speaking not on his authority but on Christ's, had removed all such excuses.[66] No room on this account for a daughter to seek divorce with the right of remarriage because of the compulsion of her father.

A letter of Pope Leo the Great, datable to around the year 458, addressed the distinction between wives and concubines. In the process of answering this question Leo asserted that women are without fault who have, "by reason of the judgment of their fathers," married men who also kept concubines.[67] As John Noonan has pointed out, "[t]hat the girls might not have wanted to marry the men possessed of concubines was not considered as a point telling against the validity of their marriages."[68]

The Christian Roman emperors of the fourth and fifth centuries maintained the same set of presumptions about the role of the family in making a marriage as had their non-Christian predecessors and, indeed, as did contemporary theologians and popes. The Emperor Constantine ruled in 332 that a father or guardian was not permitted to betroth his daughter to another after betrothing her to a soldier.[69] The official interpretation attached to this decree made clear that where the soldier had entered into a betrothal agreement with the girl's father, the marriage should normally occur within two years, and only if it was delayed by reason of the young man's dilatoriness (*tarditate*) or negligence (*negligentia*) might the girl's father make other plans.[70]

On its face, Constantine's policy was to protect the expectations of soldiers, who might be living in remote locations. But a subtext is also clear: the decision to marry involved considerations extraneous to the wishes of the parties. The daughter had no voice in these arrangements. She was presumed to consent to whatever arrangements her father made on her behalf.

Ninety years later, a decree of Honorius and Theodosius addressed the problem of a father who died after betrothing his daughter but before the marriage could take place.[71] The father's plans were not to be overturned and the judgment of the guardian substituted.[72] Indeed, the emperors observed, the judgment of the guardian might have been swayed by a cash payment, or by the influence of the girl herself, who may not know what is in her own best interest.[73] Again, the official interpretation made the point even more clearly: "where the father has died, his arrangements are to be overturned for no reason, nor is the girl to receive permission to marry another, even if mother, guardian, curator, or the relatives would perhaps wish to take another."[74]

The law and theology of the early Middle Ages, that roughly six-hundred-year period traditionally dated between the collapse of Roman political authority in the West and the various revivals and reforms that began to gain critical mass in the latter years of the eleventh century — from the papal reform movement to the popular response to Urban II's call for a crusade — retained the traditional teaching that it was the head of household's responsibility to arrange the marriages of his children, especially his daughters. This was the case whether one looked to the Germanic law codes of the early Middle Ages or to the Church's own teaching on the subject.

Thus, for instance, one finds a provision of the Visigothic Code declaring that "we shall in no way permit" a girl already betrothed by her father "to treat contemptuously her father's will by attempting to move to another. . . ."[75] A second provision of the Visigothic Code declared that a betrothal agreement could not be unilaterally broken, presumably subjecting both unemancipated sons and daughters to their parents' wishes.[76]

Early medieval church councils repeated this sentiment. A Council held at Arles around 541 warned men that they should not copulate with girls lest it be concluded that they have taken the girls captive. And if they did this prohibited thing, the Council continued, they should suffer "the severity of excommunication."[77] The Council fathers seem never to have contemplated the possibility that such young persons might have validly married against their parents' wishes. A Bavarian council, held at Ratisbon around the years 740-750, cautioned that betrothals must not be lightly entered into and advised that the "advice and consent" (*consilio et voluntate*) of parents and even the relatives should first be obtained.[78]

Early canon-law collections also endorsed the decisive significance fatherly consent played in the making of marriage. Regino of Prüm, "a jurist of wider learning than most of his contemporaries,"[79] compiled his collection of church law in the years just after 900.[80] An excerpt attributed to St. Jerome, bearing the rubric "On Legitimate Marriages" (*De Legitimis Conjugiis*), stated that the Bible recognized three types of legitimate marriage, all of which required paternal consent: first, a father might hand over his chaste virgin daughter "in her virginity" to a man he has legitimately selected. Second, a man might take a virgin to the city and there forcibly copulate with her. If the father of the girl approved of the relationship, he would then provide his daughter with a dowry and bless the marriage. Third, where a man has abducted a girl and the father disapproves, "he will take the girl from the aforesaid man, and he will hand her over to another, and he will give her a dowry, and she will be his legitimate bride."[81]

Texts included among the infamous forged Isidorian decretals, traceable to the mid-ninth-century Church of Rheims, also accorded the father a decisive role in approving or disapproving the marriages of his offspring, especially his daughters. Thus a forgery falsely attributed to Pope Evaristus declared:

Similarly we hold it to be conserved and handed down, that a wife may be legitimately joined to her husband. For we find it something other than legitimate marriage, as we have received it from the Fathers and the holy Apostles, and the tradition of their successors, if a wife is not sought from those who have control over the girl and custody of her, and she is betrothed by her parents or nearest relatives. . . .[82]

Lyndon Reynolds is correct in urging caution when approaching a document such as this because of its forged status.[83] But if we use the text merely as evidence of social expectations, of what generally counted as binding norms of conduct among the expected audience of the forged decretals, we can learn a good deal. It is clear, when seen in this limited light, that it was still the expectation that fathers should control the selection especially of their daughters' husbands.

Hincmar of Rheims (archbishop 845-882), the greatest theological writer of his day,[84] also endorsed a decisive role for the father in marital formation. Epistle 22 concerned a case that had come before a local synod in 860. A certain Stephen, count of Auvergne, had sought the hand of the daughter of Count Raymond of Toulouse.[85] Stephen, in a "delicate youthful state" (in fragili juventutis aetate) and following the custom of his ancestors (more praedecessorum), obtained the consent of his own parents as well as Count Raymond.[86] In this way, he declared before the Council, he sought "legitimate marriage" (legitimum coniugium).[87] Stephen, however, came to fear that marriage to Raymond's daughter would cause him to run afoul of the rules prohibiting consanguineous relationships — he was apparently related to Raymond's daughter in the fourth degree — and on the advice of his confessor he chose to disavow the relationship.[88]

In the course of responding to this problem, Hincmar found the following to be "necessary" to legitimate marriage:

We are led to state that this only is necessary: among equals, legitimate marriages occur when the girl is sought from and legally betrothed and endowed by her parents, who have an interest, and that when the girl is properly honored and joined in the public ceremonies of marriage, then from two a single body and a single flesh is effected. . . .[89]

Hincmar discussed these themes as well in his treatise on marriage written on the occasion of King Lothar's effort to divorce his queen, Theutberga.[90] How is marriage initiated? Hincmar asked.[91] Both the Old and New Law, the Old and New Testaments, speak with one voice to this question, Hincmar continued. Look at the betrothal of the Blessed Virgin to her husband Joseph.[92] This was accomplished, Hincmar continued, in the same manner described by Pope Evaristus, "the fourth Roman pope," whose letter Hincmar took as genuine.[93] Hincmar followed this assertion with a lengthy quotation from pseudo-Evaristus, including the passage indicating that a wife is to be "betrothed by her parents and nearest relatives."[94]

For a thousand years the Christian tradition accepted and promoted the idea that it was the responsibility of fathers to arrange the marriages of their children, especially their daughters. The requirement that children receive the approval of their parents had roots in Roman law, but it received powerful legal and theological impetus in the early Middle Ages. The Germanic law codes, the early medieval Church councils, early canonical compilers such as Regino of Prüm, all took the rule for granted. Theologically, Hincmar of Rheims completed this line of development: the Blessed Virgin, whose marriage was "legitimate" and perfect in every way, must have received the blessing of her "parents and nearest relatives" (*parentibus aut propinquioribus*). Only in this way, was an effective and legitimate marriage with Joseph her husband brought into being. A large and imposing edifice of doctrine and rules, the teaching of pagan Romans, of Germanic kings in the process of becoming Christian, the learning of esteemed doctors of the Church, stood for the proposition that marital consent belonged to parents and family, that such a decision was simply too important to be entrusted exclusively to youthful and immature parties.

Part II: Gratian's Revolution

Gratian on the "Power to Choose"[95]

Gratian was the heir of this thousand-year-old tradition favoring, indeed even mandating, the consent of parents to the marriage of their children, especially their daughters. Yet Gratian was to set in train a series of legal developments that would have the effect of toppling this legal and theological edifice.

The hypothetical question with which Gratian commenced *Causa* 31 posed a set of facts dense with legal implications. Suppose, Gratian began, some man "played around" — Gratian's verb *constupravit* supports this translation — with another man's wife.[96] With her husband dead, the adulteress and the adulterer married.[97] The adulterous second husband then swore to give the daughter born of his new union to a certain man as his wife; the daughter refused assent.[98] Her father, the former adulterer, then promised his daughter to yet another man.[99] The first man, who had originally been promised the daughter, subsequently demanded the girl's hand in marriage.[100]

Quaestio one addressed the legal problems implicated in the effort by the adulterous pair to enter a legitimate union.[101] *Quaestio* two then turned its attention to the daughter's plight: "May an unwilling daughter be given to another in marriage?"[102] *Quaestio* three, finally, asked whether it was possible for a daughter to marry another after her father has consented to a betrothal.[103]

Quaestiones two and three are relevant to our concerns. Gratian opened *quaestio* two with a simple declaration of principle, drawn from "Ambrose," probably, as John Noonan points out, "Isaac, the first Latin commentator on Paul."[104] "That a girl is not to be compelled to marry a man," Gratian announced, "Ambrose testifies to this in his [commentary] on the First Letter to the Corinthians: Let a widow marry whom she wills, only in the Lord. That is, let her marry whom she thinks apt, because unwilling nuptials usually have bad outcomes."[105] Noonan notes the limitation inherent in Gratian's teaching: while "[t]he reason seemed cogent to all marriages[,] Paul spoke . . . only of widows, whose emancipated condition clearly distinguished them from unmarried daughters."[106]

Paul and his commentator Isaac can be read as asserting, in the limited case of a widow of presumably adult years, the principle of free consent to marriage. Gratian, in a remarkably one-sided commentary, expanded upon this exception until it swallowed the general rule of parental consent. Gratian opened his analysis with a letter of Pope Urban II (1088-1099), written only a half-century before and addressed to a papal legate charged with hearing the marriage case of the daughter of Jourdain I, ruler of Capua.[107]

Prince Jourdain, the pope noted, had alleged that under heavy pressure and with great regret he betrothed his daughter to a certain Rainaldo Rodell.[108] Jourdain's daughter, a little girl (*infantulam*), did not wish to go through with the union, wept, and resisted with all her might. The authority of the law and the canons, Urban responded, did not approve of such betrothals, but, the pope continued, lest those ignorant of the law consider his judgment harsh, he would permit Prince Jourdain to complete the marriage he had started, provided the consent of daughter, mother, and the close relatives was obtained.[109] His legate, Urban instructed, ought to hear both sides, and if no proof was offered by Rainaldo regarding the validity of the marriage, the daughter should not be prohibited from marrying another man "in the Lord."[110]

Urban II, Noonan has shown, was making a sharp break with tradition. While he asserted that Roman and canon law stood behind his conclusion, Urban "gave no citations to any such authority and his self-consciousness suggested the degree in which he innovated. . . ."[111] Noonan has observed that this decretal made weak authority for Gratian's case.[112] The father was under as much pressure as was the daughter. Pope Urban furthermore offered a compromise to Jourdain and Rainaldo that depended upon the consent not only of the daughter, but also of the mother and other close relatives. "The text," Noonan concluded, "proved nothing about the case of a daughter willingly married off by her father."[113] The question remained open: suppose that her father was not under compulsion himself, might his daughter's resistance to a proposed match, standing alone, be sufficient to invalidate consent?

Gratian followed this text with a second decree of Urban II.[114] Written to Sancho Ramirez, king of Aragon, the letter concerned a betrothal the king had arranged on behalf of his niece. "Concerning the marriage of your niece, whom you have pledged under the pressure of necessity," the pope began, "we have determined that if, as has been alleged, she altogether resists and persists in the same firmness of will, so that she will deny herself in marriage to him, in no way should she, unwillingly and resisting, be compelled into marriage."[115]

Urban offered not a legal but a theological justification for this conclusion. "Those whose body is one ought to be of one mind (*animus*)," Urban asserted.[116] Urban's choice of *animus* — translated as "mind" but carrying as well the sense of deep, heartfelt feeling — captured well the shared thought and purpose the new marital theory seemed to demand of couples. Copulation with an unwilling virgin, the pope continued to build his argument, violated the teachings of Christ and St. Paul and led to divorce or the crime of fornication.[117] Furthermore, the pope added, the evil of such sins redounded to the one who compelled the girl into an unwilling marriage.[118]

This letter, Noonan asserts, constituted somewhat sounder authority for Gratian's defense of marital freedom. "This case, too, was distinguishable — an uncle's, not a father's authority was at stake, and the uncle had himself been forced. Yet the reasons given were not unpersuasive precedent for Gratian's conclusion."[119] The rationale Pope Urban proposed for his ruling — the couple's unity of mind and purpose and its effectuation by their free consent — could be seen as a principle potentially threatening to the venerable old custom of arranged marriages.

The final authority Gratian mustered was a letter of the ninth-century Pope Nicholas I to two French legates charged with hearing the famous divorce case of Queen Theutberga.[120] Among Theutberga's points of appeal was that King Lothar had compelled her to give false testimony against her marriage.[121] The pope instructed his legates to examine the veracity of these claims and to set aside the confession if Theutberga was found to have been the victim of coercion.[122] Noonan notes that although this argument was a seeming "makeweight" — it was a compelled confession, not a forced marriage, that Pope Nicholas invalidated — it was in fact decisive to Gratian's defense of free consent.[123] What was crucial to Gratian's argument was the need for "authority that a result effected by coercion could be set aside."[124]

With this one-sided analysis, Gratian concluded: "By these authorities it is shown that coupling with another is not possible unless by free will."[125] The abruptness of this analysis must have startled early editors of Gratian's work. A *palea* inserted at an early stage in the formation of Gratian's text and attributed to Pope Hormisdas qualifies Gratian's teaching: a father might not compel his adult son into marriage where the son "in no way consents," but where the son has not yet reached the age of discernment the father might pledge him in marriage and the marriage will be valid provided the son subsequently ratifies it when he comes of age.[126] No mention of adult daughters was made.

Gratian's brief treatment of *quaestio* three, whether one is free to marry another after one's father has already arranged a betrothal, tended to support the position laid down in the subsequently-inserted text attributed to Hormisdas. The *quaestio* consisted of a single text, a passage from the fourth-century Council of Elvira, that declared that parents who broke the betrothals they have arranged on behalf of their children should be deprived of communion for three years.[127]

Gratian, however, proposed that the teaching of these texts must be qualified: only where children have consented to betrothals may the parents be prohibited from breaking their prior arrangements.[128] By this qualification, Gratian changed the focus of the law from parents who had broken faith with other heads of household (and thereby disrupted dynastic strategies) to parents who had violated arrangments to which their offspring have assented.

This analysis, however, must be read against the background of other texts, found elsewhere in the *Decretum* and placed there quite possibly by Gratian's own editing, that seem to take for granted the possibility of a decisive parental role in the formation of marriage.[129]

In *Causa* 36, Gratian repeated the teaching attributed to St. Jerome and handed on by Regino of Prüm that marriage by taking a young girl captive followed by paternal consent was a legitimate form of marriage.[130] He followed this passage with local conciliar legislation altogether prohibiting marriage between a girl and the man who seized her, even with paternal consent.[131] Gratian's own response to this conflict among the sources was a nuanced response to the various pressures that must have been operative in medieval European society: After an obligatory nod in the direction of St. Jerome's authority, Gratian allowed such a marriage to occur, provided the young man did appropriate penance and the girl's father did not object.[132] Here, in the extreme case of forcible abduction, parental objections but not parental consent might play a decisive role in marital formation. If one reads into this result Gratian's commitment to free consent, one is entitled to conclude that the girl must also be given the opportunity to express her free consent at some stage in the process.

Elsewhere in the *Decretum*, Gratian also discussed the prerequisites for the formation of "legitimate marriage" (*legitimum coniugium*). These requirements included the consent of a daughter's father. In *Causa* 32, q. 2, c. 12, Gratian reproduced the text of Leo the Great which held blameless women whose fathers married them to husbands who keep concubines.[133] The closing sentence of Gratian's reproduction of this text began with the words *paterno arbitrio* — "those who are joined to husbands in virtue of paternal judgment are blameless. . . ."[134] Commenting on the words *paterno arbitrio*, Gratian continued the thought:

> When it is said by paternal judgment women [are] joined to men it is given to understand that paternal consent is desirable in marriage, nor should legitimate marriage take place without it, as is said by Pope Evaristus: "It is otherwise not a legitimate marriage unless she is handed over by the parents."[135]

The reference to "Pope Evaristus" in this passage was to the same forged text that had circulated in the days of Hincmar of Rheims.[136] The difficulty with this passage lies in the term "legitimate marriage." A requirement for a legitimate marriage need not be a requirement for a valid marriage. The canonists distinguished between licit acts and valid acts. According to canonistic reasoning an act might be illicit, that is, illegally performed, but nevertheless be valid and binding upon the person who committed the act. The forgers who produced this text clearly intended to equate legitimate marriages with valid marriages. But Gratian had in his preceding *causa* endorsed the idea of free selection as the basis of marital formation. It is entirely possible, indeed likely, that his sense of the term "legitimate" was intended to refer to the licit character and not the validity of such marriages, even though the text is not free of ambiguity.[137]

Late Twelfth-Century Decretists and Theologians

From the beginning, the decretists moved their commentaries in the direction of maximizing the freedom that Gratian acknowledged belonged to couples seeking to marry one another. The author of the work attributed to Paucapalea briefly reaffirmed Gratian's teaching that no coupling ought to take place except by "free will" *(libera voluntate)*.[138] The work attributed to Paucapalea also opened its commentary to *Causa* 31 by referring to Gratian's prior treatment of clandestine marriages, asserting that although "clandestine marriages ought not to take place, once contracted they nevertheless cannot be dissolved."[139] Although the author of this text did not explicitly make the connection, it seems clear that he considered one of the consequences of greater matrimonial freedom to be the possibility of clandestine marriage, a type of union he disapproved of but did not for that reason consider invalid.

Rolandus, for his part, sought to remove any ambiguity in Gratian's teaching on the subject of parental consent to marriage. He commenced his gloss to Gratian's words *paterno arbitrio* by reciting the story of the marriage of Isaac and Rebecca.[140] Although her parents advised her to stay a little while longer with them, Rebecca freely made the decision to travel with Abraham's servant to meet with Isaac.[141] It was thus permitted, Rolandus asserted, using Scripture as his guide, to all adult women to marry whom they wish, whether or not their fathers consented. Rolandus closed by noting that Gratian's apparent approval of parental consent in some circumstances governed only the betrothals of girls under the age of twelve, who nevertheless were also to give their free consent to marriage, once they have reached the appropriate age.[142]

Rufinus also chose to gloss the words *paterno arbitrio* in order to make the point that parental consent was unnecessary to the formation of marriage.[143] Paternal consent, in Rufinus's estimation, was needed for "a more respectable and honest marriage" (*ad verecundiorem honestatem coniugii*), but was not required for a marriage's validity.[144]

The *Summa, 'Elegantius in Iure Divino'* asked, "Why is compulsion opposed to marriage?" and answered the question: "Because compulsion breaks the will and so also consent and marriage."[145] Where "consent is compelled, it is not truly consent and marriage does not operate."[146] Quoting from Urban II's letter to Prince Jourdain, which showed the daughter "weeping and resisting with all her might," the author of the *Summa* indicated that different standards of evidence might be used in assessing claims of compulsion by daughters as opposed to sons: "tears or exclamations" might suffice as proof where a daughter was under pressure, but one might have to show evidence of physical force such as a beating where a son was concerned.[147]

The *Summa, 'Induent Sancti'* stated directly that "it is certain that no one is to be compelled to contract marriage [citations omitted], and if marriage is contracted through coercion or fear without consent it is entirely (*omnino*) without force."[148] This rule was so, the author of the *Summa* continued, despite the maxim of Roman law that taught that even a coerced will nevertheless counted as a will.[149] Such a coerced will, the *Summa's* author concluded, was "ineffective" (*[i]nefficax*) to contract marriage.[150]

By the time one arrived at Johannes Teutonicus's *Glossa ordinaria* in the early thirteenth century, the principle of free consent was well established. At the outset of his commentary to *Causa* 31, *quaestio* 2, where Gratian established the primacy of free consent, Johannes wrote: "Here it is asked whether a woman might be compelled to marriage and it is responded no; because in marriage the mind ought to enjoy full liberty."[151] And at *Causa* 32, *quaestio* 2, c. 12, where Gratian's source spoke of "legitimate" marriages, Johannes made it clear that parental consent was a matter of liceity — "the common solemnity" associated with marriage — and not required for validity.[152]

Theologians of the mid- and late-twelfth century came to accept the basic premises laid down by Gratian and the decretists. Peter of Poitiers (1130-1205) proposed that the sacrament of marriage consisted of the consent of two souls and was completed by carnal coupling.[153] Indeed, Peter argued, the "consent of souls" had sacramental significance in that it represented the spiritual union that was created by matrimony.[154] Borrowing from Aristotelian vocabulary, Peter declared that this consent was the "efficient cause" of marriage, and that it had to occur, as the canonists had argued, in the present tense between the parties themselves.[155] Although Peter did not take up the issue of coerced consent, it seems that such consent was altogether excluded from a theory of marriage formation that looked to marriage as a freely-formed spiritual union of two souls.

The *Summa Sententiarum* (ca. 1150), a work attributed by Migne to Hugh of St. Victor but borrowed in its relevant part from Walter of Mortaigne, leaned more explicitly than had Peter on the canonists.[156] Reviewing Gratian's sources and arguments, the author of the *Summa* asserted that "in the time of grace" that had commenced with Jesus' ministry it was the "legitimate consent of two suitable persons" that constituted a marriage.[157] The author noted that Roman law seemed to allow for coerced consent, but he responded by citing Pope Urban II's response to the king of Aragon.[158] "From this authority," the author concluded, "marriage comes into being among those who consent freely, not among those who object and are unwilling."[159]

Peter Lombard, the twelfth-century theologian whose works formed the obligatory starting point of the scholastic tradition, similarly endorsed Gratian's vision of freedom as the foundation of marital consent. "It is required," Peter began, "that conjugal consent be free of coercion."[160] As authority for this proposition, Peter summoned Gratian's sources. Pope Urban II's letters to Prince Jourdain and Sancho Ramirez were quoted in their relevant parts.[161]

Peter concluded from these sources: "From these it is apparent that marriage comes into being among those who consent and are willing, not among those who resist and are unwilling."[162] Peter recognized the possibility that those who were unwillingly joined might nevertheless ratify their marriages where they had been given "the faculty of departing or reclaiming their old way of life" and elected instead to remain together.[163] In these circumstances, Peter noted, where free consent is subsequently exchanged, the effects of the prior compulsion are removed.[164] Thus Gratian's teaching came to form not only the foundation of the canonistic tradition but also the scholastic.

Part III: The Triumph of the Principle of Free Consent

Papal Legislation

Popes, from the time of Alexander III (1159-1181), began to make it their steady policy to promote the cause of marital freedom.[165] Three papal decretals were especially significant. Alexander III issued *Cum locum* to resolve a dispute between two men of Pavia.[166] Each man had sought to marry a certain girl (*puella*) and apparently each had brought pressure to bear upon her. Alexander opened his decretal with the broad statement of principle that "since consent has no place where fear or compulsion intervenes, it is necessary where someone's assent is required that the stuff of compulsion be removed."[167]

To protect the girl's freedom, Alexander ordered that she be placed in a secure house until she should decide freely on a spouse. *Cum locum* can thus be seen as crystallizing in the Church's positive law the principle articulated by Gratian. It recognized that true consent can only be voluntary and that coercion has no place where consent is a requirement of the law. What is missing from *Cum locum*, however, is corresponding legal protection of those whose rights to free consent are violated. Pope Alexander III sought to protect the girl in her freedom, but did not propose to invalidate a decision that resulted from force or fear.

A second decretal of Alexander III's, however, *Veniens ad nos*, responded to this concern.[168] *Veniens ad nos* legislated the remedy for coerced marriages by declaring that such marriages were invalid. The decretal also articulated the legal standard to be used in judging whether a particular marriage was brought about through impermissible coercion. This was the "steady man" (*constans vir*) test.[169] Concerning this legal standard, John Noonan has written that "a 'steady man' was a fictional man of average fortitude who served in fear cases much as a 'prudent man' is used to measure negligence in modern tort law."[170] Where a steady man would have been overwhelmed by fear or unable to resist the force brought to bear against him, the marriage was to be declared invalid.

Gregory IX's decretal *Gemma* is the third significant text.[171] Gregory IX responded to a betrothal agreement that contained a penalty clause requiring the party breaching the agreement to forfeit a fixed sum. Gregory labelled the clause "attempted extortion" and invalidated it in the name of the principle that marriages ought to be free (*libera matrimonia esse debeant*).[172] This decretal acknowledged that fear need not be the product only of physical threats. Financial and other concerns might also give rise to an impermissible fear.[173]

Subsequent Commentary

Subsequent commentators accepted the basic premise of this legislation. Even before the *Liber Extra* appeared in published form, Tancred in his *Summa* on marriage had distilled some of the essential elements of the papal legislation found in Pope Gregory IX's collection. Violence, Tancred argued, constituted an impediment to marriage.[174] This was because violence, by its nature, excludes matrimonial consent. "For where fear and coercion intercedes, consent has no place."[175] And so, Tancred continued, "if consent has no place, neither is there any marriage, because [marriage] is contracted by consent alone."[176] There was a difference between great force or fear, which cannot be resisted, and "light" threats, which did not exclude matrimonial consent.[177] But where fear is sufficient to sway a "constant man," matrimonial consent was thereby excluded.[178]

This sort of analysis came to be generally accepted. Commenting on Alexander III's choice of the term *virum constantem* ("steady man"), Bernard of Parma explicitly connected this doctrine with the liberty necessary to contract marriage by stating that "he who consents ought to be free."[179] In explaining Alexander III's decision to allow even the plaintiff in *Veniens ad nos,* who must have been guilty either of adultery or fornication, to take advantage of the steady man doctrine, Bernard stated that a person's fault was irrelevant in determining whether he was the victim of force and fear.[180] Bernard also agreed with the outcome in *Gemma,* noting that financial compulsion can be sufficient to invalidate consent.[181]

Some decretalists essentially echoed Bernard's commentary. Innocent IV largely restated Bernard's analysis, although with occasional elaboration. Thus Innocent observed that force and fear exerted against third parties might also invalidate consent. He illustrated this point with the example of a father who, threatened with death or captivity, arranges a marriage for his daughter. The daughter, to relieve her father's fear, followed through with the wedding against her own wishes. Such a marriage was invalid, Innocent reasoned, unless the daughter consented freely.[182] Hostiensis reiterated this accepted position with little in the way of original commentary, although he also noted that a "lesser fear" might vitiate a woman's consent.[183]

Raymond of Peñafort, however, stands out in the way in which he developed what might be termed a whole psychology of human compulsion which allowed him to engage in a refined analysis of force and fear cases. In considering the sort of force and fear that might generally invalidate oaths, Raymond asked: What of someone taken captive by enemies or compelled by robbers by the "gravest sort of fear that can befall a steady man"?[184] What if by reason of this force he swore that he would pay a thousand pounds or hand over some castle? Is he obliged to fulfill the terms of the oath?

Raymond considered the various ways in which this problem might be addressed. On the one hand, the captors and the robbers might improperly benefit from their wrongdoing through the fulfillment of the coerced oath. Furthermore, the oath itself should not become a means of enforcing iniquity.[185] To this point, Raymond seemed more concerned with preventing unjust enrichment than with absolving the party whose oath had been coerced. Raymond heightened the tension by looking to St. Augustine, who had declared that a coerced will was still a will and that an oath that can be observed without threat to one's salvation should be kept.[186] He resolved this tension by pointing to Roman law, which declared that the praetor should not ratify what has been done by reason of force and fear.[187]

Having raised the possibility of legally invalidating the effects of a coerced promise, Raymond applied this analysis to marriage. He noted that the law made clear that coerced matrimonial consent was no consent at all.[188] Like Tancred, Raymond placed force and fear among the marital impediments.[189] Raymond asserted furthermore that grave force and fear excluded the possibility of marital consent, "by reason of nature itself," even in the absence of ecclesiastical law.[190] Although a "light fear" did not excuse one from one's marital promise, Raymond noted, the sort of fear that might sway a steady man did.[191] Among the examples of such fear Raymond cited were fear of death, of torture, of immorality, and of enslavement.[192] Raymond, however, also cautioned that force and fear should not be confined to these examples. Rather, he said, all sorts of proofs of force and fear might be admitted because of the variability of the effects of force on the human person. The judge, Raymond admonished, will take account of "the diversity of persons and places, the quality of fear, and will adjudge a [union] to be marriage or not."[193] Grounded on the natural law, focused on the particularities of the individual and his or her susceptibility to coercion, Raymond appreciated that the constant man standard had to be applied with sensitivity to the actual persons before the court.

The "Faculty" of Contracting Marriage:
A Zone of Protected Freedom

Gratian's *dicta*, the legislation of the popes, and the analyses of the decretists combined to create a zone of freedom. This zone of freedom was not to be intruded upon by those not a party to a marriage. The area of protected liberty came routinely to be called a *facultas* ("faculty") by the medieval canonists — the "faculty of contracting marriage."[194]

Modern analyses of rights are concerned especially with emphasizing the role rights play as a limitation on state action. Richard Flathman, for example, states that "[v]ery prominent in the modern tradition of rights is the notion that rights should protect not freedom in general but specifically freedom from excessive interference on the part of the state."[195] The thirteenth century presented a different situation. Governments were not yet seen as potentially all-pervasive mechanisms of coercion. Rather, government was seen by many as a source of stability and order. This is not to say, however, that rights were not sometimes asserted against governmental entities; such assertions of right were a common feature of the medieval legal landscape. But the larger point is that government was not invariably seen as the greatest threat to personal freedom.

Of great importance to thirteenth-century life was the potentially coercive role of the family. The father in his role as the head of the household, according to medieval canon and Roman law, exercised the right of paternal power, which carried with it real legal authority and responsibility.[196] Dynastic considerations, including arranged marriages, were a large part of family life, especially among the aristocratic and moneyed elements of society.[197] The free faculty of contracting marriage, supported by the ultimate sanction of invalidity, was an important "trump" to play in this context. Matters of dynastic policy could be frustrated by the free assertion of the individual right to contract marriage.

The basic freedom to contract marriage was protected not only by the force and fear doctrine, but also by the application of a rule of interpretation that allowed canonists to construe narrowly any legislation prohibiting individuals from marriage. Legislation restricting the right to marry would be considered "prohibitory edicts" (*prohibitoria edicta*). This doctrine taught that insofar as certain fundamental rights were concerned, legislation prohibiting the exercise of that right would be strictly construed.[198] Among the protected areas were the right to postulate, that is, to make known one's concerns to those with the jurisdictional authority to respond, the right to testify in court or to retain a proctor, and, of course, the basic right to enter marriage.[199] The implication for marriage of this doctrine was that all individuals not expressly restricted by the diriment impediments of canon law were to be permitted to marry.

The canonists were willing to extend this principle quite broadly. All those not clearly unable to exchange marital consent — such as the perpetually insane — or to engage in sexual intercourse — the perpetually frigid or impotent — were not to have their right of marriage denied.

Invoking this principle, Innocent III recognized in two separate decretals that deaf-mutes need not use words but might marry merely by exchanging visible rather than oral signs of consent.[200] Alexander III permitted lepers to marry if they could find willing spouses.[201] Also, Raymond of Peñafort made sure to include in *Liber Extra* a decretal of Pope Hadrian IV permitting *servi* to marry freely, even when their masters objected.[202] At least one decretist, Sicard of Cremona, grounded the right of serfs to marry on natural law.[203]

Later commentators accepted and expanded upon these categories. Bernard of Pavia wrote that according to "the ancient canons" a serf and a serving girl might not marry where their lords objected; by the "new law" of Hadrian IV, however, "the consent of the principal parties suffices, even if it takes place against their lords' objections."[204]

In glossing *Cum apud*, Hostiensis acknowledged as correct the interpretative principle used by Innocent III to uphold the marriages of deaf-mutes and tested its limits by inquiring whether someone might still marry if he or she was not only deaf and mute but also blind. Hostiensis replied in the affirmative.[205] Raymond of Peñafort defined *prohibitoria edicta* by reference to the diriment impediments: all those not restricted by one of the impediments, such as religious vow, Holy Orders, consanguinity, or some other impediment, were free to marry.[206] He also stressed that these impediments were to be narrowly construed so as to ensure maximum freedom.[207]

In glossing *Dignum*, Bernard of Parma noted that the decretal's holding, which literally applied only to marriages of *servi* or *ancillae,* could also be extended to marriages between free persons and those of servile status, provided the free parties were fully aware of their partners' legal status.[208] Bernard of Parma also narrowly construed at least one of the diriment impediments. The insane, Bernard argued, might contract marriage during a lucid interval.[209]

The doctrine on prohibitory edicts was directed against a potentially broader range of interference than the doctrine on force and fear. To be sure, the rule at least theoretically embraced families that might have forbidden their deaf-mute or blind children from marriage. Indeed, canonists at least occasionally recognized that children might bring a cause of action against their parents for interfering with their right to marry.[210]

The rule, however, was also directed against public authorities of various sorts. Bishops and pastors were not to deny marriage to those individuals within the protected classes. Feudal lords were not to prohibit their villeins from marriage. Cities and communes were not to legislate against the marriages of lepers. Comparable in its operation to the strict scrutiny standard of modern American fundamental rights cases, the rule on prohibitory edicts imposed an exacting standard on legislation restricting the right to marriage. Legislation restricting this right was automatically suspect.

What is significant for the purposes of this discussion is the role that this right played within the entire structure of the law of marriage. The basic right to marriage was not, to use Michel Villey's terminology, a "vague and subordinate" part of the law. Rather, it was fundamental to the creation of the entire sacrament of matrimony.[211] A marriage was formed by consent. That consent had to be free and unencumbered from outside interference. It was a protected freedom that might be asserted against familial authority, but it could also be asserted, in the appropriate context, against public authority. One could not be compelled unwillingly into marriage, and legislation restricting the right to marry was suspect. Deaf-mutes, lepers, serfs, and the blind were all canonically free to marry.

Clandestine Marriage

Given that the consent of the parties alone constituted a valid marriage, the question presented itself: what were the logical limits of such a doctrine? The older law, represented by a theologian like Hincmar of Rheims or a law code like the *Lex Visigothorum,* which made parental consent a constituent element of marriage, also required, sometimes by implication, sometimes explicitly, that marriage take place in accord with some specified form. Thus Hincmar wrote that in addition to parental consent there was required for a valid marriage the "public ceremonies of marriage" (*publiciis nuptiis*).[212]

It was Gratian, who had taken the decisive steps in favor of grounding marriage on the free consent of the parties, who first raised in a systematic way the possibility that clandestine marriages — secret marriages, contracted by the parties themselves in the absence of any prescribed form or public witnessing — might be valid.

Gratian commenced his treatment of clandestine marriage by citing pseudo-Evaristus for the proposition that a legitimate marriage cannot come into being unless one first sought the permission of the man who has custody of or authority over the prospective bride.[213] Such a union should take place publicly, with due solemnity; any other form of union is not only not legitimate, but presumptively adulterous.[214]

Gratian cited several authorities for this proposition: a passage drawn from Pope Nicholas I asserted the need to obtain the consent of parents as well as the couple themselves;[215] texts attributed to Pope Hormisdas and Leo the Great made much the same point. He concluded this catalogue of authorities by asserting: "By these authorities secret marriages are prohibited, and so, since these nuptials are against the law, they ought to be held to be infirm" *(pro infectis)*.[216]

Gratian, however, must have remained dissatisfied with this answer. He followed his response with two further decretals that seem only peripherally related to his concerns: a text of St. Isidore that taught that among the signs of marriage are the decision of the wife to go about veiled, since veiling was a sign of her subjection to her new husband; and the mutual decision to wear wedding rings, since this is a sign of "joining of hearts by a single pledge."[217] St. Isidore's lesson was followed by a text of St. Ambrose declaring that Rebecca and Isaac were married from the time she saw him walking toward her and submitted to his authority.[218]

Abruptly, in his *dictum* following the passage from St. Ambrose, Gratian changed his focus from the illegality of secret marriage to its apparent validity. Gratian bluntly wrote: "But it is objected to the foregoing: Many things are prohibited which, if they occur, are, from that time onward, valid."[219] "And so," Gratian continued, "clandestine marriages are against the laws, nevertheless, once contracted, they cannot be dissolved, because they are subsequently given firmness by a legitimate promise."[220] As authority, Gratian once again looked to pseudo-Evaristus: "Whence even Evaristus, when he wrote that they are otherwise not presumed marriages, but adulterous affairs, added: unless they have chosen by their own will, and their legitimate promises give them sustenance."[221]

Gratian has been criticized for the abruptness and apparent confusion of his endorsement of the simultaneous validity and illicitness of clandestine marriage.[222] Raymond Decker, for instance, has pointed to the conflict between "personal responsibility" and "institutional authority" inherent in this analysis and concluded that "Gratian seems to respond to these questions in a schizophrenic manner."[223] Gratian, as Decker sees it, wished to confer simultaneous approval and disapproval on the practice of secret marriages.

Decker's acknowledgement of the importance of "personal responsibility" in Gratian's analysis of marriage, however, is an important insight. Indeed, Gratian's analysis of personal responsibility is merely his doctrine of personal freedom seen in a different shade. Gratian's theory of marital formation, grounded as it was on personal freedom, also presupposed that that freedom would be exercised wisely. He was even prepared to acknowledge the possibility that free choices could be made wisely in the absence of the institutional framework of the Church, through the words and actions of the parties themselves, in their exchange of present-tense consent and their subsequent marital acts.

This basic tension between the freedom of consent, on the one hand, and the need to retain some institutional and parental control over the celebration of marriage remained a constant feature of high and late medieval law and life. The author of the *Summa* attributed to Paucapalea endorsed the possibility of clandestine marriage, but he also repeated Gratian's own reservations about such unions: "'they are not denied to be marriages, nor can they be ordered dissolved, but rather they are proven by the acknowledgement of both parties; but they are nevertheless [legally] prohibited, because when the will of the parties have changed, they cannot be proven by another's confession before a judge.'"[224]

Other canonists echoed these concerns, but proved unable, because of their commitment to the consent theory of marriage, to pronounce clandestine marriages invalid. Thus the *Summa Parisiensis* distinguished between two types of prohibited acts: those that were prohibited because of some "perpetual cause" (*perpetuam causam*), and those that were prohibited out of a desire for "greater caution" (*ad majorem cautelam*).[225] In essence, the author of the *Summa* had distinguished between invalid acts — acts always and everywhere wrong — and acts that, while prohibited, were not for that reason to be considered invalid. Clandestine marriage, the *Summa's* author observed, fell into the latter category. Such unions were prohibited out of a desire to safeguard the parties from ill-considered decisions and because of the difficulties of proof inherent in a secret marriage. But, the *Summa* noted, if the parties exchanged present-tense consent and if they subsequently acknowledged publicly their marital promises, they were obliged to remain together as man and wife.[226]

Rufinus, for his part, also declared to be illegal but not invalid those secret unions that took place without due solemnities, without the handing over of the bride, or her veiling, without even the presence of witnesses.[227] Such marriages, Rufinus wrote, echoing the language of the *Summa Parisiensis*, were prohibited, not for any intrinsic violation of the rules regarding marital formation — "since consent alone makes a marriage" — but only as "a precaution" *(propter cautelam)*, because they presented difficult issues of proof.[228] Where they were entered into, however, they were valid although illicit unions.[229]

In light of the triumph of the consent theory of marriage and the consequent sanctioning of even clandestine unions, *Liber Extra's* treatment of marriage contained a title "On Clandestine Marriage." The first of its three texts asserted that in clandestine marriages, the burden of proof was on the one alleging the existence of a marriage.[230] The second text conceded that where both parties acknowledged the existence of a secret union, their confessions were sufficient to prove the existence of a valid marriage.[231] A third text, an enactment of the Fourth Lateran Council, repeated the condemnation of clandestine marriage as a violation of canon law, declared that marriages should take place publicly, before a priest and witnesses, and also required that parish priests announce beforehand marriages that were scheduled to take place.[232] Penances were to be imposed on those who married in violation of these rules, even though their marriages were not for that reason to be declared invalid.[233]

A final text, recognizing that parties might marry validly but illicitly in violation of an ecclesiastical interdict forbidding the celebration of the sacraments, rounded out the legislation.[234] Again, penances were to be imposed for those who broke an interdict in this manner, and those who married under such circumstances were to be separated until such time as the interdict was lifted, but the marriages so contracted nevertheless remained valid.[235]

A consistent policy is discernible in this legislation: marriage remained the prerogative of the parties themselves, who might validly marry even in the absence of official witnesses and even in violation of positive ecclesiastical law. The canonists, however, continued to criticize the practice of clandestine marriage. Pope Innocent IV, for instance, denounced the custom as "dangerous" and likely to threaten the legitimacy of offspring.[236] But not even this canonist-pope was inclined to challenge the basic distinction between valid but illicit acts upon which clandestine marriage was accepted.

Hostiensis elaborated upon this legislation and the policy that undergirded it. In his *Summa,* Hostiensis embarked upon a lengthy and intricate analysis of clandestine marriage. He began from the premise that "the Church required consent alone as the essence of marriage."[237] Whence it sufficed to create a marriage for the parties to say to one another "we consent."[238]

The practical implication of this doctrine, as Hostiensis acknowledged, was that canon law was required to take account of and regulate clandestine marriage.[239] Hostiensis himself proposed that the category of clandestine marriages embraced between four and six subcategories.[240] These included: secret marriage in the sense that due solemnities, such as the priestly blessing and the handing over of the bride by her parents or guardians, were omitted.[241] Another type was clandestine marriage in the full sense of the term, where not only the due solemnities but witnesses also were missing.[242] Yet another type of secret marriage occurred where a party broke a betrothal to marry someone else, or where a party bound by a prior marital obligation married bigamously.[243] Male or female religious who married in violation of solemn professions of continence also fell under the category of secret marriage, as did those who married without the proper banns, or in defiance of ecclesiastical interdict.[244]

Not all of these marriages were valid — marriages of those bound by prior marital bonds or vows of continence were to be denied all legal status. But aside from these exceptions, Hostiensis was prepared to acknowledge — as his theory of marital formation demanded — that most of these situations resulted in valid unions, even where the marriages had been contracted illicitly.[245]

The practice of clandestine marriage created large social problems. Because many clandestine marriages lacked witnesses and their terms were known only to the parties,[246] they remained practically unprovable in ecclesiastical court absent admission by both parties that they had, in fact, exchanged vows. Despite the practical difficulties, however, and in the face of heavy criticism throughout the later Middle Ages,[247] clandestine marriage remained a fixture of canon law. Panormitanus, writing in the fifteenth century, thus stressed that the secrecy of the exchange of consent did not invalidate a marriage even though the parties thereby sinned.[248] Where the parties themselves asserted publicly that they have exchanged such consent, Panormitanus added, they are to be believed and understood to be properly married "in the view of the Church."[249] Their children, even if born before the "publication" of their consent, were thus deemed to be legitimate.[250]

Clandestine marriage, furthermore, remained a popular form of marriage throughout the later Middle Ages, and a fertile seedbed of litigation, as court records of the fourteenth and fifteenth centuries amply demonstrate. Thus James Brundage has written:

> Secret marriages made up a sizeable part of the case load in many ecclesiastical courts. The Synod of Nantes in 1386 complained that clandestine unions occurred daily and the records show that this was no exaggeration. Nearly half of the mid-fifteenth-century marriage cases heard by the Augsburg court, for example, involved clandestine marriages, as did about one-third of the Regensburg cases in 1490.[251]

Clearly, persons throughout the high and late Middle Ages considered themselves legally empowered to make their own choices regarding marital partners, even when, as must have happened frequently, they acceded to the wishes of parents or others. The law had carved out an area of personal freedom that the broad mass of the populace had come to recognize and utilize. One hopes that some of them, at least, were also able to exercise the requisite personal responsibility that the law also expected of those who entered a sacramental union — to maintain that union until the end of their natural days.

Part IV: Women and the Right to Marry

Law and Pastoral Practice

Women as well as men enjoyed the free exercise of the right to marry. In the decretal *Consultationi,* Pope Honorius III confronted the situation of women "who soon after the priestly benediction flee their marriages, before carnal coupling, asserting that they never truly consented to [their husbands], but were compelled by an imposed fear to utter words of consent, even though they dissented in their minds."[252] Honorius responded to this problem by extending the "steady man" doctrine to women. Where the force and fear experienced by women was sufficient to move a steady man, the pope reasoned, the marriages themselves should be ruled invalid.[253]

This decretal received only passing reference by a number of the thirteenth-century commentators. Bernard of Parma thus noted, in glossing the phrase *in constantem,* that this rule was "the same as *Veniens.*"[254] Bernard followed this observation with a perfunctory comparison between "lesser fear" which did not vitiate consent, and the sort of grave fear, such as danger of death or bodily torture, that excused one from performance.[255]

At least one canonist, however, despite the use of "male" language in *Consultationi,* argued that the impact of force and fear on women might be different than on men. Hostiensis premised his analysis on the principle that fear cases must be judged by the totality of circumstances. Threats of violence might invalidate consent, but so might financial threats, such as disinheritance.[256] A good judge, Hostiensis noted, will examine the sort of person (*qualitate personarum*) alleging force and fear, the type of force or compulsion brought to bear, its time and place, whether the party so moved subsequently ratified his or her consent, or whether he or she always dissented, either "expressly or tacitly."[257]

In this context, Hostiensis continued, one factor to bear in mind was whether the party making the allegations was a woman. A woman, Hostiensis noted, was "more quickly terrified" than a man and so her consent might be impeded by a lesser fear than a man's.[258] Women are the "more fragile sex," Hostiensis continued, employing a stereotype of his day, and the Latin word for woman — *mulier* — was derived from "softness of heart" (*mollicie cordis*).[259] Indeed, a woman might not be subjected to the same range of threats as a man. It was unlikely that a father would ever kill his daughter if she did not consent, although Hostiensis seemed to think homicide was possible where a son resisted his father's wishes.[260] But a woman should not be denied a hearing merely because the compulsion she might be subjected to differed from the sorts of pressures that could be brought against men.

In evaluating Hostiensis's analysis one should not condemn his homely etymology of the word *mulier* and one should avoid the easy criticism that he is merely reflecting the kind of misogynistic worldview common to most thirteenth-century writers. In fact, Hostiensis seems to be coming to terms with the full range of possibilities presented by force and fear cases and acknowledging that women — who, in a male-dominated world, may be vulnerable to economic as well as physical threats — might in some circumstances be in greater need of judicial solicitude.

Women in the later Middle Ages were able to avail themselves both of the freedom to contract marriage and the protection afforded by the doctrine on coerced consent. It is doubtlessly true that many, probably most, marriages of the later Middle Ages were the product of at least some kind of parental arrangement.[261] Women, in particular, were often expected as a matter of social custom to obtain not only the approval of parents but also the advice and sometimes even the approval of outsiders, whether they be distant relatives or family friends or counsellors.[262] But even in these circumstances, as Shannon MacSheffrey makes clear, this social custom might be turned to good advantage:

> Although women's marriage choices were clearly circumscribed by the custom of acquiring the consent of family or others to their marriages, women could sometimes employ this apparent restriction to their advantage. Some used the convention of seeking the consent or advice of important people in their lives to prevaricate when faced with a proposal of marriage they were not yet sure they wanted to accept or reject.[263]

Women acting in ways both subtle and direct to assert their freedom to marry whom they wished had by the middle and later thirteenth century behind them the whole weight of ecclesiastical authority. The marriage liturgies that developed in the twelfth and thirteenth centuries required the Church's minister to inquire into the couple's willingness to have one another as man and wife.[264] Indeed, Michael Sheehan has observed that among the "most developed sections" of medieval *ordines* were the questions priests were directed to ask in order to determine the parties' "intention to marry."[265]

Handbooks for pastors also reminded priests of the importance of the parties' freedom to consent.[266] Summarizing the teaching of Richard Wetheringsett, who authored a *summa* for confessors in the years between 1215 and 1222,[267] Jacqueline Murray states:

> Wetheringsett was . . . clear in his defense of the freedom to consent. He not only counseled priests to assist people who wanted to marry in spite of opposition from either family or lord, but he also warned priests to refuse to preside at the marriages of unwilling people. He stated that under no circumstances were priests to acquiesce to threats and solemnize a union unless the couple freely consented; it was the wills of the couple that ought to be joined.[268]

Another leading penitential writer, Thomas Chobham, who was active in English ecclesiastical affairs in the first three decades of the thirteenth century,[269] made clear that different levels of fear operated on persons differently, depending on circumstance:

It is nevertheless to be noted that some fear is great for one person and slight for another person. Whence it is read in a certain decretal that a little girl who was under her parents' power was compelled by them through certain threats and certain terrors, so that at the door of the church she consents to a certain young man; and when it is asked of her, "do you wish to have this man?" she responded, weeping, "I do." And she was crying when led to the church and after she said that she would never have him as husband, nor did she wish to enter his bedroom. And the lord pope in this decretal said that her tears sufficed to prove violence. For a modicum of fear can compel a tiny, young girl to confess that she wished to have him whom she did not consent to in mind.[270]

"We That Ought of Very Ryght to Be Moost To-gether": *Case Studies of Marital Freedom in the Later Middle Ages*

The degree to which such freedom was actually claimed by the parties is illustrated by a famous case from fifteenth-century England, that of Margery Paston. The Paston family had emerged from relative obscurity at the end of the fourteenth century to become one of the leading families of Norfolk and, by the middle decades of the fifteenth century, one of the great gentry families of England.[271] They are well-known today because of the large and comprehensive cache of their letters and documents that have survived, preserving for future scholars all manner of detailed evidence concerning business and family dealings.[272] While "neither Lancastrian nor Yorkist by tradition or conviction," the Pastons were to be found during the Wars of the Roses supporting one or the other of these families, usually as the result "of their own private interests and the postures of whatever great noble . . . they depended on at the moment for patronage."[273]

The Paston women were probably not unusual among fifteenth-century gentry in the degree to which they were required to exercise their own independent judgment in the management of family affairs.[274] Margaret Mautby Paston may be taken as an example. Born sometime in the early or mid 1420s, she was the only daughter of a local lawyer who "belonged to an old, large, and well-connected Norfolk family."[275] With her marriage to John Paston in 1440, she brought into the family wealth, connections, and a powerful set of skills for overseeing the day-to-day operations of large landed estates. Regarding the range of responsibilities Margaret undertook, Ann Haskell has observed:

Typically, her routine involved such activities as interviewing workers, hearing complaints, arbitrating disputes, and supervising rent-collections. The condition of the crops and their most advantageous markets were her concern; one of her biggest responsibilities was procuring supplies, sometimes an entire season in advance of their use, including such provisions as weapons for defense of the castle and manorial buildings. She was particularly astute in obtaining and analyzing news of local trends, political and otherwise, and of reporting them to her husband in London with appropriate precautionary advice when necessary. The most celebrated single event in Margaret Paston's long career as a manager is her withstanding an organized siege by 1,000 armed men, which literally removed the wall of a room she was occupying and drove her and twelve members of her household from the building before it was razed.[276]

John and Margaret's teenage daughter, Margery, however, would gain fame not for the astute management of the family manor or her grace under fire, but for her insistence upon marrying whom she wished. Decisions to marry in fifteenth-century England, among wealthy and aspiring gentry, included careful considerations of dynastic ambition, family alliance, wealth, and prestige.[277] The expectation was that one would marry, at the very least, a social equal, if not someone of higher station.[278]

The Paston family clearly saw the advantages of a proper marriage for Margery. In 1454, when Margery would have been about five or six, a letter from John Fastolf to "my ryght wellbelovyd cosyn John Paston" proposed a marriage for Margery in order to cement a family alliance.[279] One finds another letter, written probably four years later, in about August 1458, from Margery's uncle William Paston to her mother Margaret indicating the possibility of another marital alliance.[280] A third letter, from Margaret to John, written probably in November 1463, indicated that she had been approached by representatives of the family of Sir John Cley, who was interested in opening negotiations concerning a marriage between his son and Margery.[281]

Margery, however, who must have been a very independent personality, had different ideas concerning marriage. In May 1469, it became apparent to the family that Margery had entered into a clandestine marriage with Richard Calle, the family bailiff.[282] Calle, it has been noted, "had been an able, loyal, upper-level servant for fifteen years," who had served the Paston family interests well.[283] But his marriage to the highly prized Margery, who through the right match might have secured an important political or economic alliance for the Paston family, was simply unthinkable.

The family's response to the news was to attempt to break up the relationship. "Their initial tactic was simply to ignore the vow and to keep the girl incommunicado. . . ."[284] Margery and Richard, however, remained devoted to one another. In a letter intended to encourage Margery to remain steadfast in the face of familial disapproval and isolation, Richard wrote sometime in 1469:

> Myn owne lady and mastres, and be-for God very trewe wyff, I wyth herte full sorowefull recomaunde me unto you as he that can not be mery nor nought schalbe tyll it be otherwice wyth us thenne it is yet; for thys lyff that we lede nough is nowther plesure to Godde nor to the worlde, concederyng the gret bonde of matrymonye that is made betwix us, and also the greete love that hath be, and as I truste yet is, betwixt us, and as on my parte never gretter. Wherefor I beseche Almyghty Godde comfort us as sone as it plesyth hum, for we that ought of very ryght to be moost to-gether ar moost asondre. . . .[285]

In the emotionally charged language of this letter one finds reiterated the themes of this chapter: moved by love, Richard and Margery freely chose marriage to one another. "By very ryght," as Richard puts it, those that ought to be "moost to-gether" have been kept apart from each other through the Paston family policy of keeping Margery isolated.

Eventually, Margery and Richard would have their day in court. Richard was successful in convincing the bishop of Norwich of his obligation to intervene in the case. The bishop sympathized with the Paston family and their dynastic needs.[286] In a letter dated September 10 or 11, 1469, Margaret Paston described the bishop's examination of the parties.[287] As Margaret recalled the scene, the bishop roundly scolded Margery:

> And the Bysshop seyd to here ryth pleynly, and put here in remembrawns how sche was born, wat kyn and frenddys that sche had, and xuld have mo yf sche were rulyd and gydyd aftyre them; and yf sche ded not, wat rebuke and schame and los yt xuld be to here. . . .[288]

Margaret then recalled that Richard and Margery were examined separately by the bishop. The bishop's concern was a specifically legal one and focused on the issue of consent: "[The Bishop] seyd that he woold wndyrstond the worddys that sche had seyd to hym, wheythere yt mad matramony ore not."[289] Margery responded by informing the bishop that if her words did not constitute matrimonial consent she would be sure to re-state her intention in a way that did make a true marriage.[290]

Richard was also subjected to examination and "here worddys and hys acordyd, and the tyme and where yt xuld a be don."[291] Reluctantly, the bishop agreed that the parties were married. The family's response was "so-cial ostracism. . . . Following the inquiry she was permanently barred from home."[292] Richard "remained in the Pastons' family employment for several years," but the relationship between him and the family was kept at a proper, emotionally distant level.[293]

Margaret died in 1484, two years after her daughter Margery had passed away. In a will dated February 4, 1482, she made a gift of twenty pounds to Margery's offspring by Richard.[294] Independent to the end, and availing herself of the right granted to her by canon law to be buried apart from her husband, Margaret further specified that her body should "be beried in the ele of the cherch of Mauteby byfore the ymage of Our Lady there, jn which ele reste the bodies of divers of myn aunceteres whos sowles God assoile."[295]

While unusual, the case of Margery Paston was hardly unique. Within the Paston family one encounters as well the example of Elizabeth Paston, daughter of William Paston and Margery's aunt. While in her late teens, she was betrothed to a certain Stephen Scrope, an "old battered wid-ower of nearly fifty," who had been disfigured by disease, probably small-pox.[296] Elizabeth rejected this match. For her temerity, she was kept in iso-lated quarters — "for sche may not speke wyth no man, ho so ever come . . ." — and beaten regularly — "betyn onys in the weke or twyes, and som tyme twyes on o day, and hir hed broken in to or thre places."[297] Even-tually, however, the family would find other, more agreeable matches for Elizabeth, "first to Robert Poynings for three years, and eventually to Sir George Browne for ten, alliances that made her one of the wealthiest women in England."[298]

One hundred years before the Paston family tribulations, the case of the Fair Maid of Kent also illustrated the extent to which women might ex-ercise real freedom in choosing marriage partners, where they so desired. "Joan Plantagenet, the Fair Maid of Kent . . . [was] the granddaughter of one king of England and the mother of another."[299] Joan was unusual in her time and in light of her station in life, Karl Wentersdorf has noted, be-cause both of her legitimate marriages were contracted clandestinely.[300]

Born in 1328, Joan was twelve years old when, in 1340, she entered her first clandestine marriage, with Thomas Holland, a knight of no small martial prowess at the Court of King Edward III.[301] According to what can be learned about the petition he subsequently made to the papal court at Avignon, Thomas entered into his clandestine union with Joan "shortly before May 1340."[302] Thomas immediately spent the better part of a year on active military campaign, first in France, then in the Baltic defending the East European frontier against attacks by the Tartars.[303] During this time, Joan's family, unaware of her clandestine union to Thomas Holland, or simply dismissing it out of hand, arranged for her to marry a certain William Montague, "son and heir to the earl of Salisbury."[304] Joan and William subsequently exchanged marital consent in a public ceremony, duly solemnized by the Church, and proceeded to live together as man and wife.[305]

It would take Thomas another seven years to bring his petition to the papal court. Although his petition apparently is not extant,[306] Pope Clement VI's response, issued in May 1348, has survived and has been edited and published by Karl Wentersdorf.[307] We learn from the papal response the gist of Thomas's complaint: he had married Joan Plantagenet, he averred, in words of present tense, before witnesses but did not solemnize the union by ecclesiastical ceremony.[308] The exchange of consent was subsequently consummated by carnal copulation.[309] Thomas, "with his conscience urging him on, now intended to prosecute his right before the Apostolic See."[310]

The litigation lasted over a year, but was concluded in Thomas's favor.[311] The evidence Thomas produced must have been convincing because the pope was led to decree that "the aforesaid Thomas and Joan did and have truly contracted [marriage],"[312] and "ought to render to each other conjugal *obsequia*."[313] The pope repeated the term *"obsequia"* — "services," "duties" — several more times in the body of his decree, apparently preferring this term to the term *ius,* but making it clearly known that he expected the parties to treat one another as marriage partners.[314] In conformity with the pope's decree, Thomas and Joan seem to have ratified their marriage in a public ecclesiastical ceremony,[315] and remained man and wife until Thomas's death in 1360.[316]

Shortly after Thomas's death, in 1361, Joan entered a second clandestine marriage, this time with Edward III's son, also named Edward, the Prince of Wales.[317] The king attempted to break up the relationship and had good legal grounds to do so: "the bride and groom were related within the prohibited degrees of consanguinity, since they were both descended from Edward I, and they were also related by [affinity], since [the Prince] was the godfather of her first son, Thomas."[318] Eventually, however, it seems that the king was dissuaded from his plans, apparently by the couple's affection for one another, and chose instead to seek on their behalf the papal dispensation that would allow the two of them to live openly as spouses.[319]

Extensive legal documentation of this relationship also survives in the papal archives, thanks to Edward III's effort to regularize the union.[320] Again, one learns that "matrimony was contracted between them in words of present tense."[321] The union was entered into "not in contempt of the Church's [power of] the keys, but in the hope that Apostolic grace and dispensation might be mercifully obtained."[322] In the event, the pope granted the request for dispensation,[323] and the couple remained married until the prince's death in 1376.[324] "Joan herself died in 1385," and stipulated in her will "that her body be laid to rest not beside the prince of Wales but next to her first husband, Sir Thomas Holland. . . ."[325]

Clandestine marriage, clearly, was a tool that both the humble and the mighty might utilize in order to assert matrimonial freedom. The Church's ambiguous position on this practice — simultaneously condemning it as illicit and a violation of Church teaching, but upholding the validity of marriages entered into in this manner — allowed the practice of clandestine marriage to flourish, even though it would always necessarily remain a shadowy practice.[326]

Coupled with the teaching on force and fear, ecclesiastical teaching strongly supported the individual's freedom to enter marriage and, as demonstrated by the cases of Margery Paston and Joan Plantagenet, tended to side with parties seeking to validate such unions, even in the face of great countervailing pressures — whether it be the wealth and influence of the Paston family or the dynastic plans of the English royal house. In this way, to be sure, dynastic plans might be frustrated, but the parties themselves might assert, as Richard Calle declared, "the greete love that hath be, and . . . is be-twixt us."[327]

Part V: Early Modern Criticism and
Survival of the Principle of Marital Freedom

Protestant and Catholic Reform

There was gathering criticism of the institution of clandestine marriage on the eve of the Protestant Reformation. In his defense of the sacramentality of marriage, in the context of his commentary on Paul's Letter to the Ephesians, Desiderius Erasmus raised the issue of clandestine marriage.[328] Although arguments might be made against marriage's sacramental status — why, for instance, should virginity, which according to St. Jerome was superior to the married state, not be a sacrament while marriage was accorded such recognition? — Erasmus was prepared to confer on it such status.[329] There was, however, an important exception in Erasmus's mind: marriages that were "hidden and secret" (*arcanum et secretum*) should be denied sacramental standing as "being far removed from the nature of the sacraments."[330]

Erasmus was far from alone in criticizing clandestine marriage. With the outbreak of the Protestant Reformation in 1517, the critics grew especially vocal, especially among the Reformers. Martin Luther sought to restore the central role of parental consent to the making of marriage, at least for children still under the governance of their parents. "Parents, Luther wrote, are 'apostles, bishops, and priests to their children.'"[331] It was the responsibility of children's parents, or their guardians where parents had died or otherwise disappeared, to judge the fitness of their offspring for marriage and the suitability of any prospective union.[332]

Luther saw as well particular value to marriage ceremonies performed in public settings. A public celebration served "as an invitation for others to aid and support the couple, a warning for them to avoid sexual relations with either party, and a safeguard against false or insincere marriage promises made for the purpose of seducing the other party."[333] Marriage, in Martin Luther's theology, was a public institution, in which not only the couple themselves, but the entire community participated.

Other Reformers were even more emphatic. Martin Bucer denounced the "dogma" of "the Roman Antichrist" who, "against the laws of God and the Church," teaches that "marriage is made by the contracting parties [exchanging] words of present-tense consent," even where their parents remained "unaware or opposed."[334] The Roman law, the law of nature, the law of God, and the law of all nations stood against this teaching.[335] Quoting Genesis 2:24 ("For this reason a man will leave his father and mother and cling to his wife"), Bucer asserted that the natural relationship that should prevail between parents and their children demanded that children seek their parents' consent prior to marriage.[336]

In a passage that recalled but did not cite such authorities as Hincmar of Rheims, Bucer asserted that "the ancient Churches" defined rape to include someone who attempted to join himself matrimonially to a woman without the awareness and consent of the parents, "even if the woman consents."[337] Parental consent was necessary to the formation of marriage, in Bucer's estimation, and where such consent was not forthcoming for malicious reasons, the proper remedy was admonition of the parents by friends, neighbors, and the elders of the Church.[338] Children most emphatically were not to take matters into their own hands through contracting secret marriage.[339]

The challenge of the Reformers did not go unnoticed. Even before the Protestant Reformation had broken out, forces for renewal and reform were active within Catholic circles. "Early modern Catholicism," to use the term endorsed by John O'Malley,[340] already by the opening years of the sixteenth century, and in spite of widespread lack of respect for the papal headship of such men as Rodrigo Borgia (Pope Alexander VI), had experienced a remarkable rebirth in the form of new religious orders and renewed spirituality.[341] The impulse toward reform quickened with the challenge raised by the Protestant reformers, but it was present even before Martin Luther announced his Ninety-five Theses challenging Roman authority.[342]

On the agenda at the Council of Trent (1545-1563), convoked by Pope Paul III (1534-1549) in order to answer the Reformers' assault on much of the theology and the institutional structure of the Catholic Church, was the question of parental consent to marriage.

In the event, the Council compromised between those who wished to follow the Protestant Reformers in requiring parental consent and those who wished to retain the basic right and freedom of the parties to determine for themselves whom they wished to marry.[343] In a decree known as *Tametsi*, published in the twenty-fourth (and second to last) session of the Council, in November 1563, the Council fathers made clear that parental consent was not necessary for the making of a marriage.[344] Those who "falsely affirm that marriages contracted by the children of families, without the consent of their parents, are invalid" must be condemned by anathema.[345] Marriage, the Council asserted, could only come into being through the free consent of the parties themselves.[346]

But if the Reformers, in their enthusiasm to restore parental control over their children's marriages, were condemned, so also was the old system of clandestine marriage. The Council made clear that clandestine marriages entered into prior to the effective date of the decree were not to be judged invalid.[347] But the Council also took notice of the abuses that clandestine marriage fostered. The practice of secret marriage had given rise to many grave sins, not least the practice of some men who, while married to one woman, agreed secretly to marry a second woman and, still more sinfully, agreed openly to marry a third woman.[348] Such men, the Council averred, "lead lives of perpetual adultery."[349]

The remedy for this abuse was not the restoration of parental control over the marital decision-making process. Rather, the Council decided to require, for the validity of marriage, a public ceremony to occur "in front of the church" (in facie ecclesiae), where the couple's pastor might ask questions about their freedom and fitness for marriage, and where at least "two or three" witnesses might memorialize the agreement.[350] The parties were to exchange present-tense consent, followed by a priestly blessing conferred in the name of the Holy Trinity.[351] Henceforward, in those countries which received Tametsi as law, clandestine marriage was effectively abolished.[352]

In one country, at least, clandestine marriage remained a live possibility until the middle of the eighteenth century. Although the English rejected the jurisdiction of the Roman Church with the adoption of the Act of Supremacy of 1534, they did not follow the Protestant Reformers of the Continent in making parental consent a requirement for valid marriage. Despite criticism from a variety of sources — "from parents and ratepayers, from some parochial clergy, from common lawyers; from Members of Parliament, and from literary and artistic satirists" — the practice of secret marriage persisted as a legal reality in England until 1753.[353] Only at this late date did Lord Hardwicke's Marriage Act succeed in outlawing the practice.[354] But even then the sinuous life of secret marriage was not at an end. From England, clandestine marriage took on still another form in the American colonies, where it became known as "common-law marriage."[355] And common-law marriage remains even today part of the domestic relations law of a number of American jurisdictions.

Survival of the Doctrine of Force and Fear

Within Catholic circles, the doctrine of force and fear received further impetus at the end of the sixteenth century, thanks to the masterful work of

Tomás Sánchez. Sánchez's treatise, *De Sancti Matrimonii Sacramento*, "On the Holy Sacrament of Marriage,"[356] has been called "a standard Roman Catholic guide to marriage problems until the mid-twentieth century."[357] A lawyer, who was "[s]ometimes betrayed by a lawyer's vices of which he was not free — a fondness for distinctions, a formalism which attempted to win substantive points by the rearrangement of abstract concepts,"[358] Sánchez was also "a grave and just and subtle spirit,"[359] who mastered the entire medieval tradition of matrimonial law and theology "with the suppleness and firmness of a supreme craftsman or artist."[360]

Sánchez considered whether the rule invalidating coerced marriages was the product of the natural law.[361] He found compelling arguments for reaching such a conclusion: if the ends of marriage include "the procreation of children and the mutual self-gift of the spouses by love," then coerced consent would seem to be the very antithesis of marital consent.[362] Extending this argument, Sánchez explored "the quality of matrimony as a free gift."[363] "Every handing over through which 'dominion' is transferred," Sánchez wrote, "ought to be fully free, for [the word] gift speaks of generous giving (*dationem liberalem*), and where it is extorted by fear there is an obligation to make restitution."[364]

Sánchez arrayed against the arguments a generally unconvincing set of claims justifying the position that the rules on coerced consent were the result of positive legislative enactment by the Roman pontiffs. Thus he wrote, answering his own argument that coerced consent vitiated the principal ends of marriage, that the goods of marriage are rendered "inconvenient" (*incommoda*) by coercion, but that coercion should not be seen as destroying the "essence" of marriage.[365] Similarly, Sánchez backtracked on the subject of gifts when he wrote that while "a gift signifies generous giving, namely, that there has been no price placed on the thing received, it need not nevertheless be entirely free."[366]

Sánchez himself seemed unconvinced of these claims. He asserted that the claim that by natural law coerced consent was no consent was "strongly probable" (*valde probabilis*).[367] Nevertheless, he concluded that the claim that it was derived from the positive law of the Church was "truer" (*veriorem*).[368] Nearly four centuries later, the teaching of the canonists, in the 1980s, seemed to move decisively but not without dissent in the direction favoring the natural-law basis of the invalidity of coerced consent by making it clear that non-Catholics are able to rely on the rules governing force and fear when petitioning for the nullity of their marriages.[369]

Sánchez also took up a concern that at various times had troubled, among others, Thomas of Chobham and Hostiensis: whether women, because of their special circumstances, might require a special solicitude in force and fear cases. Sánchez analyzed this question as part of his larger treatment of reverential fear. Reverential fear, that natural respect and awe that a subject feels toward a superior, such as a son toward his father, or a wife toward her husband,[370] was insufficient, by itself, to invalidate a marriage.[371] Only when accompanied by outward actions, such as threats or beatings, which have the effect of inducing fear in a constant man, might reverential fear be considered an invalidating factor.[372] To this point, there was very little to suggest that Sánchez might depart from an already well-worn path.

Sánchez understood, however, as Chobham and Hostiensis had before him, that different levels of fear might operate differently on different persons, depending on their condition. A son of adult age might respond differently to threats than a daughter who is a mere girl, or a son who is underage.[373] What of a daughter who is subjected to her father's wrath (*indignatio*)? Is mere fear of a father's wrath sufficient to invalidate consent?

One sees in Sánchez's answer to this question both his "fondness for distinctions" and his keen awareness of the complexity of human emotions and their impact on free consent. Sánchez commenced his answer conventionally enough: "If a daughter contracts marriage without precedent threats, but only because of the fear she might incur her father's wrath, it is valid, since this fear is not accounted as moving a steady man."[374] But, Sánchez continued, a distinction is necessary. If it is likely that the father's wrath will not long endure, and there is hope of reconciliation, this is one thing; but where it is probable that a father's or a husband's wrath will endure a long time, or forever, in such circumstances, Sánchez believed, the fear would be sufficient to invalidate.[375]

In this way an analysis of force and fear sensitive to the individual person, both male and female, and to particular circumstance, was carried forward into the sixteenth and seventeenth centuries. The right of women under the law to consent freely to marriage was thus preserved in a way that was sensitive to the manner in which family authority might be asserted in the early modern era. And, through Sánchez, modern canon law came to inherit a developed theory of force and fear and its potential impact on matrimonial consent.

2

The Right of Paternal Power
(ius patria potestatis)

Medieval theology and law conferred on the father broad authority over his household. His wife, his children, and other members of the household were entrusted as a matter of law, in the first instance, to the good judgment of the father, who enjoyed what the canon and Roman lawyers came to call the "right of paternal power." This was a right grounded on the scriptural teaching that the husband was the "head" of his wife, but it was not a right that was to be used abusively. Rather, it was intended to be utilized in conformity with a broader Christian understanding of the family as a kind of spiritual womb, where children were to be taught above all to know and love God, and spouses were to minister to each other with "marital affection."[1] A study of rights and the medieval family must properly consider both the powers accorded the father under the rubric of this right of paternal power (ius patria potestatis), and the limitations placed on the scope of this right.

Part I: Historical Context

The Classical Background

The canonists and civilians of the twelfth and thirteenth centuries did not create their law of domestic relations on a blank slate. They were instead the inheritors of a substantial body of law and teaching from late antiquity which sometimes even made use of rights language to describe domestic relationships, although these usages were never worked through systematically.

Paternal power (patria potestas), in classical Roman law, meant the authority the head of the household asserted over its members. Typically, this authority was exercised by the father, but Roman law was nearly alone among ancient societies in providing that a father did not automatically lose power over his children when they "matured and established independent households."[2] In theory, "[e]ven a grandfather and a senior magistrate of the Roman state could be in his own father's power,"[3] although in practice, in light of marriage patterns and life expectancy this must have happened only infrequently.[4]

Paternal power conferred on the head of household the power of life and death (*vitae necisque potestas*) over those under his authority. This power was apparently used by fathers early in the history of the republic where sons had violated the martial discipline of Rome, although these incidents were only recorded much later.[5] This power was also retained by the Augustan age legislation, the *Lex Julia de Adulteriis,* which permitted fathers to put to death daughters in their power who had become involved in adulterous relationships, together with their illicit lovers.[6] Jurists, however, in an effort to limit the scope of this power, argued that a father was only justified in killing daughter and lover where he caught them in the actual act. Circumstantial evidence and seemingly compromising situations were insufficient.[7]

The power of life and death was exerted in a different context as well — the exposure by parents of unwanted children, usually infants.[8] Exposure, it seems, was practiced as a form of birth control throughout much of the Greco-Roman world.[9] Exposure must often have resulted in the death of the children so exposed, and death must frequently have been the intended result, especially where the children showed obvious handicaps.[10] But exposure did not automatically conclude in the death of the child, and a social problem emerged in early imperial Rome regarding free-born children who had been exposed but reared as the slaves of those who took them in.[11] Further complicating the legal situation was the fact that paternal power need not be lost in cases of exposure.[12] A father might reassert his paternal authority at some later date or a child might seek to claim his or her birthright. The Emperor Trajan and his successors ruled that where proof was obtainable, such children were to be allowed to petition for restoration to free status. Nevertheless, in spite of these social problems, in spite of the probability of the child's death or enslavement, the paternal right to abandon one's children remained intact throughout the pre-Christian period.[13]

Fathers who had the right to abandon their children also possessed the right to sell them. Such sales, it seems, were frequently the result of pressing economic hardship and, again, involved the reduction of free-born children to slave status.[14] Only late in Roman legal history did emperors legislate to prevent such transactions.[15] In this one sense, then, *patria potestas* was somewhat restricted, so as to prohibit "fathers [from making] slaves of free-born offspring."[16]

The expansive understanding of *patria potestas* was taken to be a unique creation of civil law and was a right enjoyed only by Romans. The second-century treatise-writer Gaius's explanation of paternal power is important on this score, both because he reveals the standard Roman understanding of the power's scope and because his work subsequently influenced Justinian's analysis of the subject. Paternal power over children born of legal marriage *(iustae nuptiae),* that is, marriage with another Roman citizen or another with whom one might legitimately marry, was a right pertaining to Roman citizens *(ius . . . civium Romanorum),* Gaius argued, because nearly no other people in the world claim such broad powers over offspring as did the Romans.[17]

Justinian's definition of *patria potestas,* found in the *Institutes,* closely resembled that advanced by Gaius: "In our power," the *Institutes* declared, "are our children, whom we have brought forth from legitimate marriage."[18] This "right of power" *(ius autem potestatis),* the *Institutes* continued, closely tracking Gaius, "is proper to Roman citizens, since scarcely any other people, who have power over their children, have the sort of power we have."[19]

Paternal power was not only the power of life and death over one's offspring, but embraced as well a broad set of responsibilities for the management of the Roman *familia,* commonly but mistakenly translated as "family."[20] The *familia* was essentially the household. Ulpian thus defined the *familia* as a group of persons united, either by natural relationship or by law, under the power of a single individual, usually a male, but sometimes a female.[21] This grouping might include slaves and other retainers, as well as sons and daughters, grandchildren and great-grandchildren, provided they had not been emancipated.[22] The *paterfamilias,* however, namely, the male head of household who exercised paternal power over this assemblage, was himself excluded from Ulpian's definition since he stood outside and over the household as its head.[23] On this definition, Ulpian added, there might be a *paterfamilias* who lacked offspring himself but who nevertheless governed a household.[24]

Whether the wife of a *paterfamilias* was required to submit to paternal power was subject to varying answers at Roman law. In the law of the late Republic, two types of marriage were recognized — *in manu* marriage, that is, marriage where the wife was placed "in the hands" of her husband and subjected to his paternal power;[25] and *sine manu* marriage, "outside the hands" of her husband.[26] This latter type of marriage, known commonly as "free marriage," became, during the empire, the dominant form of marital union.[27] A wife in "free marriage" might remain subject to her own father's authority, but she also might be fully emancipated — *sui iuris* in the terms of Roman law — and thus a master of her own affairs.[28] A wife in free marriage might thus manage her own property and might also divorce her husband as freely as he might leave her.[29] By the fourth century the practice of *in manu* marriage had disappeared, surviving only in a deliberately archaizing literary source like Symmachus.[30]

The reasons for the triumph of *sine manu* marriage appear to be various. The rise of new philosophical movements, especially Stoicism, challenged the traditional paternal despotism of Roman family life.[31] "So too, the freer style of life, characteristic of Roman society in the early principate, doubtlessly rendered the *patria potestas* ever more intolerable for women."[32] But the chief factor contributing to the prevalence of *sine manu* marriage, David Herlihy suggests, was the desire of wives and their families to retain some control over the management of the dowry.[33]

The Impact of Christianity

Christianity, in its earliest forms, adopted and adapted some aspects of the Greco-Roman synthesis on marriage and rejected other aspects altogether. It has been observed that many early Christian metaphors tended to be subversive of the language of authority that surrounded the Roman legal conception of the family.[34] Where Roman law emphasized hierarchical power and submission, Christian metaphors focused on equality. In a frequently analyzed passage, after all, St. Paul boldly proclaimed that "There is neither Jew nor Greek, there is neither slave nor freeman, there is neither male or female. For you are all one in Christ Jesus."[35]

But the same St. Paul who proclaimed the equality of all believers in Christ also taught that wives should be "subject to their husbands as to the Lord; because a husband is head of the wife just as Christ is the head of the Church. . . ."[36] It was in the tension between these competing commandments, both held simultaneously in the mind of St. Paul, that a Christian theology of marriage developed — one that raised profound challenges to the Roman model and would eventually supplant it altogether.

The authority of the patriarchal Roman father did not remain unquestioned in Christian circles, particularly when it came to the exposure of infants. Even before the rise of Christianity to a position of prominence in Roman society, some non-Christian jurists had cautioned Roman fathers not to abuse their power of life and death. The jurist Marcianus thus reported that the Emperor Hadrian had exiled a father who had killed his son after the son had had an affair with his stepmother, his father's wife, on the ground that he had used his paternal right (*patris iure*) as a thug (*latronis*) might, not as a real father. Even in a case like this, where a son had betrayed his father's own bed chamber, Hadrian reasoned, a father should show *pietas* — paternal devotion — rather than savagery (*atrocitas*).[37]

But it is one thing to kill a fully mature son whom one had named and nurtured and supported through life. It is quite another to expose an infant. Roman practice, like Greek practice before it, had even allowed a certain period of time between childbirth and the acceptance of a child into a family to determine whether such an acceptance should take place.[38] It was this kind of routine practice, this kind of uncritical acceptance of the practice of exposure, that Christian theologians, lawyers, and emperors began to challenge.

From the earliest, Christian theologians denounced the practice of exposure. Athenagoras, a second-century Greek apologist for Christianity, placed his attack on exposure in the context of a larger defense of Christian attitudes about the sanctity of life. The pagan criticisms that Christians practice ritual murder or cannibalism are scurrilous, Athenagoras asserted, in the light of the fact that Christians avoid gladiatorial games as akin to taking part in homicide, condemn abortion as the taking of human life, and treat as murderers fathers who expose their offspring.[39] Clement of Alexandria, in the early third century, likewise condemned the exposure of infants as a species of homicide, admonishing that those who did not want offspring should not have engaged in lustful intercourse in the first place.[40]

Justin Martyr, writing in the second half of the second century, for his part, feared that exposure would lead to all sorts of wicked social consequences. Most children who are exposed, Justin lamented, are rescued from death only to be treated as so much cattle, put out for prostitution, or even castrated to satisfy aberrant sexual pleasure.[41] Exposure also led to the risk of incest, since one would not know whether one was having intercourse with close relatives.[42] Minucius Felix, a Latin church father of the third century, agreed, asserting that promiscuous Romans, who leave the fruits of their relations on the doorsteps of others, must inevitably have intercourse with blood relatives.[43]

Tertullian combined both strains of thought in his condemnation of exposure. Those who expose their offspring risk their deaths by cold, or by hunger, or by being torn apart by dogs, a crueler fate than simply taking the sword to them.[44] And should these offspring survive, promiscuous Romans will unknowingly have intercourse with their own children, and will spread their incest through family blood lines.[45]

It was perhaps inevitable, then, that a Christianizing empire would ultimately begin to modify its legal regime to accommodate these new insights about the sanctity of human life and the fear of incestuous pollution. A decree of the Emperor Constantine, found in the *Theodosian Code,* provided that a father who exposed his child immediately lost power over that child, with paternal power passing to those who took the child in.[46] John Boswell notes, concerning this decree, that it "changed the legal position of abandoned children not only among Romans but throughout the realms in which Roman law would be known for the next millennium."[47] Any vestigial paternal claims over an abandoned child were henceforth abolished. The decree, however, was also in some respects a product of its times. It continued to permit those who took in foundling children to raise them either as free or as slave. But it radically altered the landscape where paternal power was concerned, eliminating the right of birth parents to reclaim their children, a possibility that the pre-Christian law had offered.[48]

A second decree of Constantine, found in Justinian's *Codex,* declared in passing that fathers had once possessed the right of life and the power of death over their children, with the clear implication that this power had lapsed.[49] John Boswell is correct in noting that the paternal power of life and death had been left undisturbed by Constantine's first decree, but it must be noted, *pace* Boswell, that the second decree clearly called its continued existence into question.[50]

Its theoretical foundations undermined by Christian theologians, its legal status questioned by the first Christian emperor, the paternal power of life and death over offspring was finally outlawed by a decree of the Emperors Valentinian, Valens, and Gratian (AD 374). If anyone, male or female, killed an infant, this was a "capital evil" (*capitale . . . malum*) and amounted to homicide, the relevant text provided.[51]

Christian theology played a major role in transforming conceptions of the Roman family in other respects as well. On the one hand, Christian writers encouraged a more emotional, affective view of the relationship of husband and wife. One sees this development, for instance, in Tertullian's *Exhortation* to his wife. A Christian husband and his wife, Tertullian asserted, become two persons sharing one flesh.[52] They share a single hope, a single discipline, a single spirit.[53] Equally *(pariter)*, they participate in the Church of God, in God's own banquet. Equally as well, they share in the persecutions and hardship of the Church. Christ rejoices in such as these.[54]

A second strand of theological thinking, however, proved far more conducive to a continued exalted position for the husband as head of his wife and bearer of paternal authority. Woman, St. Augustine taught, taking Genesis literally, was to serve as man's helpmate, especially with respect to the generation of children.[55] In his treatise on Paradise, St. Ambrose wrote that woman and man were created from the same material and shared an original equality, but that this was lost as the result of original sin.[56] In justifying St. Paul's subordination of women to male headship, Augustine rejected his old teacher's dictates that man and woman were equal, albeit only in Paradise, to argue that woman's formation from Adam's rib signified her continuing derivative relationship with respect to man.[57]

St. Jerome's treatise *Ad Jovinianum*, directed against the errors of a certain Jovinian who had proposed the married and celibate states to be equal, echoed this theology much more acerbically.[58] Virginity, Jerome asserted, was always to be preferred to the lusts of married life. A wife was at best a distraction, who would prevent her husband from aspiring to a life of learning and letters, at worst, an occasion for sin, as when a man loved her more than was proper.[59] Elsewhere, in his translation of the Bible, Jerome built the case, through a series of mistranslations, that "subjection and subordination of the woman" should be the norm.[60]

This sort of misogynistic reasoning continued to be countered by "a strong and enduring tradition that maintains the spiritual equality of women. . . ."[61] In the high Middle Ages, it was challenged as well by a cult of the Virgin Mary which exalted womanhood and revered, especially, the sort of non-sexual "spiritual" marriage which Mary was believed to have enjoyed with Joseph.[62] But even Mary, whose marriage was considered true in every respect save carnal union, was presumed to have subjected herself to Joseph's benevolent authority.[63] In light of this sort of reasoning, the subjection of wife to the authority of husband, theologically and legally, would become an expectation of medieval domestic relations.

It is in the tension between these two competing visions, of spiritual equality and deep marital affection, on the one hand, and relationships of authority and subordination on the other, that a theological and legal analysis developed; at times this analysis emphasized real equality between the sexes, at other times it exalted the male headship of the family. The exact contours of this complex debate do not lend themselves to easy summary. Indeed, in some respects the very terms of the discussion differed from author to author. Much of the remainder of the next two chapters is dedicated to examining the scope of the tension between these two views and the resolutions that the medieval Christian and legal communities proposed.

Part II: Medieval Analysis of Paternal Power

Paternal Power (ius patria potestatis): A Natural Right?

Roman authors generally tended to avoid theorizing about the nature or purposes of marriage. Yet they did succeed in bequeathing to later generations certain basic ideas. From the time at least of the Augustan marriage legislation, marriage for the purpose of bringing into being a new generation was officially favored, at least among Roman upper classes.[64] Roman emperors of the fifth century, such as Majorian, continued to endorse this proposition.[65]

Justinian's compilation in the sixth century preserved this principle and conferred on it the sanctity of natural law. "Natural law," the Institutes declared, "is what nature has taught all animals, for this law is not proper to human kind, but to all animals, which reside in heaven, on earth, or in the sea. From it descends the joining of male and female, which we call marriage, and thence the procreation and education of children."[66] A text of Modestinus, found in the Digest, elaborated on this idea. "Marriage," Modestinus declared, "is a joining of male and female, a sharing of one's entire life, and a participation in the [demands of] divine and human law."[67]

Marriage, the Christian theologians of the patristic era made clear, was grounded on naturalistic premises and featured procreation and spousal companionship as essential features. Thus St. Augustine proposed that marriage is found among all nations (omnibus gentibus) for the purpose of procreation.[68] St. Augustine also built an elaborate structure on the idea that marriage was grounded on lifelong companionship. Marriage, he wrote in his treatise On the Good of Marriage, arises from human sociability and the human capacity for friendship.[69] Marriage is a good, Augustine continued, not only because it provides an outlet for human sexuality, but because it creates a larger "order of love" (*ordo caritatis*) between the parties.[70] Recognition of the enduring nature of this love allowed Augustine to posit the existence of an enduring, sacramental bond between parties to a Christian marriage.[71] Ultimately, St. Augustine conceded, despite the friendship that must prevail between the parties, the male is the head of the family unit.[72] Even here, however, Augustine followed St. Paul in acknowledging equality between the spouses with respect to the sexual "debt" they owed one another.[73]

Gratian and the twelfth-century decretists were heirs of this line of naturalistic reasoning. Echoing Roman law as reproduced through the medium of Isidore of Seville, Gratian included in his *Decretum* a definition of the natural law (*ius naturale*) as the law common to all nations, such as the joining of male and female and the education of children and their succession to the estate and place of their parents.[74] Stephen of Tournai agreed with this description,[75] as did Rufinus, who added that the Roman law was in agreement on this point with the Genesis command to "increase and multiply."[76] Johannes Teutonicus emphasized the instinctive aspect of the natural law, calling the urge to copulate and procreate a "kind of natural stimulus" arising from "sensuality."[77]

The canonists and theologians of the thirteenth century, for their part, explored in deeper and more sophisticated ways the demands natural law placed on married couples. Justinian's *Institutes* had declared that the joining of male and female had been taught by nature to all animals, but this definition failed to take account of marriage's transcendent dimension. Even Modestinus's reference to marriage as a partaking in the requirements of natural and divine law went only so far in capturing marriage's special, sacred qualities.

Hostiensis sought to address this problem by distinguishing between two types of natural law: the first was that common to man and beast alike, the second that which was unique to rational creatures.[78] Marriage was the product of this latter type of natural law, the "rational natural law" (*de iure naturali rationabili*).[79] Beasts, Hostiensis noted, like human beings, can join their bodies in an act of copulation, but only humans can unite their souls as one. This is why, he explained, marriage is "an individuated way of life," possible only between one man and one woman.[80] The union of souls one finds in marriage, Hostiensis declared, mirrored the union of the faithful believer with God, while the union of bodies mirrored Christ's marriage to the Church.[81]

Hostiensis's treatment of the naturalness of marriage was echoed in other sources. The theologians provided particularly rich understandings of marriage's origin in and conformity with the natural law. William of Auxerre distinguished among three types of natural law — "special," "universal," and "most universal."[82] Marriage belonged to the category of special natural law because, unlike coupling among the animals, human marriage demanded fidelity and unity, and reflected the marriage of Christ and the Church.[83]

Thomas Aquinas's defense of the naturalness of marriage amounted to an elaboration of themes found in Hostiensis and William. Marriage, Thomas argued, belonged to the natural law in a special way because it was made in conformity to human reason and free will and looked not only to the procreation and upbringing of children, but to the "association" of man and woman.[84] Indeed, just as man was "naturally political" and lived in community, so also male and female were required to live together, because this much was demanded by the requirements of human life.[85]

Canonists and theologians agreed as well that the wife should be subject to the authority of her husband. Gratian included a whole series of texts in the *Decretum* to justify male headship. St. Augustine was quoted as declaring that "it was manifest that the law wished woman to be subject to man."[86] A second quotation from St. Augustine announced that "the natural order . . . is that women should serve men, and children their parents, and in these things there is justice, that the lesser serve the greater."[87] Yet another passage, attributed to Augustine, attempted to justify this stance through biblical citations.[88]

A passage from St. Jerome indicated that woman is subject to man, just as man is subject to Christ, and that any woman not so subjected to a man was guilty of a crime.[89] St. Ambrose was quoted as restating the "agreed-upon" view that woman is subject to male lordship, and so may not hold authority, or teach, or act as a witness, or pledge security, or judge.[90] Other passages from yet other patristic sources were mustered to lend further support to an interpretation of Christian tradition that supported male headship in the family and in society at large.[91] Gratian concluded this line of authorities with the observation that "it is most evidently apparent that the man is head of the woman. . . ."[92]

Gratian was firmly within the mainstream of canonistic thought in advancing these claims. Indeed, he had culled many of these texts especially from his predecessor Ivo of Chartres.[93] And Gratian was followed in these claims by decretist authors who were eager to provide further justification for male headship. Rolandus agreed with Gratian that his texts "manifestly proved" that a woman is always subject *(semper subesse)* to her husband.[94] Rufinus once again looked to Genesis to justify Gratian, pointing out that God in Genesis had declared to Eve that "you will be subject to the power of your husband."[95]

The *Summa Parisiensis,* on the other hand, posed a hypothetical question: If a woman took a vow of abstinence without her husband's permission, the vow would be invalid, the author declared. But, he continued, if the husband gave his permission and afterward tried to revoke it, the husband, not the wife, would sin.[96] In this way, the author of the *Summa* seemed to indicate that paternal power was not to be used arbitarily and that its capricious and unpredictable use could ultimately affect the husband's spiritual well-being.

Johannes Teutonicus, with patristic sources apparently in mind, explained Gratian's texts by noting that woman had been created from man's body and so, presumably, enjoyed a merely derivative relationship to man.[97] Johannes understood St. Ambrose to mean that all "virile duties" were taken away from women, and that therefore they should be subject to their men and enjoy no authority to govern.[98] Johannes concluded that men therefore have power over their wives, but are also given many responsibilities concerning them.[99]

The scholastic writers provided further support for the proposition that the male should rule the household. Albert the Great, in his *Commentary* to Aristotle's *Politics,* distinguished between three types of power — the lordly power of political rulers, the paternal power of fathers with respect to offspring, and the "nuptial" power of husbands *vis-à-vis* their wives.[100] The hierarchical relationship of man over woman was brought into being, Albert continued, by woman's "moist" nature, which inclined her toward inconstancy. William of Auxerre, on the other hand, preferring the authority of St. Augustine over the authority of prevailing biological learning, stated that the "dignity of the sexes" *(dignitas sexus)* required that "the man be the woman's head, and not the converse."[101]

Thomas Aquinas also maintained that within the family "[t]he husband must direct domestic affairs, provide for the necessities of the domestic life, and be solicitous for the care of his wife and chldren, and for the temporalities which serve for their upkeep."[102] The power of a father within his household, Thomas asserted, was comparable in many respects to that of a lord over his kingdom.[103] Not only within the household, but in "civil and ecclesiastical societies" generally, women were to be subject to men.[104] But an essential inequality did not prevail between man and woman, in Thomas's view. "Thomas never states as a starting principle that all women must be subject to some man."[105] Furthermore, his theory of creation, which followed Genesis in declaring that man was created in the image and likeness of God, entailed that women also shared in those attributes in which men imitated God, such as reason and an immortal soul.[106]

The decretalists also stressed that women were ordinarily to obey their husbands. Citing Gratian's texts on the subject, Hostiensis reiterated that "man is woman's head."[107] He posed a hypothetical question to consider the extent to which a wife was subject to her husband's authority: suppose a wife has taken a vow of abstinence (not, apparently, a solemn vow of chastity).[108] Would she sin mortally by breaking the vow at her husband's insistence? Hostiensis replied in the negative: she obeys God by obeying her husband's authority, since in this matter he acts with the authority of law/right.[109]

Following Roman law, the decretalists tended to call this male authority over wife and household the *patria potestas*. Frequently, they employed a rights-vocabulary, calling it a "right of paternal power" (*ius patria potestatis*). It would seem logical that such a right would be considered a natural right. After all, the sources employed by the decretalists, especially the patristic authors reproduced in Gratian's *Decretum,* repeated the claim that male dominion represented the natural order of things.

To the extent that the thirteenth-century decretalists wrote explicitly on this question, they tended to agree that this was a natural right. Hostiensis understood this right as arising from the rational natural law by which man and woman married.[110] While addressing the subject of infidel rights, not domestic relations, Innocent IV also suggested in passing that the right of paternal power was a natural right.[111] A scholastic writer like Thomas Aquinas also presupposed a naturalistic understanding of this right when he wrote of the right of Jewish fathers to direct the upbringing of their children.[112] Although the canonists were more concerned with analysis of the scope and content of this right than with its origins, they agreed that the right of paternal power originated in nature.

There was, however, a group of jurists far more preoccupied with understanding the origin of the right of paternal power as a creature not of the natural law but of the legislative power of the Roman state. These jurists were the civilians — commentators who wrote not on the received texts of canon law, but on the texts of Justinian.

It will be recalled that the Justinianic texts had taught that *patria potestas* was a right that belonged uniquely to citizens of Rome.[113] The civilians of the twelfth and thirteenth centuries tended to agree with their sources that the right of paternal power belonged uniquely to Roman citizens. Thus Placentinus defined *patria potestatis* as a "certain right" *(quoddam ius)* which belonged to "us parents" *(nos parentes)*.[114] It was in virtue of this right that a father educated his children, provided for their welfare, and even saw to their marriages.[115] In return, a son *(filius)* owed his father "every type of reverence" *(omnimodam reverentiam)* in speaking and acting.[116]

Other Romanist authors agreed. Azo, for instance, wrote that *patria potestatis* was a certain kind of right which those subject to the Roman *imperium* have over their natural and legitimate children.[117] No other men, Azo noted, agreeing with his sources, enjoyed such a right.[118]

This did not mean that those who were not eligible for *patria potestatis* were left powerless in their own families. Placentinus, in particular, made clear that all parents possessed a certain type of authority over their children. This authority, where non-Romans were concerned, was known as *potestas dominica* — "lordly power."[119] This was the same sort of power, Placentinus continued, one might exert over slaves, although it was not a power that should be used abusively.[120]

To speak of Roman citizenship in this context was not entirely anachronistic. In the world of medieval urban life, particularly in the north Italian communes, the idea of "Roman" citizenship was a valuable legal fiction that served to define the rights and privileges as well as the obligations of the communal elites and set them off from aliens, both within the community and outside it.[121] For our purposes, however, which are focused on the rights-vocabulary that the canonists and civilians employed, rather than on the details of communal family life, this treatment stands as evidence that the *ius patria potestatis* need not always be regarded as a natural right. It might also, depending on the circumstances, be regarded as a right arising from the civil law and so could not be used to describe the legal status of those fathers, within the community or outside it, who did not enjoy the privileges of citizenship.

It should not be understood that the power of fathers in the Italian communes was somehow legally disadvantaged by this analysis. Indeed, it is highly doubtful that any civilian would have agreed with the proposition that because the Roman *ius patria potestatis* was grounded on the civil enactments of emperors its scope was somehow more limited than that offered by canon law. In practice, the civilian arguments meant only this much: that the rights fathers could claim under Roman law were seen as

arising from conventional, legislative sources rather than reflecting the natural order of affairs. This stance was taken, furthermore, not to diminish
the position of the Roman father, but to exalt it.

The Right to Govern the Family

The *ius patria potestatis,* as the canonists understood the term, embraced
the governance of the household. This included not only the expectation
that the husband should be the wife's head, responsible for leading and
guiding the spousal unit of man and wife in accord with basic principles of
Christian love. It also included responsibility for the nurture and disciplin-
ing of children subject to paternal power.

   The position of children in the medieval family has been the subject
of a large body of scholarship through the last forty-odd years. At the beginning of this line of development, Phillipe Ariès confidently wrote in
1960 that "it seems more probable that there was no place for childhood in
the medieval world."[122] Because of high rates of infant mortality and other
factors, Ariès argued that medieval parents regarded their children's welfare
with an indifference utterly shocking when compared to our own high
level of solicitude. Indeed, this level of disregard was so high, Ariès claimed
that "the concept of family was unknown in the Middle Ages [and] originated in the fifteenth and sixteenth centuries."[123]

   Since Ariès published his *Centuries of Childhood,* scholars have continued to refine our understanding of childhood in the Middle Ages. Ariès's
thesis, in particular, has come under sustained fire. Contrary to Ariès's
claims, Danièle Alexandre-Bidon and Didier Lett have discovered numerous documents attesting that maternal and paternal love were both
strongly felt throughout the Middle Ages and demonstrating that parents
were far from indifferent where their offspring's welfare was concerned.[124]

   Nicholas Orme, for his part, has shown that medieval parents took
seriously their parental responsibilities, that the laws of the Church and
secular society alike took special account of their needs, and even that a
separate children's culture can be identified, which featured "toys, games,
and literature," and the chance for children to play "away from their elders."[125]

   Shulamith Shahar has shown that even though "the lot of most
adults" in the Middle Ages "was [not] a happy one," even though it was a
violent and poverty-stricken age, in which "disease and epidemics" were

rampant, parents still made efforts to provide for their children.[126] More geographically specialized studies of family and childhood in medieval England and Germany have reached similar conclusions.[127] A recent collection of studies and sources of medieval children's literature has also called attention to a wide body of materials traditionally neglected by scholars who have erroneously tried to place the origins of writing for children in Puritan England.[128]

The medieval Romanists and canonists were not unaffected by these larger currents and were not indifferent to the welfare of children. Once again, the Romanist writers tended to follow their classical sources and permitted relatively harsh treatment of some categories of offspring. Although the civilians were certainly fully integrated into the Christian culture of the time, in this instance they determined to follow the implications of the Justinianic texts upon which it was their duty to expound. The canonists, on the other hand, synthesizing the demands of Christian charity with a canonical tradition solicitous of children's welfare, offered the Church and the world a far more expansive set of legal and moral aspirations. The right of paternal power was not to be used abusively, but was to be employed for the building up of a network of Christian familial love. In reaching these conclusions, the canonists also criticized their civilian contemporaries for failing to appreciate the demands of the Gospel.

A principal right and obligation of medieval fathers was to provide for the nurture of their offspring. "Natural reason *(naturalis ratio)*," one medieval text began, required a father to provide food and drink for his children, to see that they are properly clothed, and that they have shoes to wear.[129] Romanist and canonist authors, however, disagreed over whether the obligation extended not only to one's legitimate children, but also included those born outside of marriage.

A decree of Antoninus Pius, preserved in the *Codex,* announced the broad principle that it was "just" *(iustum)* that parents provide their children with the necessities of life.[130] That this obligation of justice had its limitations was made clear by the Christian emperor Justinian, who declared that offspring from forbidden intercourse, known as "spurious" children, had no claim to support.[131] In keeping with this dictate, Justinian's *Institutes* had defined children subject to paternal power as those born of "just marriages."[132] Children born outside such unions were not subject to their fathers' authority and were not entitled to claim any measure of support.[133]

The Romanist authors echoed their classical sources. The same text which declared it a requirement of natural reason that fathers support their children, subsequently limited the requirement of support to "legitimate" children.[134] Azo had earlier asserted that a father had no obligation of support to children born outside "just" intercourse, although the mother might be so compelled.[135] Odofredus was even harsher: citing Justinian's *Novel* 89, he pronounced that sons born of "nefarious intercourse" were not really sons at all and were therefore not deserving of support by their fathers.[136]

The canonists, however, repudiated this whole line of reasoning.[137] For their sources, the canonists could consult a wide and deep theological tradition. As early as the fourth-century Council of Gangra an anathema was proclaimed on parents who abandoned their children, or failed to provide them with proper sustenance, or omitted to see to their necessities. Parents, the Council taught, were not to use the name of "piety and religion" to justify the neglect of their responsibility. The language of Gangra was broad enough to protect children not only of legitimate birth but also children born outside wedlock.[138]

In an argument reminiscent of the principles established by the Council of Gangra, Bernard of Parma proposed perhaps the most thorough refutation of Romanist limitations on the rights of children born out of wedlock. Bernard began by noting that parents and offspring were obligated to see to each other's welfare in time of need, but justified this assertion not by Roman law, but by Gratian's discussion of natural law.[139] He then followed this assertion with a series of citations to Roman-law texts, noting the contrast between canonistic teaching and the narrowness of the Roman law, which limited its concern to legitimate offspring.[140]

The rigors of the civil law, Bernard averred, represented an approach which sought to punish illicit sexual intercourse, motivated by a "hatred of crime."[141] Canon law, however, took a more generous approach (*de benignitate*) because the canons sought to fulfill the requirements of the natural law.[142] The upbringing and education of children, Bernard noted, was an obligation of the natural law and this *ius* — this law, this right — he concluded, took priority over the civil law of Justinian.[143]

Other canonists echoed this sentiment. Hostiensis posed a striking hypothetical case: suppose a child were born of an incestuous relationship.[144] This child was not to receive support under the terms of the civil law but, Hostiensis added, the civil law here represented merely the rigor and the subtlety of the world's law (*legum secularium*).[145] Canon law, however, where the kindness and equity of the natural law prevails, required that such children always receive sustenance.[146] This is because natural *ius* ought always to prevail, in time and in dignity, over all other forms of *iura*.[147]

It has been shown by scholars that medieval canonists made real efforts to apply these teachings in the ecclesiastical courts. Richard Helmholz has indicated that in England of the high and late Middle Ages the ecclesiastical courts were prepared to make awards of child support for spurious offspring where paternity could be established.[148] Because of difficulties of proof, furthermore, Helmholz notes that the evidentiary rules employed were "weighted slightly in favor of the child."[149] Acceptable proofs included evidence of sexual relations between the parents, including continuing access and opportunity, "the common fame of the community, prior admissions against interest by the father, and care for the child as one's own, even if not coupled with a claim of paternity."[150] Ecclesiastical records, furthermore, demonstrate that courts did make awards of support where such evidence was forthcoming.[151] Other scholars have agreed with these findings.[152]

A second area where the canonistic analysis of the *ius patria potestatis* modified the ancient Roman law concerned the exposure of infants. Already by the end of the fourth century, the Christian emperors had largely done away with the ancient "right of life and power of death" that Roman fathers might exercise over their children.[153] The twelfth- and thirteenth-century canonists were even more stringent than their late antique predecessors in their condemnations of the exposure of young children.

Thus a letter of Pope Gregory IX, following the tradition established by the Emperor Constantine, decreed that a father who exposed his child, or knowingly assented to that exposure was to lose his right and power over that child.[154] The same rule applied to children of serfs or freedmen — they would immediately be freed of their masters' authority.[155] The same rule applied, Gregory asserted, where a parent has "impiously" denied nourishment to a child, thus threatening the child's very well-being.[156] Under these circumstances, those who find such children may take them in, but will not thereby acquire any right (*ius aliquod*) over them, by which he clearly meant the rights of ownership or other forms of servitude.[157]

The commentators on this text reinforced Gregory's condemnation. Bernard of Parma observed first that exposure might occur either with the lord's or father's knowledge and approval, or with them kept in the dark.[158] Where the lord or father was aware of the exposure, all rights in the child were immediately lost and the responsible party must be accounted a homicide. Where they were unaware, they had ten days to assert their rights or forfeit all claim.[159]

So also, Bernard added, for children who have been denied sustenance. They should be freed of paternal control and be considered effectively abandoned (pro derelictis).[160] Echoing Gregory's decretal, Bernard emphasized that both exposed children and those who have been grossly neglected should be presumed to be free, not servile, with the result that their new parents may not acquire or transfer rights in their persons.[161]

Hostiensis reiterated that one who has been exposed is immediately freed from all paternal power.[162] He added for good measure that a father who has knowingly assented to the exposure of his child should not only be accounted a homicide but might even be subjected to the death penalty.[163] Furthermore, all paternal rights ceased upon abandonment, or when a child has been found in a condition of starvation. Starvation, Hostiensis asserted, amounted to constructive abandonment.[164]

In the fourteenth century, Johannes Andreae turned his attention to the question of abandonment. The "crime" of abandonment, standing alone, Johannes asserted, sufficed to "destroy" paternal power.[165] There were three acts that might legally constitute exposure within the meaning of the decretal, Johannes thought: these included actual exposure; gross neglect; and denial of nourishment.[166] Exposure, Johannes explained, usually occurred to infants, but children of any age might be victims of neglect or of starvation.[167] And, presumably, such children might move or freely be moved to new living situations.

Some Roman lawyers also commented on the subject of exposure. Thus the Romanist Odofredus, who had written that fathers had no responsibility toward spurious offspring since they should not really count as children at all, explained that he did not mean that parents had a right to kill their offspring. A parent should not deny sustenance to a child where such denial results in death, nor should a parent expose a child.[168]

Accursius had similar things to say about exposure and neglect. A father who denied nourishment to his child was to lose paternal power.[169] The same rule applied to a master who denied sustenance to a slave, Accursius added: the slave was to be freed at once.[170] Following his Roman-law sources, Accursius stressed that the loss of parental rights was complete and included the loss of the right to reclaim the infant (ius vendicandi).[171] Elsewhere Accursius added that if parents could not take care of their child, the infant should be delivered to a hospital or placed before the gates of a church to allow the child a chance at survival.[172]

As the ecclesiastical courts enforced the requirement of supporting illegitimate offspring, so also they were active in attempting to stamp out the practices of exposure and infanticide.[173] Richard Helmholz, studying late medieval English records, has demonstrated that infanticide, whether "by drowning, burning, or exposure,"[174] remained a continuing social problem, but that Church courts were vigorous in prosecuting such offenses. Indeed, Helmholz has shown that courts prosecuted parents not only for intentionally killing their children, but also for acts of culpable negligence that led to death. He concluded: "[T]he Church courts were not concerned solely with the sin of the parent. The safety of the child was also important."[175] In this way, also, an important restriction placed on the right of paternal power by Christianized Roman emperors was extended and given force by medieval canonists.

The scholastic writers tended to follow the canonists in giving voice to the moral requirement that parents and society at large respect children's rights to basic sustenance and support. Over the course of three centuries of scholastic speculation, this obligation of respect was transformed into a set of correlative rights and expectations which parents and children alike enjoyed.

The vehicle the scholastics employed for the exploration of rights of parents and offspring was a steady focus on the implications of the three marital goods. It was, of course, a truism of medieval scholastic marital theory that marriage existed to serve three goods — children, fidelity, and lifelong sacramental unity. The good of children, furthermore, meant more than simple procreation. Gandulf of Bologna, for instance, spoke of the good of children not only as including their material support but also as embracing a loving relationship with their parents (*amanter suscipiatur*) and training in the proper worship of God (*ad cultum Dei educandae*).[176]

Thomas Aquinas developed the good of children in some important ways. This good, Thomas wrote, must be understood not only in terms of procreation, but also in terms of the child's *educatio* — his or her upbringing and training in the virtues. Indeed, Thomas stressed that both parents were to share in the effort to provide their children with a proper education because it was for this reason that they were joined in marriage. This much was the endowment — "the treasure" (*thesaurizant*) — that parents left their offspring.[177]

Thomas reinforced this point with a citation to chapter 12 of St. Paul's Second Letter to the Corinthians. In that letter, St. Paul anticipated his upcoming visit to the church at Corinth, reminded his readers that he had not been a burden to the church in his prior visits, and added that he did not expect to become one on his forthcoming visit.[178] Comparing his position to that of a parent, St. Paul continued:

> Now I am ready to come to you this third time. And I will not be a burden, for I want not what is yours, but you. Children ought not to save for their parents, but parents for their children. I will most gladly spend and be utterly spent for your sakes.[179]

Obliquely, through the citation to St. Paul that he incorporated by reference, Thomas made the point that parents must expend themselves on behalf of their children in the same way St. Paul spent himself in endowing the church at Corinth. Thus according to Thomas sacrificial giving should characterize the parent's relationship with the child.[180]

St. Bonaventure, the great Franciscan contemporary of Thomas, made similar points about the necessity of seeing to the upbringing of children. In his treatise on evangelical perfection St. Bonaventure wrote that marriage has a "useful end." His choice of the word *utilitas* to express this concept might even be translated as "social utility."[181] This usefulness consisted in the procreation of children who would engage in the proper worship of God.[182] St. Bonaventure made a similar point in his *Commentaries* on the *Sentences* of Peter Lombard. "Right reason," St. Bonaventure announced, teaches that both parents (*parentes ambo*) must see to the training of their children.[183] Procreation, noted the Seraphic Doctor, was the result of the generative power, but marriage involved more than procreation. Children should be educated in the virtuous life, so as to receive their proper heavenly reward.[184]

In the early fourteenth century, Hervaeus Natalis, a notable Dominican theologian who was elected as master-general of that order in 1318, and whom a modern writer described as "glowing with enthusiasm for St. Thomas," recast this traditional solicitude for children in an explicit rights-based vocabulary.[185] The context was the dispute then raging over the nature of Jesus Christ's poverty. Radical "spiritual" Franciscans had advanced the claim, bolstered by papal encyclicals from the late thirteenth century, that Jesus Christ had followed perfect poverty, renouncing all but "simple factual use" of goods necessary to sustain life.[186] In 1321, Pope John XXII "invit[ed] theologians and canonists to debate publicly the question, 'Whether it is heretical to assert that Christ and the apostles had nothing singly or in common.'"[187] This invitation touched off enormous controversy. Among the works drafted against the Franciscan position on evangelical poverty was Hervaeus's *Quaestio de Paupertate Christi et Apostolurum* (1322).[188]

Franciscan opponents of Hervaeus had argued that superiors, such as monasteries in relation to their monks, fathers in relation to their sons, or masters in relation to their *servi*, might have the duty to see to their welfare, "to provide the monk, the son, the slave, with the necessities of life," but that no correlative right could be asserted by the monk, or the son, or the *servus*.[189] Hervaeus answered by invoking the concept of a *ius in re*, a term which had a history traceable to late Roman legal writers and which had come into common canonistic usage as a means of signifying the right of a property holder to the unencumbered use and disposition of his lands or goods.[190]

Hervaeus began from the premise that all persons had a basic right to sustenance. As he put it, there was "a right, dominion, and property that belonged to the one licitly using goods useful to human life."[191] This right amounted to a *ius in re* and might be exercised by the individual directly or by someone acting on his or her behalf. This right included the power to determine where one was to live, and decisions about what to eat or what to drink.[192] A prelate exercised this right in the name of the community he was charged with overseeing, but this did not mean that the community thereby lost the right. "Similarly," Hervaeus continued, "a son and a *servus* have a right to the necessaries of life to be administered by his father or his master, who are the principal lords of their goods."[193]

A son, Hervaeus continued, differed also in some respects from a monk.[194] A monk in no event may enjoy the capacity of property ownership, but not so with a child, who has such a capacity. Furthermore, the child may come to be emancipated, with the consequence that he or she becomes fully *sui iuris* and able to enjoy simple dominion over property.[195]

In the fifteenth century, the Spanish writer Juan Lopez (1440-1496), synthesizing canonistic, Romanist, and theological strands of thought, deepened and strengthened arguments on behalf of the rights of offspring by focusing in a clear and sustained way on the foundation of these rights in the natural law.[196] Lopez premised his analysis on the natural-law foundation of marriage: relying on Justinian's *Institutes,* Lopez declared that natural law was what was common to all nations; hence marriage was a part of the natural law since the joining of man and woman, the procreation and education of children, and children's succession as the next generation were the results of "natural instinct" (*instinctu naturae*).[197]

But, Lopez continued, there were different types of natural law: one type of natural law could be understood as the natural causes of earthly phenomena — in this way fire ignites from heat.[198] A second type of natural law, however, embraced natural inclinations but also required the intervention of free will — such as the acquisition and exercise of the virtues. Marriage, Lopez asserted, fell into this latter category.[199]

Lopez waxed eloquent about the good of children in this context. Children must be taken up and "religiously educated" (*religiose educetur*). This is because the good of children, the *bonum prolis,* is not good simply because of the numbers of children produced, but is good only insofar as it results in children who are properly reared and trained.[200]

Having laid a proper foundation, Lopez proceeded to inquire into the nature of polygamous unions. The question he asked was: might the good of children be retained in such relationships? His response to this question laid bare a set of natural-law based rights that children were entitled to assert.

At the beginning, God made Adam and Eve, male and female, and he instructed Adam to cling to Eve as his wife, and "not to wives."[201] Lopez followed a path already trod by the canonists and by Peter Lombard and other scholastic writers in noting that God had permitted the biblical patriarchs — Abraham, Jacob, and others — to take more than one wife,[202] but he noted, again following a well-worn path, that this was done by divine dispensation in a time of necessity to allow the rapid multiplication of believers.[203] It was not a model for Christian believers in the new dispensation to follow.

Lopez, however, next asked whether one woman might under any circumstances take more than one husband. He found no historical example of this arrangement ever having occurred. The Old Testament characters who had taken numerous spouses had all been men. Polyandry, furthermore, would have a huge adverse impact on the good of children: their procreation, their education, their very support, would all be disturbed gravely because the wife of more than one husband would never be certain of paternity.[204] The result of this confusion would be the confounding of the whole institution of matrimony and the loss, by the child, of the support to which he was entitled under the natural law.[205] With a horse, with a cow, with a goat, it was possible that the mother alone could nurture the young, but not so with humans: the presence of both parents was required. Hence, Lopez concluded, children were entitled by reason of natural law to receive proper training, food, and support, and to have the attention of two parents, who were male and female. Such a standard could not be dispensed with, Lopez stressed. In stating that these expectations arose "by *ius naturale,*" Lopez seemed to embrace both the objective of law and the subjective dimension of right in the same phrase.[206]

The final restatement of this line of development is found in the work of Domingo de Soto, the great sixteenth-century Spanish Dominican theologian and moralist, who made the relationship of the rights of parent and child a central part of his general analysis of rights. At the beginning of Book IV of his treatise *De Justitia et Jure,* Soto asked whether *dominium* ("dominion" or "lordship") was the same as *ius* ("right") and *facultas rerum* ("faculty over things").[207] It seemed, Soto said, that these three terms were equivalent: *ius,* after all, was the same as the "faculty of freely disposing of one's goods."[208] And, furthermore, when mendicant preachers exercised the right of using food and clothing and other goods consumable in use they were said to have *dominium* over these things. On the other hand, Soto said, there was the relationship of master and servant: a master was said to have a "right of command" over servants, but did not thereby acquire dominion, ownership, of the servants.[209]

Following the writings of civilians and canonists, Soto proposed that *dominium* be understood as "the proximate power of taking things not one's own for one's resources, or for licit use, in accord with reasonably enacted laws."[210] This meaning contrasted with *ius,* which possessed in a sense a "higher and deeper meaning," since *ius* also signifies "the object of justice."[211] The examples Soto gave of rights that were also the objects of justice were drawn from the law of domestic relations. Thus, Soto observed, a wife has power over her husband, because "a man does not have power over his body." Soto was here alluding to St. Paul's First Letter to the Corinthians.[212] And so also, Soto continued, a son has a right in his parents, because they are obliged to care for him.[213] By the same reasoning, Soto concluded his point, a subject has a right in a prelate by whom he is governed.

Soto then took issue with an argument of a certain Conrad, probably Conrad Summenhart, who asserted that all rights held by a superior against an inferior should really be counted a form of *dominium*. "I will not concede this point easily," he responded.[214] He then went on to say:

> For a father has a right in his sons; moreover, if this is properly called *dominium*, that is not the same thing. I say that it is fair and just and therefore *ius* that a father command the sons whom he loves, and instructs, and establishes in life, toward the good. *Dominium*, moreover, does not always signify right and power, but rather that we are able to

use some thing in accord with our wishes, toward our own private utility, because it gives us delight.[215]

On Soto's analysis both child and parent possessed certain rights. The
child had a right to be cared for and educated and nurtured by his parents;
the parents, in turn, had a right to govern the child, a right that was conditioned on the obligation to love and to nurture, to educate and support.
These were "rights," furthermore, and not a species of lordship (dominium)
precisely because they aimed at mirroring the right ordering of society. This
set of mutually entailing rights and duties sought to achieve what was "fair
and just" (aequum et iustum). Soto emphatically denied that these rights existed merely to advance the private utility or the personal enjoyment of the
possessor of the right. In this way Soto made a point not only about the
right ordering of the family unit but also about the nature of rights: rights
created a zone of freedom, to be sure, but it was a zone of freedom that conferred on the right-holder the discretion to act in a way consistent with
building up, not tearing down of society.

The canon law of the twelfth and thirteenth centuries also recognized
the existence of a right of correcting one's offspring. This right was articulated originally in Roman law, which spoke of a ius domesticae emendationis
("right of household correction") that a father enjoyed by "paternal right"
(iure paterno).[216] This right of Roman fatherhood, it is now established, did
not mean that fathers might behave arbitrarily or viciously toward their
young. Social, if not legal pressures, would have seen to that. While Roman
parents were known to rely on beatings to ensure discipline, "only the bad
parent resorted to corporal punishment for light offenses."[217]

While Roman law was silent on the degree of force allowed in chastis-
ing one's children,[218] relying instead on the force of social ostracism, the
canon law was not so reticent. The boundaries the canonists set around the
"right of domestic correction" are illustrated by the facts of a case found in
a decretal of Pope Clement III.[219] In Ad Audientiam Apostolatus, a certain
priest was called upon to discipline a member of his family. He struck the
offending child with a belt and apparently opened a wound on his back. Although the child lived for a while, he eventually took ill and died, quite
possibly of infection.[220]

Bernard of Parma noted that it was permitted to members of the family, even clerics (who were greatly restricted in their right to carry arms or
use force), to engage in limited (leviter) discipline, but that the right of correction (ius emendationis) was clearly exceeded in this case.[221] Hostiensis

also used rights language to analyze this case. Discipline is "well-approved" *(bene licet)* where "restrained means" *(modo temperato)* are used but, Hostiensis went on, one must not use one's right "immoderately," as the cleric in *Ad Audientiam Apostolatus* clearly had.[222]

In practice, it seems, the punishment of offspring could sometimes be severe and the laws against it largely a dead letter. In examining coroner records from late medieval England, Barbara Hanawalt noted that "no one has reported a case in which the jurors intervened in the case of children."[223] In such a context, Hostiensis's admonition that one must not use one's right "immoderately" stood as important social criticism, and as a reminder of an ideal that must often have been violated in practice.

In light of these examples of the law showing solicitude for the welfare of children, it is probably best, on balance, to side with the critics of Ariès's thesis in *Centuries of Childhood*. In demanding that children receive proper nurture and support, in condemning the practice of exposure, in cautioning that only moderate forms of discipline were tolerable, the law was setting certain minimal expectations. The rules laid down by the canonists constituted a floor, not a ceiling. These minimal expectations were not always observed, as in the case of excessive discipline. Yet ecclesiastical courts made significant efforts to enforce these precepts, especially in matters of child support and exposure. But even where the law was not directly implemented, its continuing presence stood as important social criticism and as a declaration of ideals about the proper ordering of family life.

The scholastic writers, furthermore, by the end of the Middle Ages, had developed a rich and sophisticated appreciation that the good of children was not to be measured in mere numerical terms, by the number of offspring produced, but embraced other values as well — religious education, training in the virtues, nurture and support. These concerns and values, also, were clothed in the language of rights.

A review of these teachings and rules and their practical implementation suggests that it is fair to conclude that the medieval canonists and theologians took substantial notice of children's needs. And this notice was taken through the manipulation of the vocabulary and concept of rights. The paternal right to govern the family contained within itself not only the freedom to judge how best to raise one's children and the authority to act upon one's judgment, but the obligation that this be done adequately and appropriately. The *ius patria potestatis* was thus a right, but a duty also, to see to the proper care and sustenance of hearth and home.

Loss of the Right of Paternal Power

The right of paternal power might be lost, first, by fault. Fault was preeminently associated with the commission of a grave crime, especially the exposure of one's children.[224] Such exposure, it was the teaching of the popes, who themselves were following the dictates of the Christian Roman emperors, resulted in the termination of paternal rights. Self-evidently, paternal power might also be lost through the father's death.

Paternal rights might be lost in other ways as well. Emancipation was always available as a means of severing parental rights and duties toward their offspring. Classical Roman law provided that parents might petition judges or magistrates for the emancipation of their offspring, who then became *sui iuris,* "masters of their own affairs," literally "of their own right."[225] Additionally a son might be emancipated by law where he had been given patrician status by imperial grant.[226] Accession to other high office, however, even the consulate, had no effect upon one's relationship to paternal power.[227]

In the thirteenth century, the Romanist rules on emancipation retained practical significance especially in the south of France and the northern Italian city-states.[228] Historians once argued that emancipation was used chiefly as a means of controlling sons and punishing them for their indiscretions — a father might, on this reading of the sources, emancipate a son so as to limit further legal obligations toward him. More recently, however, historians have come to understand emancipation as a form of honor granted to offspring, enabling them to exercise the same array of rights their parents enjoyed, such as the power of transferring property, or the right to make a will.[229]

The canonists were particularly concerned with one aspect of emancipation — its relationship to legal acts taken by the child, such as the taking of vows, or the reception of ordination, that would have the effect of placing the child under the control of some third party not of the family's network of power. Might offspring still under the control of their parents take a vow? Go on pilgrimage? Receive holy orders? Could a child be effectively emancipated or paternal rights lost without fault in circumstances such as these?

In answering these questions, the canonists drew several distinctions. The first was between the solemn vows that one was to take upon professing permanent membership in a monastery or convent, and other types of vows. Regarding solemn religious professions, the decretalists took as determinative two conciliar texts found in Gratian's *Decretum*. An excerpt from the Tenth Council of Toledo held that parents were permitted to invalidate their children's decision to enter monasteries up to the age of ten, but that otherwise parents were understood to consent to the vows.[230] A decree of the Council of Tribur allowed parents to invalidate their daughter's vow, provided she was under the age of twelve and the parents did not delay in acting longer than a year and a day.[231] The presumption in these cases was that vows had been made without parental knowledge.[232]

No mention of a right of paternal power was made in these texts,[233] and the decretalists merely accepted the rules laid down without further elaboration.[234] But when it came to lesser vows — vows of abstinence, of fasting, of pilgrimage, or of some other ascetic practice — the decretalists understood paternal rights to be very much implicated. In his *Summa*, Hostiensis proposed two complementary reasons why children still in the power of their parents were not permitted to take such vows. Such children, he asserted, lack the free will (*liberam voluntatem*) that the taking of a vow demands.[235]

Furthermore, Hostiensis added, a child, like a wife, like a monk, like a *servus*, was not *sui iuris* and so was not a master of his or her own affairs.[236] Thus not only vows which effectively terminated paternal power, but even those which effectively diminished it or which resulted in scandal should not be observed where one's father objected.[237] As if to reinforce the point, Hostiensis reiterated that this was because a son was obligated to his father by right of paternal power (*iure patrie potestatis*).[238]

The explanation for the disparate treatment accorded entry into religious life and the taking of other types of vows might simply have been customary practice: in a society where youthful religious vocations were still a feature of life, where oblate children might be commended to religious houses at very tender ages,[239] parents were deemed to consent to their offspring's choices. But where the fulfillment of vows might cause continuing complications for household governance, such decisions were to be given a higher level of scrutiny.

Ordination, finally, was treated differently from vows. Innocent IV and Hostiensis both considered this question in some detail. Innocent began with the proposition that prelates and clerics ought to be entirely freed from paternal power. They belong to a "sacred order" (*sacer ordo*), and this elevated status ought to be incompatible with any kind of subservience to external authority.[240]

But, Innocent continued, this may not be entirely practical. A bishop, he acknowledged, must be freed of all paternal power, but a subordinate cleric need not be, at least not in all respects.[241] Such a subordinate cleric, he conceded, might wish to come into his inheritance, or litigate over matters concerning his patrimony.[242] His father, however, must be restricted in the governance he can exercise over his son. While the father may retain a say in the management of his son's worldly goods (in bonis prophanis), he must not be given a say in the management of the Church's goods.[243]

Hostiensis's analysis reached similar conclusions, but through a different chain of reasoning. Some have argued, said Hostiensis, taking aim at certain unnamed opponents, that ordination automatically freed one of paternal power.[244] But this argument, he continued, depended upon a flawed analogy to Roman law, which freed those elevated to the patrician class from paternal power.[245]

This analogy did not hold, Hostiensis contended, because paternal power originated in the rational natural law — Hostiensis once again made the case that paternal power was a natural right — and this sort of natural relationship cannot be severed, even by ordination.[246] Like Innocent, though, Hostiensis did not believe that the cleric's father continued to exercise unfettered control over his son. A father might retain authority over matters pertaining to the son's "patrimony," but not over ecclesiastical affairs.[247] A bishop, however, should never be subject to another's authority, since he is given the power to correct and coerce others.[248]

The right of paternal power might thus be lost through fault, through emancipation, or through operation of law. The canonists preserved as well from their Roman-law sources a fourth means of losing the right of paternal power, although they took care to hedge in its force. Following his Romanist sources, Hostiensis conceded the possibility that a father, "induced by the necessity of hunger," might sell his children.[249] Hostiensis was careful to restrict this freedom substantially: such a sale is generally prohibited, and it is only allowed in time of general want. Mothers, furthermore, may not sell offspring because a son is not in a mother's power in the same way he is in a father's.[250] The survival of this rule may speak to the desperation that still prevailed in some corners of Europe even in the mid-thirteenth century.

Summary

To summarize: What one sees in the decretalist analysis of the right of paternal power is a careful reworking and systematization of Roman-law sources in the light of Christian revelation and the demands of Christian charity. Rejecting the analysis of their contemporaries, the civilians, at least some canonists maintained that paternal power was a right derived from natural law. Building on naturalist foundations, synthesizing law with Christian teaching about the worth of all individuals, the canonists imputed to fathers rights and responsibilities toward their spurious offspring which the Romanists denied.

Parents, furthermore, were not to expose their children. This would amount to criminal wrongdoing. Parents were to discipline their children with moderation and affection. Because paternal power was a natural right, furthermore, it was not easily lost. The reach of this power meant that children could not take steps which jeopardized its continued integrity. Thus children were not to take vows that gravely prejudiced paternal power or brought their father into public scandal. It also meant, as Innocent IV and Hostiensis made clear, that not even ordination could entirely destroy paternal power, as a father might continue to retain a say in the management of the things pertaining to his son's patrimony.

The scholastic writers, in particular, stressed the grounding of these rights in natural law. While some writers like Thomas Aquinas and St. Bonaventure stressed the obligations of parents with respect to their children, other writers — like Hervaeus Natalis or Juan Lopez or Domingo de Soto — indicated that children had correlative rights — rights to a proper upbringing, to sustenance, to training in the faith of their fathers.

The right of paternal power, finally, was not absolute. It was conditioned by a series of other rights and obligations. Although women were ordinarily subjected to the authority of their husbands, the law recognized certain areas of equality. Although children were subject to the authority of their fathers, the law recognized that they enjoyed the freedom to make certain choices, such as the decision to marry. Although fathers possessed a certain freedom to dispose of their property through a will, this testamentary right could not be exercised to the detriment of their children. These issues will be explored further in subsequent chapters.

∽ 3 ∾

The Right of Women (ius mulierum)

As has already been intimated, where the legal status of women was concerned a basic tension can be identified in the canon law between a set of principles and rules that subjected women to the authority of men and a different set of beliefs and ideas that stressed a radical equality between men and women "in Christ Jesus." This equality was evident most prominently in spiritual matters: women and men were recognized as spiritual equals, who benefited equally from Christ's salvific acts. Men and women alike and in equal measure have gained eternal life through Christ's death and resurrection.

Equality, however, was not confined solely to spiritual matters, but was also translated into legal categories in several respects. Men and women were considered equal with respect to their legal capacity to claim the conjugal debt. This equality, and the conception of the conjugal debt as a right that should not ordinarily be lost through no fault of the parties,[1] provided a sturdy foundation for the analysis of many aspects of the marital relationship. A second area of equality might strike the modern reader as odd: the right of women, as well as men, freely to select their own place of burial. But when viewed against the backdrop of early medieval experience, which had a very different set of expectations, the change in this area of law was dramatic and total and represented the triumph of a principle of equal and free choice. Finally, there is the matter of the decision to leave one's spouse where it appears that the marriage is invalid, or at least unlivable. Again, the lawyers conceptualized this aspect of the marital relationship as a right that could be equally exercised by male and female. Other areas of equality can be identified as well, such as the right of men and women alike to contract marriage freely, a topic already addressed in Chapter One.[2]

Part I: Historical Development of the *ius mulierum*

Early Christian Background to the Canonists' Discussion

Women in the early Christian world enjoyed a wide variety of opportunities and functions. The New Testament itself offers a number of examples of the various roles women played. One sees Mary Magdalene, cured by Jesus Christ of demon possession,[3] following him faithfully to his crucifixion.[4] To her belonged the honor of being the first to find the empty tomb on Easter Sunday.[5] One encounters Elizabeth, mother of John the Baptist.[6] And, of course, there is also Mary, Elizabeth's kinswoman and Mother of Jesus Christ.[7]

One encounters prominent women also in the primitive Church, as portrayed in the Pauline epistles, in Acts, and in other sources. Throughout those letters of Paul generally accepted as genuine, one sees references to women playing leading roles in the Church. There is Phoebe, "called by Paul the *diakonos* of the churches in Cenchreae and *prostatis* of many and of Paul himself."[8] There is also Prisca, called by Paul a "co-laborer" (*synergos*) in the building up of the Church.[9] And there is Chloe, who was the leader of a faction in the Church at Corinth.[10] In Acts, one finds Mary and other women praying in the upper room with the eleven named apostles following the Ascension of the Lord.[11] One finds as well evidence that women engaged in mission activities and may even have made their homes available for assemblies of local Christians.[12]

Women, clearly, performed a variety of functions in the early Church. Scholars have called attention to the diversity of these responsibilities. Junia, mentioned in Romans 16:7, was called by Paul an "apostle," presumably because she enjoyed a vision of the resurrected Christ.[13] Phoebe, as noted, was called a "deacon" and Chloe was a faction-leader, while other women were noted as performing a prophetic function in the primitive Church.[14]

By the end of the first century, as the pastoral epistles were undergoing their final redaction, the role of women was simultaneously being more clearly defined and more severely restricted in scope. The First Letter of Timothy declared that women may not "teach or have authority over men."[15] Women are advised "to learn in silence with all submission."[16] This was because Adam was created first and Eve formed from his rib. Furthermore, it was Eve who succumbed to temptation, not Adam.[17] Similarly, one sees the prophetess of the book of Revelation portrayed as an evil seductress.[18] But even in this context, writers of the subapostolic age continued to prescribe an important role for women, including notably virgins and widows, in the early Church.[19]

Still other early Christian texts, not part of the biblical canon, continued to stress well into the second century the leading role played by women in the founding of Christianity. One particularly noteworthy text is the *Protoevangelion* of James. Purporting to have been written by James, the son of Joseph by his first marriage, and half-brother of Jesus, this work provides a moving portrait of the Holy Family.[20] The purpose of this work, according to scholars, "is to glorify Mary by telling of her birth, childhood, and marriage."[21]

It is the role of women in the conception and birth not only of Jesus, but also of Mary herself, that is at the center of this work. St. Anne, Mary's mother; Elizabeth, Mary's kinswoman and mother of John the Baptist; and a Hebrew midwife who attended Mary during her labor, figure crucially in this narrative of the Savior's birth. An extremely popular work among the Eastern Churches,[22] this work fell out of general circulation in the West following St. Jerome's criticism of the text.[23]

This early experience, and these early layers of texts and sources, only served to enhance some of the tensions inherent in the Christian message about women. Women, to be sure, according to a major strand of Christian theology, were to be subject to their husbands' authority, and to fill the subordinate but necessary role of helpmate. But another strand of thought that emphasized a radical equality between the sexes drew support from depiction of powerful women in canonical and some non-canonical sources — beginning with Mary, the Mother of Jesus, but also including Mary Magdalene, Phoebe, Chloe, St. Anne, and others.

This tension continues to be on display in the writings of the great doctors of the Church of the patristic era — men like St. Jerome and St. Augustine. Jerome exalted the state of being a celibate male, denigrated marriage, but still found room to speak highly of individual women he knew. Thus he praised his friend Paula's pilgrimage to the Holy Land, the generosity she showed toward the unfortunate, and the hospitality she furnished to travellers.[24] And he expressed similar high regard for Marcella, who, inspired by the desert fathers, chose to lead an ascetic life following her husband's untimely death.[25] Marcella reminded Jerome of the great women of the New Testament, who should be judged by their virtue, not by whether they are male or female.

St. Augustine, similarly, could declare man to be the sovereign head of woman, but also made room in his theology for a certain equivalence between male and female. Thus when answering the question whether male and female are both made in the image and likeness of God, he was able to answer in the affirmative. They are alike, he asserted, in their *spiritus mentis,* their "spirit of mind,"[26] which is "the most spiritual aspect of the human being."[27] Augustine praised individual women, such as his mother St. Monica, for their ability to reason. Of Monica, St. Augustine wrote: "Mother, you have grasped the summit of philosophy."[28] He also singled out women as the morally stronger partners in marriage, thereby criticizing their husbands for various transgressions, especially the keeping of concubines and the frequenting of prostitutes.[29]

One continues to see this acknowledgement of essential equality between the sexes in the writings of the early scholastics. Thus Peter Lombard, in explicating the Genesis account of the creation of woman from man's side, speculated that God chose to mold Eve from Adam's rib in order to emphasize the equality and companionship he expected to see prevail between the sexes. God did not make woman from man's head, so that she might dominate him. God did not make her from man's foot, to show the subjection of female to male. Woman is neither to dominate man, nor to be his slave, but to be his "companion" *(socia)*. And so man and woman should remain side-by-side as they were made.[30]

This sense of spiritual equality, a recognition of women's capacity for virtue, and the praiseworthy qualities of individual women formed as much a part of the Christian background that shaped the world of the twelfth- and thirteenth-century canonists as did the sense of male superiority explored in the preceding chapter. It is the appreciation of male and female as being created side-by-side in the image and likeness of God that helped inform the canonists' discussions of the *ius mulierum,* the "right of women."

"So it will be found that the right of women in many cases is of diminished condition."[31] When Hostiensis wrote this passage, he may well have had in mind a passage of Azo, a teacher of Roman law at the beginning of the thirteenth century. Azo wrote that "men and women differ in many respects, because the legal condition of women is less than men."[32] Azo proceeded to list a variety of ways in which women were of diminished capacity: they were prevented from exercising governmental power, judicial power, guardianship, and from enjoying a variety of other rights or powers.[33] Azo himself was not original in making this observation about the status of women. His acknowledged source was the classical Roman jurist Papinian, who wrote that "in many articles of our law the condition of women is inferior to that of men."[34]

Hostiensis, however, moved significantly beyond his sources. Where Azo and Papinian spoke in objective terms, referring simply to the juridic condition of women, or to the law pertaining to women, Hostiensis spoke in terms of subjectve rights — the *ius mulierum,* best translated as "the right of women."

As Hostiensis himself conceded, for the most part the right of women was of "diminished condition." Women were subject to male headship. They lacked the legal capacity to undertake any number of activities. Nevertheless, there were areas in which they enjoyed a significant measure of equality. It is to these areas of equality that we turn next.

Part II: The Woman's Conjugal Right *(ius coniugale)*

The Conjugal "Debt" or Duty in Scriptural and Patristic Sources

The notion of a conjugal debt has its origins in St. Paul's First Letter to the Corinthians:

> Let the husband render to the wife her due, and likewise the wife to the husband. The wife has not authority over her body, but the husband; the husband likewise has not authority over his body, but the wife. Do not deprive each other, except . . . by consent, for a time, that you may give yourselves to prayer; and return again lest Satan tempt you because you lack self-control. But I say this by way of concession, not by way of commandment.[35]

The term that is translated above as "due" is the Greek word *opheile. Opheile* unambiguously meant what was owing. It was a debt.[36] In the Vulgate, it was translated as *debitum,* "debt."[37] The notion of sexual reciprocity as a moral obligation owed to the other party thus remained the primary meaning of the passage.

The patristic authors subsequently made the conjugal debt a part of their theology. In the fifth century, St. Augustine developed a theology of marriage which saw the union of man and woman as embodying three great goods: procreation, lifelong fidelity between the spouses, and the sacramental sign of Christ's union with the Church.[38] Augustine went on to identify marriage's end, or ultimate purpose, as the promotion of love between the parties.[39] This goal toward which marriage strove stood apart from the marriage's goods, but the goods aimed at the fulfillment of the end.

In this context, St. Augustine distinguished between two types of sexual intercourse within marriage: that undertaken for procreative purposes, which was entirely blameless;[40] and that undertaken to satisfy the Pauline debt, which amounted to a pardonable wrong on the part of the one seeking sexual satisfaction.[41] As Augustine put it, those who have intercourse "inflamed with passion are using their *ius* (right) intemperately," but may nevertheless be forgiven their excesses.[42]

While Augustine here made use of rights language in describing the conjugal debt, the idea of the conjugal relation as a right assertable by the parties to a marriage was by no means a prominent part of his thought. Indeed, it is clear from other passages in his works that Augustine thought of the sexual relationship primarily as a duty that was to be fulfilled even in spite of a personal desire to pursue ascetic ends. This notion of marital sexuality as an onerous responsibility comes across especially clearly in Augustine's letter to Ecdicia, a married noble woman who had rashly made a vow of continence without first consulting her husband.[43]

Ecdicia, it seems, had subsequently succeeded in securing a mutual vow of chastity from her husband, but Ecdicia took her husband's consent as license to pursue a life of radical spiritual autonomy. She gave away family property, took a widow's garb, and otherwise displayed her fundamental independence. Her husband responded by breaking his vow of continence and becoming involved with another woman.[44]

St. Augustine wrote to call Ecdicia back to her responsibilities as a Christian married woman. As Augustine interpreted First Corinthians, St. Paul had admonished his readers to render to each other the conjugal debt so that the weaker party in a relationship, the party more inclined to yield to sexual temptations, might be given a legitimate outlet for sexual expression.[45] God, Augustine asserted, will impute the good of continence to a reluctant spouse acceding to his or her partner's requests for sexual intercourse but not demanding it for oneself.[46] Ecdicia sinned in her pride by failing to acknowledge the significance of this obligation. Absent from this discussion is any notion of Ecdicia's husband having a right to sexual relations. The focus, rather, is on obligation and the rewards that await its fulfillment.

St. Augustine's duty-centered approach to the conjugal debt is found in other writers of the patristic and early medieval period. Two centuries before Augustine, Tertullian argued that chastity was the highest good although the conjugal relationship provided an acceptable outlet for those too weak to pursue a higher calling.[47] In this context, the conjugal debt was portrayed as something onerous, something a man (or woman) should be glad to be freed of, whether by the death of a spouse or the mutual renunciation of sexual relations. "Cease to be a debtor, you, oh happy man," Tertullian announced.[48] Seize the opportunity to be free of that debt which you must satisfy when it is demanded of you.[49]

This mode of thinking about the conjugal debt persisted into the early Middle Ages. Thus Hincmar of Rheims in the middle of the ninth century explicated Paul's admonition by looking chiefly to St. Augustine: Marital intercourse should chiefly serve the good of procreation, but it is possible that couples might engage in "immoderate" intercourse (*immoderate coeundi*) for the sake of avoiding adultery.[50] Indeed, Hincmar asserted, St. Paul's teaching, which permitted marital intercourse for the purpose of assisting the frailer spouse avoid illicit unions, created a "kind of mutual servitude" (*mutuam quodammodo servitutem*) in the parties which they were not free to renounce. Marriage, Hincmar reiterated, served both the purpose of procreation and as a remedy against concupiscence, and spouses were not free to deny either aspect of the relationship lest they tempt Satan and fall into "damnable corruptions."[51] Hincmar's conception of debt was driven chiefly by conceptions of underlying obligation and duty.

Throughout this period, it seems, the idea of the conjugal relationship as a debt was preserved. The suggestion that this was a right was barely, if ever, acknowledged.[52] Patristic and early medieval writers made clear that the highest calling was a life of chastity, dedicated to the worship of God and spiritual development. Marriage was a concession to those who could not fulfill these counsels of perfection, but it nevertheless carried the promise of spiritual growth, particularly for the reluctant spouse who allowed his or her spouse to claim the conjugal debt, but who had the strength to refrain from demanding it for oneself.

From a Duty to a Natural Right: Redefining Conjugal Relations

At best, the idea of the conjugal duty as a rightful claim assertable by the parties to a marriage was weakly held by patristic and early medieval writers. What was emphasized rather was the sense of obligation that bound parties together. It would be the canonists and theologians of the twelfth century who would transform this *debitum* from a moral obligation founded on scriptural exhortation into a judicially enforceable right.

This transformation commenced in earnest with Gratian's discussion of the subject. Gratian grounded his treatment of the conjugal debt on the standard medieval suspicion of unrestrained sexuality.[53] Before the Fall, Gratian noted, the marriage bed was "immaculate," but expulsion from Paradise brought with it sexual urges, necessary for reproduction but also capable of abuse.[54] Whence, averred Gratian, St. Paul instructed the Corinthians that marriage was the proper outlet for these impulses. Marital intercourse, Gratian wrote, following Augustine, was blameless, but intercourse for the satisfying of lust was a pardonable transgression.[55]

Recognizing that St. Paul had counseled couples that they might separate for a time in order to give themselves over to prayer, Gratian tested the limits of the Apostle's advice. Even though St. Paul had mentioned only the possibility of temporary separations — permanent renunciations, Paul taught, tempted Satan — Gratian asked whether a man might take a vow of (presumably perpetual) continence without his wife's approval.[56] He commenced his response with St. Augustine's condemnation of such unilateral arrangements: a spouse preferring continence, Augustine counseled, should always render the debt, but not seek it. This much will count for "perfect sanctification" before God.[57]

Other texts striking similar chords were also cited, including two excerpts from St. Augustine's letter to Ecdicia.[58] Summarizing his sources, Gratian concluded that either spouse may renounce the debt, provided the other one freely consented.[59] In such circumstances, although the marriage bond endured, the sexual rights thereby created ceased to be operative. And so, Gratian continued, one who has absolved his or her partner from their right (*a suo iure*) may not thereafter summon him or her back to this obligation.[60]

It seems that the decretists were initially slow in picking up Gratian's use of rights language to characterize the marital relationship. The work attributed to Paucapalea noted that Gratian's teaching was in accord with the teaching of the Church as found in Augustine and other sources.[61] Rufinus emphasized how important it was to obtain spousal free consent for a perpetual vow of chastity.[62] The *Summa Parisiensis* stressed that a vow entered into without permission was invalid.[63] Johannes Teutonicus observed that it belonged to neither the man nor the woman in a marriage to "prejudice" the conjugal debt.[64] In the *Summa*, '*Induent Sancti*,' however, one encounters the invocation of rights: where a man has taken a vow and thereby injured his wife's right, the anonymous author of the *Summa* wrote, she is able to seek judicial redress.[65]

This right came eventually to be seen as a natural right. This is evidenced most clearly in the canonistic and theological debates over whether infidels might validly marry. Dialectically, Gratian began by stating a strong case, grounded on scriptural and patristic authority, that marriage among unbelievers was impossible. St. Paul had taught everything that did not take place "by reason of faith" was sinful.[66] Marriage between non-Christians was outside the faith and hence infidel marriages could not exist without sin.

Similarly, Gratian read St. Augustine as having taught that marriage among infidels lacked the *pudicitia* — "honesty," "modesty" — required of marriages. Hence, for this reason, too, they should be counted as invalid.[67] St. Ambrose was cited as demonstrating from the Book of Esdras that "foreign wives" (*uxores alienigenas*) should be dismissed. This was yet another reason, Gratian asserted, that such marriages might be invalid.[68] And, once again, Augustine was cited, this time for the proposition that there could be no marriage without God, and infidels clearly failed to meet this criterion. By all these authorities, Gratian asserted, unions among infidels failed to meet the criteria of valid marriage.[69]

Gratian, however, did not leave the argument here. He added a whole series of contrary examples, indicating Jesus Christ's apparent recognition of the validity of marriages of non-Christians.[70] He then elicited further examples from Paul, demonstrating Paul's willingness to countenance marriages between Christian and non-Christian spouses, for the "sanctification" of the non-Christian party.[71] And so by these authorities, Gratian continued, it seemed that the marriages of infidels, and especially marriages between infidels and Christians, ought to be counted as valid, at least in certain circumstances.[72]

Gratian, however, had merely framed his argument between these two poles of the debate. He followed these assertions with a series of texts focused particularly on the issue of marriages between believers and unbelievers. Such relationships were to be disapproved, Gratian insisted, whether they involved Christians marrying Jews or heretics.[73]

Gratian's conclusions, however, had broader implications. There were, he asserted, three types of marriages. The first type, "legitimate marriage" (*legitimum coniugium*) was the type of marriage most frequently found among unbelievers. This was marriage in accord with the legal forms of the community, but such a union was not *ratum* marriage, that is, it was not indissoluble, since the parties to the marriage reserved the right to divorce. The marriage therefore lacked the added strength provided by grace.[74]

This sort of marriage stood in contrast with the two types of marriages that believers might enter into: legitimate and ratified marriages (*legitima et rata coniugia*), that is, marriages that have observed proper legal form and that are, because of the beliefs of the parties and the act of consummation, indissoluble;[75] and ratified, but not legitimate marriages (*rata coniugia*), where the solemnities of marriage were avoided, as in clandestine marriage, but where, because of the intent of the parties and the act of consummation, a valid and indissoluble marriage has nevertheless come into being.[76] A Christian marriage was, on this account, essentially characterized by its *ratum* aspect, its sacramental quality, whether or not it had legal standing; non-Christian marriage could at best be characterized as "legitimate" as to external form.

Nevertheless, by proposing that infidels might enjoy legitimate marriages, Gratian opened the door to considering the rights of infidels in such unions. The decretists followed Gratian in his division of marriage into legitimate and *ratum*. Rufinus thus agreed with Gratian that infidels might have "legitimate and perfect" marriage, but might never have *ratum* marriage because Christ and the sacrament of the Church were always absent from their unions.[77] Rolandus proposed to analyze infidel marriages through a complex set of distinctions. Among infidels, Rolandus asserted, there might be legitimate (*legitimatum*) marriage of two types: *initiatum* (marriage to which the parties consented but that has not yet been consummated); and *consummatum*. Infidel marriage, however, could never be "ratified" (*ratum*) in the same way as Christian marriage, and hence might never be rendered indissoluble.[78]

For the most part, as the arguments of Rufinus and Rolandus suggest, the canonists, being practical men, focused on the insecurity of infidel rights in the case of Christian marriage. Rufinus dealt with this question directly. Suppose, he argued, an infidel woman tried to compel her Christian husband to practice idol worship or other crimes.[79] Her husband should cease cohabitation with her, and seek judicial dismissal, including release from any obligation to render the conjugal debt.[80]

It would, however, be the theologian Hugh of St. Victor, a close contemporary of Gratian, who would consider in greatest detail the marital right of non-Christians. There are some, Hugh began, who would deny that legitimate marriage was possible "without faith" (*sine fide*).[81] Hugh, however, would repudiate this way of thinking. Where an infidel has taken a wife for purposes of procreation, has kept faith with her, loves her as a companion, nurtures and takes care of her, and, so long as she lives, does not abandon her, he has done nothing against divine command.[82] In such a case, Hugh asserts, a legitimate marriage has come into being.

Pagans as well as Christians, Hugh acknowledged, share in the *ius matrimonii*, the body of rights that accompany marriage.[83] That this is so, Hugh asserted, is proven negatively by the fact that the dissolution of a pagan marriage is said to result in the dissolution of the *ius matrimonii*.[84] It is the duty of every spouse, Christian and non-Christian alike, Hugh argued, to keep the *ius et debitum* of marriage inviolate.[85] Pagans, however, destroy this right when they show contempt for God, particularly where their spouses have converted to Christianity:

> Your wife says to you: "You have become a Christian, I will not follow you. Because you do not worship idols, because you have thrown away the rites and customs of your parents, I go another way, and if I do not go another way, at least I do not go with you, I do not acknowledge you as husband unless you deny Christ." You understand this: injury to the Creator dissolves the *ius matrimonii*.[86]

In Hugh's treatment one sees both the universality that canonists and theologians were willing to ascribe to the marital right, as well as the special standing enjoyed by Christian marriage. The natural law was inscribed in the hearts of all persons, St. Paul had taught. In Hugh's teaching about the potential sanctity even of the marriages of non-Christians one sees this expansive vision of the natural law at work: all persons of good will, Christians and non-believers alike, might share in the fruits of marriage and enjoy marital rights, provided they kept in mind the need to respect the basic Augustinian goods of marriage — procreation, fidelity, and lifelong companionship. And where a non-Christian failed in these respects or, even more fundamentally, spurned Christ or prevented a Christian spouse from the practice of his or her faith, then the *ius matrimonii*, the "right of marriage," might be dissolved in favor of the faith. Non-Christians thus might share in the rights of marriage, but this participation was qualified by the requirement that their marriages conform to the expectations of Christian theology and that they not interfere with their partners' Christian faith.[87]

Formal Equality and Actual Inequality:
The Right to Consummate a Marriage

Canonists and theologians built on these invocations of rights-language an impressive structure of mutually entailing rights and obligations. The structure of rights that was brought into being was, however, not without its limitations. Because the canonists conceptualized rights as a set of correlative claims which parties might freely assert and duties which could not legitimately be denied absent some showing of fault, they encountered a particularly serious problem when they addressed the question of the reluctant bride — a woman who consented to marriage but subsequently refused to consummate the union. This problem led some writers to advocate extreme solutions, demonstrating that a formal equality of rights might bring about some highly unequal results. But the canonists' reliance on rights language also had its advantages. The conjugal right could serve as a check on the exercise of arbitrary power and could even — as in the case of the spouse who contracted leprosy — require truly heroic conduct for the benefit of the ill spouse.

The problem of the right to consummation arose because of the triumph of the consent theory of marriage. Consent, not consummation, made a marriage,[88] and sexual relations, although conferring a special indissoluble firmness to a marriage, were not essential to the union's legal survival.[89] After all, even though Joseph and Mary were legally married, and the very paradigm of holy matrimony, they never consummated their union.[90] But because consummation did confer a special strength on marriage, and because procreation was one of the fundamental goods of marriage, the sexual relationship could not be ignored. Thus the question: By what right did parties consummate their unions? Furthermore, might a marriage be forcibly consummated where one spouse resisted?

Rolandus, a mid-twelfth-century decretist,[91] saw marriage as consisting in two *fides* — "faiths" — which came into being by different acts. The *fides* of the matrimonial contract arose from the exchange of consent between the parties, while the *fides* of carnal joining brought about a "mutual servitude" for the purpose of discharging the debt.[92] Left unspoken by Rolandus was whether the husband had a right to consummate the marriage and whether his bride had a right to resist.

Master Honorius, who authored a treatise on marriage law in the closing years of the twelfth century, asserted that marriage consisted of two "bonds" (*vincula*), one of mutual "chastity," the other of mutual "servitude" (*servitutis*).[93] The first bond, the bond of "chastity," represented unity between Christ and the soul of the faithful believer and is dissoluble. The second bond, the bond of "servitude," was indissoluble and represented the union of Christ and his Church.[94] It was the second bond which gave rise to the conjugal debt.[95] Prior to consummation, the parties were governed only by the first bond, that of chastity, which might be dissolved by the decision to take a vow of continence and enter a monastery.[96] During this time, the husband had the power of requesting the conjugal debt, but the wife was not under "the necessity of rendering it," because the second bond had not yet come into being.[97]

Huguccio, for his part, proposed a theory of marital rights which cast doubt on the analyses of Rolandus and Honorius. It has been argued, Huguccio observed, that the right of demanding the conjugal debt (the *ius exigendi debitum*) arose only after the first act of intercourse.[98] Distinguishing between a right and that right's execution, Huguccio maintained that the right to demand the debt was a part of marriage itself and arose from the exchange of promises made by the parties, but that its execution only occurred after the bride was handed over or the nuptial blessing conferred.[99]

Even before consummation, Huguccio taught, neither party was free to enter a monastery without the permission of the other because the conjugal debt was present from the beginning (*a principio*).[100] Huguccio explained what he meant by execution when he compared the right to demand the conjugal debt to the powers of a priest under interdict to hear confession or the right of a creditor to demand payment on a certain date and not before.[101] In both instances, a right has been vested in the party by reason of a certain past act, such as priestly ordination or the exchange of promises that created the debt.[102] But the authoritative power to exercise this right can only be conferred by a subsequent occurrence — that is, by the lifting of the interdict, or by the arrival of the date on which the debt has come due.[103]

Bernard of Pavia, who wrote a treatise on marriage law at the dawn of the thirteenth century, contrasted these two schools of thought on the origin of the conjugal debt.[104] Some have argued that the debt arises with the first act of sexual intercourse, but the problem with this school of thought, according to Bernard, is that if the parties fail to consummate the marriage the right never comes into existence.[105] With Huguccio obviously in mind, Bernard noticed that certain "others" have claimed that the right arises from the exchange of promises, but the right is not activated until the handing over of the bride.[106] It is this latter school of thought which had more appeal for Bernard. Either the handing over of the bride or, even better, the nuptial blessing, should be seen as effectuating a completed marriage after which the parties could equally claim the conjugal debt and were no longer free to leave the union or pursue a religious vocation.[107]

Both Huguccio and Bernard, however, avoided the very real problem presented by a wife who was genuinely unwilling to go through with the consummation. The author of the anonymous Summa, 'Induent Sancti,' however, was not so reticent. The author agreed with Huguccio that a marriage was created from the moment faith was pledged and likened the status of spouses to that of parties to a contract of purchase and sale who have incurred mutually entailing obligations.[108] The author, however, parted company with Huguccio by proposing that prior to consummation either party was free to enter religious life without the other's consent.[109] For this proposition, the gloss cited Alexander III's decretal Ex Publico, which had allowed a bride, who had given present-tense consent but had not consummated her marriage, two months to decide whether to enter a convent.[110]

But, the author continued, suppose that her husband has chosen to consummate the marriage "violently" (violenter), before she has entered religious life?[111] He has merely used his right (ille enim usus iure suo).[112] He has brought force to bear without deceit. Indeed, the force he has used can be called just, and is comparable in its justness to the force used by the magistrate.[113] Citing a second decretal of Alexander's, the author conceded that a woman may enter a convent prior to consummation even without her husband's consent, but only so long as there has not been sexual intercourse.[114] But here there were sexual relations. The husband did have carnal contact with his espoused in virtue of his right, even though his partner resisted.[115] Furthermore, the author added, it was a mortal sin for the woman to refuse her husband in these circumstances, unless she was prepared to enter a monastery at once.[116]

It seems that subsequent canonists were unwilling to press the logic of the right of demanding the conjugal debt as far as did the author of the Summa, 'Induent Sancti.' Nevertheless, it remained the case that a party might be compelled to consummate a marriage. Hostiensis made this point in his commentary on Ex Publico.[117] Hostiensis first observed that some have argued that the first act of intercourse should be considered "free" (gratuita), since prior to consummation either party is free to enter religious life and neither has power over the other.[118] Hostiensis, however, rejected this proposition: "the contrary is true," he asserted, and followed this terse claim with cross-references to three decretals that stood for the proposition that it was the Church's prerogative to enforce marriage contracts made in the present tense.[119] Absent from Hostiensis's analysis is any sense of the rough justice and self-help of the *Summa, 'Induent Sancti.'* But his analysis still allowed the official weight of the Church to be brought to bear on the spouse who refused to consummate a marriage but who also refused to enter religious life.

Scholastic writers also considered the question of the reluctant bride. Alexander of Hales's analysis reveals the same sort of equivocation present in some of the canonistic sources.[120] Referring to the canonistic texts, Alexander asked about a husband who "oppressed his wife with force."[121] "It seemed," he said, that "this use was according to his right and the marriage was consummated."[122] Alexander considered both sides of this debate. Some would concede that the woman retained her liberty *(libertas)* to pursue a monastic vocation since there had been no coming together of the soul.[123] Others say, however, that even though there had been no true "delight in carnal coupling" *(non . . . delectando in carnali copula),* the wife had promised, by consenting to the marriage, not to "dissent" *(non dissentire)* from sexual relations. Hence, according to this second school of thought, the marriage should be counted as consummated. Alexander, for his part, did not see fit to choose between these competing schools of thought.

It is highly unlikely, though not impossible, that Thomas Aquinas would have read an obscure *Summa* on Gratian's *Decretum* written three-quarters of a century before his time. Thomas did, however, return to the issues of self-help presented so baldly in the *Summa, 'Induent Sancti,'* asking whether the kind of forcible consummation commended by that text amounted to a species of rape.[124]

Rape, as Thomas defined the term, was committed whenever violence was used illicitly to deflower a virgin.[125] What, then, of a man betrothed to a girl? Does he commit the crime of rape by forcibly consummating the marriage? Thomas answered in the negative: he has a kind of right in the betrothed *(aliquod ius in sua sponsa).*[126] Hence, although he commits a sin by bringing violence to bear against his betrothed, he is excused from the crime of rape.[127] Thomas did, though, succeed in turning the tables on the author of the *Summa*. No longer would the woman sin by resisting her attacker. It was the attacker who sinned and put his immortal soul in jeopardy by his violent sexual coercion. The woman's ultimate remedy, however, was not in the criminal courts of the external forum, but before the throne of God.

At the end of the Middle Ages, Panormitanus returned to these themes. *Ex publico,* as Panormitanus understood the text, justified the use of public authority to compel consummation and the continued cohabitation of the spouses. The first act of consummation was not "gratuitous," Panormitanus stressed, and the penalty of excommunication might be imposed on one who refused to permit it to take place.[128] As with Hostiensis, so with Panormitanus: both recommended that the institutional weight of the Church be brought to bear against the reluctant bride.

How did so many canonists and theologians come to a conclusion so obviously wrong? How did they manage to import the idea of forcible consummation into a relationship that should be defined by love and mutual self-giving? The reasoning process by which they reached this result may be emblematic of some deeper, more general hazards of rights-discourse. Their argument was premised, first, on a radical equality between the parties — a wife, as well as a husband, at least theoretically, might consummate a marriage by force. But this was not the end of their analysis.

At least two other components were crucial to making this argument work. These included, first, a sense that the possession of a right was a license to engage in "rightful" behavior. The consent of spouses to marriage meant a surrendering of personal control over their bodies. Second, there was the sense that it was wrong for one to defraud an innocent party of his or her right. Applied mechanically, these principles led to outrageous results. The best answer Thomas Aquinas could muster in response to this rights-based logic was the admonition that the use of violence to achieve one's way sexually was mortally sinful, although it could not be prosecuted in this world.

A recent account of the history of the "marital rape exemption" by Jill Hasday has properly challenged "[t]he notion that a husband's conjugal rights were not contested until the late twentieth century."[129] Hasday's study acknowledges the possibility that the marital rape exemption — the exemption of men from criminal prosecution for sexually forcing themselves upon their wives — has its source in medieval canon law.[130] She sees the earliest challenges to the general acceptance of the rule that a husband might with impunity have forcible sexual relations with his spouse as dating to the nineteenth century. In fact, as this study makes clear, the story of the marital rape exemption is not a linear one, moving from a more restrictive past toward a more open future, and neither is it free of the ambiguities of history. Different canonists and theologians might simultaneously acknowledge the rights-based nature of spouses to the conjugal debt, either endorse or disapprove of its forcible exercise, and sometimes, as in the case of Thomas Aquinas, even see its violent imposition as a mortally sinful act, although not one amenable to resolution by the external forum. An account of the marital rape exemption and its demise ought not to start with the common-law heritage of nineteenth-century American courts, but should begin with this complex canonistic background.

Equal Access to the Conjugal Debt in Marriage

If the notion of the right to the conjugal debt could disadvantage the female party to a marriage prior to consummation, this right might also advantage her in other situations. In a consummated marriage, the right to the conjugal debt was one of the very few areas of equality between husband and wife.[131] Theologians and canonists were agreed on this point. Thus the theologian Peter Lombard wrote: "It should also be known that although in all other respects the man is placed above the woman, at her head, for 'the man is the head of the woman,' nevertheless in satisfying the debt of the flesh they are equal."[132] Gandulf of Bologna seconded Peter's view when he asked directly whether man and wife were equal with respect to the conjugal debt and answered in the affirmative.[133] Citing St. Paul and St. Ambrose, Gandulf concluded that "spouses are equal in demanding the conjugal debt," even though he acknowledged that "in other matters the husband is superior."[134]

The canonists concurred with the theologians. Echoing St. Paul, Hostiensis noted simply that "such is the effect of a consummated marriage, that a woman has no power over her body, but her husband, and also the reverse."[135] While in other respects the husband is to be obeyed, neither party may take an action, such as changing one's status in life, or entering religious life, which has the effect of damaging the other party's claim to the conjugal debt, without the other's free consent.[136] The conjugal debt, furthermore, was a permanent feature of the sacramental union: a valid marriage gave rise to a sacramental bond which might be dissolved only by death, and by no other occurrence, "such as one party becoming a heretic, or becoming blind, or leprous, or encountering some other horrible thing."[137]

Hostiensis was not saying anything new in laying down these conditions. Indeed, Tancred in the early thirteenth century had made many of the same points in his *Summa* on marriage.[138] These teachings had simply become the common deposit of faith among the canonists on the matter of marital relations.

This concern for the equality and permanence of the conjugal right would come to color much of thirteenth-century analysis of marital relations. By the thirteenth century, the *ius coniugale* had achieved a settled meaning as the right to claim conjugal relations within a legitimate, consummated marriage. The operation of the *ius coniugale* can be compared to the correlation of rights and duties described by David Lyons. Lyons identified a "familiar class of cases" where a tight correlation exists between a right and a duty.[139] For example, A lends B ten dollars. A tight correlation exists between A's right, or claim, to payment, and B's obligation to pay. A may assert this claim, defer it, or renounce it altogether, but should A assert it, B is duty-bound to satisfy A's claim. Lyons proposed a formal definition for this type of correlation, stating that "[t]he rule is that the expression of the content of the right is related to the content of the obligation as the passive is related to the active voice."[140] Thus, for example, A's right to be obeyed correlates with B's duty to obey.

The decretalists' understanding of the *ius coniugale* satisfies Lyons's formal definition. The content of the *ius coniugale* is the expectation that each party will be obeyed when requesting sexual intercourse from the other. The right of one spouse to demand the debt correlated strictly with the other spouse's obligation to render it. In theory, it did not matter whether the one making the demand was the wife or the husband. The equality of the *ius coniugale* lay in this recognition — that both parties enjoyed this right and each was equally obliged by the correlative duty.

By the thirteenth century, the Church was able to exercise real and exclusive jurisdiction over marriage cases throughout western Europe.[141] The *ius coniugale* became the means by which the decretalists regulated relations between the parties to a marriage.[142] A maxim of canon law taught that no one was to be deprived of his or her right without fault — *sine culpa*.[143] In the area of marriage, in particular, the decretalists engaged in extraordinary efforts to protect parties from unjust deprivations of the *ius coniugale*. This effort can be seen in three areas in particular: renunciations of rights; the protection of the rights of a spouse with leprosy; and protection of married persons from interference in their conjugal relations by public, especially feudal, authority.

Special Circumstances

Renunciation of the Ius Coniugale

The conjugal right, like most of the rights the canonists recognized, could be renounced by the parties. This was especially the case when one or the other party wished to enter religious life. From an early time in the life of the Church, there were always some married persons who wished to change their condition in life, to enter a monastery, and there pursue the counsels of perfection.

Because entry into religious life required a vow of continence, it had the effect of depriving the other party of his or her conjugal right. Therefore, the deprived person's free permission had to be obtained before the departure of the other spouse would be allowed. Additionally, since a consummated marriage made a husband and wife "one flesh," from the time of Gregory the Great it was taught that the second party, the one who had not taken the initiative in seeking to renounce the debt, should also lead a life apart from the world, preferably in a monastic setting.[144]

These rules were workable so long as both parties freely renounced the *ius coniugale* and were prepared for all that such a renunciation entailed. But title 32 of *Liber Extra*, which dealt with the entry of married persons into religious life, stands as ample testimony to the fact that parties to a marriage sometimes objected vigorously to the departure of their spouses to the higher calling of a religious vocation. The decretals found in this title, and the commentary that grew up around them, stand as a practical elaboration of the rule that no one was to be deprived of his or her right without fault.

A number of circumstances might give rise to invalid renunciations. For example, the decretal *Veniens* illustrates that both force and fraud could render a renunciation invalid.[145] In *Veniens,* a certain husband, called L., pressured his wife by threatening that he would render himself useless both to himself and to the whole world if she did not agree to renounce her right and allow him to enter religious life.[146] Priests accompanying L. failed to tell his wife that she would also be expected to enter religious life after renouncing her right.

Innocent III found "not a little fault" — *non modicum deliquisse* — in L.'s conduct.[147] When L.'s wife did not enter religious life as expected, but instead took a series of lovers — *amatores* — L., fearing his wife's incontinence might be imputed to him, sought advice as to whether to remain in the monastery.[148] Innocent III admonished L. that under the circumstances he should remain in the monastery he had chosen for himself. He also refused to restore L.'s wife to her marital right since she had had several extra-marital affairs following her renunciation. Her adultery prevented a claim for restitution.[149]

Commentators immediately recognized that the wife would have been able to obtain restitution of her marital right had she not engaged in adultery. Bernard of Parma asserted that L.'s fraud would have been sufficient to void the agreement had his wife remained continent.[150] He also noted that had the wife not prejudiced her claim, the permission she granted to L. would have been invalid because of L.'s threats.[151] Coercion had no place in the renunciation of marital rights. Hostiensis noted that the woman only seemed to have renounced her right at the time of L.'s coercion, but that by her fornication she lost her right completely (omne ius suum perdidit).[152] Indeed, it was clear that the husband's vows would have been invalid had the wife not engaged in misconduct herself.[153]

A second of Innocent III's decretals, Accedens, dealt with even more overt pressure.[154] After twenty years of marriage, a certain husband, V., sought to leave his wife and enter a monastery. He first approached his spouse "humbly and piously" seeking her agreement, but then resorted to beating and threatening her. After repeated blows and threats, she acceded to his demands and entered a convent herself, but did not assume a habit or take any vows. With the passage of time, the man found that religious life was not to his liking and withdrew from the monastery. His wife then left the convent and sought to have her husband restored to her, apparently in spite of his previous misbehavior.[155] Innocent III ruled that, if the facts were as alleged, husband and wife should be restored to one another.[156]

The commentators focused their energies on whether the husband, given his prior renunciation, might again be able to seek as well as render the conjugal debt. Bernard of Parma argued that the husband lacked the capacity to seek the conjugal debt because he had renounced this right by entering the monastery, but that he was still obliged to render it when it was demanded of him.[157]

Hostiensis agreed with Bernard, stating that the man had renounced his right and was therefore unable to make any claims on his wife, but that he remained obligated to satisfy her demands.[158] The commentaries of Bernard and Hostiensis remained among the standard restatements of the law where one party withdrew from the marriage in order to enter religious life but subsequently returned to the world.[159]

These rules may seem like a bizarre way to regulate marital relations, but they illustrate the connection the canonists perceived between due process and rights. As matters of principle, the canonists recognized that a person was free to renounce his or her own rights, but could not prejudice the rights of another person.[160] They also recognized as a basic principle that one ought not to lose a right through no fault of his or her own.

The rules on the restoration of rights in cases of coerced renunciations were simply an elaboration on these first principles. L.'s wife had committed adultery following her separation; hence, she was no longer without fault, and could not seek restitution. But the wife in *Accedens* was blameless, and so was able to seek restitution and claim the conjugal debt once her husband was restored to her. Her husband, however, who had freely renounced his right, could no longer make a claim for sexual relations. This was because a person was free to renounce his or her rights but unable to prejudice another's. The logic of rights had its own consequences, whatever the practical implications for the marital relationship.

A Spouse with Leprosy

The limits of the desire to protect marital rights were tested in the case of a spouse who had contracted leprosy. Leprosy was a dreaded and fearful disease in thirteenth-century Europe, chiefly affecting rural areas and extending north as far as Scandinavia.[161] Lepers, who were without hope for cure and were thought to pose the risk of deadly contagion, were ostracized socially and legally.[162] Lepers were segregated from the larger society, sometimes living in isolated encampments, sometimes housed in leprosariums that came to be established in the larger dioceses of western Europe during the twelfth and thirteenth centuries.[163] The separation of lepers from the larger society was often accompanied by considerable liturgical pomp, including a symbolic burial.[164] A comprehensive set of legal regulations governing this separation developed.[165] Some monarchs, however, dispensed with legal niceties and executed lepers in various grisly ways.[166] Throughout Europe, lepers were required to wear distinctive clothing, to live in isolation, and to warn the healthy of their presence with rattles, bells, or other instruments.[167]

Marriage, with its commitment to lifelong sacramental fidelity and its accompanying conjugal right, a right that could not be lost except through voluntary renunciation or through wrongdoing, represented a conceptual problem for this policy of isolation. Already in the twelfth century, Pope Al-

exander III proposed in two decretals that a healthy spouse was not to separate from a spouse who had contracted leprosy. In *Pervenit,* Alexander
condemned a local custom that permitted separation.[168] Because husband
and wife are made of one flesh, Alexander reasoned, the healthy spouse was
to remain with the leprous one and to minister to him or her with conjugal
affection.[169] In *Quoniam,* Alexander asserted that, as separation was permitted only on the ground of adultery, spouses may not separate merely because one of them had contracted leprosy.[170] Furthermore, Alexander
added, if the leprous spouse requested the conjugal debt, the healthy partner was obliged to render it. To Alexander's mind, Paul's exhortation in
First Corinthians did not brook exceptions.[171]

Alexander, it seems, arrived at these conclusions through a kind of
biblical literalism. The Matthean divorce text recognized adultery by one of
the spouses as the only ground for separation,[172] and Paul had seemed to
allow no exceptions to the rule that parties were obliged to render the conjugal debt. Alexander must have assumed that he was doing no more than
applying clear scriptural texts to an obvious case.

The decretalists, however, analyzed the problem in terms of rights.
Might a leprous spouse continue to demand the conjugal right, and might
the healthy spouse be compelled to render it? This question was made even
more urgent by the close connection many medieval writers drew between
leprosy and sexual contamination.[173]

Goffredus of Trani articulated the revulsion and fear that many must
have felt at the thought of lepers married to healthy partners. He announced that he considered prior leprosy to be an impediment to marriage
that effectively dissolved all subsequent betrothals.[174] Where a married
person has contracted leprosy, Goffredus went on, the parties should be
separated but the healthy spouse should continue to reside in the vicinity,
so as to tend to the leprous spouse's needs as well as to render the conjugal
debt.[175]

Bernard of Parma asserted that the healthy spouse need not be compelled to share the same bed or the same house with the leprous spouse.[176]
Furthermore, the leprous spouse should not be overly wicked in exacting
his or her right.[177] Bernard, however, concluded that if the healthy spouse
refused the leprous one completely, he or she could be compelled to render
the debt. This was because the leprous spouse was not to be defrauded of
the conjugal debt.[178]

Innocent IV, for his part, taught that a healthy partner was obligated
to tend to his or her spouse's needs, but that they were not to dwell to-

gether in the same house.[179] Innocent distanced himself from those who rigidly required fulfillment of the conjugal right: others argued that parties are to be strictly compelled to render the debt, he observed, but out of kindness (*de benignitate*) some other arrangement might be tolerated.[180]

Hostiensis, finally, staked out a position that recognized at once the sanctity of the right at issue but that also tempered rigidity with a sense of compassion for the difficult situation created by a diagnosis of leprosy. Marriage, Hostiensis began, was instituted by God to make two parties into one flesh, and Scripture permitted separation only in the case of adultery.[181] Turning to the wording of the papal decretal, Hostiensis explained that by "minister" Alexander meant that the healthy spouse was to provide the leprous spouse not only with the necessities of life, but also with the conjugal debt.[182] Hostiensis agreed with Bernard of Parma that the parties should not share the same bed or the same house, but that they should not live at such a distance that the ill spouse was effectively defrauded of the debt.[183] Although Hostiensis was not explicit, it seems that his understanding of the conjugal debt must have embraced more than mere sexual relations and should probably be understood as also encompassing some larger notion of emotional love and material and spiritual support.

Hostiensis was both more explicit and more nuanced than Bernard as to the level of compulsion that could be brought to bear on the healthy spouse. He acknowledged that complete refusal to render the conjugal debt would amount to a mortal sin. Nonetheless, he was also reluctant to employ the sanction of excommunication against the healthy spouse.[184] The healthy spouse might simply be incapable of rendering the debt because of the horror of the disease, and one should not be held to do the impossible under a sentence of excommunication.[185] In laying down these criteria, Hostiensis seemed to be taking account of the demands of pastoral reality: it was highly unlikely that ecclesiastical sanctions could or should be utilized to compel intercourse between a healthy and a leprous spouse. But by the same token the ill spouse was not to be deprived of some of the other necessary attributes of married life, such as support and sustenance.

Panormitanus, in the fifteenth century, stressed that "supervening leprosy does not dissolve a marriage or the effects of marriage. And so the couple should treat one another with marital affection or be induced to a perpetual vow of continence."[186] Panormitanus's use of the term "marital affection" in this context underscored the element of interpersonal love hinted at by Hostiensis.[187] Where, however, the couple failed or refuse to vow continence and the ill party sought the healthy partner's sexual companionship, the healthy spouse should be firmly compelled to render the debt.[188]

In practice, the decretalists' teaching must have been difficult to realize. Statutes of the leprosaria of the late twelfth and thirteenth centuries make it clear that men and women, wives and husbands, were supposed to avoid contact with one another. The statutes of the leprosarium of Saint Lazare of Meaux, published at the end of the twelfth century, declared that men and their wives should be separated and the healthy and the sick were not to have conjugal relations.[189] In 1239, the leprosarium in Lille legislated that "fatuous love or suspect relations" were to be punished by temporary or permanent exclusion from the home and that those who married were to be banished permanently.[190] The leprosarium at Brives, on the other hand, made a modest effort to accommodate itself with canon law. Wives and husbands, it was declared, ought not to be received into the hospital except with the license of the bishop, even where they wished to remain together as man and wife.[191] An exception was thus carved out in an otherwise inflexible rule.

The decretalists' analysis appears to represent a decided shift away from Alexander's biblical literalism.[192] The decretalists confronted the issue of the leprous spouse by reference to their understanding of due process and rights. The leprous spouse was not to be defrauded of his or her right. He or she should be restrained in seeking marital satisfaction, but where it was demanded the healthy partner was obliged to render it. Even though canonists like Innocent IV and Hostiensis ultimately proposed means by which the rigor of this rule might be mitigated, they engaged in strenuous efforts to uphold the basic principle that no one was to be deprived of his or her right without fault. Even though in practice these ideals were often honored in the breach, the canonists were not willing to sacrifice the principle that a right derived from natural and divine law was to be arbitrarily denied an innocent party, even in the case of the most dread disease of the age.

Interference from Feudal Authority

Frederic Maitland has observed concerning the medieval serf that "[a]s regards his lord, the serf has, at least as a rule, no rights."[193] Social reality, on the other hand, suggests that there was substantial variety in the ways in which the medieval serf related to his lord. Lords might behave in a violent fashion toward those subject to manorial authority. Paul Freedman, following earlier work by Marc Bloch, noted the survival of evidence of "mutilation, torture, and burning" of villeins by their lords.[194] On the other hand, even Freedman agrees that "it is unlikely that [serfs] were completely cowed, given their control of the immediate circumstances of cultivation."[195]

The Latin word for serf was *servus*, which might also mean slave. This ambiguity of terminology creates continuing confusion as to whether the decretalists, when discussing the status of *servi*, actually had in mind slaves or serfs. Although this is a complex question, some cursory observations are in order. "[T]he last vestiges of slavery," Michael Sheehan notes, as it was understood in the classical Roman world, "were disappearing in northern Europe" in "the late eleventh and twelfth centuries."[196] Nevertheless, in other parts of Europe, in portions of Spain, in Valencia, in Portugal, in southern France, and in Venice and Genoa, one can detect the survival of Roman forms of slavery throughout much of our time period.[197]

The practice of serfdom was itself a complex matter. The classical distinction between serfdom and slavery is that serfs were bound to the land while slaves were the chattels of particular owners. This distinction, however, was sometimes blurred in practice.[198] But however blurred the boundary lines might become, it was increasingly difficult in large portions of Europe for persons to be thought of as chattel property. Made in the image and likeness of God, serfs might occupy a servile status and be restricted in a number of respects,[199] but they nonetheless retained "a certain minimal human dignity and, related to that, a certain minimal human freedom or immunity from arbitrary domination by others."[200]

In the realm of marriage, *pace* Maitland, the canonists were prepared to recognize that serfs had significant claims of right, and the lawyers accordingly struck a balance between the right of serfs to claim or render the marital act, on the one hand, and the demands of feudal overlords, on the other. Lords had a *ius*, a right, in their serfs, but so too did their wives.[201]

Bernard of Parma, in balancing the claims of lords and servile families, was willing to give priority to the claims of wives, at least in most circumstances. Bernard discussed the conflicting priorities that existed when a lord demanded *servitium*, service, from a serf and the man's wife demanded the conjugal debt at the same time. Some say the lord should be obeyed, Bernard began, unless it is feared that the wife will fornicate or otherwise be prejudiced greatly by her husband's service.[202] Bernard, however, thought the priorities should be reversed. The serf-husband should ordinarily render the debt first, since the lord would only be slightly prejudiced by the modest delay that this would cause.[203] The only exception Bernard acknowledged was where the serf was obliged to render immediate personal assistance to the lord.[204]

Bernard's answer did not go unchallenged. Innocent IV responded by seeming initially to agree with Bernard: if the wife seeks the debt at the same time the lord demands some service, the lord would appear to behave maliciously if he did not allow the serf a modest amount of time to satisfy his wife.[205] Nonetheless, Innocent continued, citing Roman law, since the serf is legally unable to prejudice a prior obligation, namely his duty to render service to his lord, the man ought to obey his lord first, unless there is significant possibility the wife might commit adultery.[206]

In his *Summa,* Hostiensis generally agreed with Bernard. Where a lord will be greatly prejudiced by his *servus's* absence, as, for example, when he is under attack, the *servus* ought to render service first to his lord.[207] Otherwise, the lord should be obligated to wait a little time for his *servus,* since there is no great loss in a short wait.[208] In his *Lectura,* Hostiensis continued to build a case in favor of the *servus* by criticizing the position of Innocent IV: there are some who say that when a wife and lord request satisfaction at the same time, the lord should be obeyed first, since the feudal obligation is prior in time.[209] But, Hostiensis continued, with a degree of emphasis missing from Innocent's text, where there is danger of fornication, it is clear that the teaching of God and St. Paul must be given priority.[210]

Hostiensis bolstered these claims by an appeal to general principle. Calling his readers' attention to the bold language of the decretal letter on which he was commenting, Hostiensis stressed that marriage — like baptism, confirmation, the Eucharist, confession, and Extreme Unction — was counted among the sacraments.[211] Why should *servi* be disqualified from this sacrament when they may freely receive the others? Hostiensis noted that the decretal served to amend Roman law, which had limited those of servile status to sexual relationships of lesser status than marriage, relationships characterized by the Roman lawyers as *contubernia.*[212] Henceforward, provided they have freely consented, *servi* might, like all others, join together matrimonially in valid marriages.

Raymond of Peñafort, for his part, provided a set of detailed policy recommendations responding to the decretal's acknowledgement that, while the marriage of *servi* may not be impeded by their lords, the couple's lords nevertheless remained entitled to their "customary services" (*consueta servitia*).[213] Where the lord has consented to a servile marriage,

Raymond argued, he should be presumed to have consented to the exercise of the conjugal rights that are a part of marriage.[214] But where the marriage took place against the lord's wishes, or where the lord was unaware, then the lord's orders should ordinarily be obeyed first, except where there is danger of adultery.[215] Turning the marital rights argument on its head, Raymond noted that in the latter case it is the lord who through no fault of his own should not be deprived of the service he is owed.[216]

What is significant in this discussion is the balance that the decretalists struck between competing sets of claims. Both lord and wife were understood to have valid claims. The decretalists did not automatically yield to the lord's claims merely because he occupied a more favorable position in the medieval hierarchy. Rather, the decretalists were quite willing to balance the lord's claims against the wife's in an effort to ensure that both parties were not deprived of their rights. Once again, the relationships generated by rights are clearly visible at work together with an operative concept of due process.

This review of the role that rights played in the conjugal relationship is not comprehensive. One can identify yet other areas where the canonists sought to safeguard the conjugal right, such as the frosty reception Pope Innocent III's decretal *Ex Multa* received.[217] By the terms of this decretal married men were allowed to take the crusading vow without their wives' consent. Hostiensis, echoing prevailing sentiment, observed that this was "a most special case" *(specialissimus casus)*, since it seemed to make the crusading vow even more important than the vow of continence, for which spousal permission had to be obtained.[218] By this oblique criticism, the preeminence of the conjugal right was maintained, even in the face of contrary papal legislation.

The canonistic analysis of the *ius coniugale* illustrates the powerful hold claims of right had on the legal imagination of the thirteenth century. The violence of a forcible consummation was nearly completely masked by the invocation of rights language in a work like the *Summa, 'Induent Sancti.'* Even Thomas Aquinas, who was willing to analyze forcible marital intercourse under the rubric of rape and to condemn transgressors as sinners, concluded that a husband's forcible intercourse with his newly-wed bride did not amount to the crime of rape because he had "some right" to take this action.

On the other hand, claims of right might insulate married women — as well as men — from the worst depredations of medieval life. The marital rights of female serfs were to be protected. Women and men were to be safeguarded from arbitrary renunciations of marital rights by their partners. And in an extreme case, a spouse with leprosy was to be protected in his or her right. Indeed, the invocation of marital rights became the means by which Church leaders could exhort the healthy spouse to minister to the ill spouse's needs. Thus the marital right might even provide some small measure of comfort in the face of the onset of one of the most fearsome diseases of the age.

Part III: The Woman's Right to Select Her Place of Burial

Burial was not viewed in the Middle Ages merely as the disposal of dead bodies no longer part of the Christian community.[219] Death and the disposition of the dead formed an integral part of communal existence that was closely connected to the central Christian belief in the resurrection of the dead and the transcendence of death itself at the time of the Last Judgment.[220]

In its origins, Christianity placed an emphasis on the resurrection of the dead that was new in the Greco-Roman world. Pagan writers, and even pagan tomb inscriptions, often commented wryly on the absence of any afterlife.[221] Jewish theology of the sixth and fifth centuries BC, furthermore, lacked a well-formed conception of an afterlife, although a few biblical texts, most of them of somewhat late provenance, promised a more hopeful future.[222]

Christianity, however, with its belief in a Savior who rose from the dead following his execution by Roman authority, and who promised eternal life to his faithful followers, made belief in the resurrection of the dead a central part of its teaching.[223] A powerful commitment to the idea of the resurrection of the body permeated early Christian texts and shaped the way burial itself was conceptualized.[224] Gradually, Christians came to reshape antecedent Jewish and Roman burial practices.[225] In the process there developed a powerful new set of beliefs and practices concerning the proper disposition of the dead that reflected Christian expectations.[226]

From an early date, Christian burial places were integrated into the devotional life of the larger community. The practice of burial *ad sanctos* — literally, burial within the church at the side of the saints — grew up in the fifth and sixth centuries as a means of seeking the intervention of the anointed of God at the time of final judgment.[227] Those who could not be buried at the side of the saints — that is, the great majority of the Christian community — came to be buried in the yard surrounding the parish church. By the eleventh century, "[t]he church and its cemetery are regarded as a unity in Christian practice."[228]

During these early centuries of Church history, in a development parallel to the growth of Christian burial practice, there developed a theology of Christian marriage that emphasized the enduring unity of the married couple.[229] Male and female were made one flesh at the time of coupling,[230] and neither party was thereafter free to shatter this unity.[231] The unity was not perfect. It did not endure into the next life. In the life to come, they neither marry nor are given in marriage.[232] Thus a widowed spouse might be free to remarry, although the praiseworthy course of action might be a life of consecrated chastity or some other form of spiritual pursuit.[233]

The Early Medieval Context: Obligation of a Woman to Follow Her Husband

The law, as found at the dawn of the second millennium, invoking the essential oneness of the married couple, asserted the obligation of the woman to follow her husband in choice of burial place. Burchard of Worms included four texts in his collection making this point. A passage of St. Jerome noted that the three great patriarchs — Abraham, Isaac, and Jacob — were all buried with their wives and that Adam and Eve were also buried together.[234] In the excerpt reproduced by Burchard, Jerome next turned to the Book of Tobit for support, noting that Tobias counseled his son to bury his wife next to him, since they had spent their lives together.[235] A second excerpt from Jerome then asserted that "those who were joined together in life should be joined together in a single tomb, because they have become one flesh and what God has joined together, man should not separate."[236]

These passages were followed by an excerpt from St. Augustine noting that "every woman should follow her husband, whether in life or in death."[237] Rounding out the four excerpts was a passage from Gregory the Great noting that St. Benedict's sister, St. Scholastica, who had chosen with St. Benedict to follow the monastic vocation, should become one and the same flesh with her brother in a single tomb since they had been of one mind in the Lord during their lifetimes.[238] The implication was clear: those who followed the same path in life should remain together, side-by-side, in death. The inclusion of the passage about St. Scholastica, who was not married to St. Benedict but as his sister shared his way of life, only moved this point to a higher, spiritualized frame of reference in which soul and body become united forever, thanks to the parties' singleness of purpose.

Burchard, furthermore, was not alone in deploying these texts to make the case that women were obliged to follow their husbands in choice of burial ground. Two hundred years before Burchard, the local Irish compilation of law known as the *Collectio Hibernensis* deployed several of the same texts to make the same claim about a woman's obligation to follow her husband.[239] Burchard and the Irish Collection represented deeply-held social expectations.

That the teaching of Burchard and the Irish canons represented the social ideal toward which married persons were expected to strive in the early Middle Ages is evidenced by the historical record and by hagiographical accounts. Gregory of Tours, in his *History of the Franks,* tells the story of Iniuriosus and Scholastica, the "two lovers" (*Duos Amantes*).[240] Hailing from a senatorial family, Iniuriosus married well, but discovered on his wedding night that his bride wished to consecrate the two of them to a spiritual marriage, free of the pollution and stains of a sexual union. Iniuriosus agreed to this proposal and the two of them embarked upon a close and spiritually fruitful marriage.[241]

Eventually, each of them died, Scholastica first, followed quickly by Iniuriosus. Iniuriosus was buried close by Scholastica's tomb, but with a wall separating the two of them. Miraculously, however, the wall was removed so that the two of them, companions in life, now also companions in death, might be joined together as they await the resurrection of the dead on the last day.[242]

In his *Glory of the Confessors,* Gregory recounted the story of Reticius, who had enjoyed a virginal marriage during the lifetime of his wife and who was elected bishop of Autun following her death. Reticius had promised his wife on her death-bed that they would be buried together,[243] and when at last he died it proved impossible to remove his body for burial until it was recalled that he was to be interred side-by-side with his wife.[244]

In all likelihood, Iniuriosus and Scholastica never existed, or at least the miracle that accomplished the removal of the barrier separating them in death never occurred. Similarly, the miracle by which it was called to mind that Reticius was to be buried next to his wife probably did not happen in the way that Gregory recalled it. But awareness of Gregory's role in embellishing these stories only heightens the sense in which burial side-by-side, spouses following one another in death as well as life, was a real social ideal of the early Middle Ages. Unity in one's resting place thus confirmed the enduring quality of marital oneness, a unity that should be preserved until Christ comes again.

The story of St. Ida of Herzfeld, a ninth-century holy woman, provides further illustration of the enduring strength of the tradition that spouses must be buried together.[245] Unlike the stories of Iniuriosus and Scholastica, or Reticius and his wife, there is no suggestion in the hagiography that St. Ida was involved in a virginal marriage. Indeed, her hagiographer took pains to point out that her marriage was consummated.[246] St. Ida was a young noblewoman who fell in love with a certain Count Egbert, whom she married after nursing him back to health following an illness.[247] Following Egbert's death, Ida built a chapel to honor his memory and dedicated herself to a life of austere sanctity and charity toward the poor.[248] She eventually ordered a marble tomb be built for both of them,[249] where "[t]heir bodies are united in the grave forever."[250]

Recognition of the "Equal Faculty" of Selecting a Burial Site

That these expectations were deeply-entrenched at the dawn of the second millennium is not surprising. In an enchanted world, where the boundary lines between the living and dead were not clearly drawn,[251] where a whole spirit world seemed palpable and nearly within reach,[252] the social ideal of husbands and wives remaining side-by-side, awaiting eternity, probably seemed like an altogether natural extension of lived reality.

The case of the burial of Peter Abelard and Heloise, a case some of the decretists might even have known about, illustrates how deeply entrenched this ideal remained in the first half of the twelfth century. Abelard (1079-1142) was, as is well known, one of the dominating intellects of his time, the author of works on logic, biblical criticism, and Christian theology.[253] Heloise was one of Abelard's prize pupils, entrusted to his care by her uncle, Fulbert. The romance that this couple embarked upon set in motion one of the great dramas of the twelfth century:[254] Heloise's pregnancy by Abelard; their secret marriage, a union in which the parties only rarely saw one another;[255] and Abelard's ultimate castration brought about by Fulbert, who was fired by a desire to take revenge for the embarrassment Abelard had caused him.[256]

Following these events, Abelard and Heloise eventually retreated to separate monasteries.[257] They clearly remained emotionally and spiritually close, even though physically separated for most of their remaining days. Indeed, one of his recent biographers has observed that the aging Abelard addressed his final statement of faith not to St. Bernard of Clairvaux and the Council of Sens, who were demanding it as part of their investigation into Abelard's suspected heresy, but to Heloise, "'once dear to me in the world, now dearest in Christ.'"[258]

It is their burial, however, that is relevant to our concerns. At the end of his days, Abelard had taken refuge at the monastery of Cluny, whose abbot at the time was Peter the Venerable, famous for his works on Islam.[259] When he died, Peter made sure to return the body to Heloise for proper burial.[260] Exquisitely, Peter the Venerable wrote of the carnal bond that had once connected Abelard and Heloise, and the "much greater bond of divine charity" which subsequently joined them in their mutual service to the Lord.[261] When she died in 1164, Heloise was laid to rest next to Abelard.[262] Side-by-side, they remained, even after their tomb was relocated to Paris following the French Revolution.[263] Their burial place remained a prominent tourist destination until modern times.[264]

Not surprisingly, therefore, this understanding of eternal togetherness also remained deeply embedded in the law at the beginning of the twelfth century. The law of burial at the time of Abelard's death had been conveniently restated by Ivo of Chartres, who included in his *Decretum* the same four texts that Burchard and the Irish compilers had relied upon, making it clear that the teaching on wives following their husbands remained intact.[265]

Gratian, too, made use of these texts.[266] The overarching concern of *Causa* 13, *quaestio* 2, where he inserted these references, was with the proper ownership of tithes and other fees payable to the Church, including fees payable upon burial.[267] Gratian opened his analysis by inquiring into the possession of the *ius funerandi,* by which he meant not the right of the individual to choose a place of burial, but the right of the Church to collect its fees.[268] Following St. Jerome, Gratian stated that married persons were obligated to be buried in a single grave.[269] Though Gratian did not explicitly draw the conclusion, presumably he thereby intended that a deceased husband's pastor would also bury his wife, thus allowing the parish to collect fees for both funerals.

Gratian, however, also articulated principles that stood in seeming contradiction to a hard and fast rule requiring women to follow their husbands in the choice of burial places. Immediately after reproducing Gregory the Great's description of St. Scholastica seeking burial in her brother's tomb — used by Burchard for the principle that those of one mind should not be separated in death — Gratian posed the issue of the proper burial place of adult children.[270] Are such children obligated to choose the burial place of their parents? It seemed, Gratian initially replied, that they were.[271] After all, it is recorded that St. Philip built a tomb for himself and his family.[272] And St. Severus, archbishop of Ravenna, built a tomb for himself, his wife, and his daughter.[273]

But not everyone chose to be buried with his or her parents. Isaac was buried next to Abraham, but Ishmael, Abraham's son by his servant girl, was not.[274] Nor were Adam's children all buried with Adam. Indeed, this would have been impossible, given that the whole multitude of the human race could not be accommodated in such a small burial site.[275] If children are free to make this choice, one might reason, though Gratian did not, why not wives?

Gratian continued his analysis by including a text of Gregory the Great holding that the final wishes (the *ultima voluntas,* or "last will") of a decedent should in all respects (*in modis omnibus*) be obeyed.[276] He followed this text with one from the Council of Tribur allowing Christians to choose to be buried at the episcopal see, or with congregations of canons, or monks, or nuns, or at the parish where they paid their tithes.[277] Acknowledging the possibility of choice, Gratian returned his analysis to the issue of children electing to be buried apart from their parents: it is one thing, he reasoned, when the choice is the result of pride, and quite another when it is based on some reasonable cause.[278] Citing Gregory the Great yet again, Gratian concluded that the freely chosen last will of the decedent to seek "new hospitality" for his body ought to be respected.[279] As he had done with the choice of marital partner, so also with the choice of burial ground, Gratian injected a principle of freedom into the law. It remained to others, however, to work out the implications of this liberty in a consistent fashion.

The early decretists had relatively little to say on the subject of women following their husbands in death. The *Summa Parisiensis* merely noted that it was Rachel who was buried next to Jacob,[280] while Stephen of Tournai called attention to the physical dimensions of the tomb of the patriarchs.[281] Rufinus, in contrast, emphasized the importance of honoring the final will of the decedent, "since there is no greater duty owed to men than" giving effect to decisions which can no longer be altered.[282]

It is possible that this reticence was the result of changing social expectations. The twelfth century, as is now understood, was a period of blossoming "individualism."[283] This transformation is definitively evidenced by a decretal issued by Pope Lucius III (reigned 1181-1185) declaring that a wife should have a free faculty equal to her husband in choosing her place of burial (*liberam . . . aequalem . . . facultatem*).[284] In a choice such as this, Lucius continued, the woman should be released from her husband's governance (*mulier solvitur a lege viri*).[285] The teaching of Jerome and Augustine that a wife should follow her husband was thus rejected in favor of the principle of free choice, which Gratian had introduced into his analysis of selection of burial sites but had not applied to wives. By choosing the word *facultas*, furthermore, Pope Lucius connected this freedom of choice with an emerging rights vocabulary that stressed individual discretion in matters fundamental to one's spiritual development.[286]

Lucius's decretal became the foundation stone of thirteenth-century canonistic analysis of choice of burial ground. Goffredus of Trani asserted simply that one might freely choose one's place of burial provided the appropriate fees were paid to the deceased's parish.[287] Standing on the principle of free selection, Goffredus refrained from commenting on the matter of wives choosing to be buried apart from their husbands.

Bernard of Parma, however, was less reticent. He opened his summary of the decretal by observing that just as the husband is free to choose his place of burial, so also is his wife.[288] There is no difference between them because in this respect the wife is released from her husband's rule.[289] Glossing the word *aequalem*, Bernard raised as an objection Jerome's invocation of Matthew 19:6: "What God has joined together, man may not separate," and replied that Jerome's exegesis only operated where the wife had not chosen her place of burial.[290] Where she has chosen to be buried apart from her husband, the ruling of Pope Lucius's decretal ought to prevail.[291]

Although he abstained from committing himself to one or another viewpoint, Innocent IV, in his *Apparatus*, proposed two possible ways to reconcile Lucius's decretal with the teaching of St. Jerome and St. Augustine, as preserved in Burchard and Gratian.[292] It is possible, Innocent reasoned, to see Jerome and Augustine as establishing the socially proper course of conduct (*de honestate*), while Lucius's decree set a kind of legal minimum (*de iure*).[293] Borrowing from Vincentius Hispanus, Innocent had conceded as a general principle that every adult of "discrete" capabilities was free to choose his or her place of burial, provided the selection was not made "maliciously."[294] But it was also possible, the canonist-turned-pope reasoned, to accept the admonitions of Jerome and Augustine as applicable in those cases where the wife has not herself chosen a place of burial.[295]

Thus the default position, where a wife had not elected to be buried apart from her husband, was burial side-by-side. Innocent, it seems, was here attempting to reconcile the general principle of freedom as found in Pope Lucius's decree and Vincentius Hispanus's teaching with what must have remained the powerful social expectation that husbands and wives should ordinarily be buried together.

Raymond of Peñafort, for his part, also borrowed from Vincentius to support free choice in one's place of burial. Commencing his analysis, Raymond declared broadly: "I say . . . that any living adult of sound judgment can choose to be buried where he or she wishes. . . ."[296] Raymond went on to make clear that wives, as well as husbands, enjoyed this freedom: "About the wife whose husband has died, I say that she is able to choose to be buried apart from her husband. But if she dies without selecting a place of burial, then I believe she ought to be buried with her husband."[297]

Hostiensis offered perhaps the most complex and thorough defense of Lucius's decretal, and in the process displayed his own virtuosic command of Roman law. He began his gloss to the word *aequalem*, found in Lucius's decretal, by noting that Scripture seemed to stand against the pope: "What God has joined together," Hostiensis said, quoting the first half of Matthew's text, expecting his readers to fill in the rest.[298] But, Hostiensis continued, citing a phrase in Justinian's *Novella* 22, it is death, which dissolves all things, that separates the couple in the instant case, not man.[299] Hostiensis then noted a seemingly contradictory rule of Roman law: wives, he observed, are immunized from suits charging the plundering of an estate because they are their husbands' helpmates, "both in human affairs and in their heavenly home" (*quae socia rei humanae atque divinae domus*).[300]

If, then, women share a heavenly residence with their husbands on the authority of Roman law, how might one preserve Pope Lucius's teaching? Did the older imperial decree require that man and wife be buried together? Hostiensis answered these concerns by turning first to Innocent IV's distinction between conduct that is *de honestate* and that which is legally permissible (*de iure*).[301] Lucius's teaching might be the strict law, but propriety teaches women to follow their husbands in death as well as in life. Hostiensis, however, suggested an even better answer (*vel melius dic*).[302] Where a husband has chosen to be buried in his own church, or even in another church, and his wife has not specified a place of burial for herself, she should be seen as following her husband.[303] This much, Hostiensis made clear, through a series of cross-references to Roman-law texts, was the dictate of the ancient law.[304]

Where, however, a wife has chosen her own place of burial, her choice must be respected (*electioni suae standum esset*), whatever the disposition of her husband might have been.[305] This conclusion should be seen simply as a practical elaboration of Gregory the Great's principle that the last will of the decedent must be observed.[306] Hostiensis reiterated this point in his gloss to the word *facultatem:* a wife is obligated to remain under her husband's authority, but this authority is dissolved by death.[307] She is accordingly free to select her own place of burial.[308]

Pope Lucius's decree, fortified by the teaching of the thirteenth-century decretalists, became the established teaching of the Church.[309] Johannes Andreae, writing in the fourteenth century, took the prior commentary for granted when he wrote that "a married woman can freely choose her place of burial."[310]

An *additio* to Panormitanus's text similarly took the principle embodied in Lucius III's decretal for granted when it asserted that a wife who had several husbands and did not make clear her burial preference was deemed to prefer burial with her most recent husband.[311] The norm was freedom. Burial side-by-side, however, remained the socially expected choice where a wife had not made other arrangements.

Luis de Molina, the great Portuguese Jesuit, writing at the end of the sixteenth century, reached a similar conclusion.[312] Every living person, Molina asserted, is able to select his or her own place of burial, even if it meant rejecting the family burial plot, or selecting a place that is "less holy."[313] A wife thus enjoyed the same independence as her husband in selecting a place of burial, although she was obligated to follow her husband where she had not made a choice.[314] A wife, Molina noted, might have good reason to choose to be buried apart from her spouse. She might be divorced from her husband, or she might have married a man of lesser social status, or her husband might have died a long time ago and she now wished to be buried in her father's family tomb.[315]

The canonist Johannes Paulus Lancelotti (1522-1590) agreed with what had become, since the late twelfth century, the new tradition of Christian burial. A wife is not to be judicially compelled into following "her head," her husband, in choice of burial site.[316] Rather, she has an "equal faculty of choosing" and is "freed of her husband's governance" in this matter.[317]

The principle of free selection came to be incorporated as well into the great seventeenth-century treatise on cemetery law written by Peter Murga.[318] Peter simply took it for granted that a wife might select her own place of burial, even if her husband was still alive.[319] Just as her husband is free, so also his wife is free to make this choice. There was no difference between male and female here, Murga reasoned, relying on Lucius's decretal, since the wife was understood to be released from her husband's authority in this matter.[320]

Modern canon law preserves the same rule.[321] Today, this rule seems like a self-evident proposition, but the law might have taken a very different course had it not been for the efforts of Pope Lucius III and the thirteenth-century canonists to establish a parity of rights between men and women on the subject of Christian burial.

Part IV: The Right of Women to Accuse a Marriage and to Seek Divorce

The ancient Jewish law permitted husbands freely to divorce their wives, but gave women no reciprocal set of rights.[322] Although divorce was possible wherever "[a wife] finds no favor in [her husband's] eyes,"[323] Jewish prophetic literature condemned such arbitrariness as immoral.[324] Nevertheless, the Jewish law of the first century AD, at the time of Jesus' public ministry, continued to confer on husbands the power to divorce freely, while withholding any comparable power from wives.[325]

It seems that pre-classical Roman law also denied women the capacity to pursue divorce, although this limitation was restricted to *manus* marriages, in which the wife came to occupy a position in the household legally akin to that of a daughter of the *paterfamilias*.[326] In *sine manu* marriage, however, women, as much as men, enjoyed the capacity to seek divorce and Percy Corbett has noted that by the time one reaches the age of Plautus and Terence, in the second century BC, this was very much a lived social reality.[327]

It is in this context that Jesus' teaching, as recorded in the Gospel of Matthew, that a man may divorce a woman only in case of *porneia* ("fornication," "immorality") must be placed.[328] Because of the hardness of the people's hearts, Moses permitted men to divorce their wives, but this concession violated the original unity of male and female, a unity that was made complete through marriage. Thus, because male and female have been made one flesh in marriage, a husband may only divorce his wife where she has committed a serious crime against the marriage.[329] Mark emphasized, even more powerfully than Matthew, the principle that marriage made a couple two in one flesh with the consequence that divorce was forbidden entirely.[330] Luke, however, merely recorded Jesus as saying that anyone who puts away his wife to marry another commits adultery.[331]

Only in Mark was the prohibition on divorce absolute, and this was because of the essential oneness of the married couple. Matthew repeated Mark's proclamation that a married couple became "two in one flesh," but nevertheless retained the Jewish tradition that allowed men to divorce their wives, but now only in a limited class of cases, i.e., those involving adultery or gross immorality. On close reading, Luke seemed to allow divorce, but this allowance was limited to men and further restricted by the requirement that those who have left their wives not marry again. The idea of a woman divorcing or remarrying was outside the cases contemplated by the evangelist.

Paul's teaching on divorce, however, moved in a complementary but somewhat different direction from the Gospels. "To those who are married," Paul wrote, "not I, but the Lord commands that a wife is not to depart from her husband, and if she departs, that she is to remain unmarried or be reconciled. . . . And let not a husband put away his wife."[332] Paul gave additional instructions to Christians, male and female, who were married to unbelieving spouses. They should not leave their unbelieving spouses simply because of their lack of faith, Paul counseled, but where the unbeliever has departed, the Christian should "let him depart."[333]

It is on these foundations that subsequent generations of Christian writers built the rules concerning when and how and by whom divorce was permitted. The *Shepherd of Hermas,* an early-to-mid-second-century work that was assigned great authority by some early Christian writers,[334] added to the teaching of Matthew by not only permitting but affirmatively requiring a man who has caught his wife in adultery to divorce her lest he become implicated in her sin.[335] The *Shepherd* went on to advise that a marriage between a Christian and one who relapses into paganism is a form of spiritual adultery and thus impossible to maintain. Hence the believing spouse should depart under those circumstances too. The *Shepherd's* choice of pronouns (masculine for the relapsed spouse) made clear that women were empowered to depart from their husbands where the marriage or the faith had been betrayed.[336]

St. Ambrose represented a significant advance on this view. In his treatise *De Virginitate* ("On Virginity"), he noted that a marriage could not be dissolved, except for fornication.[337] No mention here of a husband leaving his wife. The act of adultery, apparently by either party, sufficed for dissolution. And in his *Expositio Evangelii Secundum Lucam* ("Commentary on the Gospel according to Luke"), Ambrose drew a distinction, important for the entire history of marriage law, between valid marriage ("marriage from God") and invalid marriage ("marriage not from God").[338] A union between a Christian and a non-Christian, Ambrose asserted, was not of God and mere "copulation." Hence, either party was free, indeed, it seems, required to depart, although Ambrose refrained from drawing such a potentially socially disruptive conclusion.[339] Ambrose's use of the feminine form of the noun *Christianae* in this passage drew attention to his desire to see women, as well as men, share in this power.[340]

Thus Christian practice moved in a direction different from both Jewish law and the practice of the early Roman Republic: it restricted generally free accessibility to divorce previously enjoyed by men and also opened up the possibility that women might in some circumstances take the initiative in leaving their husbands. One might detect in the rules that were handed down a certain double standard: women were at greater risk of committing adultery, but also at greater risk of falling back into paganism because of the spiritual lapses of their men. But it is also probably not surprising that a proselytizing faith, living in the midst of indifferent, even hostile "gentiles," should adopt such rules, particularly regarding marriages between believers and unbelievers, which conferred on women as well as men the power to dissolve such marriages. Their souls, after all, were in equal peril from such spiritual contamination.

It remained to St. Augustine to connect these developments to the larger principle of the indissolubility of Christian marriage. In his treatise "On the Good of Marriage" (*De Bono Coniugali*) Augustine commenced by asking whether it was ever possible for a man who has left his wife because of adultery to marry another.[341] He noted that St. Paul advised a wife who has left her husband that she should remain unmarried or be reconciled to him. He noted as well, reading this Pauline passage in light of the Gospel, that a wife should only leave in cases of adultery.[342] Elsewhere in his work, St. Augustine defined adultery broadly, to include disbelief or relapse into paganism.[343]

Thus both men and women may depart from marriage under certain circumstances. Christians, however, may not remarry. This is because Christian marriage creates a bond of companionship (*sociale vinculum*) between the parties that is so strong not even a desire to fulfill the good of procreation by leaving a barren wife and moving to one capable of bearing children suffices to rupture it.[344] The marriage covenant (*foedus*), once entered into, possessed a sacramental quality, St. Augustine asserted, referring to the way in which it symbolized Christ's unity with the Church. Hence, even in the case of divorce brought about by the fornication of one of the parties, the couple remained married in the eyes of God and so may not move to new spouses.[345]

In the Roman law of the Christian emperors of the fourth and fifth centuries some effort was made to restrict free access to divorce, but it seems that the ideal of indissolubility was never adopted. Constantine's reform of Roman divorce law, thought by many scholars to be "among the most 'Christian' of his laws,"[346] began by announcing that a wife, moved by "depraved fantasies," may not divorce her husband by alleging merely that he was a drunkard, or a gambler, or a womanizer, nor may a husband allege trivial pretexts (*quascumque occasiones*).[347] A wife, Constantine continued, may only divorce upon proof that her husband was a murderer, a sorcerer (literally, a *medicamentarius*, i.e., one who gives potions), or a violator of tombs. A husband may only divorce where his wife has been proved to be an adulteress, a sorceress (*medicamentaria*), or a procuress.[348] Men and women were thus allowed the opportunity to divorce, but on different but equally serious grounds.

In his reform of the marriage law, *Novella* 22, Justinian expanded the grounds for divorce.[349] Recognizing the possibility that parties might separate from "common consent" (*consentiente utraque parte*), Justinian focused his legislation on a second type of divorce, that for "reasonable cause."[350] Both women and men could seek divorce: a woman's reasonable causes might include a demonstration that her husband has committed murder, or adultery, or has administered poison; she might also divorce on grounds that the husband has committed forgery, violated tombs, participated in the theft of goods or livestock, plotted treason, or has led a debauched or dissolute life, carrying on with other women, especially married ones.[351] A husband might divorce on many of the same grounds, but also on some others, such as his wife's associating with improper guests or spending the night away from home without her husband's permission.[352]

The canonists of the twelfth and thirteenth centuries, confronted with these disparate elements of a theory of divorce, brought both coherence and consistency to the subject, and fitted it within their larger conception of the domestic relationship as a structure of integrated rights and duties.

An understanding of Gratian's theory of divorce must begin with his renewed commitment to the ideal of indissolubility. James Brundage has observed that "an attentive reading of [Gratian's treatment of indissolubility] makes it clear that [he] considered marriage came into being, not as the result of a single action, but rather as a two-stage process."[353] In *Causa* 27, *quaestio* 2, Gratian proposed to consider whether a girl (*puella*) betrothed to another might renounce this relationship. To answer this question, Gratian resolved that he needed to define the marital relationship and to identify what it was that brought marriage into being.[354]

Marriage, Gratian argued, borrowing his definition from Roman law, was a "joining of male and female, who kept a common way of life."[355] Was this relationship brought about by the consent of the parties? It seemed, Gratian observed, that this was so. A text attributed to John Chrysostom and a decree of Pope Nicholas I were brought to bear on this point.[356] It seemed that the consent of the parties, in and of itself (*inter istos consensus . . . solus matrimonium facit*), was what made a marriage.[357]

Other texts were mustered in favor of this conclusion. St. Ambrose had taught that it was not the deflowering of a virgin, but the marital agreement (*pactio coniugalis*) that made a marriage.[358] Isidore of Seville and St. Augustine were quoted as declaring that it was the first "pledge of faith" (*prima desponsationis fide*), not sexual intercourse, that made a marriage.[359] The teaching of the Old Testament that one who violated a woman betrothed to another was guilty of adultery was put forward as further evidence.[360] The example of the marriage of Mary and Joseph was elicited as yet more evidence that it was consent that made a marriage.[361] Gratian could thus conclude: "By these authorities they are proven to be spouses."[362]

Gratian was thus able to establish that consent made a marriage. But he was not content to leave his analysis here. He felt the need to show that consummation was also a decisive factor in marital formation. St. Augustine was quoted as asserting that there can be no doubt that a woman does not belong to a marriage until there has been sexual relations.[363] Pope Leo the Great was then cited as declaring that the marital union (*societas nuptiarum*) cannot be said to have begun until the parties have been joined sexually.[364] Gratian followed these texts by repeating St. Paul's teaching on the conjugal debt.[365]

Gratian followed his citation of St. Paul with several texts elaborating on the conjugal debt,[366] and followed these texts with several others on the distinction between ratified marriage and a mere betrothal.[367] He then returned to the Augustinian and Leonine texts just cited to formulate his own distinction between consummated and non-consummated unions. St. Augustine and Pope Leo were to be understood, Gratian asserted, as speaking about marriages that have been ratified, or "perfected" by intercourse.[368] There was a difference, Gratian asserted, between a marriage so perfected and a mere betrothal that looked forward to marriage at some future date.[369] There was also a difference between a consummated marriage, and a non-consummated marriage, which might still be brought to a close by the unilateral decision of one of the parties to enter religious life.[370] The marriage of Mary and Joseph, finally, should be considered unique because, although they did not have intercourse, they nevertheless realized "the good of children" through the birth of the infant Jesus.[371]

Having restated the indissoluble ideal and distinguished between marriages that have been ratified by sexual intercourse and those that have not been so strengthened, Gratian proceeded to articulate a theory of Christian divorce based on a theory of impediments to valid consent or successful consummation.[372] A consummated, ratified union, Gratian taught, might only be dissolved where it could be shown that one or the other or both of the parties were gravely impeded from consenting to the marriage or from fulfilling the terms of that consent.

Gratian proposed a dense network of rules and regulations governing when and how matrimonial consent might be impeded. Blood relationships, known generally under the rubric of "consanguinity," violated the natural law as a species of incest and so prevented marital formation.[373] Affinity, a spiritual relationship between the parties formed through baptismal or confirmation sponsorship or through the prior marriage of close relatives ("in-laws"), also impeded a marriage,[374] as did a relationship by adoption.[375] Marriage contracted with an insane person (*furiosus* or *furiosa*) was not possible, but, Gratian cautioned, persons so married should not be separated.[376]

Mixed marriages between believers and non-believers were entirely prohibited,[377] and so also were marriages with those bound by the obligations of solemn religious profession or Holy Orders.[378] Error, especially error induced by the fraud of one of the parties, invalidated marriage,[379] as did "crime," by which was meant sexual relations between the parties prior to marriage, especially where the relations were involuntary.[380] Prior and perpetual impotence also sufficed to invalidate a marriage because it made it impossible to render the debt, thereby effectively depriving one of one's marital right.[381]

An earlier generation of canonists might have prepared such a list of impediments as a means of instructing the clergy on who may or may not be permitted to enter marriage, with little thought given to the question of

separating parties once joined in matrimony.[382] Gratian, however, was prepared to move in a new direction by advocating the availability of ecclesiastical divorce, sometimes coupled with the right of remarriage where the
first marriage was proven to be invalid.[383] Non-consummated marriages
presented the easiest case. So long as a good cause could be identified, particularly entry into religious life, a non-consummated marriage might be
dissolved.[384] This power of choosing marital dissolution, Gratian made
clear, might be exercised equally by male or female. Couples who had consummated their marriages were also free mutually to renounce their marital right in favor of the higher calling of religious life.[385]

Gratian also permitted marriages to be dissolved in the case of perpetual impotence. As Gratian put it, the "impossibility of rendering the
debt dissolves the bond of marriage."[386] Gratian made clear that this rule
pertained to women as well as men when he asserted that a woman whose
husband suffered from the "impediment of the curse" (a favored euphe-
mism for male impotence) may be separated from her husband.[387]

Gratian showed greater reluctance to countenance separation in cases
of consanguinity and affinity, "especially if the relationship was unknown
or had been concealed by one party at the time of the marriage."[388] Gratian
acknowledged that the ecclesiastical rule prohibiting marriage within
seven degrees of consanguinity was difficult to maintain in practice and he
preferred that the Church's power of dispensation be utilized to allow couples distantly related to one another to cohabit peacefully.[389] On the other
hand, he was not eager to permit the marriage of close relatives.[390] Although Gratian did not specifically declare that females as well as males
had an equal right to seek the dissolution of such unions, a declaration he
had made where non-consummation and impotence were at issue, his analysis did not foreclose such a conclusion.

Regarding marriages between Christians and non-believers, Gratian
proposed that different circumstances required different treatments.[391]
Gratian's doctrine of fraud in the inducement, Brundage notes, was broad
enough to embrace the case of a non-believer who deceived his or her
Christian spouse into marriage by asserting that he was also of the faith or
planned to convert.[392] Gratian also included texts that made the case that
Christians should not marry Jews or infidels and that such unions were
wholly improper.[393]

But Gratian also turned his attention to the problem St. Paul had confronted — that of a Christian convert whose spouse remained committed
to his or her old "errors." Gratian commenced his analysis of this question

with several texts that made the point that an unbelieving spouse who did not wish to remain in conjugal intimacy with a believer should be allowed to depart.[394] As one of Gratian's texts put it, this was merely the practical working out of Paul's teaching on relations with unbelievers.[395]

A more difficult question was posed by the possibility of the Christian party remarrying. Two texts were brought forward: a passage of St. Ambrose declaring that a husband whose non-Christian wife left after his baptism may not remarry;[396] followed by a passage from Gregory the Great counseling Christians who have been abandoned by their non-Christian partners that they are free to enter new marriages since the act of departure showed contempt for the Creator and thus dissolved the *ius matrimonii* itself.[397]

Gratian compromised between these two venerable sources: where the non-Christian party had abandoned the family, the Christian might remarry, but where the non-Christian wished to remain with his Christian spouse, the Christian spouse might separate but not remarry, since their marriage had become indissoluble.[398] The choice of language by Gratian's sources, as well as Gratian's own terminology, made clear that both men and women could avail themselves of these rules.

Gratian also considered the possibility of divorce in case of adultery, the original ground for divorce established in the Gospel of Matthew. Following his sources, Gratian expanded on Matthew's text, permitting both men and women to divorce by reason of adultery. He included a number of texts in his *Decretum* that supported the claim that this was a right that belonged to women as well as men.

A text of St. Jerome's reiterated Jesus' command that divorce was forbidden except where the wife has commited adultery and added that whatever is taught regarding men applies also to women since "an adulterous wife may not be dismissed but an adulterous husband retained."[399] A letter of Pope Nicholas I to the Bulgarians instructed that women who leave their husbands for any reason other than adultery are to be shunned.[400] A letter of Pope Innocent I lamented the fact that men are more quickly listened to when bringing charges of adultery; adultery is a crime whether committed by men or women, and should be appropriately punished by denial of communion.[401] A text of St. Augustine made it clear that men, because they are the "head" (*caput*) of their wives, sin more grievously than women when they commit adultery.[402] Gratian's position was obvious: men as well as women might commit the crime of adultery, and members of both sexes were free to leave an adulterous spouse.

But since such marriages were presumptively valid, consummated marriages, Gratian also made clear that the parties were not free to move to second marriages so long as their former partner was alive. They might obtain an ecclesiastical divorce (*a mensa et thoro,* "from bed and board," a subsequent generation of canonists would describe it), but they nevertheless remained married in the eyes of God, connected by an enduring sacramental bond. This rule applied to both men and women. Gratian's inclusion of a fourth-century text from the Council of Elvira stressing that a woman who left her adulterous husband may not remarry made the point emphatically.[403] Both men and women might leave one another on account of adultery but remained obliged equally by the sacramental bond of marriage.

Gratian's reworking of the law of divorce has remained the basic framework for ecclesiastical annulments and separations since his time. It was a structure that, through the medium of the Anglican canon lawyers of the seventeenth and eighteenth centuries, influenced the early American approach to divorce and remarriage.[404] Its basic outlines can still be seen in the Catholic canon law on the subject today.[405] It was a framework that would dominate the analysis of separation and divorce throughout the Middle Ages.

Twelfth-century scholastic writers and canonists were in basic harmony with Gratian's treatment of divorce. Under the rubric "man and woman use the same right" (*eodem iure utitur vir et mulier*), Peter Lombard considered the question of the right of men and women to divorce where the other party has committed adultery.[406] Peter noted that when the Lord granted that a husband might put away his wife for adultery, he did not intend that men and women should be treated unequally: women, as well as men, might seek divorce on the basis of adultery.[407] Following the text of Jerome also utilized by Gratian, Peter declared that a female adulteress should not be dismissed and a male lecher held on to.[408]

Gandulf of Bologna, for his part, examined the question whether a husband — and, by extension, a wife — was obliged to separate from his or her spouse where that spouse had been caught in adultery.[409] Quoting from the writings of St. John Chrysostom, Gandulf declared that "it is cruel and unjust to dismiss the chaste, but foolish and wicked to keep a whore. For one becomes a patron of turpitude who conceals the crime of one's wife."[410] Gandulf admonished that those who wished to remain together after such a crime were obliged to do penance. He stressed that the husband who continued to have relations with an unchaste wife who had not done penance sinned mortally as did she.[411] He added that the adulterous party — man as well as woman — lost the right to claim the conjugal debt upon commission of the crime of adultery and that the other party was thereupon free to leave,[412] although the matrimonial bond endured.[413]

The decretists echoed this sentiment although they did not engage in detailed analysis. Rolandus stated that the wife as much as the man might seek a separation on account of adultery, and stressed the importance of not departing from one's spouse without first obtaining an ecclesiastical decree of divorce.[414] Rufinus simply noted that a woman might depart from her husband, just as a husband might leave his wife for the same offense.[415] Johannes Teutonicus agreed with these basic propositions.[416]

The thirteenth-century decretalists refined certain portions of Gratian's treatment but retained the essential framework. Bernard of Pavia, in his *Summa Decretalium*, written at the beginning of the thirteenth century, explored the basic equality that prevailed between men and women on this subject. After treating the topic of marital formation, Bernard proposed to consider the ways in which marriages might be "divided" (*dividantur*).[417] Both husband and wife, Bernard asserted, may denounce their marriage, on account of the adultery of the other spouse.[418] Regarding this power, Bernard observed tautologically, husbands and wives are equal because in such matters there is no inequality.[419] Bernard supported this assertion with several texts drawn from Gratian's *Decretum*.[420]

Furthermore, Bernard added, a wife equally with a husband (*tam uxor quam maritus*) may accuse a marriage on other grounds except where forbidden by law.[421] The prohibitions on the right to separate or divorce that Bernard had in mind, furthermore, were not driven by considerations of the sex of the parties, but by their conduct before or within the marriage. Thus one who knew from the beginning that a marriage was invalid but concealed that information in order to enter marriage should subsequently be precluded from accusing the marriage on the ground of that invalidity.[422]

Other canonists endorsed these categories. Some writers, such as Tancred, contented themselves with largely repeating or slightly embellishing on the categories devised by Gratian and Bernard of Pavia. Thus Tancred simply declared that any one may accuse a marriage who is not prohibited by law, and that this included wives as much as husbands.[423] Hostiensis spoke of the "right of a husband" (*ius mariti*) to divorce his wife for adultery, a right he grounded on Matthew's Gospel, but he also allowed women a similar right.[424] Raymond of Peñafort wrote more generally about the right to divorce in his *Summa* on marriage. Anyone not expressly forbidden, Raymond wrote, may accuse a marriage.[425] In speaking of adultery,

Raymond stressed that both husband and wife could equally bring a charge of fornication and misquoted Matthew, which had spoken only of men departing from adulterous wives, to support this claim.[426]

The right of divorce, the canonists made clear, could not be lost through prescription, a Romanist doctrine roughly comparable to the Anglo-American concept of statutes of limitations. Tancred, in his *Ordo Iudiciarius* — a procedural manual intended for canonists — gave as an example of a spiritual right against which prescription did not run cases where parties have been wrongly separated or joined in marriage.[427]

Near the close of the thirteenth century, William Durandus proposed a further refinement of divorce law that followed the basic outline of the impediments. There were two types of impediment, Durandus asserted, those arising from defect (*ex defectu*) and those resulting from the sin of the parties (*ex peccato*). Impediments of defect included prior and perpetual female frigidity or male impotence, and other such matters outside the control of the parties.[428] Where impediments of this sort were concerned, only the parties to the marriage themselves had the right to bring an accusation. Those outside the marriage, Durandus stressed, lacked an "interest" in impugning the union.[429]

Sinful impediments included such matters as consanguinity, which resulted in the affected parties living in an objectively immoral relationship. Anyone not otherwise prohibited may be admitted to accuse the invalidity of such a marriage because of the public interest in ensuring the integrity of the marital relationship.[430]

Divorce itself also came to be seen by twelfth- and thirteenth-century canonists as involving the assertion and the termination of rights.[431] This was so, whether one speaks of the termination of marriage between infidels by "favor of the faith," or of other forms of separation.

The decretal *Quanto Te,* issued by Pope Innocent III, established the ground rules regarding what came to be known to canonists as the "Pauline privilege" — the right of a convert to Christianity whose spouse has abandoned him or her on account of the faith, to obtain an ecclesiastical divorce with the right of remarriage.[432] Innocent limited this privilege to marriages where both of the parties were non-believers (*infideles*). But where this condition was satisfied, and one of the parties has converted to the Catholic faith while the other party sought to disrupt the marriage because of the faith — whether through blasphemy or through pulling the Catholic party into "mortal sin" — in these circumstances the marriage itself was dissolved. The Catholic was thereby freed to proceed to a new marriage. As Innocent put it, echoing the language of Gregory the Great that Gratian had also repeated, "contempt for the Creator dissolves the *ius matrimonii*."[433]

The decretalists, following Pope Innocent III, continued to refer to this process as a dissolution of the marital rights of the prior infidel union. Bernard of Parma repeated the language of the decretal indicating that the *ius matrimonii* itself was dissolved and asserted further that the maxim "no one was to be deprived of a right without fault" had no bearing on the outcome of this case.[434] He noted as well that the first marriage was dissolved by the act of departure by the unbelieving spouse — it was this act of contempt, not any formal judgment by the Church, that freed the believer to marry again.[435]

Innocent IV, paraphrasing the text of the decretal, questioned whether a truly ratified marriage could even come into existence among infidels. They lack the sacraments, they are infidels, and in marriage they employ the *ius* of infidels *(iure infidelium utuntur)* in their relationships.[436] Here the word *ius* seems to carry both objective and subjective meanings at one and the same time: it can be seen as referring both to the rules that govern infidel marriages but can also refer to the rights and claims arising within such unions. Their marital rights, Innocent seemed to suggest, were weaker because they lacked a sacramental understanding of the marital relationship. Innocent IV went on to conclude that such infidels may freely divorce even without the judgment of the Church. And where one of the parties has converted to the Catholic faith and the marriage is dissolved for that reason, the Catholic party may freely move to another marriage.[437]

Raymond of Peñafort, on the other hand, argued that marriages among infidels, especially Jews and Saracens, were true marriages.[438] But, Raymond went on, if one party converts and the other does not wish to cohabit peaceably, or blasphemes, or tries to draw the Christian party back into his or her old religion, "in these three cases contempt for the Creator dissolves the *ius matrimonii*."[439]

Hostiensis agreed with Bernard of Parma in stressing that it was the unbeliever's act of contempt for the Creator, not any official act of the Church, that dissolved the matrimonial right.[440] Hostiensis specifically wished to repudiate those who maintained that only the believer's second marriage or entry into religious life could dissolve the first marriage.[441] The act of the unbeliever's departure, without more, sufficed to dissolve the union.

Divorce without the right of remarriage also came to be seen as the severance of marital rights. The canonists eventually established three grounds for such divorce. We have already reviewed divorce based on the adultery of the parties. It remains simply to note that like other rights, this was a right that could be lost through the fault of the parties.[442] Raymond of Peñafort, in fact, provided a list of circumstances that would disqualify a spouse from seeking separation.[443] A party convicted of fornication was unable to divorce his or her spouse on this ground.[444] A husband who employed his wife as a prostitute could not thereafter complain of her infidelity.[445] And, one who forgave his or her spouse and reconciled could not thereafter seek separation on account of that offense.[446]

Eventually, the decretalists developed two further grounds for divorce — "spiritual fornication," by which they meant a lapse into heresy or a conversion to Islam or Judaism; and *saevitia,* "wildness," that is, unrestrained violence on the part of one of the parties.[447] Divorce on either of these grounds also resulted in the loss of marital rights but the affected parties were not thereafter free to remarry.

The concept of heresy as a form of spiritual fornication was as old as the *Shepherd of Hermas,* although it was not used as a legal category by the author of the *Shepherd.* The use of "spiritual fornication" as a legal term of art, with specific juridic consequences for one's marriage, can be found in Rufinus, active around the year 1160,[448] and in the *Summa, 'Elegantius in iure divino,'* composed probably around the year 1169.[449] The author of the anonymous *Summa, 'Elegantius'* commenced his analysis by referring to passages of St. Ambrose and St. Augustine that compared heresy and idolatry and even *avaritia* — "greed" or "avarice" — to fornication.[450]

The anonymous author went on to compare the ways in which spiritual as opposed to carnal fornication differed and were similar.[451] There was no doubt, the author asserted, that a wife may be dismissed for spiritual as well as for carnal fornication. But "according to the common teaching" *(iuxta multorum traditionem)* there were at least two differences in the ways in which these cases ought to be treated: a spiritual "fornicator," one who has committed the sins of heresy or idolatry but who has now repented, ought to be received back by her or his partner; and, secondly, a spiritual fornicator who does not disturb the faith of the Christian partner should be allowed to remain in the union, as St. Paul had taught. An incorrigible carnal fornicator, however, should in no way be tolerated.[452]

The law governing spiritual fornication took definitive shape in *Quanto Te,* the same decretal in which Innocent III established the ground rules for the operation of the Pauline privilege.[453] Innocent distinguished between the case of two infidels, one of whom converted, causing her or his marriage to become intolerable or otherwise cease; and a marriage of two Christians, one of whom lapsed into heresy sometime after the wedding. In the first of these cases, the party may remarry, but in the second, the faithful Christian spouse may not. This is so, Innocent asserted, even if the faithful Christian spouse wished to marry again to fulfill the good of procreation. This rule obtains, Innocent explained, because among faithful Christians a marriage is a sacrament, a sign of the faith, a bond which, once established, may never be broken.[454]

At the close of this analysis, Innocent addressed a rights-based argument that must have been raised before him at the time he rendered this decision. Nor is it an objection, Innocent asserted, as if to answer some curial lawyer, to say that the Christian spouse is thereby deprived of a right "without fault" (sine culpa).[455] Sometimes such deprivations are unavoidable, Innocent argued, but in this case a much greater evil is thereby avoided. The whole bond of marriage would be threatened if the Christian spouse were allowed to move to a new marriage because then couples, dissatisfied with their marriages, might feign heresy in order to move to new unions.[456] The sanctity of marriage would then be subjected to manipulation.

Bernard of Parma focused his analysis on Innocent's use of the maxim: no one may be deprived of his or her right, "without fault." Glossing the words sine culpa, Bernard noted that one should not be deprived of a right without fault, but that one might lose a right for cause (si causa subest).[457] And in the case of the heretical Christian spouse, the innocent spouse has lost his or her right, presumably to preserve a greater good, that is, the integrity of the matrimonial bond.

Innocent IV, for his part, simply considered the importance of baptism in the making of a valid marriage. Those who have been validly baptized may not move to other spouses, even where their first spouse has become a heretic.[458] Innocent did not consider the rights language used by Innocent III and commented upon by Bernard.

Like Innocent IV, Hostiensis stressed that baptism was central to the making of a truly ratified and indissoluble Christian marriage.[459] Hostiensis went on, however, to consider a hypothetical case: what of heretics, who have been baptized according to heretical form? Can they have a valid and indissoluble marriage?[460] Hostiensis stressed that either their baptism took place in conformity with the Church's teaching (in forma Ecclesiae) or it did not.[461] If it did not, he observed, they use "the law/right of infidels" in their marriages and their marriages may be dissolved in favor of the faith.[462] But where their baptism was validly administered, so also their marriages were indissoluble.

Raymond of Peñafort added little except to state that the term "spiritual fornication" included conversion to a heretical sect, to Judaism, or to "the error of the gentiles," that is, to Islam, and that allowance should be made for the guilty party to return to the faith before finalizing a divorce.[463]

The final ground for divorce, *saevitia,* "savagery," developed technically not as a reason for marital separation, but rather as an equitable remedy of the ecclesiastical courts when confronted with an abusive marriage. Where a wife fled her abusive husband, courts simply would not restore marital rights to the abusive husband. The foundation of this doctrine included a decretal of Alexander III and a decretal of Innocent III.[464] Each decretal involved actions by husbands to seek the judicially-ordered return of their wives. In each case, the pope indicated that the physical well-being of the wives must be protected. Innocent III, in particular, stressed that restitution was not to occur where there was the threat of grave violence (*magna saevitia*).[465]

Bernard of Parma treated these decretals as representing no more than an equitable means of blocking judicially-mandated restitution.[466] Hostiensis noted that Roman law allowed savagery as a ground for divorce and proposed further that if couples have been separated for this reason, this is all the more reason their marital rights should not be restored to them.[467] Raymond of Peñafort, on the other hand, continued to treat *saevitia* as a sort of equitable principle allowing courts discretion in determining whether rights were to be restored to a violent spouse. Where a husband's savagery has been such that a woman fears that inadequate security will be available and her husband harbored a "deadly hatred" (*odio capitali*) toward her, then, according to Raymond, this was good cause why his rights should not be restored.[468]

Saevitia, however, had its limitations as a grounds for divorce. Johannes Andreae considered the question whether a husband might divorce his wife where the wife has murdered the couple's child and responded that a separation ought not to be granted for that reason, although the wife has in this instance sinned gravely and should be held *in odium.*[469] *Saevitia,* it seems, was to be limited to the situation of ongoing, unmanageable violence between the parties themselves.

Saevitia nevertheless remained a viable ground for separation to the end of the Middle Ages. Panormitanus wrote that a wife should not be restored to her husband if she could not reside with him safely and without risk to her person. Indeed, such danger was sufficient cause for removing her from her home and declaring a separation from bed and board.[470]

Summary

The anonymous author of the *Summa, 'Elegantius in iure divino'* asked "in what is a husband preeminent and in what is he equal to his wife?"[471] The author of the *Summa* responded to this query with some of the standard principles of male headship. The husband is the head of his spouse and, "as it were, her reason and her good judgment" *(quasi ratio et consilium)*.[472] The man was created in the image and likeness of God, and the woman was created in the image and likeness of her husband.[473]

Of course, as this chapter makes clear, there is more to the answer than the one-sided reply of the *Summa, 'Elegantius.'* In a sense, this chapter has been an effort to understand the fullness of the canonists' response to the issues raised by such a document. In most respects, the man was indeed preeminent, as the *Summa's* author asserted. As Hostiensis observed some decades later, the right of women was, for the most part, of "diminished condition." Women were legally disadvantaged compared to men and restricted from a variety of activities. They were not to govern, nor to judge, nor to exercise any number of spiritual offices and responsibilities.

Nevertheless, women retained certain areas of legal equality within the canon law. The theology of creation espoused by the *Summa, 'Elegantius,'* viewing the wife as created in her husband's image, had to be balanced with a theology of creation that stressed male-female complementarity. As Peter Lombard had observed, woman was made from man's side, not his foot, so as to be his associate, not his slave. These two competing theological visions, one emphasizing male headship, the other emphasizing the complementarity of man and woman, are evident in the work of the canonists. For the most part, headship prevailed, but at other times, in certain circumscribed areas of the law, equality was the norm.

Thus women, like men, were allowed to choose their marriage partner freely. Women and men were equal in the right to claim the conjugal debt. Women as well as men were able to choose their own place of burial, and to seek divorce where that seemed to be the only solution to pressing marital issues. The relationship that was to prevail, legally, between men and female thus featured, to be sure, a significant degree of male domination, but this domination was always tempered by other considerations.

These other considerations tended to be put in a vocabulary that emphasized rights and equality. The canonists explicitly invoked rights when they spoke about the freedom to choose one's marital partner, or to claim the conjugal debt, or to obtain a divorce, or to seek a proper burial for one's mortal remains. At times, this equality was only theoretical. And this theoretical equality could even lead to monstrous results, most especially in the case of the right of forcible consummation. But it could also require spouses to lead lives of heroic virtue, as illustrated in the rules governing the rights of a leprous spouse.

The canonists' recognition of an equality of rights in certain areas of medieval life was the result of their efforts to reconcile two theological demands: that of male headship and that of a radical equality between the sexes in terms of their dignity and worth as human persons. As St. Paul had put it, there was neither male nor female in Christ Jesus. The canonists were forced, in short, to address the theological insight that man and woman were brought into the world side-by-side. The law was, in part, a product of this insight, as much as it was the product of a strong commitment to the principles of male headship. In certain areas, at least, of medieval law and life, man and woman were clearly equals — sometimes in theory, sometimes in reality.[474]

❧ 4 ❧

Testamentary Freedom and
the Inheritance Rights of Children

Testamentary freedom is assumed by many to be a cardinal principle of the American law of wills and estates. The idea that one who drafts a will should be free to dispose of his or her property as it seems best, without regard to ties of natural affection, has had a strong hold on the American legal imagination, although it has never conquered the field.[1] Traditionally, however, this right has not been seen as fundamental or constitutional in character, but rather as dependent upon statutory, conventional sources.[2] Although the United States Supreme Court recently had occasion to question the proposition that the right to make a will is of statutory origin, and not the product of natural or constitutional right, commentators have for the most part continued to urge that the right may be limited, or even abrogated, by statute.[3]

If the American legal system considers testamentary freedom to be the product of statute, not fundamental law, the same can also be said for the obligations, such as they are, that American law imposes on testators with respect to their offspring and their spouses. In modern American law, testators are generally free to disinherit their children.[4] Various statutory and judicial doctrines have developed to mitigate the harsher aspects of this rule,[5] but it remains the case that in most American jurisdictions, "a child or other descendant has no statutory protection against disinheritance by a parent."[6]

Spouses, on the other hand, generally receive more generous provision under the dictates of American law. In most American jurisdictions, spouses are allotted an "elective share," which permits the surviving spouse to choose "[to] take under the decedent's will or [to] renounce the will and take a fractional share of the decedent's estate."[7] Commentators have expressed surprise at this seemingly inconsistent feature of American testamentary law — the idea that even though spouses are generally grown and mature and able to take care of their needs, they should receive superior protection at law than children, whose needs are often significantly greater.[8] This sort of differentiation in treatment has typically been premised on the belief that "the surviving spouse contributed to the decedent's acquisition of wealth and deserves to have a portion of it."[9]

This set of legal arrangements presupposes a narrowly economic and utilitarian vision of the family unit: the exercise of testamentary freedom is appropriate where children are concerned because they presumably have contributed little to the economic well-being of the family and have cost much. It should thus be in the discretion of the testator whether to bestow further economic benefits upon them. The surviving spouse, on the other hand, was in a sense an economic partner with the decedent, and so is entitled to receive the benefit of the bargain.

The testamentary law the canonists devised, on the other hand, while rights-based, was structured in a way calculated to protect not only the freedom of the testator — which the canonists labeled a right, the *ius testandi*, "the right to make a will" — but also to safeguard the interests of the more vulnerable members of the family unit. Thus children were entitled to a share of the estate. Indeed, the claims children might make on a parent's estate were grounded on natural law and were typically referred to as a "natural right," or a "claim based on natural law." Spouses, too, were given the protection of the law, although their inheritance rights will not be a focus of this chapter.[10]

The system the canonists devised was one that integrated basic human freedom — the freedom to dispose of one's property through a last will and testament — with the obligations any testator possessed of valuable property would necessarily have with respect to the rest of the family unit. The canonistic system was not grounded, like modern American law, on a libertarian, individualistic conception of the members of a family as independent economic actors, but rather on a Christian vision of family that expected rights to be exercised against a backdrop of mutual and reciprocal love. This system and its reliance on a vocabulary of natural rights, especially with respect to the standing of children to inherit, will be the subject of this chapter.

Part I: The Right to Make a Will *(ius testandi)*

Roman Law Background

Roman law employed various terms to describe the capacity to make a will. Two excerpts from Gaius contained in the *Digest* referred to the "right of making a will" *(testamenti faciendi ius)*.[11] A practical equivalent of this term was *testamenti factio*, "the making of a will," with the term *ius* or some equivalent suppressed.[12] More frequently, one encounters the pairing of the words *facultas* — "faculty" — with some variant of the word *testamentum*, "will." Thus Modestinus in the *Digest* spoke of a "faculty of making a will" *(testamenti faciendi facultas)*.[13] Similarly, the Emperor Leo, in legislation preserved in the *Codex*, spoke of a "free faculty of making a will" *(testandi . . . libera facultate)* given as a favor to clerics still under paternal power where they are of "orthodox faith" and of "proven morality and chastity."[14] Emperor Leo's choice of words hardly stands alone in the *Codex*. One finds frequently repeated in other legislation found in the *Codex* various forms of the expression *facultas testandi*, "the faculty of making a will."[15]

The law, in late Republican Rome, confined the power to make a will to Roman citizens.[16] The insane were denied the capacity to make a will, as were those who suffered from significant disabilities, such as deaf-mutes.[17] Women were able to make a will but only with the consent of guardians who should not have a direct interest in the will.[18]

Justinian's *Institutes* defined those who might possess the right of making a will negatively, by proposing that there were certain groups who must be denied the *testamenti faciendi ius*.[19] The capacity to make a will was primarily denied to those under another's power *(alieno iuri subiecti sunt)*, including even children given permission to make a will by their parents.[20] Emancipation, not parental permission, carried with it the right to make a will. The sole exception to this rule concerned soldiers, who benefited from special provisions because of the dangers of their calling and the likelihood that relatively few of them knew how to write.[21] That slaves, who by definition were subject to another's power, lacked the capacity to make a will seemed too obvious for Justinian to mention.

Other groups excluded from testamentary capacity included those who had not yet reached the age of puberty;[22] the insane, who might, however, make a will during a lucid interval;[23] the "prodigal," i.e., spendthrifts who had lost the right to manage their own affairs;[24] perpetual deaf-mutes, although an exception was made for "literate and learned" men who subsequently lost the capacity for hearing or for speech;[25] the blind;[26] and those held captive by Rome's enemies.[27] If a consistent thread can be discerned running through these prohibited categories, it was the idea that to make a will one must be capable of reasoned and free deliberations regarding the disposition of one's estate.

The teachings of the jurists collected in the *Digest* elaborated on these provisions of the *Institutes*. The making of a will (*testamenti factio*), Papinian taught, was a public, not a private right.[28] A will, as Modestinus defined it, was the "just expression of our will concerning that which we wished to happen after our death."[29] By its nature, Labeo added, a will required that the testator possessed "soundness of mind, not health of body."[30]

An excerpt from Gaius's *Institutes*, retained in the *Digest*, indicated that the first order of business in determining the validity of a will was to ascertain whether the testator possessed *factio testamenti*.[31] Both males and females who reached the age of puberty, Ulpian taught, might make a will where they have otherwise satisfied legal requirements.[32] Regarding testamentary capacity, the jurists repeated the categories of persons whom the *Institutes* excluded from the making of a will.[33] The lawyers stressed, however, that even though slaves, children, and deaf-mutes lacked testamentary capacity, they nevertheless retained the right to benefit under the terms of another's will.[34]

The legislation of the *Codex* did not significantly add to these requirements. One encounters there reiteration of long-standing principles — those in another's power, such as an unemancipated child, lacked testamentary capacity.[35] One also encounters efforts to introduce a certain fact-sensitive sophistication to the rules. Thus one finds, for instance, the Emperors Diocletian and Maximian ruling that a testator who subsequently committed suicide because of unendurable pain or "raging" insanity should not have his will invalidated if he was of sound mind at the time the will was executed.[36]

The Roman authors, who abhorred general theory, never discussed the purposes behind these rules nor the philosophical presuppositions that supported them. Nevertheless, some consistent principles are discernible, embedded within the rules themselves. The capacity to make a will was connected, first of all, to free status. Only those who were *sui iuris*, masters of their own affairs, met the threshold for consideration. Children and slaves were thus excluded as well as those subject to coercive control by Rome's enemies. It also required clear judgment and the capacity to express oneself. Hence the mentally infirm and those unable to express their desires clearly and intelligibly were similarly excluded.

An unspoken utilitarianism thus undergirded this set of rules: the management of property was an important economic and social end. The *familia*, the household, was itself conceived in large measure in economic terms.[37] The disposition of household property, understood as a solemn and sacred trust, could be entrusted only to those with the freedom and foresight to see to its prudent transmission from one generation to the next.

The Canonists and Testamentary Capacity

Early Medieval Theology and Law: The Transcendent Dimension of Testamentary Freedom

Christian writers of the late empire were required to come to terms with the Roman law on inheritance. For the most part, the basic structure of the law remained unchanged during this time, but the law of inheritance took on a social dimension it had previously lacked. Theologians thus stressed that the right and freedom testators enjoyed — their *testamenti faciendi ius* — ought to serve certain social goods. Chief among these were the support of the Church and satisfying the needs of the poor.

From an early date, some Christian theologians at least connected the reception of death-bed penance with the making of a final will and testament. Thus Caesarius of Arles considered the case of someone who has "always led a bad life."[38] This man has waited until the hour of his death to make amends, hoping that he might through a single penance discharge a lifetime of sins.[39] He has made no effort during his life to share his ill-gotten earthly goods with Christ's Church. Caesarius fretted that such a character would be denied entrance into paradise, although he conceded that only God could judge him according to his true merits.[40] Such a man, as a sign that he has now received God's grace, should take to heart the teaching, "By their fruits you shall know them," and take proper remedial steps — such as giving his wealth to charity.[41] Otherwise things will likely go badly for him in the next world.[42]

Not all early Christian writers were as explicit, or as crude, as St. Caesarius was in his expectation that those who genuinely desired absolution for their sins would also exercise testamentary freedom in order to bequeath at least a certain measure of their earthly goods to the Church. But one nevertheless finds the patristic authors connecting ideas of testamentary freedom and the desirability of exercising that freedom on behalf of pious causes.

Thus one sees in St. Augustine's sermon "On Christian Discipline" (De Disciplina Christiana) sustained reflection on the problem of the "wealthy Christian." "Perhaps you say," St. Augustine began, "I am rich. That man is poor. Do you walk together or not?"[43] St. Augustine observed that in these circumstances it is the rich Christian, not the poor one, who is burdened. "Release your chains," St. Augustine admonished, "lighten your bags of money."[44] "Have you not read, have you not feared, [the Gospel saying], 'whatever you do to the least of mine, you do to me?'"[45]

St. Augustine proposed one way in which the man overburdened with wealth might become more pleasing in the eyes of God. "Behold one who is wanting, do you count him among your sons? Count your sons, and add one to your sons, your Lord. You have one son. Let [the Lord] be a second. You have two sons. Let Him be a third. You have three. Let Him be the fourth."[46] In this way, St. Augustine proposed, a wealthy Christian paterfamilias might provide not only for his family but also for the poor with his testamentary dispositions.

St. Augustine emphasized these themes in a second sermon as well:

> Make a place for Christ among your sons. Let the Lord become part of your family. Let your Creator become part of your offspring. Let your brother be numbered among your sons. . . . You have two sons, compute a third; you have three, count four; you have five, say you have six; you have ten, let there be eleven. I do not wish to say more. Keep a place for your Lord as one of your sons. For what you give your Lord, you will also offer your sons. . . . You will thus give one portion, which you designated for one of your sons.[47]

Salvian, a mid-fifth-century theologian known as the "presbyter of Marseilles," carried these arguments to an extreme.[48] In his "Four Books of Timothy to the Church" (Timothei ad Ecclesiam libri IV), Salvian measured the competing claims of heirs to one's worldly goods as compared to one's own eternal salvation.[49] "I say this specially, and I admonish with a particular admonishment,"[50] Salvian began grandly. "No one is to prefer any material good, even the most dear, to his soul. Nor is it unjust for any Christian to gather up less in this world even for legitimate heirs, provided one is assisting oneself by various ways [to gain] eternity, because it is easier for one's sons to do without in this life than for parents in the future life, and because a present indigence is a much lighter [burden] than eternal poverty. . . ."[51]

And so, Salvian continued, "each person must take counsel concerning his soul and his salvation, and renounce all," although some provision should be made for our sons — "to whom we naturally owe more" — and our neighbors.[52] "Justice and the worship of God," concluded Salvian, required generosity and sharing.[53]

Salvian's argument has been criticized as "crude egoism" by one twentieth-century Christian writer.[54] A second modern critic has noted that Salvian must be understood in terms of his ascetic desire to see all Christians partaking in the counsels of perfection.[55] Certainly Salvian appears to be deeply radical when placed alongside a Christian realist like St. Augustine. In his challenge to Christians to place the things of the Lord ahead of all earthly concerns, even the responsibility to provide well for one's family, Salvian had few followers. But in voicing a desire for freedom from the traditional bonds of children and household with respect to postmortem dispositions Salvian had few equals.

This tension between testamentary freedom, often exercised on one's deathbed, on the one hand, and the call of family responsibility, on the other, can be discerned in some early medieval legal texts. Thus a text found in Regino of Prüm's collection admonished parish priests, upon learning that a member of their flock had become seriously ill, to attend at once to that person's spiritual needs.[56] They should hurry at once to the afflicted one's home, sing the Psalms, and recite prayers for the ill.[57] They should also hear the afflicted one's confession and encourage him or her to promise to amend his or her life should good health return, and also to make a bequest from their "substance" to obtain the forgiveness of sins (*ut peccata sua eleemosynis redimat*).[58]

This theme was picked up again by Burchard of Worms, who similarly admonished the local pastor to rush quickly to the side of an ill parishioner, to meet the spiritual needs of the afflicted, singing psalms and saying prayers, and to hear confession.[59] Repeating Regino, Burchard also admonished the pastor to encourage the parishioner to make amends through the making of an appropriate charitable bequest.[60]

A modern reader might place an entirely cynical interpretation on these texts: absolution conditioned on the promise of charitable bequests made on one's deathbed hardly seems appropriate. Indeed, a modern reader might even question the level of true freedom involved in the extraction of such promises. Furthermore, any law that even suggested the possibility that forgiveness of sins required the payment of money veered ominously in the direction of simony — prohibited commerce in spiritual goods. The impulse toward reading these texts cynically, however, must also be balanced with the realization that early medieval writers saw acts of charity, including charitable giving on one's deathbed, as important spiritual acts that also happened to be necessary for the continued smooth running of whatever rudimentary social services existed.

That testamentary freedom was also to be encouraged in other contexts comes across clearly in other legal collections. An Irish collection, dating to the first half of the eighth century, at the latest,[61] admonished testators to think about dividing their patrimony into three parts: a third should go one's sons; a third to "Caesar"; and a third "to the Church."[62] Where the testator did not have a church, he should give to the poor; if he did not have "a Caesar," he should divide his worldly goods among his sons and the Church; and if he lacked both church and Caesar, he should divide his belongings between his sons and the poor.[63]

Wills surviving from the Anglo-Saxon period in England reveal how this freedom was exercised in practice. One finds, for example, the following dispositions in the will of Thurketel of Palgrave, executed sometime before 1038:[64] For the benefit of his soul, he granted his estate known as Palgrave to St. Edmund's, and also bequeathed the estate Whittingham, half to St. Edmund's and "half to the Bishop."[65] Thurketel then decreed that his men are to be free "and each is to have his homestead, and his cow, and his corn for food."[66] Thurketel went on to bequeath other estates to his wife and to his brother's sons, and to make other dispositions with respect to his nephew and other kinsmen.[67] The range of freedom Thurketel exercised to endow family, church, and loyal retainers was not unusual, at least insofar as is reflected in Whitelock's collection.[68]

The Canonists on the Right to Make a Will (ius testandi)

Gratian and the Decretists This idea of testamentary freedom, exercisable to the benefit of the Church but also to the benefit of one's natural heirs, one's feudal lords, and one's retainers, stands behind the notion of the canonistic right to make a will.

Gratian's *Decretum* contains relatively little information on wills and testaments, at least when compared with his thirteenth-century successors.

His definition of *testamentum* is found in the context of his treatment of burial law. Gratian had juxtaposed three texts, the first by Gregory the Great, the second from the Council of Tribur, the other attributed to Pope Melcias.[69] Gregory the Great wrote simply that "the final will (*ultima voluntas*) of the dead should in all respects be conserved."[70] Tribur specified further that this freedom included choice of one's place of burial,[71] although the text attributed to Melcias declared that it would be the "height of temerity" for one to choose a burial site other than one's own church, except for narrowly specified causes.[72]

In a *dictum* following these texts, Gratian set forth his understanding of testaments and testamentary freedom. It was a rudimentary understanding which brought together issues that might have been better kept apart — the proper disposal of dead bodies and the disposition of one's belongings following death.[73]

Limiting the reach of the decree attributed to Pope Melcias, Gratian conditioned the application of his restrictions to those who have committed the sin of pride in choosing a particular burial place, thus maximizing freedom.[74] Gratian then considered Gregory the Great's use of the term *ultima voluntas* ("final will"). According to some, Gratian acknowledged, the expression "everyone's final will should be free" (*libera est ultima voluntas cuiusque*) pertained to the disposition of one's property in contemplation of death.[75] Gratian, however, questioned how free individuals were to dispose of their property following death in light of St. Augustine's admonition to count Jesus Christ among one's heirs.[76] Far from seeing this teaching as a source of potential freedom, allowing the testator to direct at least a part of the family resources to charitable causes, Gratian saw it as a potential constraint on even greater testamentary generosity on behalf of charity.

Gratian made mention of wills and testamentary capacity in a few other places in the *Decretum*. Two further papal teachings, one by Gregory the Great, the other by Gelasius I, endorsed the need to respect the "pious wishes" (*piae . . . voluntates*) and "just disposition" (*iusta dispositione*) of testators.[77] It was taught further that those who interfered with dispositions made to the Church should be punished with an appropriate sanction, such as excommunication.[78] In this way, Gratian not only affirmatively endorsed testamentary freedom, but also provided a means by which it could be effectuated in the case of gifts made to the Church.

Gratian also considered whether monks possessed the "license of testation" (*licentia testandi*).[79] He summoned two texts of Gregory the Great to bear on this question[80] and concluded that monks who have entered community life, made solemn profession, and given everything away lacked this right, although hermits, who lived isolated lives and might still own some belongings, could bequeath their possessions to others.[81]

Henri Auffroy, author of one of the definitive treatments of the law of wills and testaments in the Middle Ages, has asserted that Gratian's analysis, despite its relatively undeveloped appearance, stood at the cusp of a sea change in the relationship of the Church to the enforcement of wills and testaments.[82] Gratian had begun to raise the sorts of questions — about testamentary capacity, and the need to enforce testamentary choices — that would dominate future analysis. And he raised these questions in the context of the emergence of ecclesiastical courts empowered to enforce the Church's own jurisdiction over wills and testaments.[83]

It was in the generation after Gratian, however, that a body of law grew up to protect the exercise of this freedom and the freedom itself came to be conceptualized as a "right." By the time one arrives at Rufinus one sees a sophisticated effort made to understand testamentary freedom and its limitations.

Rufinus began his commentary by emphasizing the importance of testamentary freedom.[84] He agreed with the sentiment of Gregory the Great that the "final will" of the decedent should be respected. Nothing, Rufinus asserted, is more owing to men than that their final will be kept, since they are afterward unable to alter it.[85]

Rufinus was particularly concerned with the impact on the freedom to make a will of St. Augustine's teaching that one should regard the Lord as entitled to a share of the inheritance equal to one of the paterfamilias's children.[86] In taking up this question, Rufinus implicitly challenged Gratian's treatment of the text.

It seemed, Rufinus opened, that St. Augustine's teaching was opposed to the principle of testamentary freedom.[87] St. Augustine, as Gratian had arranged his texts, seemed to place a limit on what a head of household might give the Church by limiting the bequest to a single son's share, although other laws taught that where a father had decided to enter a monastery, he should give all he owned to the Church, provided he had not defrauded his children of their share of the estate.[88] Rufinus reconciled the seeming contradiction by concluding that St. Augustine was not prohibiting the giving of more than a son's share to the Church. He was rather giving practical advice that in ordinary family circumstances a testator may not wish to give more to the Church than the share owing to one of his sons.[89]

Rufinus also appreciated that testamentary freedom came with its own set of responsibilities. He made this point in commenting on a text of St. Augustine, contained in the *Decretum,* which cautioned the *paterfamilias* against disinheriting a son in a fit of anger.[90] A "pious deliberation of mind," Rufinus declared, should precede all donations to the Church.[91] One should not make a donation to the Church out of a fit of anger against a son. Testamentary freedom presupposed a sound and solemn and benevolent mental intention undisturbed by the passions of the moment.

Papal Legislation and Decretalist Commentary   Testamentary freedom and its limitations became a subject of papal legislation by the end of the twelfth century. Bernard of Pavia's collection of papal decretals, the first of the "Five Old Compilations" of decretal legislation which preceded Gregory IX's *Liber Extra,* contained a title "On Testaments and Last Wills."[92]

All but one of the decretals Bernard included in his collection would subsequently make their way into Gregory IX's larger collection. These decrees took for granted a certain fundamental freedom and built a latticework of rules on top of this foundation. A number of decretals dealt with the capacity of priests and bishops to dispose of property belonging to their own patrimony, as opposed to the ecclesiastical goods and grounds entrusted to their stewardship. Thus a bishop as well as a priest was free to make bequests by will out of their property.[93] Another decree established that only two or three witnesses need be present for the execution of a valid testament.[94]

Still other decretals contained in title 26 of Book Three of *Liber Extra* made much the same point. A decree of Pope Gregory the Great asserted that legacies supported by "bare words" were nevertheless to be treated as valid.[95] A decree of Innocent III allowed that one who as his last will committed his disposition to another should not be considered as dying intestate.[96] Yet another decretal commanded that executors who failed to fulfill their office should be compelled to do so.[97] In this way the legislation of popes built a structure of law upon a foundational belief in the freedom of testators to direct the disposition of their goods.

The decretalists explored the issue of what it meant to possess testamentary freedom in fresh and important ways. Bernard of Pavia, who authored a commentary on the law in addition to his decretal collection, noted that the last will and testament was a matter of divine law, spoken of in both the Old and New Testaments.[98] Bernard defined the testament as "the disposition by which one arranges what he wishes to have done with his goods following death."[99] Hence, Bernard concluded, the "testament is so-called as if [derived] from *testatio mentis,* that is, a manifestation of will."[100] In this way testamentary capacity was linked to divine command and simultaneously connected with intentionality and freedom from coercion.

Bernard also laid down ground rules as to who possessed this freedom. He adhered to Romanist principles in stating that no one in another's power, such as a servant, or a son still within his father's power possessed the capacity to make a will.[101] Bernard followed the dictates of Roman law again in adding that those excluded from the *factio testamenti* also included those lacking completely *(omnino)* in speech and hearing,[102] and indicated that the prohibition also embraced those who renounced the right to make a will, such as monks, nuns, and canons regular.[103] All those not otherwise prohibited, Bernard concluded, had the capacity to make a will.[104]

Goffredus of Trani, like Bernard, stressed the element of intentionality in the making of a will. He defined the testament as "the just expression of our will" concerning what we wished done following our death.[105] Hence, Goffredus agreed with Bernard, a will is so-called because it is the "testimony of our mind."[106] And furthermore, Goffredus added, "the will of the testator is law."[107]

Bernard of Parma described this capacity as the "free power of making a will" *(liberam potestatem testandi).*[108] Hostiensis defined the capacity of making a will by referring his readers first of all to his discussion of gifts.[109] There, he spoke of the *ius donandi,* "the right of making a gift," which belonged to the *paterfamilias* and others who exercised *dominium,* the highest form of property ownership.[110]

Hostiensis made clear that one exercising the right of giving had to act freely: a gift could not be other than "free" *(sponte),* he insisted, because no one can truly be generous when compelled by necessity.[111] Measured by this standard, a final will and testament made under compulsion was entirely ineffective as a disposition of property. Hostiensis, furthermore, accepted Goffredus's definition of a testament as "the just expression of our will" and the derivation of *testamentum* from *testatio mentis* proposed by Bernard of Pavia.[112] A will, Hostiensis added, was "ambulatory" — the testator might freely change its terms until the hour of his death.[113] Since a will was subject to revocation or cancellation during the testator's lifetime, it was only at the testator's death that rights in the disposition might be established.[114]

In this body of writing one saw the emergence of a sophisticated defense of an idea of testamentary freedom premised on the capacity of the human person to know and judge how his affairs should be ordered. This freedom was conceptualized as a right. The freedom to make a will, to put one's affairs in order in contemplation of death, included the admonition that one make some kind of contribution to the Church. One should thus be concerned not merely with dynastic affairs, the canonists taught, but also with matters of the spirit, although both the law and ecclesiastical teaching allowed considerable latitude in the kind and amount of the contribution given.

Family obligations, however, were also an important part of making one's final will and testament. Indeed, children as well as spouses had certain rights that they could press against the estate. Children, in fact, had a claim grounded in natural law to a certain portion of their parents' estate. Testamentary freedom, far from being absolute, had to be exercised within a larger network of competing interests and rights. It is the scope of this natural right of children to succeed to a share of an inheritance that is to be taken up next.

Part II: The Natural Right of Children to Claim an Inheritance

In taking up the right of children to claim from their fathers' estates, one must be clear whether one is speaking of the legitimate biological children of the decedent; adopted children of the decedent; or illegitimate children sired by the decedent.[115] Each class of children had a different set of claims they might (or might not) be able to press against their fathers' wills.

These claims were understood by the Roman lawyers and, to a much greater extent, the canonists, to be grounded in natural law. The natural relationship of the family led to certain expectations and responsibilities on the part of all concerned. Children were expected to behave with "piety" (*pietas*) toward their parents. Parents were expected to reciprocate by honoring their children's natural right to inherit. Testamentary freedom, far from being an absolute right, was conditioned on the moral obligation of testators to provide bounteously for their offspring.

Legitimate Biological Offspring of the Decedent

Classical Roman Law

The *lex Falcidia*, promulgated in 40 BC, probably as a revenue-collection device and not a child-welfare ordinance, restricted the right of testators freely to dispose of their property by requiring that one-fourth of the estate (the "Falcidian fourth") be set aside to pass to the children.[116]

The second-century lawyer Gaius offered his own historiography of this law. The Twelve Tables, he noted, had provided for absolute testamentary freedom.[117] A testator might choose to exercise this right by bequeathing all of his property in the form of special legacies, leaving nothing for those entitled by law to take except the empty title of "heir."[118] And under Roman law, this meant that estates would frequently fail, because heirs, faced with the administrative costs of managing an estate without prospect of reward, would renounce their rights.[119] The *lex Falcidia*, on this account, was simply the final step in a series of legislative experiments meant to give heirs incentive to succeed to estates.[120] The *lex Falcidia* was apparently successful, as it was the law of Gaius's day,[121] and remained so until Justinian's.

An excerpt of Paulus, contained in the *Digest,* provides a summary of this law. This decree, as reproduced, recognized that testators had a "free faculty of bequeathing" *(liberam legandi facultatem)* up to three-fourths of their estate.[122] "All Roman citizens," the text went on, "shall have the right and power *(ius potestasque)* of conferring legacies of money or property" on whomever they wished, provided the bequests be so given that "the heirs shall take not less than one-fourth."[123]

Justinian's *Institutes* laid out rules concerning the way in which the *lex Falcidia* was supposed to interact with the related ideas of testamentary freedom and the right of testators to disinherit whom they wished. The *Institutes* began by spelling out the way in which disinheritance was to take place. A testator, the *Institutes* determined, must either name his son an heir of his estate or expressly disinherit the son.[124] Where the testator merely omitted a son in silence, the *Institutes* added, the will's provisions were rendered null and void *(inutiliter).*[125]

The *Institutes* also settled a long-standing debate among lawyers as to the status of daughters and other heirs whose names had been omitted from the will. Gaius had taught that the rule requiring the naming of a disinherited heir applied only to the disinheritance of sons and that a general clause such as "let all my remaining heirs be disinherited" sufficed to remove daughters and grandchildren from the line of succession.[126] Justinian, on the other hand, required testators to declare expressly whether daughters or other, more remote descendants were to be counted as heirs or were to be considered as disinherited.[127]

Sons and daughters and other heirs thus disinherited, however, were not without legal recourse. Justinian's *Institutes,* under the caption *"De*

Inofficioso Testamento" — the "inofficious will," that is, a will that fails to perform its duties *(officia)* — observed that such recourse was sometimes necessary "because for the most part *(plerunque)* parents disinherit or omit their children without cause."[128]

Children who had been "wickedly" disinherited or passed over were thus enabled to press a claim against their parents on the ground that they were not of sound mind.[129] It was not that such parents were actually insane, Justinian added. Rather, they had drafted a will that appeared superficially valid, but which failed "the duty of piety" *(ex officio pietatis)*.[130] The justification for the action — the presumed insanity of the testator — was a classic example of a legal fiction that served to reconcile the tension inherent in a system that prized both testamentary freedom and an almost transcendent duty to transmit wealth to the next generation.[131]

Pietas, the "piety" to which the law referred, was one of those richly-textured Latin words that signified responsibility toward others. Cicero defined *pietas* as "the duty one is reminded to keep with respect to nation and parents and those joined by blood."[132] In this sense, *pietas* was distinguishable from religion *(religio)*, which was the awe and ceremony owed the gods. *Pietas*, rather, pertained to right conduct and proper respect within the hierarchically-structured earthly relationships of hearth and home and country.[133]

Regarding the role of *pietas* in the Roman family, Richard Saller has written: "At the center of the Romans' ideal view of familial relations was the virtue of *pietas*, represented by the image of Virgil's Aeneas carrying Anchises on his shoulder."[134] But Saller has also pointed out that at least in the classical Roman legal literature there was a reciprocal quality to *pietas*: children certainly owed duties to parents, but parents also had obligations toward their offspring.[135] This was especially evident in the testamentary obligations parents and children had toward one another.[136] Where these obligations were breached without adequate justification, the legal remedy of the action on an inofficious will was available.

This action on an inofficious will, Justinian noted, was introduced out of "respect for nature" *(ad verecundiam naturae)*, and was available where those entitled to share in the "Falcidian fourth" had been completely disinherited.[137] Where provision had been made for offspring in the will but the amount set aside proved less than the statutory one-fourth, heirs might still bring an action, but they could not allege an inofficious will.[138] The remedy for an inofficious will was draconian: the invalidation of the entire will, which could have the effect of upsetting years of careful testamentary planning.[139] It has been observed by one modern commentator that the lex Falcidia's threat of invalidation was so severe that it "must have influenced the power structure within the Roman family."[140]

The language the Roman lawyers used to describe this action relied heavily on naturalistic premises and a belief in the bonds of affection that must bind a family together. Marcianus emphasized that the children's allegation in an action against an inofficious will that the testator was of unsound mind should not be taken as literally true but rather as evidence of the unnaturalness of the testator's denial of the "duty of piety" (ex officio pietatis).[141] Papinian stressed that although parents did not have a claim to their children's estates in the way children did with respect to their parents' earthly goods, nevertheless, because of the "solicitude" (votum) and "love" (caritatem) that prevailed between parent and child, a parent should be allowed to succeed to a dead child's estate "where the natural order of mortality has been disturbed."[142] Saller's assessment of the reciprocity embodied in the lawyers' conception of pietas is confirmed by these texts.

The Christian emperors drew the connection between natural affection and the inofficious will even more compellingly than their pagan predecessors. Constantine stressed that children alleging a will to be inofficious must demonstrate that they regarded their parents at all times with "due obsequium."[143] Obsequium was one of those exquisitely difficult, almost untranslatable Latin terms. It might mean "respect"; it might mean "obedience"; it might also mean a kind of "obeisance," a sense of deference shown to those family elders who had brought the younger generation into being and given it proper nurture and guidance. The official interpretation of a second decree of Constantine, found in the Codex Theodosianus, combined the ideas of pietas and obsequium in stressing that a son who had brought a complaint of an inofficious will against his mother had to establish that he had in no way damaged the pietas that should prevail between mother and child and that he had at all times showed obsequium.[144]

But if children were expected to comport themselves with piety, honor, reverence, filial duty, and due deference, they also had a claim against the estate that was justified by recourse to language of natural obligations and rights. Paulus for instance, spoke of "that which nature owes by way of inheritance."[145] The language and metaphor of naturalness was used as well in Justinian's legislation concerning inofficious wills. Thus a rescript of Justinian contained in the Codex condemned delays in the delivery of the amount "naturally owing" (debito naturali) to an heir entitled to share in the "Falcidian fourth."[146] Justinian made use of the cognate expression *debetur ex natura* in *Novella* 1, which contained further legislation on the Falcidian share.[147]

In *Novella* 115, Justinian declared he would bring order to the law concerning disinheritance of children by identifying behaviors that might disqualify ungrateful children from their natural share in the inheritance. These reasons included the obvious: children who committed acts of violence against their parents, or who made an attempt on their parents' lives were deemed ungrateful by law, as were children who became chronic criminals.[148] The law also disapproved of certain sexual relationships within the family, especially incestuous ones. Thus a son who had sexual relations with his father's wife, or with his stepmother, or with his father's concubine, was thereby subject to disinheritance.[149]

Another reason for disinheritance reflected the violent and chaotic circumstances of the time: children who delayed or who failed altogether in ransoming parents who had fallen into captivity were to be disinherited.[150] Detailed provisions were also included about children who either were not Catholic or who had lapsed from the faith. If a parent "sensed" (*senserit*) that his children had fallen from communion with the Catholic faith, that parent was most strongly (*maxime*) encouraged to disinherit the suspect children.[151] Provision was subsequently made to protect the assets of children returning to the faith and to address situations where only some but not all of the children had fallen into heresy.[152] These gross forms of misconduct clearly breached the bonds of *pietas* that should govern the home and disqualified children from their share of the estate. But by setting such limits, Justinian also made it evident that the usual frictions of family life were insufficient reasons for disinheritance.[153]

The amount due to children entitled to share in the Falcidian fourth and who did not commit ungrateful acts justifying disinheritance came to be known variously as the "legitimate portion" (*legitima portio*) or "due portion" (*debita portio*). Justinian used this term repeatedly in legislation found in the *Codex* and the term acquired a specialized significance that it would retain well into the Middle Ages.[154]

The Roman lawyers, finally, were required to come to terms with the relationship of the Falcidian fourth to the *fideicommissum*, loosely translated by modern writers as "trust." The use of the *fideicommissum* was governed by a law known as the *lex Trebelliona*. The *lex Trebelliona*, promulgated as a *senatusconsultum* in about AD 56, summarized by Ulpian in the *Digest,* established the basic framework for analyzing the relationship of the *fideicommissum* and the natural obligations testators had toward their heirs.[155] Although this law underwent massive revisions by Justinian, the canonists nevertheless continued to refer to the legal principles represented by this decree as the "trebellonian law."

Most importantly for our purposes, Justinian's reorganization of the *lex Trebelliona* accomplished two goals: first, it made the *fideicommissum* binding upon an heir.[156] The *fideicommissum* was not merely a moral obligation, which heirs were free to disregard, as generations of Roman lawyers had understood it to be. Where a testator indicated that a *fideicommissum* should confer some bequest on a third-party beneficiary, the heir or heirs, who succeeded to the entire estate, were obliged to meet the terms of the bequest.[157] This rule, however, was conditioned on fulfillment of the law's second objective: the preservation of the Falcidian fourth. Prior to satisfying the terms of a *fideicommissum,* the heirs were entitled to withhold as much as was needed to equal one-fourth of the estate.[158]

The Medieval Canonists

The canonists were the heirs of this body of testamentary doctrine. The law of wills that the canonists constructed in the twelfth and thirteenth centuries depended heavily on the conceptual apparatus created by the ancient Roman lawyers. In revivifying the old Roman forms, however, and applying them to the governance of the universal Church in circumstances very different from those that prevailed in ancient Rome and Byzantium, the canonists were forced to rethink portions of the old learning. Two decretals, *Raynutius,* issued by Pope Innocent III,[159] and *Raynaldus,* issued by Pope Gregory IX,[160] represented fundamental advances in the canon law of wills and testaments in the way in which they connected the language of natural rights to the share children were entitled to take from their parents' estates.

In *Raynutius,* Pope Innocent III had to sort his way through a series of complex transactions. By his wife Clera, Raynutius, the testator whose will was at issue, had two daughters, Alterocha and Adiecta. In his will, he left a house and a garden to Alterocha, and "certain other goods" to Adiecta.[161] The terms of the will instructed Adiecta's guardians to give her possession of her goods should she marry.

Following her marriage to a certain Peter, Adiecta's guardians, following "Lombard law," transferred the goods to the couple.[162] Adiecta and Peter lived together for four years and had a son. Adiecta then died.[163] Only then did Alterocha challenge the distribution of property, alleging that she and her son were owed a portion of the *fideicommissum* that had apparently been established to benefit Adiecta. It seems that their claim was predicated on the failure of the testator to set aside sufficient property to satisfy the Falcidian/Trebellonian fourth. Peter and Adiecta's son, through a guardian, a certain Raynerius, argued that Alterocha's claim was barred by prescription.[164] Raynerius further argued on his client's behalf that the court should only calculate the amount owing to Alterocha after first setting aside two-thirds of the estate, which was alleged to have belonged to Adiecta's mother and Peter's second wife.[165]

The matter was heard by a cardinal legate who borrowed from the vocabulary of Roman law to condemn Raynerius's position. There was a "legitimate portion" (*legitima portio*) owing to Alterocha, and this was debt owed to her by "right of nature" (*iure natura debita*).[166] Raynerius as guardian, the cardinal held, was obliged to satisfy this amount. Innocent III affirmed the cardinal's decision, referring to the statutory one-fourth as the share owing "*per Trebellonianum.*"[167]

Raynaldus, the second of the two decretals, was similarly complex, involving brothers who attempted to divide an estate without taking adequate account of the "claim owing by nature" (*naturae debitum*).[168] Pope Gregory IX spoke of the necessity of keeping secure the right of institution created by the *lex Falcidia*.[169] Gregory's invocation of a "right of institution" meant to refer to the share the offspring were entitled to claim in virtue of natural law.[170] Taken together, the two decretals recognized the existence of a natural right of offspring to share in a statutory minimum of one-fourth of their parents' estate.

The emergence of the doctrine of a natural right to claim an estate coincided with the Church's assertion of jurisdiction over the administration of wills and testaments. Canonists like Goffredus of Trani had contended that jurisdiction over wills belonged to the Church. As Goffredus had put it, "the defense of testaments belongs to the Church."[171] The issuance of *Raynutius* and *Raynaldus* and their inclusion in *Liber Extra*, in conjunction with the assertion of ecclesiastical power over last wills and testaments, opened up the possibility of ecclesiastical enforcement of this newly recognized natural right.

The natural right of offspring to inherit received further definition from the pen of Hostiensis. He began his analysis by considering the nature of the action *per querelam inofficiosi testamenti*.[172] Through this action, Hostiensis announced, a will that is "broken" might be repaired.[173] Such a will is called "*inofficiosum*," Hostiensis added, "because it is made against the duty of piety."[174] This assertion was followed by a cross-reference to Marcianus's denunciation of wills made in violation of this basic familial duty.[175] Hostiensis then followed the cross-reference by emphasizing that "there is a duty between father and son, and it is called *pietas*."[176]

Hostiensis's use of the term *pietas* summoned to mind not only the classical meaning of the term but also a rich scholastic understanding that had been developing in the schools of philosophy. *Pietas* now referred not only to the maintenance of proper deference and respect in earthly relationships, but might even connote the respect and obeisance owed to God.[177]

Hostiensis invoked this rich notion of *pietas*, this idea of a transcendent familial duty rooted in the right order God established for his creation, and placed it within a broader juristic vocabulary. There is the duty between a patron and a freedman, he noted, and this is called *obsequium*.[178] There is furthermore, Hostiensis observed, the duty between God and man, called *religio*.[179] *Pietas* bore some resemblance to these two concepts, but also differed from them in the way in which it referred to the solemn obligation of love and respect that should prevail within the family.

The expectations Hostiensis associated with *pietas* were not one-sided. Invoking the Roman juristic tradition, Hostiensis insisted that children owed duties to their parents, but that parents also owed duties to their offspring. Indeed, he concluded, the duty of piety that should prevail between father and son was a kind of natural reciprocity. As Hostiensis put it, it was "what man owed man by reason of nature."[180]

The remainder of Hostiensis's treatment of the inofficious will as found in his *Summa* laid bare the rules that governed the prosecution of one's right to inherit. Hostiensis defined the scope of the right as extending to sons, grandsons, and other descendants of the father who stood to succeed the decedent in the event of intestacy.[181] He endorsed the causes for disinheritance established by Justinian.[182] The action *per querelam inofficiosi testamenti*, Hostiensis stressed, served to ensure that disinheritance might only take place for good cause.[183] He discussed as well the status of uterine brothers, who shared a common mother but not a common father, and other specialized circumstances that might or might not result in the loss of the right.[184]

Hostiensis continued these themes in his gloss to *Raynutius*, found in his *Lectura*. He indicated that the share owing to children might under certain circumstances be a third instead of a fourth of the estate; he stressed that the share that was owed the children of the decedent was "a legitimate claim by right of nature" (*legitimam . . . debitam iure naturae*); and he insisted that parties could not be defrauded of this right.[185] He asserted that a father was not to "burden" (*in quo nec gravari*) this share of the estate.[186] He provided a detailed analysis of the proper means of computing the Trebellonian or Falcidian share, considering such issues as the proper way in which to calculate ongoing sources of income (*fructus*), and repeatedly stressed that the heir enjoyed this claim as a right "from nature."[187]

Bernard of Parma, in the *Glossa ordinaria*, repeated at several points that the legitimate portion due heirs under the Trebellonian or Falcidian laws was a claim based on natural law.[188] Innocent IV used similar language.[189] By the time one arrives at the end of the thirteenth century, the term "portion owing by right of nature" seems to have acquired the sense of a term of art. This, at least, is how Pope Boniface VIII, in legislation found in *Liber Sextus*, used the term in describing the proper disposition to be made of property where the children of a testator themselves predeceased the testator, leaving no issue.[190]

Fourteenth-century canonists continued to speak of the children's share of the estate as owing "by nature." Johannes Andreae, taking the "third" that Hostiensis spoke of as normative, declared that "in the goods of one's father or mother or grandparents one has a share in a third of the estate by reason of natural law/right of which one may not be deprived."[191]

Johannes Andreae also called attention to a potentially problematic question concerning the enforcement of the share owed by nature: how ought this canonistically-recognized natural right interact with the inheritance laws of the new kingdoms and principalities of Europe? Pope Innocent III had himself referred tangentially to this problem in *Raynutius* when he took notice of Lombard inheritance law.[192] Johannes realized that some secular legal systems might seek to protect values different from those the canon law sought to conserve. Thus, in an off-handed exercise in comparative law, Johannes noted that "Gallican law" and the law of Sicily, which followed the "law of the Franks," both made generous provisions for surviving spouses as opposed to surviving offspring.[193] So long as such provisions did not detract from the third or the fourth owed by nature to the offspring, however, such provisions did not violate canon law.

The interaction of canon law and the secular legal systems of Europe on the right to the Falcidian share was the subject of a commentary by Antonio de Butrio at the end of the fourteenth century.[194] Antonio noted that the rules and commentary that had grown up around the decretal *Raynutius* had grown exceedingly complex — "more than enough for three lectures, indeed, more than enough for three months."[195]

Antonio followed his effort at law-school humor by repeating Johannes Andreae's insistence that one-third of a decedent's estate belonged by natural right to the decedent's descendants and that this amount could not be detracted from.[196] He noted that this share was given definition by the Trebellonian and Falcidian laws.[197] Antonio asserted that not the canon law alone, but also "the law of nations [and] the civil laws mandate a father to leave a legitimate [share] to his son, which is a third, or even a half, according to the number of children."[198]

But what of those civil laws that failed to respect these requirements? Some writers, Antonio conceded, have asserted that the requirement of the fourth owing by nature — here Antonio subtly adjusted the percentage downward from his earlier claim — "might be diminished by statute or by custom."[199] These writers seem to think, Antonio asserted, that the fourth represented some kind of maximum and that civil governments were free to set some lower figure.[200] Antonio concluded by noting that this question had recently been put to "the lords of the Rota."[201] Repeating an apparently otherwise unknown rotal decision, Antonio asserted that "it was decided that a statute could not remove in the entirety the legitimate [share], but could reduce it."[202] This was because, Antonio continued, the complete removal of the legitimate share "makes war against natural equity and piety, for a parent is bound by natural law to leave something to his child for support."[203]

Canon Law and Secular Law

While canon law asserted and defended the proposition that children were entitled to share in at least one-quarter of their parents' estate as a matter of natural law, this claim of jurisdiction did not go uncontested. As Antonio de Butrio's analysis suggests, secular legal systems also asserted jurisdiction over the distribution of property by will. One might therefore consider some examples of the ways in which canon law and the secular legal systems of Europe interacted on this matter.

To write of medieval Spanish testamentary law forces one to recognize the regional diversity that prevailed on the Iberian peninsula in the period in question. The law differed from one territory to the next. The Visigothic law of the early Middle Ages, however, stood in the background and represents the starting point of future development.[204] A law of the Visigothic King Reccared favored the traditional regard for children's inheritance rights in teaching that children should not be lightly disinherited.

Such an action would seem like a "suspension of natural piety."[205] Reccared followed this condemnation with a list of reasons justifying disinheritance in certain specified circumstances — such as striking one's parents with a shoe, or a rock, or a club, or a whip.[206] A decree of King Ervig, also found in the Visigothic law, made clear that the legitimate share of offspring should usually be four-fifths of the estate, a far more generous allowance than Roman law had made or that canon law would subsequently make.[207] A testator might accordingly exercise free disposition of only one-fifth of the estate.

The Visigothic rules continued to influence the law in some parts of Spain well into the thirteenth century. Thus Stephen Bensch has indicated that Barcelona retained the Visigothic practice of requiring that four-fifths of the estate be reserved to offspring until 1284, when, under the influence of Roman and canon law, the amount that "a testator could dispose of freely" was increased "from one-fifth to seven-fifteenths."[208]

Canon law, however, would have far more direct influence on the shape of the law in the most powerful political unit in thirteenth-century Christian Spain, the united kingdom of Castile and León. Dominating the life of this realm during the middle and latter decades of the century was King Alfonso X, the Learned (1221-1284), who practiced an "astonishing patronage of letters, law, music, art, and science" within the kingdom.[209] Among the duties Alfonso wished to fulfill was that of wise law-giver.[210] To that end, he commissioned a series of legal texts, the most enduring of which is known today as the *Siete Partidas* — "The Seven Parts."[211] Canon law and Roman law — the building blocks of the European *ius commune* — were among the principal sources of this massive synthesis of the Spanish legal tradition.[212]

Canon law stood directly behind the *Sieta Partidas*'s provisions regarding the share to which offspring were entitled. Children were entitled to a *legitima parte* of their parents' estate, "and this legitimate part is called in Latin 'the part owing by right of nature.'"[213] Where there were four or fewer children, one-third of the estate was to be reserved to them, free of all encumbrances; where there were five or more, one-half of the estate was to be set aside in this manner.[214] These rules applied, King Alfonso declared, even where the father whose estate was being divided was divesting himself of his property in order to enter religious life. A father with a monastic calling was to donate to his new religious house only that which remained after he completed the preliminary distribution to the children.[215]

The *Siete Partidas*, like its canonistic and Romanist sources, recognized that there were circumstances which called for the disinheritance of offspring. Disinheritance was defined as the deprivation of a right — "the right (derecho) which one has of inheriting from his father" or some other relative.[216] The loss of this right could only be justified by some good cause.

The Siete Partidas identified a number of reasons for disinheritance. A son who pursues an undignified career — such as one who fights other men for profit — might be disinherited.[217] So also might a daughter be disinherited where she spurned a marriage her father arranged and chose instead to "lead the life of a bad woman in prostitution."[218] Children who failed to ransom a father who had been taken captive might be disinherited.[219] A Christian father was strongly encouraged to disinherit children who turned to heresy, or Judaism, or Islam.[220] The opposite rule applied, however, where the children of a non-Christian father converted to Catholic Christianity: such a parent was obliged to establish these offspring as his heirs as opposed to children who clung to the ancestral faith.[221]

Although "[t]he Siete Partidas was conceived originally as a uniform code for all of Alfonso's domains,"[222] it was "redefined in 1274 as a body of general law to be applied principally in appeals to the king's bench or in cases where royal jurisdiction [was] primary."[223] As such, it determined legal norms for the unified kingdom of Castile and León. These rules eventually passed into the legal heritage of the Spanish American southwest where they influenced development until the middle of the nineteenth century. They also passed into early Louisiana law where today they stand in back of Louisiana's continued requirement of providing children a "forced share" of the parental estate.[224]

A forced share for offspring received rather different treatment in the history of English law. A proper understanding of the English law of wills should begin with the basic distinction drawn by the English lawyers between estates in land and personalty. By the middle twelfth century it was already well-settled that land passed inexorably to the eldest son through the system of primogeniture.[225] Thus at the end of that century the treatise known as Glanvill observed that "according to the law of the kingdom of England the first-born son succeeds in totum."[226] Indeed, a modern commentator has noticed regarding the medieval rules that "[t]he descent [of land] to the heir could not be interfered with by will."[227]

Personalty, on the other hand, could and did pass by means of will. The treatise known as Glanvill, which stressed the importance of primogeniture with respect to estates in land, proposed a very different set of rules for the distribution of personalty. All of a testator's chattels *(res mobilies)* were to be divided into three equal shares: one to be given to his "heir" (presumably his child or children); one to go to his wife; and the third share reserved to the testator for his free disposition.[228] *Magna Carta,* in clause 26, contained a similar provision, declaring with respect to a decedent's chattels, that "reasonable shares are to be set aside for wife and children."[229]

This rule was subsequently endorsed in the mid-thirteenth-century treatise attributed to Henry Bracton.[230] After allowing for the payment of just debts and expenses, the personalty of the decedent was to be divided into three shares: one share should go to the children *(pueris);* the second share to the decedent's wife, if she survived; the testator, finally, retained "the free faculty of disposing *(liberam disponendi facultatem)* of the third part."[231]

At this early date in English legal history it seemingly belonged to the ecclesiastical courts to enforce these provisions. Surveying the records of the ecclesiastical courts, Richard Helmholz has demonstrated "there was a time when the right [to the *legitima portio*] was known and enforced, probably throughout England."[232] Helmholz even identified "a reference to the *lex Falcidia . . .* in a 1306 record from Canterbury."[233]

But Helmholz also made clear that in England, from the fourteenth century onward, the right seemed to be grounded more on prevailing local custom than on ecclesiastical law.[234] "[B]y the end of the fourteenth century, [furthermore], the *legitim* had been reduced to the level of a local rather than a national custom," for the most part enforceable only in the northern ecclesiastical province of York.[235]

The commentary of William Lyndwood, fifteenth-century canonist and ecclesiastical and royal administrator,[236] sheds further light on the situation in late-medieval England. Lyndwood's work, the *Provinciale,* is significant in that it takes as its subject the legislation of English ecclesiastics over the preceding two centuries.[237] In commenting on English ecclesiastical law, Lyndwood brought to bear the learning of the universal Church, as applied to the peculiarities of the English political order.[238]

Commenting on a statute of the archbishop of Canterbury, John Stratford, on the subject of inheritance rights, Lyndwood advised that recourse should be had to "the custom of the place."[239] Lyndwood acknowledged a variety of possibilities: sometimes the estate remained undivided, as when no wife or children survive; sometimes, when only the wife survived, the estate was divided in half; and where wife and children survived, the estate might be divided into thirds.[240] He called attention to the fact that his source — Stratford's decree — did not speak of a "claim based on common law" (de Jure communi debitum), but of claims grounded on customary law.[241]

George Keeton and L. C. B. Gower, writing in the 1930s, noted that as local custom, the *legitim* survived in a few parts of England until quite late.[242] It was only finally legislatively abolished in York in 1692, in Wales in 1696, and in the City of London in 1724.[243] In Scotland, which was governed by Roman law, it remained the law even at the time Keeton and Gower wrote.[244] But as a matter of general law, enforceable throughout England either in the ecclesiastical or the secular courts, it had practically disappeared during the fourteenth century.

The developing *ius commune* of Europe, as reflected in the commentataries of the glossators, urged respect for the *legitima portio*. Azo's treatment of the Falcidian fourth amounted to a small treatise on the intricacies of its operation.[245] An heir entitled to take did so by reason of "hereditary right" (iure haereditario).[246] Rules governing the proper computation of the Falcidian fourth, and issues such as advances on inheritances, were set out in great detail.[247]

Accursius defined the Falcidian fourth as "a claim by right of institution" (debita iure institutionis).[248] Like Azo, Accursius understood the right to take a portion of the parental estate as the starting point for a close analysis of rules governing the distribution of the estate in a wide variety of circumstances.

Bartolus, the greatest of the fourteenth-century Romanists, elaborated upon these themes. He corrected those canonists and others who described the right as based on the *lex Trebelloniana*. Properly speaking, Bartolus asserted, it was a "claim by right of institution grounded on the Falcidian [law]."[249] It was "most improperly" (improprissime) called the "*legitima*," although Bartolus conceded that this term had become the standard usage.[250]

Drawing comparisons between the ancient sources and his contemporaries, Bartolus implicitly criticized prevailing testamentary practice. He noted that under the ancient Roman law a son who challenged his father's disinheritance had the burden of proving he had been grateful. This order was now reversed, Bartolus observed: today, the son was presumed to be grateful and the burden of proof was placed on the father who wished to disinherit his offspring.[251]

Like his predecessors, Bartolus was also concerned with laying out the proper rules by which the Falcidian fourth might be administered. He inquired into questions such as whether an heir who was left less than his share of the fourth had the right to invalidate the entire will or only bring an action to supplement his share. Bartolus sided with the less drastic remedy.[252] Bartolus, like his Romanist predecessors, assumed the vitality of the Falcidian fourth and sought to propose means by which it could be properly governed.

One can now reach some conclusions about the degree to which secular legal systems actually observed the canonistic teaching that the *legitima portio* was a requirement of natural law. The legislative reforms of King Alfonso the Learned can be said to have conformed generally to the rules laid down by the canonists, which taught that at a minimum one-fourth of the estate was to be set aside for the children. The unreported rotal decision to which Antonio de Butrio alluded recognized that secular realms were free to set aside a larger amount for the children — as the Visigothic law had done — but a smaller amount was condemned as seeming to make war on nature herself. The Spanish experience fit this general profile.

The English rules also generally conformed with the guidelines set by the canonists, at least until one arrives at the end of the fourteenth century. Even after this date, in some places at least, the canonistic rules were preserved under the guise of local custom. But where these rules entirely neglected the *legitima portio,* as they seemingly did in many parts of England by the fifteenth century, then they could at least be accused, in the words of Antonio de Butrio, of making war against natural equity.

Although the medieval Romanists relied to a lesser extent than their canonistic counterparts on the language of natural rights, they nevertheless came to conclusions similar to their ecclesiastical brethren. The Falcidian fourth, whether understood, as the canonists conceived it, as the claim owing by nature, or as the Romanists thought of it, as a right of institution predicated on the civil law, became a central feature of inheritance law in the developing European common law. And indeed, this romano-canonistic synthesis would come to be shared by most European legal systems up to our own day.

Adopted Children of the Decedent

To speak of adopted children in the high Middle Ages requires some elaboration. Jack Goody has made an argument, widely believed by some scholars, that adoption, if not theoretically impossible in the later Middle Ages was at least actively discouraged by the Church, which viewed the practice as dangerous to its own policies on the transmission of wealth from generation to generation.[253] In fact, as will become apparent, Goody's contentions are flawed. The canon lawyers of the twelfth and thirteenth centuries developed a sophisticated body of adoption law that recognized the inheritance rights of adopted children. But in order to understand the concepts used by the canon lawyers and the social background against which they worked, one must first consider the classical and post-classical Roman law of adoption and the practice of adoption in the early Middle Ages. As with so much else regarding inheritance rights, the canonists made extensive use of these densely-technical Roman-law sources in formulating their own theories.

Adoption in Classical and Post-Classical Roman Law

The Roman law of the classical period, whose legal forms the canonists would borrow in the course of the great juristic revival of the twelfth and thirteenth centuries, had a well-developed body of adoption law. The Roman lawyers recognized two types of adoption. Gaius, in his *Institutes*, described the first form of adoption, *adrogatio*, as involving adoption by a *paterfamilias* of someone who was already *sui iuris*, a "master of his own affairs," who had been emancipated by his biological father.[254] It was called *adrogatio*, Gaius noted, because the one adopting must be asked whether he wishes as his son the one who is to be adopted, while the one who is being adopted must also be asked whether he approves of his new father.[255] This form of adoption required "the authority of the people," by which was meant the approval of the imperial authority itself.[256] Presumably, it could take place only in the presence of the emperor and only at Rome.[257]

The second form of adoption, which came to be known as "simple adoption," did not involve these formalities, and might take place in the provinces, before the provincial governor or some other imperial official.[258] Daughters could not be adopted by *adrogatio*, but might be adopted through simple adoption.[259] Children of any age might be adopted by simple adoption, although *adrogatio* was typically reserved to sons above the age of puberty.[260]

This basic distinction shaped the way subsequent generations of Roman lawyers came to conceptualize adoption. The *Institutes* of Justinian modified Gaius in some particulars, but retained the essential elements. Adoption, Justinian wrote, was of two types: by rescript issued by the emperor, or by recommendation of inferior magistrates. The former was known as *adrogatio* and the latter was known simply as "adoption."[261] Some aspects of Gaius's rules were modified: daughters as well as sons, Justinian taught, might be adopted by *adrogatio*.[262] But in the main, the old rules were kept.

Gaius declared further that the power to adopt a child was reserved to men as an aspect of their right of paternal power.[263] This teaching, however, was modified in a rescript of Diocletian and Maximian.[264] In response to a petition for adoption brought by a woman the two emperors ruled that while it is impossible for a woman to adopt, as she cannot exercise paternal power, nevertheless an accommodation might be made in her case. As solace *(solacium)* for the children she had lost, she was to be given the privilege of raising her stepson as her own, just as if he had been born from her *(ex te progenitum)*.[265] The *Institutes* of Justinian represented a careful paraphrase of elements of both Gaius and this later imperial rescript as it asserted the impossibility of women adopting but also conceded the possibility of imperial authority making exceptions where the felt demands of human nature required relaxation of the rules.[266]

The texts of the legal commentators preserved in Justinian's *Digest* laid out further principles and rules on the subject of adoption. "Sons are made not only by nature, but also through adoption" was the broad principle laid down.[267] The law regarding those who might adopt was broadly conceived. Javolenus laid down the boundary lines within which adoption might occur when he stressed that it might take place among all those who could theoretically share the natural relationship of father and son.[268] Within these borders adoption was broadly permitted. Thus Ulpian declared that even the blind might adopt or be adopted.[269] Similarly, Paulus added, an unmarried man might adopt.[270] Rules were also enunciated regarding the adoption of children into families where there were already living children.[271]

A decree of Justinian found in the *Codex* specifically addressed the inheritance rights of adopted children.[272] Justinian asked whether a son who was given by his natural father in simple adoption to someone who was not a blood relative might nevertheless retain inheritance rights through his natural father. Justinian responded in the affirmative.[273] This was because the adoptive father might emancipate his new son, thereby dissolving the inheritance rights he enjoyed within his new family. Without protection of law, the son would effectively be disinherited with respect to both his old and new families.[274] The bonds of adoption are so fragile, Justinian wrote, that one can, on the very same day, be made a son through adoption and a stranger through emancipation.[275]

For this reason, Justinian wrote, the rights of such a child must be kept intact (iura integra) within his original family; and so, Justinian decreed, the son retained the right to inherit through his natural father and even retained the right to bring an action inofficiosi querellam should his natural father disinherit him without cause.[276] Having established that a son given in such an adoption retained rights within his family of origin, Justinian took the next step of decreeing that where a son was adopted by one who was not a blood relative, any provisions in the will made by the adoptive father on behalf of his newly-adopted son were entirely a matter of grace, not obligation.[277]

But, Justinian continued, what if the adoptive father died intestate? In such circumstances, the adopted child might nevertheless inherit from his adoptive father, while also taking under his natural father's will.[278] In these circumstances, Justinian emphasized, the rights acquired by adoption (iura adoptiva) are superimposed on the child's enduring natural rights (iura integra naturae) to take under his birth father's will.[279]

Justinian closed his decree by considering the rights of a child who was adopted not through the simple form, but by means of adrogatio.[280] Such a child, presumably above the age of puberty, had consented to adrogatio as had his adoptive father. Such a child became the adoptive heir of his new father and was counted as a member of the family.[281] Justinian elaborated on this point in the Institutes: a son adopted through adrogatio was entitled to share in the Falcidian fourth of his adoptive father's estate.[282]

Adoption, in ancient Rome, was conceived chiefly as serving dynastic needs, either political or economic. This much is revealed through even a casual reading of a work like Suetonius's Lives of the Caesars.[283] Adoption might also be seen as a means of resolving pressing family crises, such as providing within the extended family for children for whom the natural parents have found it impossible to care. This explains the many references in the law to adoption by blood relatives of the children. It seems, however, that adoption was not viewed as a means of resolving the pressing problem of abandoned or exposed children.

Adoption in the Early Medieval Church

Both the Old and New Testaments admonished believers to see to the needy in their midst, especially the widows and orphans.[284] Adoption as a theological and legal concept, however, took shape not in reflection on the proper ways to serve the needs of orphaned children, but as a means of explaining the relationship of believers to the Godhead. In several passages in the letters known to have been written by Paul one finds the concept of adoption used to explain the relationship followers of Jesus Christ share with the deity.

Thus in his letter to the Galatians, St. Paul announced that in the fullness of time God sent his Son, Jesus Christ, "that he might redeem those who were under the Law, that we might receive the adoption of sons."[285] In Ephesians, Paul proclaimed that "[God] predestined us to be adopted through Jesus Christ as his sons, according to the purpose of his will."[286] And in his letter to the Romans, St. Paul added that all who are led by the Spirit of God are sons of God. This relationship is created by adoption and allows us to call to God, "Abba, Father."[287]

Paul's letters put adoption at the heart of the Christian message. Through our faith in Christ, we have been transformed. We have been adopted as God's own children and thereby brought into a direct relationship with the Godhead in a process that has ensured our salvation. This endorsement of adoption as a part of the Christian message remains a central feature of Christian belief today. Over the centuries, it has provided a model by which Christians might pattern their own familial relationships. The working out of this process, however, was a gradual one.

The theological condemnations of infant exposure, well-documented above for the patristic period,[288] continued into the early Middle Ages and were backed by the force of the canon law and the laws of the Germanic peoples as they came under the influence of Christianity. Not suprisingly, infanticide was also regularly condemned. The evil of child-killing is a depressingly frequent theme of the penitential literature of the early Middle Ages. This literary genre was a new creation of the early Middle Ages and was intended to "provide[] guidance for confessors in dealing with sinners who wished to be reconciled with God and make their peace with the Church."[289] The earliest penitentials were Irish, but this literary form "spread from Ireland in the late sixth century to England in the seventh century and thence to the Continent during the eighth century."[290]

A woman who killed her son, the *Canons of Gregory* declared, was subject to fifteen years' penance, although the next canon qualified this assertion: where the killing was done by "a poor little girl" (*paupercula*), she should be liable to seven years' penance.[291] These provisions would be repeated in the *Penitentiale* of Theodore.[292] A provision of the *Valicellanum* penitential taught that where a woman killed a small child before baptism, seven years' penance should be imposed, including three years on bread and water.[293] Variations on these sorts of offenses and penalties were frequently repeated.

In addition to the penitential literature, the early canonical collections also denounced the crime of infanticide. The early tenth-century canonist Regino of Prüm included several texts in his collection of laws condemning the murder of children by their parents. If a woman willfully (*voluntarie*) killed her son or daughter, she should be accounted a homicide and serve a ten-year penance, one text recorded.[294] A second text declared that women who conceive children in fornication and try to conceal this fact through infanticide should in justice be deprived of communion until the end of their days, but in mercy might be returned to the table after ten years.[295]

The law of the Germanic kingdoms condemned child murder in equally harsh terms. Thus a passage in the law of the Visigoths began by stating that "persons can be possessed of no more shameful form of madness than those who, unmindful of their duty (*pietas*), are murderers of their own children," and went on to outlaw infanticide.[296] Not all Germanic law reflected this value. The *Lex Frisionum*, for instance, continued to reflect pre-Christian attitudes when it provided that among those who can be killed "without compensation" are infants taken from the womb and killed by their mothers.[297] But where Christianity succeeded in inculcating its respect for the sacredness of human life, infanticide came to be seen as a grave crime.

At least in the minds of some, adoption could be viewed as a remedy for this callous discarding of children. A letter of St. Boniface, the great eighth-century Anglo-Saxon apostle to the Germans and the English, proposed adoption as an alternative for some of the gross excesses he witnessed in English convents. He reported that he was horrified to see members of these convents, more "prostitutes than nuns," killing the offspring of their wombs, thereby choosing "not to fill the churches of Christ with adopted sons, but instead filling the graveyards with corpses of infants and the netherworld with their pathetic souls."[298]

Ecclesiastical legislation similarly drew a connection between infanticide and what might best be termed "informal" adoption. The Council of Vaisons, held around 490, decreed infanticide was the equivalent of other forms of homicide and laid down rules by which a parent might expose a child with some hope of that child being found and raised.[299] Noting in a preamble that children, who should be the object of human mercy, must not be left exposed to the elements to be torn apart by wild dogs, the Council enacted the following rules: (1) finders of such children are encouraged to take them in and raise them; (2) they should, furthermore, notify their pastor of their discoveries; (3) pastors are to announce such discoveries at Sunday Mass; (4) should the children be claimed by those responsible for the abandonment, compensation should be made to the finders; (5) if no one came forward to make a claim, the finders are presumably free to raise the children as their own.[300]

Rules of this sort and the guiding principle behind them, that innocent life was worthy of legal protection, came to be the established policy of canon law. Regino of Prüm included in his collection a decree, misidentified as belonging to the Council of Rouen,[301] recognizing that sometimes, because of the persuasiveness of the devil or the weakness of human flesh, a mother will desire to kill the offspring of her womb.[302] Pastors should announce to their congregations that women feeling such pressures should leave their children on the church's doorstep.[303] The pastor was then to seek someone from the congregation who would take it in and nourish it and raise it up. In this way the child's life will be kept safe and secure from the clutches of the devil and the woman will avoid being judged a homicide.[304]

The finding of a child, it seems, might sometimes result in a commercial exchange taking place. This sort of commercialization can be seen in Visigothic law. "If someone, bearing in mind the demands of mercy, picks up an abandoned child and provides sustenance and afterward the parents are found," they may, if they are free-born, redeem their child by providing the finders with a slave or paying the equivalent.[305] But where the birth parents fail to pay compensation, and their claim had to be resolved by the judge of the territory, then the birth parents, "the authors of this breach of parental duty" (*impietatis*), might be condemned to perpetual exile.[306] In this text, one sees blended together an appeal to motives of love and mercy as well as a frank profit motive, and a concern that the penal law be fulfilled.[307]

Given the reduced living standards that prevailed throughout western Europe in the early Middle Ages, most of these informal adoptions doubtless did not involve transfer of wealth from one generation to another to any significant degree. They were not, in short, the product of what we might call a worked-out testamentary plan. Most adoptions were probably motivated by a mixture of mercy and pity, on the one hand, and self-interest, on the other, as parents with few or no children sought the assistance that sturdy young arms and legs might provide.

But the historical record also makes clear that adoption continued at high levels of society. Thus Gregory of Tours recorded that in 577 King Guntramnus of the Franks, who was childless, assembled his leading nobles so that he might obtain their advice and consent.[308] Because of his sins, Guntramnus confessed, God had left him childless. He now wished, he petitioned the assembly, "that this my nephew be to me as a son," a request that was granted.[309] Childebert, Guntramnus's nephew, was made heir to the kingdom and eventually succeeded his adoptive father on the throne.[310]

Childebert subsequently repeated this process by adopting his nephew.[311] It has been observed that Frankish royal adoptions sometimes occurred outside blood lines as well. "Sigebert III, for example, Merovingian king from 633 to 656, had no children and, pressured by his Grimoald mayor, he adopted a son from him who, to bind himself to the Merovingian dynasty, took the name of Childebert, the traditional anthroponym of the Merovingians. 'Childebert l'Adopté' reigned from 656 to 662."[312]

The survival of Merovingian-era formulary procedures by which an adoption might be effectuated is further evidence of the seriousness with which this practice was regarded and the efforts made by better-established adoptive parents to provide for offspring by will. One such formula recorded the reasons why someone might adopt and why someone else might agree to be adopted. Long deprived of sons, burdened with weakness and ill-health, the prospective father viewed adoption as a kind of bargain: the adoptive parent will provide food and clothing and shoes in return for the services of a son. After death, the formula promised, neither the adoptive father by his will nor any of his natural heirs shall remove the adoptive son from his preferred status.[313]

The sort of informal adoption that must have been commonplace in the first millennium is well-illustrated by the story of St. Peter Damian's life. Born close to the year 1000, Peter Damian was one of the leading advocates of Church reform in the middle eleventh century.[314] His biographer relates that Peter was orphaned while still a small child.[315] He went to live first with an older brother who mistreated young Peter and sent him out to the fields to work as a laborer.[316] "Barefoot, with his hair unkempt," he tended the swine.[317] Despite this maltreatment, Peter grew both in the virtues and in his religious faith.[318] Finally, as an adolescent, he was rescued from this series of "calamities" by another older brother who was a cleric.[319] This brother appreciated Peter's abilities and saw to his education.

And Peter, for his part, returned the favor by entering religious life himself and so immersing himself in study that he "became a marvel among his professors."[320] This story, one suspects, is unusual only in its outcome, which saw its protagonist rise from humble circumstances to become one of the doctors of the Church.

Adoption and Inheritance Rights in Twelfth- and Thirteenth-Century Law

This system of informal adoption constituted the background against which Gratian and the decretists operated. Gratian's *Decretum* viewed the practice of informal adoption as a means of relieving the problem of exposure. An excerpt from the Fourth Council of Toledo included by Gratian in the *Decretum* provided that a child who had been abandoned in front of the church might, "out of mercy," be picked up by anyone.[321] A blood relative of the child had ten days in which to contest the informal adoption, after which time the new parents might rest secure.[322] Should someone come forward to claim the child after the time period had elapsed, that person should be accounted guilty of homicide.[323]

The decretist commentators agreed with and elaborated upon the rules laid down in this text. Stephen of Tournai emphasized that if some "lord" (*dominus*) — by which term he seemed to embrace not only fathers but also lords of the manor and others in positions of authority and power — abandoned a child, he would immediately lose all rights to that child. The ten-day period to reclaim a child, Stephen thought, should be allowed only where the abandonment had occurred without the father's or lord's knowledge.[324] Stephen also emphasized that the words "rest secure" did not mean that the child became the servant of its new parents, but only that the parents could not be compelled to return him or her.[325]

Other decretists concurred with this teaching. The anonymous *Summa Parisiensis* echoed Stephen in declaring that the ten-day waiting period applied only where the birth parents were truly unaware of the abandonment, and added that in appropriate circumstances this period might be increased.[326] Rufinus, in his commentary stressed that no child so "collected" should subsequently be reduced to bondage.[327]

The anonymous *Summa, 'Induent Sancti'* stressed that Gratian's text even applied to those of servile birth who have been exposed by their masters.[328] After the requisite ten days have elapsed, the lord is prevented from seeking the return of the child and the child is thereafter to be treated as if born free, since all persons are presumed to have been born into the state of liberty.[329]

The commentary of Johannes Teutonicus, authored in the early thirteenth century and accepted as the "ordinary" gloss on the *Decretum,* distinguished two reasons for child abandonment. One might abandon a child "spontaneously," which resulted in the immediate termination of parental rights.[330] But one might also be so pressured by extreme necessity, such as the inability to feed a child, that one might for that reason abandon the child, although it was preferable to leave the child at a home for foundlings. Only where necessity motivated the abandonment did the ten-day limit apply.[331]

For the remainder of the thirteenth century, there was little in the way of commentary on Gratian's *Decretum.* Guido de Baysio, however, took a fresh look at this basic work in his commentary known as the *Rosarium,* authored at the end of the thirteenth century.[332] He accepted Johannes's teaching regarding necessity and also endorsed his predecessor's suggestion that leaving children at a *hospitale* was preferable to abandonment.[333]

The decretal of Pope Gregory IX, discussed above in relation to the termination of the right of paternal power,[334] was the chief official legislative enactment on informal adoption. That decretal allowed both for the termination of parental rights in cases of abandonment or extreme neglect, and also permitted the practice of informal adoption to continue.

In addition to informal adoption consequent upon actual or constructive abandonment, the canonists also integrated into their thought-world the system of adoption devised by the ancient Roman lawyers. The vehicle by which this whole legal apparatus of adoption was introduced to the canon law was an unlikely choice: the analysis of the impediment to marriage created by the entry of an adopted child into the family.

Gratian included in his collection an excerpt from Pope Nicholas I's letter addressed to the Bulgarian church around the year 866, in response to inquiries about correct religious observance.[335] Among the Bulgarians' concerns was the proper understanding of the impediments of marriage: what were the rules by which two parties might marry, while other parties were prevented from marriage?

Pope Nicholas responded by considering the different types of relationship that prevailed among persons. In taking up the issue of relationship, he was concerned with the larger question of what constituted incest. There were relationships, he instructed, based in blood, but there are also spiritual relationships, which have made us spiritual brothers and sons, which are grounded on a "grace-filled holy communion."[336] Marriage is impossible, Nicholas continued, among persons who enjoy such spiritual relationships. "Those whom adoption joins," Nicholas concluded, may not marry one another for this reason.[337]

Nicholas's prohibition became the teaching of the Church. The decretists accepted Gratian's rendering of Nicholas's text and used it as a vehicle for exploring the question, what constituted a valid adoption? It was in this context that the canonists introduced the old Roman-law categories into the canonistic analysis of adoption.

Rufinus distinguished among three categories of children with whom adults might have a legal relationship — natural children, who are the offspring of one's natural relationships and for whom one is the natural parent. His use of "natural" here connoted those whom one has naturally conceived, apparently either within or outside wedlock. There were also "spiritual children," with whom one is related through the sacrament of baptism, where one has served as sponsor. Finally, there were "adopted children," "who are not one's own by natural childbirth, but are made into one's own children so as to be installed as heirs."[338]

In explaining what was meant by adoption, Rufinus reiterated the old Roman-law categories. Adoption might be effected through "adrogation," by which children who either have no father or who have been emancipated by their parents are placed under the paternal power of another.[339] But it might also be accomplished through simple adoption, in which the adopted child remained "in the power of the natural parents."[340]

This general treatment of the issue came to be widely accepted by the canonists. In speaking of familial relationships, the *Summa, 'Induent Sancti'* distinguished between "legal relationship" (*legalis proximitas*) and "spiritual relationship" (*[proximitas] spiritualis*).[341] Adoption fell into the category of legal relationship while relationships established through sponsorship at baptism or confirmation constituted spiritual relationships. Huguccio, meanwhile, defined a "natural son" (*naturalis filius*) as a child legitimately born from the "flesh of his father and mother, in contradistinction to one who has been adopted."[342]

By the thirteenth century, a well-developed doctrine of legal adoption was in place. Raymond of Peñafort might be taken as representative. Raymond used the occasion of commenting on the marital impediment of adoption to lay down a strict set of rules governing the operation of this institution. Adoption, as Raymond defined the term, "is the legitimate assumption of a 'foreign person' (*extraneae personae*) as a son or grandson."[343] Those who may adopt included heads of household who are "able to generate."[344] Eunuchs and the perpetually impotent were thus barred from adopting, as well as women, who were unable to exercise the paternal power required of heads of household.[345]

As intimated by Rufinus's remark that adoption occurred to facilitate the installation of heirs, the canonists also turned their attention to the subject of inheritance rights in adoptive relationships. Tancred's *Summa de Matrimonio* treated the rights of adopted children at some length.[346]

Tancred followed the Roman law distinction between simple adoption and *adrogatio*. The effects of simple adoption included, according to Tancred, "being accounted . . . as the son of the one adopting, with the result also that one may succeed in intestacy."[347] *Adrogatio*, however, conferred on the one adopted a broader array of inheritance rights. "One difference between one who is arrogated and one who is [simply] adopted," Tancred wrote, is that the father who has arrogated a child is obliged to leave him a share in Falcidian fourth.[348] A father who obtains a child through simple adoption, on the other hand, "is obliged to leave nothing, unless he wishes to."[349]

Tancred's analysis represented the basic distinction the canonists maintained on the subject of inheritance rights of adopted children. Thus one sees Raymond of Peñafort distinguishing between *adrogatio* and simple adoption.[350] One may only be arrogated, he stressed, if one did not have a father, or was otherwise emancipated from paternal power.[351] Simple adoption, on the other hand, occurred where the child being adopted was in another's paternal power.[352] Echoing Tancred, Raymond declared that one who has been adopted in simple form may succeed his adoptive father in intestacy, but that an adoptive father was not required to make provisions in his will for the child. On the other hand, a child who has been arrogated must be left a share in the Falcidian fourth by will.[353]

The Romanist civilian writers of the twelfth through fourteenth centuries were largely in agreement with this analysis. Placentinus observed, following his Roman-law sources, that there were two means of adoption, *arrogatio* and "what is commonly called 'adoption.'"[354] One who is adopted in simple form, Placentinus asserted, remained under the paternal power of his father (*genitoris*), but may nevertheless share in the inheritance of his adopted father should that father die intestate.[355] One who has been arrogated, however, was thereby transferred to the power of the arrogator, and was counted among his children, presumably entitling him to full inheritance rights.[356]

Azo, for his part, proposed competing definitions of adoption. "Some have defined adoption," Azo wrote, "as a legal action introduced to give comfort *(solatium)* to those who have no children. . . ."[357] Azo, however, proposed as well a second definition: "Adoption is the legitimate act through which one who is not a son is held to be a son."[358] The second definition was to be preferred because adoption was available even to those who had children of their own.

"Briefly," Azo noted that *adrogatio* resulted in the one arrogating being accounted "in all respects" *(per omnia)* as the child's new father.[359] Implicitly, a child so situated shared in full inheritance rights. Azo noted explicitly that a child adopted in simple form might inherit where the adopted father died intestate.[360]

Odofredus, active in the 1230s and 1240s, defined adoption in terms similar to Azo's. "Adoption," he wrote, "is the legitimate act by which one who is not by nature a son is made one by law; and in this it imitates true nature."[361] He noted that the principal distinction between simple adoption and *adrogatio* was the fact that simple adoption involved the transfer of a child to a new home even though he also remained under his birth father's paternal power. *Adrogatio*, on the other hand, involved the assertion of paternal power over a child who was at that time *sui iuris*.[362]

Odofredus dealt at length with the relationship that should prevail between the adoptive child and his natural as well as adoptive parents. Because one adopted in simple form remained under his birth father's paternal power, Odofredus felt compelled to ask "Who is responsible for feeding a child who has been adopted?"[363] Reviewing the legal debate that had occurred, Odofredus noted that some had argued that the natural father retained the obligation of support. Others, however, have said that this obligation passed over to the adoptive parent. Realistically, Odofredus observed, the natural father may be in no position to provide sustenance. He might be *inops* — "without resources."[364] From the standpoint of social reality, Odofredus felt that this was an obligation that ought to be assumed by the adoptive parents.

Odofredus, furthermore, provided a much more complex analysis of the inheritance rights of adopted children than had his predecessors. He was particularly interested in the problem of a son adopted out in simple form by a natural father who subsequently omitted him from his will. If this son was subsequently emancipated by his adopted father, it seemed he might effectively be left without an inheritance.[365]

Odofredus looked to Justinian's legislation in the *Codex* for guidance on this point. Where a son has been adopted by a family relative, such as his grandfather, the adoption effected a transfer of paternal power from natural to adoptive parent, and the child became eligible for a share in his adoptive father's estate. As Odofredus put it, "natural rights and civil rights concur in one."[366] But where the son has been adopted by a stranger, not a member of the extended family, then he will be deemed to remain under his natural father's paternal power, at least for purposes of inheritance. His original rights, in this latter case, Odofredus asserted, must "remain intact" (*integra iura*).[367]

Cino da Pistoia, finally, stressed that by means of arrogation children have acquired "the right of taking the fourth" (*cum iam quaesitum sibi ius habendi quartam*).[368] Cino, however, drew one important difference between children who have been arrogated and legitimate children born into a family: through emancipation, he noted, a child is restored to a "pristine state." Since the right to take the Falcidian fourth was not a part of this pristine, or original, state into which an arrogated child had been born, such a child, unlike those born into a marital union, lost the right to claim his or her share of the fourth.[369]

This extensive debate over the inheritance rights of adopted children is important for our exploration of the relationship of natural rights to marriage and the family. The Falcidian fourth had come to be understood as a natural right; it was, the canonists were fond of asserting, a "claim owing by nature." Adoption posed an interesting set of questions for such a claim. To what extent were the natural rights to inherit the product of blood relations? To what extent could these natural rights come into being through the legal action of adoption?

In answering these concerns, one must be sensitive to the distinctions the canonists and civilians drew among different types of adoption. There were three types of adoption recognized by law: informal adoption; simple adoption; and arrogation. Arrogation, which represented a total severance of rights within one's original family coupled with a transfer to a new family, conveyed the highest level of rights to the adopted child. Indeed, some of the sources asserted that such a child had a claim to the Falcidian fourth — such a child could share, in other words, in the natural rights enjoyed by biological members of the family. The writers of the medieval *ius commune*, canonists and civilians alike, also emphasized that because *adrogatio* represented a severance of old familial ties and complete incorporation in a new household, it belonged to the prince to ratify the process.[370] Informal adoption, as well as adoption through the simple form, did not require the same level of legal solemnity, nor did they carry the same effects as *adrogatio*. The inheritance rights of children adopted through these latter two forms were less than complete. But even here, canonists and civilians were willing to extend some inheritance rights to children brought into the family by adoption.

Adoption in the Later Middle Ages

Jack Goody has argued that the triumph of Catholicism in early medieval Europe ensured the practical disappearance of adoption as an institution.[371] Goody based this claim on surmises about the testamentary implications of certain statements of St. Jerome and other early Christian writers.[372] Especially influential, in Goody's opinion, was the teaching of the fifth-century priest of Marseilles, Salvian, whose statements about inheritance are quoted and analyzed above.[373] Salvian "encourag[ed] parents to leave their wealth to [the Church] rather than to their offspring, on the plea that it is better for the children to suffer in this world, than that the parents be damned in the next."[374] Since adoption, Goody surmised, was principally about "strategies of heirship," the institution of adoption could not have survived in such a hostile thought-world.[375]

The danger of relying on Salvian's texts as representative of the Church's teaching on the law of adoption or inheritance should by now be abundantly clear. Salvian's texts simply never constituted part of the legal tradition of the Church. Goody's claims are further refuted by the evidence suggesting that adoption remained a regular feature of life throughout the medieval period. It is true that feudal law declared that "an adoptive son does not succeed to a fief."[376] Nevertheless, it is also a fact that archival evidence supports the conclusion that adoption remained a viable practice through the thirteenth, fourteenth, and fifteenth centuries.

James Brundage has marshaled evidence demonstrating that the courts of canon law continued to recognize adoption in the thirteenth century.[377] This much is illustrated by William Durandus's inclusion in his procedural treatise of standard forms to be used in adoption proceedings.[378] Adoption, Durandus's recommended form began, served "to comfort (*ad solatium*) those who do not have sons."[379] As part of its recommended language, the form further declared that "every natural right of paternal power" was transferred to the adoptive father.[380] Nor was Durandus alone in providing forms for adoptions. Geoffrey Barraclough has shown that notaries in the papal chancery also made use of standard forms to expedite adoption proceedings.[381]

René Aubenas, in an important early study of notarial records in Provence, has shown that adoption was a regular feature of fourteenth- and fifteenth-century life.[382] Notaries, from the fourteenth century onward, employed a standard-form contract for "the reception of a son" in order to effectuate adoptions.[383] These contracts recognized the existence of reciprocal duties on the part of the one adopting and the one being adopted. Acceptance of these duties, Aubenas noted, "establish[ed] a fictive bond of paternity, a definitive and perpetual bond."[384] Aubenas supported these contentions with an appendix containing a series of adoption contracts, the earliest dated June 1418, the latest dated August 1538.[385] The majority of these documents are from the fifteenth century.[386]

A survey of legal sources by Kristin Gager lends further support to the survival of adoption practices in the later Middle Ages.[387] She cites evidence that adoption was a feature of Spanish law and life in the thirteenth century.[388] Adoptions took place in eleventh-century and fifteenth-century Brittany, and in Paris in the fifteenth and sixteenth centuries.[389] The "fourteenth-century treatise, *La Somme Rurale* [by] Jean Bouteillier[,] claimed that adoptions, although rare, were practiced in the north of France as well as in the southern, Roman-law regions of the country of his time."[390] Franck Roumy has shown that French jurists of the fifteenth and sixteenth centuries — Jean Maseur and Guillaume Benoit — argued that adopted children could not serve as their parents' heirs in intestacy because they lacked the necessary blood relationship.[391] Gager, on the other hand, notes that the Church continued to give approval to "dynastic adoptions" as late as the fourteenth and fifteenth centuries.[392]

Also standing against Goody's contentions are the thorough analyses by canonists and Romanists of adoption in both its less formal and more formal senses.[393] It is simply an error to conclude, on the basis of one fifth-century writer's comments about heirship, that the institution of adoption disappeared from European life for a millennium and a half. The error in Goody's misplaced reliance on Salvian's text as evidence of a thousand years of ecclesiastical hostility to adoption is especially clear when one realizes that Salvian's arguments were never picked up by the canonical writers.[394] Salvian was neglected by the canonists, one can surmise, because he simply never reflected medieval reality.

The canon law of adoption and heirship that evolved in the twelfth through fourteenth centuries remained the teaching of the Church through the early modern period. Tomás Sánchez probably represents the best restatement of the Catholic teaching. He proposed two alternative, but complementary definitions of adoption. Following the jurists, he stated, one might define adoption as "the legitimate act, nearly imitating nature, through which one who is not a son or grandson is made one."[395] Or alternatively, one might define adoption, following St. Thomas, as "the legitimate assumption (*assumptio*) of an 'extraneous person,' i.e., one who is not a blood relative, as a son or grandson."[396]

Sánchez moved in a thought-world where motives were conditioned at least as much by consideration of succession to great estates as by the possibility of real love between father and adopted offspring. Indeed, Sánchez explained the motive for adoption as the desire to supply for an heir. In this vein, adoption was seen as "a kind of legal or artificial generation."[397]

Sánchez also explained the distinction between *adrogatio* and simple adoption chiefly by reference to the different inheritance rights attached to each. *Adrogatio* was "perfect adoption," in which the one adopted was placed under the paternal power of the one adopting and was made a necessary heir of his new father.[398] Sánchez furthermore added that a child adopted by *adrogatio* could not be excluded from sharing in the Falcidian fourth which Roman and canon law required a father to leave to offspring.[399] This much was required in the case of *adrogatio*, Sánchez wrote, because one so adopted "stood in the position of a natural son" (*instar filii naturalis*).[400] One placed in this position within the family thus shared in the natural rights of a biological son.

Simple adoption, in contrast, did not result in a child being transferred from the power of one's natural father over to the authority of the adoptive father.[401] Rather, one so adopted remained in the power of his natural father and was not made a necessary heir of his adoptive father.[402]

Children Born out of Wedlock

To understand the testamentary rights of children born out of wedlock it is necessary first to explore the Roman-law institution of concubinage and its ultimate fate at the hands of Christian rulers and canonists. It is also necessary to consider the three types of legal categories Roman jurists devised in order to categorize children according to the relationships they had with their mother and father. These included children born within "lawful (*iustum*) matrimony"; those born as the result of concubinage; and those born of forbidden intercourse.

*Concubinage and the Rights of Children Born
out of Wedlock in the First to Fifth Centuries*

Concubinage, as an institution in pre-Christian Rome, had a protean quality, depending variously on what an upper-class Roman thought he might
be able to get away with and on what frequently hostile observers wished to
see. "A Roman governor or emperor might have a whole seraglio of slave or
freed mistresses, according to hostile sources, and these are called
concubinae."[403] On the other hand, a study of Roman epigraphical evidence
suggests that concubinage was often a stable and enduring relationship involving men and women of widely differing social backgrounds who were
for that reason unable to marry.[404]

The Roman practice of concubinage generally contemplated an ongoing relationship of monogamous, or near-monogamous quality, between a
well-born male and a woman of lesser birth. A passage from Ulpian high-
lights a debate within Roman juristic circles, whether a freedwoman in a relationship of concubinage with her patron might leave him without his
consent to marry another. Ulpian argued that she should remain with her
patron, although it is apparent from the sources Ulpian cited that others
disagreed.[405]

Marcianus distinguished among the different social classes from
which concubines might be drawn: freed women, those born free, and
those of obscure birth.[406] One might choose to keep as a concubine a
woman who was formerly a prostitute.[407] On the other hand, one might
also wish to keep as a concubine a woman of "proper character" *(honestae
vitae).*[408] The latter relationship must be formed openly and before witnesses. Furthermore, Marcianus added, it was better that such a pair marry
one another, lest they commit sexual crimes.[409] Marcianus, however, emphasized that concubinage itself did not result in the commission of a
crime, since it was permitted by law.[410]

Children born of concubines, at least in pre-Christian Roman law,
were unable to claim against their fathers' estates, although they were entitled to the support of their mothers. Their fathers, however, also remained
free to provide for them in their wills.[411] The capacity of such children to
succeed to their mothers' estates is clear from a portion of Gaius's commentary on the provincial edict preserved in the *Digest.*[412] That children born
of such relationships were forbidden to claim against their fathers' estate in
the absence of an affirmative provision in the paternal will is the implication of a commentary by Ulpian. Such children, Ulpian stressed, lacked the

ius cognationis, the right of legitimate blood relationship, that prevailed between father and offspring born in a marital relationship. Hence, a father was unable to succeed to a child's estate.[413] And so, by implication, children might not take by right of cognation from their fathers, although they might still seek praetorian protection to secure inheritance rights from their mother or their mother's next-of-kin.[414]

In addition to children born within a relationship of concubinage, the pre-Christian Roman law also recognized the possibility of "spurious" (*spurii*) offspring — children conceived in illicit intercourse. Such illicit intercourse might include incest or adultery or some other serious sexual crime. For purposes of claiming against their parents' estates in the absence of a will, however, these children were treated no differently from children born to concubines.[415]

The earliest Christian writers approached the issue of concubinage with surprising tolerance. The practice of concubinage was plainly inconsistent with the Christian theology of marriage, but it was not on this account immediately condemned. The practice had existed in Judaism and was pervasive in Roman society. It required a significant effort of imagination to conceive of its elimination.

Hippolytus's *Apostolic Tradition* counseled that a woman held as both a slave and a concubine should not be rejected from the communion table where she has remained faithful to a single man and raised his children.[416] On the other hand, Hippolytus admonished men who neglected to marry their concubines to do so under pain of exclusion from communion.[417] Pope Leo the Great sounded positively world-weary when confronted with the question of what to do with a priest whose daughter was given to a man in concubinage.[418] "Not every woman joined to a man is a wife," Leo began, and "not every son is his father's heir."[419] Concubinage seemed too much a feature of the Roman landscape for Leo to challenge it directly. The First Council of Toledo prohibited married men from taking concubines, although it allowed unmarried men to do so.[420]

Legislation of the early Christian emperors gradually came to recognize the possibility that inheritance rights might attach to children born in concubinage. This process did not proceed smoothly. The Emperor Constantine reflected a degree of moral suspicion where concubinage was concerned when in 336 he condemned senators or other persons of rank who wished to legitimate for purposes of inheritance children born of liaisons with slave women, freedwomen, actresses, tavern-girls, prostitutes, or other women of lesser status.[421] In 371, however, the emperors Valentinian and Gratian reversed Constantine and permitted fathers to leave up to a twelfth of their estate to children born out of wedlock where they had children born in legitimate wedlock; where they had no legitimate children, they might leave such children a fourth of their estate.[422]

This provision differed from the Falcidian fourth. Unlike fathers of children born in a legitimate marriage, who were obliged, for reasons of natural law and right, to provide for their legitimate offspring, fathers of children born out of wedlock were given the freedom — "the faculty of giving or leaving" (*donandi aut relinquendi . . . facultatem*) a portion of their estate to illegitimate offspring.[423] The legislation of Valentinian and Gratian spoke of what fathers were permitted to do, not what they were required to do. Spurious or natural children might not bring an action *querela inofficiosi testamenti* if their fathers failed to mention them in the will, but at least their fathers could, if they saw fit, provide for them.

The Emperors Arcadius and Honorius reversed this policy in 397, explicitly endorsing Constantine's rule that "natural children" be excluded from all inheritance rights and further requiring that their portion of the estate escheat to the state.[424] Eight years later, however, these two emperors, joined by Theodosius, reversed their position, allowing fathers to leave up to a fourth of their estate to children "born of any kind of a relationship."[425]

The Christian Roman emperors took further steps to make at least some provision for children born of such relationships. Theodosius and Valentinian ruled in 442 that a father who had only natural children might appoint them heirs of his entire estate.[426] In 470, the Emperors Leo and Anthemius permitted fathers to legitimate their natural children in order to make them eligible for public office.[427] And in 477, the Emperor Zeno decreed that where a man subsequently married his concubine the children he had previously had by her were legitimated by the marriage and so might succeed to their father's estate.[428]

Novella 89, issued by Justinian in the year 539, represented a comprehensive restatement of the subject. The decree opened with criticism of ancient Roman practice: Roman lawyers had failed to show any "humanity" with respect to children born out of wedlock.[429] But since the time of Constantine a more liberal approach had evolved. Justinian's purpose in writing was to bring order to various rules that had been promulgated by the emperors of the prior two centuries.

One might legitimize a child, first, Justinian wrote, by installing him as a *decurion* — a principal office of local government that carried burdensome responsibilities and was widely avoided by those who could do so.[430] Such a child might have the burdens of public office, but would also be treated as the equal of legitimate children for purposes of inheritance. Second, one might legitimate a child through a subsequent marriage with his or her mother.[431]

Where marriage was impossible, either because the man's concubine had died or because the social gulf was too wide, a father might petition the emperor for a rescript of legitimation.[432] Justinian finally indicated a third means of legitimation open to fathers: a father could declare a child to be legitimate in his will.[433] By natural law, Justinian asserted, all children are born legitimate. It is through human sinfulness — the result of "wars and enslavement" — that such distinctions first entered the law.[434] By liberalizing the law, Justinian thus considered himself to be restoring the natural condition.

This analysis, Justinian made clear, implicated a larger right, the "right of legitimacy" *(legitimum ius),* which pertained, in the first instance, to those born into legitimate marriage. The right of succession was part of the bundle of rights that belonged to legitimate status.[435] But the right of legitimacy extended to other categories of children as well. It might also be acquired by operation of law, through the three methods Justinian set forth in his reordering of the law.[436]

But roughly a hundred years before these accommodations were being made, a Christian theologian with the imagination to conceive of a world where marriage was the only legitimate outlet for human sexuality challenged the whole foundation of concubinage. St. Augustine in his treatise "On the Good of Marriage" *(De bono coniugali)* asked about a relationship in which an unmarried man and an unmarried woman become sexually involved, not for procreation but for lust, but in which the parties themselves nevertheless maintain fidelity with one another, "so that neither the man nor the woman does it with anyone else."[437]

Such a union might be marriage, St. Augustine argued, provided the pair took no steps actively to frustrate procreation. But, he continued, what if the man took a woman "for a time" *(ad tempus),* until he might find another with "honors and resources equal" to his own?[438] Such a man, St. Augustine asserted, was "an adulterer in his soul," and she might also be accounted an adulteress, at least where she has agreed to the temporary nature of the relationship.[439] Perhaps thinking of his own relationship with his former mistress, Augustine imagined a circumstance where only the man was blameworthy: if the woman remained true to the man even after he moved on to another partner, and "prepared herself for a life of continence," "I should not easily dare to call her an adulteress."[440]

St. Augustine drew out the theological implications from this set of facts. Concubinage, he concluded, violated the purposes toward which marriage was oriented: it stood against the goods of procreation, of permanence, and of lifelong fidelity. It was no marriage at all but only adultery by another name. The canonists of the twelfth and thirteenth centuries would deploy this legacy to attack the legal foundations of concubinage and so to cast doubt on the legitimacy and inheritance rights of children born of such unions.

The Decretists on Inheritance Rights of Children Born out of Wedlock

Gratian confronted these divergent traditions in his effort to reconcile the millennium of Church teaching that had grown up on the subject of the proper outlets for human sexuality. He reproduced the text from the First Council of Toledo that had taught that an unmarried man who kept a concubine "for a wife" (pro uxore) should not be kept away from the Church.[441] He repeated a saying of Isidore of Seville on the difference between the Old and New dispensations: it is no longer permitted, Isidore declared, for a Christian to keep more than one woman, although an unmarried Christian might keep a concubine.[442] In a different context, he repeated Pope Leo the Great's worldly reply to Rusticus: not every son is his father's heir; concubinage was a social reality to be accepted, albeit with regret.[443]

Gratian, however, tried to assimilate these texts to his understanding of the goods of Christian marriage as articulated by St. Augustine.[444] A concubine, as Gratian defined the term, was "one united [to a man] in the absence of legal instruments, but received with conjugal affection."[445] Brundage has observed that much is made to depend on the phrase "conjugal affection"; in effect, affection itself converts a transient sexual liaison into "a type of informal marriage."[446]

Some of Gratian's immediate successors were less kind to concubinage. Indeed, a palea inserted in early editions of Gratian's text contains a ringing denunciation of concubinage by St. Augustine: Calling on all persons — believers, catechumens, unbelievers — to hear him, calling on God and the angels for support, St. Augustine roared "you are not permitted to have concubines!"[447]

The commentary attributed to Paucapalea, for its part, genuinely equivocated on the relationship of concubinage to marriage. With a quotation from Gratian's own analysis, the gloss distinguished between "affection [that] makes a woman a spouse, and the law [that] calls [her] a concubine."[448] But the author of the commentary, when it came to make his own view clear, merely cited the decree of the Fourth Council of Toledo allowing concubines in stable relationships to take communion.[449]

Rufinus sought to provide greater systematization to Gratian's texts and analysis. He endorsed concubinage where it could be seen as a type of informal marriage, but he disapproved of other forms of sexual liaisons, which he collectively grouped under the rubric of fornication. Commenting on Gratian's dictum about the transformative power of conjugal affection, Rufinus noted that the legal instruments referred to by Gratian were merely the external trappings of a marriage ceremony: the handing over of the bride by her father, the conferral of a dowry, and so forth symbolized a deeper, more transcendent phenomenon.[450] It was conjugal affection that made one person a spouse even in the absence of such formality. Rufinus concluded that what was forbidden to all Christians was the "fornicatory affection" (*fornicario affectu*) that accompanied some forms of concubinage.[451] One was not to keep more than one sexual partner or move casually from partner to partner. Where one had established a sexual relationship with a member of the opposite sex, it was presumptively marriage with all the rights and duties appertaining thereto.

Inheritance rights of children born to such unions were nevertheless called into question. The *Summa Parisiensis* agreed that a concubine might be called a wife, but this did not mean that her "sons succeed unless to the amount their father set for them."[452] Commenting on Leo the Great's world-weary text, Stephen of Tournai was far more detailed:

> So natural children, namely those born of a concubine, who are neither servile nor legitimate heirs, do not succeed their father, unless he has perhaps legitimated them, either through the prince, or because they have been handed to the court by the father, or where the father has taken their mother as a bride [with all legal requirements] fulfilled. A father is nevertheless able to leave his natural children and their mother a twelfth of his substance, if they have been legitimated. Moreover, under the new law [Justinian's *Novellas*], if the father does not have legitimate children or parents, he may leave them [his natural offspring] his entire substance. . . .[453]

202 POWER OVER THE BODY, EQUALITY IN THE FAMILY

The Thirteenth-Century Synthesis:
Legitimacy and Inheritance Rights

By the thirteenth century the conceptual struggle against concubinage had largely been won. Where the proper terms of consent had been uttered by both parties, such a relationship might be subsumed under the category of clandestine marriage. Where the relationship lacked proper consent it was classified as criminal — fornication perhaps, or adultery, or rape, or some other offense, depending on the marital status of the parties and the sorts of sex acts they performed.

Concubinage, as it had been legally articulated in ancient Rome and even as it had been understood in Gratian's time, was disappearing from view. Marriage had become the exclusive legitimate outlet for sexual expression. Children not born within such unions were illegitimate and not eligible for the range of inheritance rights accorded to children born in valid wedlock. It nevertheless remained possible to legitimate children by using the Roman forms. Children so legitimated acquired the *ius legitimorum* — the "right of legitimates" — which included inheritance rights.

The trajectory of these developments was already evident at the time when Stephen of Tournai wrote, as his reference to the *Novellas* and his allusion to the grounds of legitimation established by Justinian made clear. The process accelerated with the collections of decretals that were appearing at the end of the twelfth century. Bernard of Pavia, for instance, collector of decretals and commentator upon them, wrote on the subject of legitimate children and inheritance rights.

Marriage, Bernard began, exists for the sake of children.[454] Having already analyzed how a marriage was contracted, Bernard now wished to turn his attention to its effects: who might be considered a legitimate child and how a child who was not legitimate might become so.[455]

A legitimate child was one born of a legitimate marriage — a marriage contracted in accord with the norms of canon law — or from a union reputed to be legitimate by virtue of having been contracted "in facie ecclesiae," in a ceremony in front of the church.[456]

But marriage, Bernard added, is not the only means of producing legitimate children. Some children, he noted, are born legitimate, but others are legitimated by operation of law. Thus, for instance, where a concubine has come to be graced with the title of "wife" — Bernard's elegant way of describing a marriage between a man and his mistress — the children of the union are thereby legitimated.[457] To support this proposition, Bernard turned to Roman law.[458] Bernard followed Roman law in other respects as well. A child, he noted, echoing Justinian, might be legitimated by being made a decurion, or by means of a rescript issued by the emperor.[459] A child finally might also be made legitimate through being named in his father's will or through some other public instrument.[460] A child thus made legitimate acquired the "right of legitimates" *(ius legitimorum),* which included inheritance rights.[461]

Other canonistic writers continued to employ Romanist concepts as the foundation of their analysis of legitimacy and the Church's power in this area. Thus Tancred noted that children born of legitimate or putative marriage, or adopted, or arrogated might in the right circumstances succeed their fathers in all their goods.[462] This rule, however, contrasted with that applied to natural children, offspring born of concubines who lived in the master's house, and who may take up to two-twelfths of the estate; it contrasted also with spurious children, born of adulterous or "vulgar" intercourse, who were entitled to nothing.[463]

The decretals that comprised Book IV, title 17 of the *Liber Extra*, "Who Are Legitimate Children," took these premises for granted. Natural children, Pope Alexander III ruled, were legitimated by the subsequent marriage of their parents.[464] Children born of divorced parents were legitimate, provided they had been conceived prior to the sentence of divorce.[465] So, too, children born in clandestine marriages, provided the union subsequently received the approval of the Church.[466]

There were, however, limits to the Church's power to legitimate children. The power of legitimation necessarily posed a threat to secular realms. The legitimation of the illegitimately-conceived child of a king or other nobleman might disrupt the dynastic plans of a kingdom or some other dukedom or principality. The power of legitimation, in short, strategically wielded, could be used by ecclesiastical authorities to control succession to the secular realms of Europe.

Pope Innocent III's famous decretal, *Per Venerabilem*, was issued in the context of a political struggle involving the king of France and explored the scope of the papal power to legitimate offspring so as to make them eligible for secular benefits.[467] Known to scholars for its sustained reflection on papal power,[468] this decretal specifically addressed the dynastic needs of a certain French nobleman, William of Montpellier, on whose behalf a petition had been taken to the pope by the archbishop of Arles.

William wished to have his sons legitimized so that they might succeed him as lord when he died. Innocent began his response with a broad statement of principle: the apostolic see has full power (*plena potestas*) over the legitimation of other than legitimate children, so that it might legitimize not only natural children, presumably born in concubinage, but even children of adulterous or other forbidden relationships.[469] The pope may not only legitimize these children, he may even dispense from the rules and allow them to succeed to spiritual office, even to the episcopate itself.[470]

Innocent heaped further proofs upon this claim. He drew a comparison between legitimation and the power of ordination to remove one from paternal power. One consecrated a bishop, Innocent noted, was automatically released from his father's power. A bishop, in turn, might even ordain a man of servile rank to the priesthood, thus releasing the man from his servitude, although the bishop would be obliged to make satisfaction to the feudal overlord.[471]

If ecclesiastical power might be used to make one eligible for episcopal ordination or to dissolve paternal power or the feudal relationship, then its scope must be very broad. Hence, Innocent continued, "it is believed more than likely and reputed more probable" (*verisimilius creditur et probabilius reputatur*) that the pope might legitimize irregularly-born children for secular responsibilities, especially in those circumstances where the person petitioning the Roman pontiff did not himself have another secular overlord possessed of the power of legitimation.[472] Indeed, Innocent concluded, "[i]t would seem monstrous that one made legitimate for spiritual acts, should nevertheless remain illegitimate for secular acts."[473] If one could legitimize for the greater responsibility, one could legitimize for the lesser. Thus, on Innocent's analysis, there would be no difficulty if the pope legitimated the illegitimate children of a king at that king's request. The king, who had no feudal overlord, might directly approach the pope without fear of interfering with another ruler's rights.

But the pope conceded that greater difficulty was involved where the person seeking legitimation had a secular overlord who also possessed the power of legitimizing offspring. To address this situation, Innocent offered a series of distinctions. It is clear, he asserted, that with respect to "the patrimony of Peter" — the papal states, where the apostolic see enjoyed both spiritual and secular authority — the pope enjoyed the "authority of legitimizing" (*legitimandi auctoritas*) not only for spiritual but also for temporal purposes.[474]

William of Montpellier had attempted to analogize his situation to that of King Philip Augustus of France, who also had sought papal legitimation of his offspring.[475] Innocent rejected the comparison. Philip had obeyed canon law in obtaining a proper separation from his wife, and had otherwise fulfilled the mandates of the Church.[476] The equities in his case were clear.

William, however, presented a very different case from Philip's. He had violated canon law in seeking a new sexual partner while still formally married to his first wife. Most importantly to Innocent, however, was the question of rights. The king of France did not have a feudal overlord whose rights might be infringed by an act of legitimation for secular purposes.[477] In the case of William, however, to legitimize his sons would do damage to the right of a secular overlord possessed of the authority to legitimize for secular affairs.[478]

Innocent, however, did not mean to renounce entirely the power to legitimize in such circumstances. Based on the equities of a particular case, Innocent declared, the papacy retained power, because of the exalted nature of ecclesiastical authority, to legitimize even for secular purposes, although he did not believe that William's case merited its use.[479]

Kenneth Pennington has observed that the first generation of canonists following Innocent III greeted with scepticism his claim on behalf of an expansive papal authority over the legitimation of children for secular purposes. Both Johannes Teutonicus and Vincentius Hispanus, for instance, asserted that the power to legitimize in these circumstances was more satisfactorily grounded not on papal power over secular affairs, but on "voluntary jurisdiction" *(voluntariam iurisdictionem)* — the agreement of all parties to be bound by the decree of legitimation.[480]

Bernard of Parma made similar arguments against the pope's claim of superiority over temporal jurisdiction. The pope might legitimize for spiritual matters, Bernard wrote, but "it is not proven that he has jurisdiction over temporalities. For legitimation belongs to voluntary jurisdiction," where the parties to the case agreed in advance to be bound by its outcome.[481] Bernard subsequently emphasized: "I believe against [Innocent's claim], namely that the lord pope is not able to legitimize someone to this extent, that one who is not [legitimate] may succeed to an inheritance as if the legitimate heir."[482]

Innocent IV noted — in his private capacity, not in his capacity as universal legislator — that legitimation might take place in the ecclesiastical as well as the civil forum and that one so legitimated enjoyed all the benefits that his superior was empowered to confer on him — he might have his good name restored, he might be allowed to testify in court, or to receive spiritual or civil honors, or to inherit in intestacy.[483] The civil authority, Innocent stressed, might legitimize for secular purposes, but could not legitimize for spiritual purposes.[484] The pope, however, might legitimize for civil as well as spiritual purposes, through the exercise of voluntary jurisdiction.[485] Innocent's analysis thus did not depart substantially from the commentaries of his predecessors.

Hostiensis, however, sought to move the debate in a different direction. He attempted, in the words of one modern commentator, "[to bring] canonists back to the real mind of the legislator."[486] Hostiensis recalled that what was at stake was nothing less than jurisdiction over the sacrament of marriage and all that pertained to it. In his *Summa,* Hostiensis commenced his response by reviewing the arguments of prior critics. "With due respect for the others," Hostiensis continued, "it seems to me that the Lord Pope has the power of legitimizing with regard to spiritualities and temporalities, and [this power belongs to] him alone, as indicated in *Per venerabilem.*"[487]

This conclusion, Hostiensis argued, was the natural consequence of the Church's responsibility to see to the sacral character of the marital relationship. "For the matrimonial cause spiritually so belongs to the Church that a secular judge is not able to take cognizance of it, even incidentally."[488] "Not even," Hostiensis added, "regarding the legitimation of offspring."[489]

Hostiensis's argument had the effect not only of restoring the claims of Innocent III to full vitality after a generation of criticism, but also shifted the premises of the argument: now, it was not a matter of raw papal power that was being asserted, but the necessity to protect marriage and all that belonged to it. Thus Hostiensis as well stripped all secular claims to the power of legitimation, even for secular purposes. It belonged to the Church to legitimize, and to make one eligible to take by inheritance.

Hostiensis added to these claims in his *Lectura.* He acknowledged that "the emperor" had power over temporalities and that "he held this power immediately from God."[490] But this power did not extend over marriage, which belonged to the natural law and the divine law, and against which no contrary custom might prevail.[491] The objection that legitimation did not involve jurisdiction over marriage, but the regularizing of children born outside of wedlock did not occur to Hostiensis, or at least remained unaddressed. His conception of ecclesiastical authority embraced responsibility for family situations of all types, even for such related matters as the passing of secular emoluments to children. This authority, Hostiensis assured his readers, was not grounded in some act of positive law — ecclesiastical or secular — which was changeable and subjected to the whim and caprice of the legislator. No amount of contrary argument could change the enduring naturalness of the pope's responsibility for marriage and all of its incidents.[492]

Hostiensis's defense of an all-encompassing papal jurisdiction over all attributes of marriage was far from universally accepted. One can gauge some sense of the opposition to the pope's position by considering the events surrounding the so-called "statute of Merton" of 1236. Bishop Robert Grosseteste of Lincoln had attempted to reconcile the canon law, which allowed subsequent legitimation by marriage, with the English royal law, which did not. "At Merton," Powicke records, "the magnates refused to listen to the canonists. They doubtless realized that many vested or settled interests would be in jeopardy if they agreed to a change in the law. They were unwilling to change the law of England. *Nolumus leges Angliae mutare*."[493]

Canonists also continued to ponder the extent of papal claims over the power to legitimate children for secular purposes. Some seventy years after Hostiensis's death, Johannes Andreae reviewed the terms of this debate. For the most part, Johannes's gloss to *Per Venerabilem* amounted to an expert summary of the arguments made by Hostiensis and his interlocutors. At the close of his commentary, however, Johannes questioned whether Hostiensis was correct to rely on the category of "marriage" as a means of asserting jurisdiction over legitimation for secular purposes.

The pope's dispensing power, Johannes conceded, was large, but it was not without limits. The pope might only dispense for cause, Johannes argued, because the pope was a man, like all other men, and capable of sin, but unlike other men he had no earthly judge.[494] Hence he, unique among all men, must act with special caution and prudence.

Furthermore, his dispensing power over marriage and other sexual unions was not complete. Johannes distinguished between relationships entirely lacking in marital consent and other types of sexual relationships. The pope lacked the power to supply marital consent where none existed.[495] Therefore, his power to legitimize children of relationships where no consent had been exchanged was limited. He might legitimize on behalf of the Church's own forum (i.e., legitimizing to make one eligible for ecclesiastical office); or in the exercise of the temporal jurisdiction of the papacy (i.e., to make one eligible for secular preferment within the papal states); or in undertaking governance responsibilities for the empire during a time of imperial vacancy (a power exercisable only in extraordinary circumstances).[496] Outside these classes of cases, however, the pope presumably could exercise only the voluntary jurisdiction attributed to him by other canonistic commentators.

Johannes Andreae made it clear that he was here discussing only sexual liaisons entirely lacking in marital consent. But there were other types of unions where marital consent existed in fact, even if not recognized in law (i.e., concubinage). There were also sexual unions forbidden by the canon law that might have achieved the status of marriage had the parties been dispensed from the impediments that prevented a valid exchange of consent (such as men and women religious under solemn vows).[497] Where these conditions have been proven to exist, the pope might exercise his power to dispense in order to legitimize the offspring, provided just cause existed.[498] Johannes's treatment, in short, was a sophisticated attempt to limit the impact of Hostiensis's all-embracing claims.

Standing at the close of this line of development, Panormitanus recited the opinions that had been developed over the prior three centuries. He described the decretal *Per Venerabilem* as a "difficult and very famous one," and conceded the greatness of papal power but, following Johannes Andreae, he asserted that the use of the dispensing power without sufficient cause was sinful. And the pope, Panormitanus assured his readers, was a man who might indeed sin.[499]

This debate had large practical consequences for the inheritance rights of children born of irregular unions. If the arguments of Hostensius had prevailed, children or their parents might have been empowered to look to the ecclesiastical courts for recourse in order to have vindicated their full array of inheritance rights. Such children might have been "legitimized," that is, made eligible to inherit not only their parents' property, but their titles, and their place in feudal society, even over the objections of secular overlords. In the final analysis, the great weight of canonistic opinion drew back from reaching such a potentially radical conclusion. Motivated, no doubt, by considerations of prudence as well as principle, canonists and commentators backed away from endorsing a position that might have allowed children born of irregular relationships to obtain their full array of rights (the *ius legitimorum*) from church tribunals but that would also have had the effect of disrupting the compromises between church and state that had allowed medieval society to function and flourish.

Even in the face of criticism, however, Hostiensis's view of papal authority persisted. Richard Helmholz has called attention to the persistent survival of Hostiensis's way of thinking about legitimation in ecclesiastical documents of the eighteenth century.[500] Pope Benedict XIV wrote of the

Church's responsibility for *miserabiles personae* — "widows, orphans, wards, and others" entrusted to the special care of the Church — that such a charge required jurisdiction, "lest it be ineffective."[501] By implication the "others" included in Benedict's legislation embraced children born out of wedlock.[502] The canonistic model of inheritance, by which offspring were entitled by natural right to a portion of the estate, survived even longer than the claimed ecclesiastical power of legitimation. Indeed, elements of it are still identifiable in the forced heirship requirements found in the law of much of western Europe, Latin America, and the American state of Louisiana.

Summary

What then was meant by the natural right of offspring to inherit? It was, first, a right that stood against another compelling right — the right of testators to dispose of their property. Contrary to Salvian's desire to see the revenue needs of the Church augmented at the expense of the next generation of Christians, neither the theological nor the legal traditions of the Church supported the idea that parents were obliged to give most or all of their property to ecclesiastical causes. St. Augustine admonished that one should treat "Christ" — by whom he meant Christ's Church — as one more son. One should provide the Church with a share equal to that of a child. One should regard the Church as placing a demand on one's wealth equal to a deserving child. One was not obliged to divest oneself of all one's earthly goods as a condition of entering paradise. It was Augustine's teaching, not Salvian's, that was picked up by Gratian and made a continuing feature of the canon law.

St. Augustine's teaching presupposed as well some awareness of what the requirements were with respect to the inheritance rights of sons — and daughters — under Roman law. It was Roman law that Augustine was familiar with. And it was Roman law, in its revived form, which provided the Church with the foundation of inheritance law in the twelfth and thirteenth centuries.

The canonists, however, did not merely incorporate Roman law, without adding their own set of ideas. The most important idea they contributed was the notion that children of legitimate marriages possessed inheritance rights as a kind of natural claim. It was the claim owing by nature, the "legitimate portion" *(legitima portio),* which was theirs by right, absent some showing of truly outrageous conduct. In developing these ideas and this vocabulary, the canonists built on a substructure of Roman law, but designed their structure of inheritance rights in new and compelling ways.

The boundaries of this claim were set by the nature of the relationship the children had with respect to their parents. Children born of legitimate marriage were fully enabled to claim this natural right. Children who had been arrogated into another family possessed the same type of natural claim as those born into the family. Those who had been adopted in simple form — and thus remained under the paternal power of their birth fathers — enjoyed a lesser range of claims, but only because they continued to enjoy rights that came from continued membership in the family of their nativity.

Children born outside of marital unions were placed in a more difficult situation. As made clear in this chapter and elsewhere, the Church enjoined on parents the requirement that such children be provided with adequate support. The canon law favored liberality, while the civil law favored strictness when it came to child support. But matters were different when it came to inheritance rights. With respect to inheritance, one's natural rights were the result of birth in a marital union, not the result of simply being born into the world. The Church might legitimize for some purposes, but legitimation for the purposes of receiving a secular inheritance was always a problematic endeavor, one that took account of practical politics as well as legal theory.

Secular legislators often drew from canonistic sources in defining the rights of heirs to take by will or through intestacy. Indeed, secular legislators and canonists inhabited the same legal universe, and moved in the same circles. It should not be surprising that the *Siete Partidas* of Alfonso the Learned borrowed the canonistic *legitima portio* to describe the share owing offspring. More surprising, and open to question, is the fact that the English moved in a direction so far removed from the Continental, and canonistic, experience.

To a modern American legal audience, conditioned by notions of unfettered testamentary freedom, and conditioned to thinking that children should inherit not by right but by the grace of the testator, these may seem like quaint arguments. But they remain the dominant way of arranging testamentary rights in much of the world. American lawyers and legislators could take a lesson from the writings of the canonists on this subject.

Conclusion

The standard contemporary account of rights, informed by a liberal philosophical tradition that distinguishes sharply between self-regarding acts that are presumed to affect only one's personal well-being and other-regarding acts that have an impact on the larger world, has come to explain rights as powers and prerogatives that an individual might assert against society. Thus individual rights have typically been seen as claims against the government, but rights might also be equally assertable against large institutions, such as universities or corporations, or even against the small units that form the bedrock of society — like the family unit. Rights seen in these terms are preeminently individualistic. They exalt the individual over and above the group, the community, or the institution.

This conception of rights has become wedded, in the course of the twentieth century, to a positivist legal theory that understands as law only the commands of the legislature and appreciates as right and just the will of superior force. One should be clear that this sort of positivistic theorizing does not usually advocate explicitly authoritarian forms of government. In contemporary American jurisprudence the Constitution, seen as an expression of sovereign will, is understood as a guarantee of essential rights and liberties and thus is thought to serve as a bulwark against tyranny. Positivists are among the most zealous advocates of respect for the Constitution and governmental restraint. But it should be stressed that a positivistic starting point serves to obstruct debate about the nature and origin of these rights and liberties. Rights have come to be seen less as natural or as transcendent than as concessions of the sovereign power or as instruments for the accomplishment of certain policies.[1]

Critics and sympathizers alike have come to see this particular com-

212 POWER OVER THE BODY, EQUALITY IN THE FAMILY

bination of legal positivism and individual rights as having its origin in the secularizing project launched by the French Revolution. John Stuart Mill, on this view, represents a nineteenth-century synthesis of these ideas,[2] while John Rawls might be seen as a more contemporary expression. Agnostic about substantive goods and goals, this modern rights-synthesis places its faith in process — the proper process, fastidiously followed, will lead to good results.[3]

Traditionally minded Catholics have been among the sternest critics of this approach to rights. Much better, it has been argued, to rely on notions of obligation and duty. Such, it is thought, is the teaching of the Church's tradition. Obligation and duty will direct us outward, to tend to our neighbor's needs. Rights are egoistic. They are self-directed, indeed, self-centered. They cause us to lose our respect for the needs and circumstances of other persons. Rights run counter to the Christian message of love of neighbor. A strong sense of obligation, on the other hand, will necessarily direct the person toward the good of others.

There is much to be said in favor of this criticism. Rights, in their modern manifestations, often run contrary to the responsibilities and the common decency we owe to others. Regrettably, however, this criticism also obscures the historical record. Rights-based reasoning has a much deeper history than is commonly appreciated. Historically, at the beginning — in the twelfth and thirteenth centuries — rights did not act as wedges that separated people from community. Rather, in their very foundation, rights were understood as grounded in community and in a shared conception of nature and of natural law. In a sense, this book has explored this older, more venerable conception of rights by focusing on one aspect of it — rights in the context of domestic relations law.

The story told in this volume is not meant to be triumphalist. Indeed, there are aspects of the medieval synthesis that we should emphatically not wish to emulate ourselves. We should not be entrapped by the logic of rights in the way, for instance, the author of the *Summa, 'Induent Sancti'* found himself cornered when he endorsed the possibility of the forcible consummation of marriage. A study of the application of rights in this context might thus serve as a cautionary tale on what are the pitfalls of over-reliance on this form of thought when we seek to achieve justice.

It must be stressed, however, that this work is primarily a work of history, not philosophical polemic. It is intended as a reconstruction and analysis of the older understanding of rights developed by the medieval canonists. One can learn a great deal from such a reconstruction. We can appreciate the ways in which a logic of rights compels particular results. We can understand how a theory of rights can co-exist with an underlying theory of natural law, that is, the naturalist premises surrounding marriage and family law. And we can conclude that rights can serve to build up community. Family and domestic relations law, in the medieval canon law, consisted of a series of interlocking rights and duties — husbands, wives, children, and others all had rights as well as obligations. The smooth running of the family depended on the continued coherence of this system.

Notes

Notes to the Introduction

1. John T. Noonan, Jr., "The Family and the Supreme Court," *Catholic University of America Law Review* 23 (1973): 255, 265, 273-74.

2. See *Eisenstadt v. Baird*, 405 U.S. 438, 443-454. As the *Eisenstadt* Court put it: "The question for our determination in this case is whether there is some ground of difference that rationally explains the different treatment accorded married and unmarried persons" with respect to contraceptives. The idea that marriage was that "ground of difference" was rejected by the Court.

A recent commentator has observed that beginning with *Eisenstadt*, "[T]he Supreme Court . . . moved toward displacing marriage from the seat of official morality." See Nancy F. Cott, *Public Vows: A History of Marriage and the Nation* (Cambridge, MA: Harvard University Press, 2000), p. 199.

3. The Supreme Court extended and ratified this manner of thinking about marriage in *Planned Parenthood of Southeastern Pennsylvania v. Casey*, 505 U.S. 833 (1992). Relying on, among other authorities, *Eisenstadt*, Justices Anthony Kennedy, David Souter, and Sandra Day O'Connor, writing for the Court, declared: "At the heart of liberty is the right to define one's own concept of existence, of meaning, of the universe, and of the mystery of human life." *Id.*, at 851. This right trumped Pennsylvania legislation that, among other provisions, required that parents of minors be notified if their children sought an abortion and required a wife to sign a statement that she had informed her husband of her intent to obtain an abortion.

4. See *Baehr v. Lewin*, 74 Haw. 530, 852 P. 2d 44 (1993): "This Court construes marriage 'as a partnership to which both parties bring their financial resources as well as their individual energies and efforts.'" 852 P. 2d at 58 (quoting *Gussin v. Gussin*, 73 Haw. 470, 483, 836 P. 2d 484, 491 [1992]). The *Baehr* Court went on to identify as marital rights:

> "(1) a variety of state income tax advantages, including deductions, credits, rates, exemptions, and estimates [citations omitted]; (2) public assistance from and exemptions relating to the Department of Human Services [citations omitted];

(3) control, division, acquisition, and disposition of community property [citation omitted]; (4) rights relating to dower, curtesy, and inheritance [citations omitted]; (5) rights to notice, protection, benefits, and inheritance [citations omitted]; (6) award of child custody and support payment in divorce proceedings [citations omitted]; (7) the right to spousal support [citations omitted]; (8) the right to enter into premarital agreements [citation omitted]; (9) the right to change of name [citation omitted]; (10) the right to file a nonsupport action [citation omitted]; (11) post-divorce rights relating to support and property divisions [citations omitted]; (12) the benefit of the spousal privilege and confidential marital communications [citation omitted]; (13) the benefit of the exemption of real property from attachment or execution [citation omitted] and (14) the right to bring a wrongful death action [citation omitted]." *Id.,* p. 59.

The understanding of marriage embodied in this catalogue of marital "rights" — many of which are not marital rights at all — might be summarized as the union of two persons joined for mutual economic advantage.

5. Lenore J. Weitzman, *The Marriage Contract: Spouses, Lovers, and the Law* (New York: Free Press, 1981), pp. xx-xxi.

6. Weitzman, *Marriage Contract,* p. xxi.

7. Weitzman, *Marriage Contract,* p. xxi.

8. Bruce Ackerman, *Social Justice in the Liberal State* (New Haven: Yale University Press, 1980), pp. 139-67; Patricia White, *Beyond Domination: An Essay in the Political Philosophy of Education* (London: Routledge and Kegan Paul, 1983), pp. 81-118; and John Holt, *Escape from Childhood* (New York: E. P. Dutton, 1974), pp. 240-48; 277-86. Cf. Stephen G. Gilles, "On Educating Children: A Parentalist Manifesto," *University of Chicago Law Review* 63 (1996), note 2 (collecting these references).

9. Ackerman, *Social Justice,* p. 160.

10. White, *Beyond Domination,* pp. 86-87: "Certain subjects . . . will be ruled out, most notably perhaps religion if taught as a faith to be accepted. Religion as a social phenomenon considered sociologically, historically and a background to the various literatures of the world will, of course, be studied in its major forms. What will not be permitted is conversion of children into good Christians, Moslems, Hindus and so on. This is because imparting and encouraging of particular faiths runs counter to the basic aim of encouraging personal autonomy and allowing children to choose a way of life."

11. Marsha Garrison, "Toward a Contractarian Account of Family Governance," *Utah Law Review* (1998): 241, 269.

12. Garrison, "Toward a Contractarian Account."

13. An early and prescient article examining some of these trends is Mary Ann Glendon, "Marriage and the State: The Withering Away of Marriage," *Virginia Law Review* 62 (1976): 663-720.

14. Judith T. Younger, "Responsible Parents and Good Children," *Journal of Law and Inequality* 14 (1996): 489, 511.

15. Rodolfo and María Valdes, "The Christian Family at the Service of Reconciliation," in *The Pontifical Council for the Family: Marriage and Family* (San Francisco: Ignatius Press, 1989), pp. 165, 167-68.

16. John Kippley, *Sex and the Marriage Covenant: A Basis for Morality* (Cincinnati: Couple to Couple League, 1991), p. 9.

17. Kippley will occasionally speak of "conjugal rights," but the use of this language almost seems like an afterthought, a borrowing from another era. See *Sex and the Marriage Covenant*, pp. 10-11.

18. Cormac Burke, *Covenanted Happiness: Love and Commitment in Marriage* (San Francisco: Ignatius Press, 1990), p. 23.

19. Gregory K. Popcak, *For Better . . . Forever! A Catholic Guide to Lifelong Marriage* (Huntington, IN: Our Sunday Visitor, 1999), p. 21.

20. Donald P. Asci, *The Conjugal Act as a Personal Act: A Study of the Catholic Concept of the Conjugal Act in the Light of Christian Anthropology* (San Francisco: Ignatius Press, 2002).

21. Asci, *Conjugal Act*, p. 287 (quoting Pope John Paul II, *Familiaris consortio* [1981], sec. 11).

22. Asci, *Conjugal Act*, p. 311.

23. Asci, *Conjugal Act*, p. 309.

24. Summarizing some of the developments is Scott Fitzgibbon, "Marriage and the Good of Obligation," *American Journal of Jurisprudence* 47 (2002): 41-69; cf. John J. Coughlin, "Natural Law, Marriage, and the Thought of Karol Wojtyla," *Fordham Urban Law Journal* 28 (2001): 1771-86.

25. *Arcanum Divinae Sapientiae*, sec. I.9.19 (reprinted in *De Matrimonio Christiano* [Rome: Pontificia Universitas Gregoriana, 1942], p. 15).

26. *Arcanum Divinae Sapientiae*, sec. I.8.18, p. 14.

27. *Arcanum Divinae Sapientiae*, sec. I.9.19, p. 15.

28. *Arcanum Divinae Sapientiae*, sec. I.5.14, p. 12 ("Summa quoque in mutuis coniugium iuribus et officiis perturbatio extitit, cum vir dominium uxoris acquireret . . .").

29. *Arcanum Divinae Sapientiae*, sec. I.8.18, pp. 14-15.

30. *Arcanum Divinae Sapientiae*, sec. I.9.19-20 ("Atque illud etiam magnum est quod de potestate patrumfamilias Ecclesia, quantum oportuit, limitaverit, ne filiis et filiabus coniugii cupidis quidquam de iusta liberate minueretur . . .").

31. *Arcanum Divinae Sapientiae*, sec. I.9.20, pp. 15-16.

32. "Ius coniugii naturale ac primigenum . . ." *Rerum Novarum*, sec. 19, reprinted in *Two Basic Social Encyclicals on the Condition of Workers* (Washington, DC: Catholic University of America Press, 1943), p. 14.

33. *Rerum Novarum*, sec. 19, p. 14.

34. See Ernest L. Fortin, "'Sacred and Inviolable': *Rerum Novarum* and Natural Rights," *Theological Studies* 53 (1992): 203, 219: ("[N]atural rights are totally foreign to the literature of the premodern period"). Fortin's thesis is that Leo borrowed heavily from contemporary secular debates about natural rights in formulating his own concept. Marital rights, however, which were conceived of variously as a species of natural and divine right, were widely known and commented upon by medieval writers.

35. Pietro Gasparri, *Tractatus Canonicus de Matrimonio*, 3d ed. (Paris: Beauchesne, 1904), vol. I, sec. 7, pp. 4-5.

36. Gasparri, *Tractatus*, sec. 6, p. 4.

37. Cc. 1111, 1917 Code of Canon Law.

38. "Contractus matrimonialis, cuius principale obiectum mutua traditio iuris in corpora in ordine ad generandum prolem. . . ." See F. X. Wernz and P. Vidal, *Ius Canonicum,* vol. V *(Ius Matrimoniale)* (Rome: Gregorianum, 1925), sec. 599, p. 700.

39. "[I]n *utroque* coniuge sit *aequale ius ad debitum coniugale* stricte exigendum, cui iuri in altero coniuge correspondet *obligatio* strictae iustitiae reddendi debitum exactum nisi iusta causa excuset" (emphasis in original). "[There is] in each party an equal right strictly to claim the conjugal debt, to which right there shall correspond in each party an obligation in strict justice to render the debt when exacted unless excused for just cause." Vol. V, sec. 599, p. 700.

40. Felix Capello, *Tractatus Canonico-Moralis De Sacramentis* (Turin: Marietti, 1950), vol. V *(De Matrimonio),* p. 5.

41. *Dictionary of Moral Theology* (Westminster, MD: Newman Press, 1962), p. 731.

42. "jus et obligationem in hanc intimam communitatem vitae. . . ." *Sacrae Romanae Rotae Decisiones, coram L. Anné,* February 25, 1969, in *Ephemerides Iuris Canonici* 26 (1970): 429.

43. Germain Lesage, "The *Consortium vitae coniugalis:* Nature and Applications," *Studia Canonica* 6 (1972): 99-113 (documenting early developments).

44. On developments in 1970s' rotal jurisprudence, see in particular David E. Fellhauer, "The *Consortium omnis vitae* as a Juridical Element of Marriage," *Studia Canonica* 18 (1979): 7, 125-52.

45. Urbano Navarette, "De Iure ad vitae communionem: Observationes ad Nova Schema Canonis 1086 sec. 2," *Periodica de re morali, canonica, liturgica* 66 (1977): 251-70.

46. See *Digest* 23.2.1: "Nuptiae sunt coniunctio maris et feiminae et consortium omnis vitae, divini et humani iuris communicatio" ("Marriage is a joining of male and female, a consortium of one's entire life, and a participating in the divine and human law"); and *Institutes* 1.9.1: "Nuptiae autem sive matrimonium est viri et mulieris coniunctio, individuam consuetudinem vitae continens." ("Marriage, or, rather, matrimony is a joining of male and female, comprising an individual way of life.")

47. *Sacrae Romane Rotae Decisiones, coram Serrano,* May 9, 1980, *Studia Canonica* 15 (1981): 285, 287. Cf. José Maria Serrano Ruiz, "Le droit à la communauté de vie et d'amour conjugal comme objet de consentement matrimonial," *Studia Canonica* 10 (1976): 271-301 (Serrano setting forth his thoughts on the nature of the object of matrimonial consent).

48. *Wightman v. Wightman,* 4 Johns. Ch. 343, 348 (1820).

49. *Id.,* at 348-349.

50. *Id.* p. 347.

51. *Davis v. Beason,* 133 U.S. 333, 343-344.

52. *Maynard v. Hill,* 125 U.S. 190, 205 (1888).

53. See *Lewis v. Tapman,* 90 Md. 294, 298, 45 A. 459 (1900).

54. *Lewis,* 90 Md.

55. *Campbell's Administrators and Heirs v. Gullatt,* 43 Ala. 57, 67 (1869).

56. Joseph Story, *Commentaries on the Conflicts of Law* (Boston: Hilliard, Gray, and Company, 1834), sec. 108, p. 100.

57. James Schouler, *A Treatise on the Law of Marriage, Divorce, Separation, and Domestic Relations*, 6th ed. (Albany, NY: Matthew Bender & Company, 1921), vol. I, p. 17.

58. On the significance of Joel Bishop's career and contributions to American law, see Stephen A. Siegel, "Joel Bishop's Orthodoxy," *Law and History Review* 13 (1995): 215-59.

59. Joel Prentiss Bishop, *Commentaries on the Law of Marriage and Divorce*, 4th ed. (Boston: Little, Brown, and Company, 1864), vol. I, sec. 322, p. 272 (quoting *Deane v. Aveling*, 1 Robertson's Eccl. Rep. 279).

60. Charles J. Reid, Jr., "The Augustinian Goods of Marriage: The Disappearing Cornerstone of the American Law of Marriage," *Brigham Young Journal of Public Law* 18 (2004): 449-78.

61. It must be stressed, however, that there was also present in nineteenth-century case law a strain of thought that emphasized the origin of marriage in the statutory enactments of the state. Thus one sees in a case like *State v. Duket*, 90 Wis. 272, 63 N.W. 83 (1895) the recognition that marriage serves "the highest interests of society and the state," and that it "[has] more to do with the morals and civilization of a people than any other institution." 90 Wis. at 276, 63 N.W. at 84. For this reason, the Court states, "[t]he power of the legislature over the subject of marriage as a civil *status* is unlimited and supreme. . . ." *Id.*, at 90 Wis. at 277, 63 N.W. at 85. It seems that natural-law and statist ideas about marriage co-existed in the minds of many nineteenth-century lawyers and judges.

62. *Ditson v. Ditson*, 4 R.I. 87, 101 (1856).

63. *Nichols v. Nichols*, 134 Mo. 187, 193, 35 S.W. 577, 578 (1896).

64. *Browning v. Jones*, 52 Ill. 597 (1894), at 604.

65. *Hardin v. Hardin*, 17 Ala. 250 (1850) at 253.

66. *Id.*

67. See, for instance, *Foot v. Card*, 58 Conn. 1, 18 A. 1027 (1889), which rejected the older common-law rule that wives, unlike husbands, could not bring suits for alienation of affection. "[T]he parties . . . in regard to this particular matter of conjugal society," the *Foot* Court wrote, "stand upon an equality." *Id.*, 58 Conn. at 8, 1 A. at 1028. The Court added: "Wherever there is a valuable right and an injury to it, with consequent damage, the obligation is upon the law to devise and enforce such form and mode of redress as will make the most complete reparation." *Id.*, 58 Conn. at 9, 1 A. at 1028. Cf. *Wolf v. Frank*, 92 Md. 138, 48 A. 132 (1900) (allowing suits for alienation of affection where "the marital rights of a woman are unlawfully invaded so as to cause this 'loss of consortium'"). *Id.* 92 Md. at 140, 48 A. 133.

68. See, for example, *Hunt v. Hayes*, 64 Vt. 89, 94, 23 A. 920 (1892).

69. *Biggs v. State*, 29 Ga. 723, 729 (1860).

70. *Nichols v. Nichols, supra*, at 193.

71. *Weigand v. Weigand*, 41 N.J. Eq. 202, 208, 3 A. 699 (1886).

72. *Id.*

73. See *Schneider v. Hasson*, 161 Md. 547, 551, 157 A. 739 (1932).

74. *Walter v. Gunter*, 367 Md. 386, 397, 788 A. 2d 609 (Ct. App., Md., 2002) (quoting William Blackstone, 1 *Commentaries on the Laws of England*, p. 435 (Chicago: University of Chicago Press, 1979) (facsimile of 1765 edition). Cf. *In re Bruce R., et al.*,

234 Conn. 194, 203, 662 A. 2d 107, 112 (1995) (relying upon Blackstone for the "deeply rooted" "obligation" to provide child support. *Id*).

75. *Moss v. Superior Court of Riverside County*, 17 Cal. 4th 396, 409-410, 950 P. 2d 59 (1998) (quoting *Lewis v. Lewis*, 174 Cal. 336, 339 [1917]).

76. See Harold J. Berman, *Law and Revolution: The Formation of the Western Legal Tradition* (Cambridge, MA: Harvard University Press, 1983).

77. Berman, *Law and Revolution*, pp. 120-64.

78. James A. Brundage, *Medieval Canon Law* (London: Longmans, 1995), pp. 47-49.

79. John T. Noonan, "Gratian Slept Here: The Changing Identity of the Father of the Systematic Study of Canon Law," *Traditio* 35 (1979): 145-72. Noonan reviews most of the available biographical data. See also Stanley Chodorow, *Christian Political Theory and Church Politics in the Mid-Twelfth-Century: The Ecclesiology of Gratian's Decretum* (Berkeley: University of California Press, 1972) (hypothesizing Gratian's political commitments from the ecclesiology implicit in the *Decretum*); and Stephan Kuttner, "The Father of the Science of Canon Law," *The Jurist* 1 (1941): 2-19.

80. Stephan Kuttner set the framework for answering these concerns when he asked: "The making of the *Concordia discordantium canonum*, its plan and structure: was it drafted and completed in one grandiose thrust, or did the original version go through successive redactions?" Stephan Kuttner, "Research on Gratian: Acta and Agenda," *Proceedings of the Seventh International Congress of Medieval Canon Law*, Peter Linehan, ed. (Vatican City: Biblioteca Apostolica Vaticana, 1988), pp. 3, 10.

81. Anders Winroth, *The Making of Gratian's Decretum* (Cambridge, UK: Cambridge University Press, 2000).

82. Winroth, *Making of Gratian's Decretum:* "Gratian's *Decretum* is not one book, but two. The *Decretum* that has been known until now was preceded by another, much shorter book, which was almost entirely subsumed into the later version. This explains many of the mysteries that have surrounded the *Decretum* and that have hampered study of this pivotal text. It also raises new questions, about the authorship of the *Decretum*, about the environment in which its author or authors worked, and about the development of legal science and scholarship in the twelfth century." P. 193.

83. See Carlos Larrainzar, "El Decreto de Graciano del Códice Fd (= Firenze, Biblioteca Nazionale Centrale, *Conventi Soppressi* A.I. 402)," *Ius Ecclesiae* 10 (1998): 421-89; José M. Viejo-Ximénez, "La Redacción Original de C. 29 Del Decreto de Graciano," *Ius Ecclesiae* 10 (1998): 148-95; Rudolf Weigand, "Chancen und Probleme einer baldigen kritischen Edition der ersten Redaktions de Dekrets Gratians," *Bulletin of Medieval Canon Law* 22 (1998): 53-75; José M. Viejo-Ximénez, "'Concordia' y 'Decretum' del maestro Graciano," *Ius Canonicum* 39 (1999): 333-47; Carlos Larrainzar, "El Borrador de la Concordia de Graciano: Sankt Gallen, *Stiftsbibliothek* MS. 673 (= Sg)," *Ius Ecclesiae* 11 (1999): 593-666; and Anders Winroth, "Le manuscrit florentin du Décret de Gratien," *Revue de droit canonique* 51 (2001): 211-31.

84. On the structure and type of reasoning found in the *Decretum*, see Brundage, *Medieval Canon Law*, pp. 47-48.

85. James A. Brundage, *Law, Sex, and Christian Society in Medieval Europe* (Chicago: University of Chicago Press, 1987), p. 233.

86. On the dissemination of the *Decretum,* see Brundage, *Medieval Canon Law,* pp. 48-49.

87. On the chief characteristics and concerns of the decretists, see R. Naz, "Décrétistes," *Dictionnaire de droit canonique,* vol. IV (Paris: Letouzey et Ané, 1949), cols. 1065-1067; and Brundage, *Medieval Canon Law,* pp. 49-51.

88. Charles Donahue, Jr., "Roman Canon Law in the Medieval English Church: Stubbs vs. Maitland Re-examined after 75 Years in the Light of Some Records from the Church Courts," *Michigan Law Review* 72 (1974): 681-82. Cf. *Miranda v. Arizona,* 384 U.S. 436 (1966); and *Henningsen v. Bloomfield Motors,* 161 A. 2d 69 (N.J., 1960).

89. Brundage, *Medieval Canon Law,* pp. 53-55.

90. On Raymond's editorial work, see Stephan Kuttner, "Raymond of Peñafort as Editor: The 'decretales' and 'constitutiones' of Gregory IX," *Bulletin of Medieval Canon Law* 12 (1982): 65-80.

91. Brundage, *Medieval Canon Law,* p. 55.

92. For a helpful thumbnail sketch of the major phases in the development of the *Corpus Iuris Canonici,* see Amleto G. Cicognani, *Canon Law* (Philadelphia: Dolphin Press, 1935), pp. 273-321.

93. Brundage, *Medieval Canon Law,* pp. 57-58.

94. J. A. Clarence Smith, *Medieval Law Teachers and Writers* (Ottawa: University of Ottawa Press, 1975), p. 46. See also Stephan Kuttner and Beryl Smalley, "The Glossa Ordinaria to the Gregorian Decretals," *English Historical Review* 60 (1945): 97-105; and Stephan Kuttner, "Notes on the *Glossa Ordinaria* of Bernard of Parma," *Bulletin of Medieval Canon Law* 11 (1981): 86-93.

95. Brundage, *Medieval Canon Law,* p. 225.

96. Brundage, *Medieval Canon Law,* p. 225.

97. A recent and important study of Innocent's career is Alberto Melloni, *Innocenzo IV: La concezione e l'esperienza della cristianità come regimen unius personae* (Genoa: Marietti, 1990). See also Clarence Smith, *Medieval Law Teachers and Writers,* pp. 45-46; Charles Lefebvre, "Sinibalde dei Fieschi (Innocent IV)," *Dictionnaire de droit canonique,* vol. VII (1965), cols. 1029-1062.

98. For Hostiensis's biography, see Clarence Smith, pp. 46-47; Charles Lefebvre, "Hostiensis," *Dictionnaire de droit canonique,* vol. V (1953), cols. 1211-1227; and Kenneth Pennington, "Henricus de Segusio (Hostiensis)," which appears as chapter 16 of Kenneth Pennington, *Popes, Canonists, and Texts, 1150-1550* (Aldershot, UK: Variorum, 1993). See also the important series of articles by Noel Didier, "Henri de Suse in Angleterre (1236?-1244)," in *Studi in onore di Vincenzo Arangio-Ruiz nel XLV anno del suo insegnamento* (Naples: Jovene, 1953), vol. II, pp. 333-51; "Henri de Suse, évêque de Sisteron (1244-1250)," *Revue historique de droit français et étranger* 31 (4th ser., 1953): 244-70; and "Henri de Suse, prévôt de Grasse (1235-1244)," *Studia Gratiana* 2 (1954): 595-617. For a review of the issues involved in dating Hostiensis's work, together with an important bibliography, see Kenneth Pennington, *The Prince and the Law, 1200-1600: Sovereignty and Rights in the Western Legal Tradition* (Berkeley: University of California Press, 1993), p. 49 and notes 45-47.

99. On the rediscovery of Justinian, see the Wolfgang Müller's important study, "The Recovery of Justinian's Digest in the Middle Ages," *Bulletin of Medieval Canon Law* 29 (1990): 1-29.

100. "Justinian's *Digest* . . . completely disappeared in the Latin West. After Pope Gregory the Great last cited it in a letter of 603, the sources remained silent for almost half a millennium." Müller, "Recovery," p. 1.

101. See, for instance, the examples collected by Ernst Levy, *West Roman Vulgar Law: The Law of Property* (Philadelphia: American Philosophical Society, 1951).

102. Harold J. Berman and Charles J. Reid, Jr., "Roman Law in Europe and the *Ius Commune*: A Historical Overview with Emphasis on the New Legal Science of the Sixteenth Century," *Syracuse Journal of International Law and Commerce* 20 (1994): 1, 3, note 2 (quoting Wolfgang Kunkel, *An Introduction to Roman Legal and Constitutional History*, trans. J. M. Kelly [Oxford: Clarendon Press, 1973], p. 162).

103. Manlio Bellomo, *The Common Legal Past of Europe, 1000-1800* (Washington, DC: Catholic University of America Press, 1995), p. 61.

104. Bellomo, *Common Legal Past*, p. 60, note 6 (quoting Odofredus, *Lectura* in D. 1.1.6, *de iustitia et iure*, 1. *ius civile* [Lyon, 1550], fol. 7rb: "Quidam dominus Pepo cepit au[c]toritate sua legere in legibus").

105. Berman, *Law and Revolution*, pp. 123-24.

106. Peter Stein, *Roman Law in European History* (Cambridge, UK: Cambridge University Press, 1999), pp. 54-57.

107. Stein, *Roman Law in European History*, p. 56.

108. Albert Gauthier, *Roman Law and Its Contribution to the Development of Canon Law* (Ottawa: Saint Paul University Press, 1996), pp. 53-62 (property ownership); pp. 63-74 (contractual obligations); pp. 83-99 (procedural norms); and pp. 31-48 (marriage and divorce).

109. Bellomo, *Common Legal Past*, pp. 167-71.

110. An important analysis of the civilian approach to marriage is Charles Donahue, "'The Case of the Man Who Fell into the Tiber': The Roman Law of Marriage at the Time of the Glossators," *American Journal of Legal History* 22 (1978): 1-53.

111. On the contributions of Roman and canon law to the formation of the *ius commune*, see Richard H. Helmholz, *The Ius Commune in England: Four Studies* (Oxford: Oxford University Press, 2001), especially pp. 10-15; and Richard H. Helmholz, *Roman Canon Law in Reformation England* (Cambridge, UK: Cambridge University Press, 1990), especially pp. 12-20.

112. At the end of the twelfth century, Peter of Blois described the resolution of "discordant canons" so that the Church might be better governed as an enterprise distinct from theological speculation. See Peter of Blois, *Speculum Iuris Canonici*, ed. T. A. Reimarus (Berlin: G. Reimeri, 1837), pp. 6-8. Cf. Herbert Kalb, "Bermerkungen zum Verhältnis von Theologie und Kanonistik am Beispiel Rufins und Stephans von Tournai," *Zeitschrift der Savigny-Stiftung für Rechtsgeschichte (kan. Abt.)* 76 (1986): 338, 339.

113. See Rufinus, *Summa decretorum*, ed. Heinrich Singer (Aalen: Scientia Verlag, 1963), p. 9. Cf. John van Engen, "From Practical Theology to Divine Law: The Work and Mind of Medieval Canonists," *Proceedings of the Ninth International Congress of Medieval Canon Law* (Vatican City: Biblioteca Apostolica Vaticana, 1997), pp. 873-74.

114. Van Engen, "From Practical Theology to Divine Law," pp. 874-75.

115. Van Engen, "From Practical Theology to Divine Law," pp. 877-79.

116. On the "individualism" of the era, one might consult: Colin Morris, *The Dis-*

covery of the Individual, 1050-1200 (New York: Harper and Row, 1972); Caroline Walker Bynum, "Did the Twelfth Century Discover the Individual?" *Journal of Ecclesiastical History* 31 (1980): 1-17; and Colin Morris, "Individualism in Twelfth-Century Religion: Some Further Reflections," *Journal of Ecclesiastical History* 31 (1980): 195-206.

117. An important work probing some of the questions is Edouard-Henri Wéber, *La personne humaine au XIIIe siècle: L'avènement chez mâitres parisiens de l'acception moderne de l'homme* (Paris: J. Vrin, 1991); cf. Alain Bourleau, "Droit et théologie au XIII siècle," *Annales ESC* 47 (1992): 1113-25 (examining the concept of personhood in canonistic and theological writing).

118. Writing from a traditional Marxist perspective, C. B. MacPherson asserted boldly that the seventeenth century witnessed the emergence of "a new belief in the value and the rights of the individual." See C. B. MacPherson, *The Political Theory of Possessive Individualism: Hobbes to Locke* (Oxford: Clarendon Press, 1962). MacPherson traced this new belief to the economic changes occurring in England in the seventeenth century and maintained that Hobbes, Locke, and other natural rights philosophers simply "projected these developments onto a hypothetical state of nature and . . . derived political philosophies congruent with their class interests." See Charles J. Reid, Jr., "The Canonistic Contribution to the Western Rights Tradition: An Historical Inquiry," *Boston College Law Review* 33 (1991): 37, 47-48.

Writing from a very different perspective, Leo Strauss and his followers have also maintained that the seventeenth century was decisive for a shift from systems of thought that emphasized transcendent and immutable principles to a way of viewing the world that placed primacy on the competition of all against all and the individual rights that flow from such an a-social struggle. See Leo Strauss, *Natural Right and History* (Chicago: University of Chicago Press, 1953), pp. 120-64. For an example of Catholic Straussian historiography, see Fortin, "'Sacred and Inviolable.'"

119. Michel Villey has made this case most emphatically. Villey's major work of synthesis on this subject is *Le Droit et les droits de l'homme* (Paris: Presses universitaires de France, 1983). For criticism of this approach, see Brian Tierney, "Villey, Ockham, and the Origin of Individual Rights," in John Witte, Jr., and Frank S. Alexander, eds., *The Weightier Matters of the Law: Essays on Law and Religion (A Tribute to Harold J. Berman)* (Atlanta: Scholars Press, 1988), pp. 1-31.

120. See especially Brian Tierney, *The Idea of Natural Rights: Studies on Natural Rights, Natural Law, and Church Law, 1150-1625* (Atlanta: Scholars Press, 1997). For a review of Tierney's contribution in the area of rights-thought, see Charles J. Reid, Jr., "The Medieval Origins of the Western Natural Rights Tradition: The Achievement of Brian Tierney," *Cornell Law Review* 83 (1998): 437-63.

121. Tierney, *Idea of Natural Rights,* pp. 56-58.

122. Brian Tierney, "Origins of Natural Rights Language: Texts and Contexts, 1150-1250," *History of Political Thought* 10 (1989): 615-46; and Brian Tierney, "*Ius* and Metonymy in Rufinus," in Rosalio Castillo Lara, ed., *Studia in Honorem Eminentissimi Cardinalis Alphonsi Stickler* (Rome: LAS, 1992), pp. 549-58.

123. "Est itaque naturale ius vis quedam humane creature a natura insita ad faciendum bonum cavendumque contrarium. Consistit autem ius naturale in tribus, scilicet: mandatis, prohibitionibus, demonstrationibus. . . . Detractum autem ei non est utique in mandatis vel prohibitionibus . . . sed in demonstrationibus, que scilicet natura

non vetat non prohibet, sed bona esse ostendit, et maxime in omnium una libertate. . . ."
Rufinus, *Summa,* D. 1, c. 1, v. *Humanum genus* (quoted in Tierney, "Origins of Natural
Rights Language," p. 632).

124. Tierney, "*Ius* and Metonymy," p. 553.

125. Tierney, "*Ius* and Metonymy," p. 554.

126. "Dicitur ius naturale habilitas quedam qua homo statim est habilis ad
discernendum inter bonum et malum: et secundum hoc dicitur ius naturale facultas —
hoc est liberum arbitrium" (quoted in Tierney, "Origins of Natural Rights Language,"
p. 634, note 76).

127. See Tierney, "Origins of Natural Rights Language," pp. 634-35.

128. Charles J. Reid, Jr., "Thirteenth-Century Canon Law and Rights: The Word
ius and Its Range of Subjective Meanings," *Studia Canonica* 30 (1996): 295-342.

129. Reid, "The Word *ius,*" pp. 314-31.

130. The work of two other scholars has also greatly broadened and deepened our
understanding of early rights-talk. Annabel Brett's *Liberty, Right, and Nature: Individual
Rights in Later Scholastic Thought* (Cambridge: Cambridge University Press, 1997) is an
important examination of the philosophical dimensions of medieval rights talk. Through
a careful reconstruction of the writings on rights of St. Bonaventure, William of
Ockham, John Wyclif, Jean Gerson, and others, Brett establishes that a vocabulary of individual rights was already well-entrenched when the Jesuits and Dominicans of
sixteenth-century Iberia employed rights language to consider the conditions of the na-
tives of the New World in the face of the European arrivals.

In a profoundly creative work, Fred Miller has demonstrated the existence of a
rights vocabulary in the ancient Greek world. Employing among other techniques, a
Hohfeldian analysis of Greek political vocabulary, Miller has demonstrated that the
Greek noun *dikaion* — "the right," or "the just" — also carried a subjective sense of
right-based claims. See Fred D. Miller, *Nature, Justice, and Rights in Aristotle's Politics*
(Oxford: Clarendon Press, 1995), pp. 93-101. Another Greek term, *exousia,* carried the
meaning of another aspect of Hohfeld's category of rights — "liberty." See pp. 101-4. Still
other Greek terms were employed to convey yet more aspects of Hohfeld's taxonomy of
rights. Thus *akuros* meant "without authority," or immunity. See pp. 105-6. Miller has
continued exploring these themes. See Fred D. Miller, "Legal and Political Rights in
Demosthenes and Aristotle," in George Anagnostopoulos, ed., *Law and Rights in the Ancient Greek Tradition* (Berkeley: University of California Press) (forthcoming). On
Hohfeld's categories, consult preeminently Wesley N. Hohfeld, *Fundamental Legal Conceptions as Applied in Judicial Reasoning* (New Haven, CT: Yale University Press, 1923),
especially pp. 36-64.

131. See Charles J. Reid, Jr., "Rights in Thirteenth-Century Canon Law: An Historical Investigation" (Cornell University Ph.D. dissertation, 1995), pp. 428-39.

132. See Bernard of Parma, *Glossa ordinaria,* X.1.2.2, v. *culpa caret.* "Paupertas,
odium, vitium, favor, scelus, et ordo. Personas spoliant et loca iure suo." The edition
consulted is *Decretales D. Gregorii papae suae integritati una cum glossis restitutae* (Rome,
1582).

133. See Reid, "Rights in Thirteenth-Century Canon Law," pp. 428-39 (collecting
examples).

134. Brundage, *Sex, Law, and Christian Society in Medieval Europe.*

135. John T. Noonan, Jr., *Contraception: A History of Its Treatment by the Catholic Theologians and Canonists*, enlarged ed. (Cambridge, MA: Harvard University Press, 1986).

136. John T. Noonan, Jr., *Power to Dissolve: Lawyers and Marriages in the Courts of the Roman Curia* (Cambridge, MA: Harvard University Press, 1972).

137. Richard H. Helmholz, *Marriage Litigation in Medieval England* (Cambridge: Cambridge University Press, 1974); and Richard H. Helmholz, *Canon Law and the Law of England* (London: Hambledon Press, 1987).

138. John Witte, Jr., *From Sacrament to Contract: Marriage, Religion, and Law in the Western Tradition* (Louisville, KY: John Knox Press, 1997).

139. Witte, *From Sacrament to Contract*, pp. 3-5, 16-41.

140. Witte also provides an important account of the reformers' criticisms of canonistic marriage in his *Law and Protestantism: The Legal Teachings of the Lutheran Reformation* (Cambridge, UK: Cambridge University Press, 2002), pp. 214-55.

Notes to Chapter 1

1. "Introduction," in C. H. Talbot, ed. and trans., *The Life of Christina of Markyate: A Twelfth Century Recluse* (Toronto: University of Toronto Press, 1998), pp. 10-15. See also Christopher J. Holdsworth, "Christina of Markyate," in Derek Baker, ed., *Medieval Women* (Oxford: Basil Blackwell, 1978), pp. 185-204.

2. *Life of Christina of Markyate*, pp. 36-41.

3. *Life of Christina of Markyate*, pp. 40-43.

4. *Life of Christina of Markyate*, pp. 44-45.

5. *Life of Christina of Markyate*, pp. 44-47.

6. *Life of Christina of Markyate*, pp. 46-47 ("[E]t eadem hora Burthredus illam in coniugem sibi desponsavit," p. 46).

7. *Life of Christina of Markyate*, p. 46.

8. *Life of Christina of Markyate*, pp. 46-49.

9. *Life of Christina of Markyate*, pp. 50-51.

10. *Life of Christina of Markyate*, p. 50.

11. *Life of Christina of Markyate*, p. 50.

12. *Life of Christina of Markyate*, pp. 50-53.

13. *Life of Christina of Markyate*, pp. 58-59.

14. *Life of Christina of Markyate*, p. 60.

15. *Life of Christina of Markyate*, p. 60.

16. *Life of Christina of Markyate*, p. 62.

17. *Life of Christina of Markyate*, pp. 62-63.

18. *Life of Christina of Markyate*, p. 64.

19. *Life of Christina of Markyate*, pp. 68-70.

20. *Life of Christina of Markyate*, pp. 70-72.

21. C. 1057, sec. 1.

22. C. 1057, sec. 2.

23. C. 1058.

24. John P. Beal, James A. Coriden, and Thomas J. Green, eds., *New Commentary on the Code of Canon Law* (New York: Paulist Press, 2000), p. 1254.

25. John XXIII, *Pacem in Terris, Acta Apostolicae Sedis* 55 (1963), pp. 257, 261.

26. *Pacem in Terris*, p. 259.

27. *Pacem in Terris*, p. 259.

28. *Id.*, p. 261: "adeoque aut sibi condere familiam, in qua condenda vir et mulier paribus fruantur iuribus et officiis. . . ." John's use of the verb *fruantur* carries with it a rich set of connotations, not only of enjoyment but even of delight and pleasure.

29. *Loving v. Virginia*, 388 U.S. 1 (1967).

30. *Id.*, at 12.

31. *Id.* (quoting *Skinner v. Oklahoma*, 316 U.S. 535, 541 (1942)).

32. Diana C. Moses uses Livy's treatment of the literary figure of Lucretia to explore the degree to which even coerced consent carried with it real consequences. See Diana C. Moses, "Livy's Lucretia and the Validity of Coerced Consent in Roman Law," in Angeliki E. Laiou, *Consent and Coercion to Sex and Marriage in Ancient and Medieval Societies* (Washington, DC: Dumbarton Oaks Research Library, 1993), pp. 39-81. See also Richard P. Saller, "The Social Dynamics of Consent to Marriage and Sexual Relations: The Evidence of Roman Comedies," in Laiou, ed., *Consent and Coercion*, pp. 83-104. "The negotiations leading to consent to marriage could be presented in terms of the father's *potestas* being obeyed out of *pietas*, or resisted and manipulated by his children's appeals to paternal *officium* and affection" (p. 104).

33. James Brundage, *Law, Sex, and Christian Society* (Chicago: University of Chicago Press, 1987), p. 33: "Roman marriage began with betrothal, an enforceable agreement between the heads of two households concerning the future union of two persons — a member from each group."

34. *Digest* 23.1.11. The references to Roman law here and elsewhere in this volume are derived from the three-volume edition of the *Corpus Iuris Civilis*, ed. Paul Krueger, Theodor Mommsen, Rudolf Schoell, and Wilhelm Kroll (Hildesheim: Weidmannsche Verlagsbuchhandlung, 2000).

35. *Digest* 23.1.12.

36. *Id.* ("si indignum moribus vel turpem . . .").

37. *Codex* 5.1.1.

38. *Codex* 5.4.20 provided that where a woman was *sui iuris* and also under the age of twenty-five, the consent of her father remained a requirement for marriage. Presumably, once she passed the age of twenty-five she was freed of this necessity.

39. *Digest* 23.1.13.

40. *Digest* 23.1.14.

41. *Digest* 23.1.4.

42. *Digest* 23.1.5.

43. *Digest* 23.1.7.

44. *Digest* 23.1.10.

45. *Codex* 5.4.1.

46. *Digest* 23.1.10.

47. See Susan Treggiari, *Roman Marriage*, pp. 93-94.

48. Treggiari, *Roman Marriage*, p. 94.

49. Treggiari, *Roman Marriage*, p. 95.

50. Treggiari, *Roman Marriage,* p. 97.

51. Treggiari, *Roman Marriage,* p. 95.

52. *Digest* 23.2.2.

53. *Digest* 23.2.18.

54. *Digest* 23.2.35 ("sine patris voluntate").

55. *Digest* 23.2.9.

56. *Digest* 23.2.9.

57. *Digest* 23.2.10.

58. *Digest* 23.2.11.

59. *Codex* 5.4.14.

60. *Codex* 5.4.14.

61. *Digest* 23.2.21.

62. *Digest* 23.2.22.

63. See p. 30, above. Cf. *Digest* 23.1.12.

64. St. Jerome to Amandus, Letter 55, PL 22: 562-63. Cf. John T. Noonan, Jr., "Power to Choose," *Viator* 4 (1973): 419, 422-23. The abbreviation PL, used here and elsewhere, stands for the *Patrologia Latina,* ed. J.-P. Migne (Paris, 1844-64).

65. St. Jerome, Letter 55, PL 22: 419, 422-23. Cf. Noonan, "Power to Choose," pp. 422-23.

66. St. Jerome, Letter 55, PL 22: 562-63.

67. Leo to Rusticus, Letter 157, PL 54: 1199. Cf. Noonan, "Power to Choose," p. 423.

68. Noonan, "Power to Choose," p. 423.

69. *Codex Theodosianus,* ed. Paul Krueger and Theodor Mommsen (Hildesheim: Weidmannsche Verlagsbuchhandlung, 2000), 3.5.5.

70. *Codex Theodosianus* 3.5.5.

71. *Codex Theodosianus* 3.5.12.

72. *Codex Theodosianus* 3.5.12.

73. *Codex Theodosianus* 3.5.12.

74. *Codex Theodosianus* 3.5.12: "[S]i humano casu, antequam puella iungatur, mortuus fuerit pater, mutari placitum nulla poterit ratione, nec habebit puella licentiam aliud faciendi, etiamsi mater tutor aut curator vel propinqui alium voluerint fortasse suscipere. . . ."

75. *Lex Visigothorum* III, 1. 2, in *Monumenta Germaniae Historica, Legum Sectio* I, vol. I (Hanover, 1902), p. 122.

76. *Lex Visigothorum,* III, 1. 3, p. 124.

77. *Concilium Aurelianiense* c. 22, in *Monumenta Germaniae Historica, Legum Sectio III, Concilia,* vol. I, *Concilia Aevi Merovingici* (Hanover: Hahn, 1893), p. 92.

78. *Concilium Baiuwaricum* c. 12, in *Monumenta Germaniae Historica, Legum Sectio III (Concilia),* vol. II, part 1 *(Concilia Aevi Karolini)* (Hanover: Hahn, 1896), p. 53.

79. Brundage, *Law, Sex, and Christian Society,* p. 173.

80. Brundage, *Medieval Canon Law* (London: Longmans, 1995), p. 32.

81. Regino of Prüm, *Libri duo de Synodalibus,* bk. II, c. 107, PL 132: 183, 305.

82. See *Decreta Evaristi Papae (Pseudo-Evaristus),* in Paulus Hinschius, ed., *Decretales Pseudo-Isidorianae et Capitula Angilramni* (Aalen: Scientia Verlag, 1963), p. 87 (= PL 130: 81). Cf. Benedict the Levite, c. 463, at PL 97: 859. Like the decrees of Pope

Evaristus, the writings of Benedict the Levite are also ninth-century forgeries. On these collections generally, see Brundage, *Medieval Canon Law*, pp. 26-27.

83. Philip Lyndon Reynolds, *Marriage in the Western Church: The Christianization of Marriage during the Patristic and Early Medieval Periods* (Leiden: E. J. Brill, 1994), p. 391.

84. On Hincmar and his contributions to marital theory generally, see Brundage, *Law, Sex, and Christian Society*, pp. 136-37.

85. Epistle 22, PL 126: 132-53.

86. Epistle 22, PL 126, col. 133.

87. Epistle 22, PL 126: 133.

88. Epistle 22, PL 126: 133.

89. Epistle 22, PL 126: 137. "Tamen dicere necessarium duximus, et inter aequales legitima fiunt conjugia, cum a parentibus, quorum interest, petita, et legaliter desponsata, et dotata, et publiciis nuptiis honorata femina conjugii copulae sociatur, et ex duobus unum corpus unaque caro efficitur."

90. Hincmar of Rheims, "De Divortio Lotharii Regis et Tetbergae Reginae," reprinted in Letha Böhringer, ed., *De Divortio Lotharii Regis et Theutbergae Reginae* (Hannover: Hahnsche Buchhandlung, 1992) (*Monumenta Germaniae Historica, Concilia,* vol. 4, supp. 1) (= PL 125: 619-772). Hincmar's defense of Theutberga's marriage was written in the context of this case. Theutberga was the queen of Lothar II (855-869), king of Lotharingia. Lothar had been compelled by reason of politics to marry Theutberga, although he remained romantically attracted to his mistress Waldrada. He had a child by Waldrada and, in order to legitimize his son and ensure a smooth succession, he sought to divorce his queen on the grounds of various alleged immoral and criminal actions. The case sparked an intense controversy that endured for several years and involved Pope Nicholas I, who decreed that king and queen must remain together. See Suzanne Fonay Wemple, *Women in Frankish Society: Marriage and the Cloister, 500-900* (Philadelphia: University of Pennsylvania Press, 1981), pp. 84-87.

91. See *De Divortio Lotharii Regis*, ed. Böhringer, p. 133 (= PL 125: 648).

92. *De Divortio Lotharii Regis*, ed. Böhringer, p. 133. Cf. Matthew 1:18.

93. *De Divortio Lotharii Regis*, ed. Böhringer, p. 133 (= PL 125: 648-49).

94. *De Divortio Lotharii Regis*, ed. Böhringer, p. 133 (= PL 125: 649).

95. This section title is borrowed from the important article by John Noonan bearing this title, "Power to Choose" (see note 64, above). My own debt to Noonan's work on this topic will be readily apparent.

96. C. 31, pr. The edition of the medieval canon law cited here and elsewhere is Emil Friedberg, ed., *Corpus Iuris Canonici* (Leipzig: Officina Bernhardi Tauchnitz, 1879). The citation system used when referring to Gratian or to other medieval canonistic sources generally conforms to that found in Brundage, *Medieval Canon Law*, pp. 190-202.

97. C. 31, pr.

98. C. 31, pr.

99. C. 31, pr.

100. C. 31, pr.

101. C. 31, pr.

102. C. 31, pr.

103. C. 31, pr.

104. Noonan, "Power to Choose," p. 419. On the identification of Isaac, see his note 1.

105. C. 31, q. 2, d.a.c. 1.

106. Noonan, "Power to Choose," p. 419.

107. See C. 31, q. 2, c. 1. Cf. Noonan, "Power to Choose," pp. 419-20 (reviewing the background of this case).

108. See C. 31, q. 2, c. 1.

109. C. 31, q. 2, c. 1.

110. C. 31, q. 2, c. 1.

111. Noonan, "Power to Choose," p. 420.

112. Noonan, "Power to Choose," p. 420.

113. Noonan, "Power to Choose," p. 420.

114. C. 31, q. 2, c. 3.

115. C. 31, q. 2, c. 3.

116. C. 31, q. 2, c. 3.

117. C. 31, q. 2, c. 3.

118. C. 31, q. 2, c. 3.

119. Noonan, "Power to Choose," p. 421.

120. Regarding this case, see above, pp. 36-37.

121. C. 31, q. 2, c. 4.

122. C. 31, q. 2, c. 4.

123. See Noonan, "Power to Choose," p. 421.

124. Noonan, "Power to Choose," p. 426.

125. C. 31, q. 2, d.p.c. 4.

126. C. 31, q. 2, c. 2.

127. C. 31, q. 3, c. 1.

128. C. 31, q. 3, d.p.c. 1.

129. See, for instance, C. 32, q. 7, c. 7 (quoting St. Jerome's letter to Amandus); C. 32, q. 2, c. 12 (quoting Leo the Great on the blamelessness of wives who are married by parental authority to husbands who keep concubines); C. 30, q. 5, c. 3 (quoting Pope Nicholas I's letter instructing his Bulgarian correspondents that at Rome marriage is celebrated with the consent of those in whose power the couple happens to be). Regarding these texts, Noonan has observed: "Gratian's freedom of maneuver was such that none of these relevant passages was brought to bear upon the question, 'May a daughter be given in marriage against her will?'" See "Power to Choose," p. 424.

130. C. 36, q. 2, c. 8. On this text, see above, p. 35.

131. C. 36, q. 2, c. 11.

132. C. 36, q. 2, d.p.c. 11.

133. C. 32, q. 2, c. 12. See also above, pp. 33-34.

134. C. 32, q. 2, c. 12.

135. C. 32, q. 2, d.p.c. 12.

136. See above, pp. 35-36.

137. See Michael M. Sheehan, "Choice of Marriage Partner in the Middle Ages: Development and Theory of Marriage," reproduced in Michael M. Sheehan, *Marriage, Family, and Law in Medieval Europe: Collected Studies* (Toronto: University of Toronto Press, 1996), pp. 87, 97. Sheehan concedes that "[i]t is true that, even in the context of

the *Decretum*, the word 'legitimate' might be read in terms of liceity rather than validity — as, in fact, it would be interpreted by later commentators"(p. 97). Sheehan, however, would prefer to read this passage as nevertheless requiring parental consent "for the validity of the marriage." It is probably better, however, to agree with Brundage that the question was simply "left open" by Gratian. See Brundage, *Law, Sex, and Christian Society*, p. 238. Read in the context of Gratian's own preference for free consent, as articulated in *Causa* 31, *quaestio* 2, it seems unlikely Gratian would have reversed field here.

138. See Paucapalea, *Summa über das Decretum Gratiani* (Aalen: Scientia Verlag, 1965), C. 31, q. 2, p. 124.

139. Paucapalea, *Summa*, C. 31, pr., p. 123. On problems with the editorial decision to credit this work to Paucapalea, see John T. Noonan, Jr., "The True Paucapalea?" in *Proceedings of the Fifth International Congress of Medieval Canon Law* (1980): 157-86. Noonan's conclusions have been questioned by Rudolf Weigand, "Paucapalea und die frühe Kanonistik," *Archiv für Katholisches Kirchenrecht* 150 (1981): 138-50.

140. See Rolandus, *Summa Magistri Rolandi*, ed. Friedrich Thaner (Aalen: Scientia Verlag, 1962), C. 32, q. 2, d.p.c. 12, v. *paterno arbitrio, etc.*, p. 168.

141. Rolandus, *Summa*, pp. 168-69. Cf. Genesis 24:53-60.

142. Rolandus, *Summa*, p. 168.

143. See Rufinus, *Summa*, C. 32, q. 2, d.p.c. 12, v. *cum dicitur paterno arbitrio*, p. 483.

144. Rufinus, *Summa*, p. 483.

145. See Gérard Fransen and Stephan Kuttner, eds., *Summa, 'Elegantius in Iure Divino'* (Vatican City: Biblioteca Apostolica Vaticana, 1969-90), vol. IV, p. 33.

146. *Summa, 'Elegantius in Iure Divino,'* vol. IV, p. 33.

147. *Summa, 'Elegantius in Iure Divino,'* vol. IV, p. 35.

148. See *Summa, 'Induent Sancti,'* C. 31, q. 2. The edition of the *Summa, 'Induent Sancti'* consulted for this work is the one prepared by Richard Fraher as part of his doctoral work at Cornell University. See Richard Michael Fraher, *Summa, 'Induent Sancti': A Critical Edition of a Twelfth-Century Canonical Treatise* (Cornell University Ph.D. dissertation: Ithaca, NY, 1978), p. 626.

149. *Summa, 'Induent Sancti,'* ed. Fraher, pp. 626-27. Cf. *Digest* 4.2.21.5.

150. *Summa, 'Induent Sancti,'* p. 627.

151. Johannes Teutonicus, *Glossa Ordinaria*, C. 31, q. 2, pr, v. *quod autem:* "Hic queritur an aliqua sit cogenda nubere et respondendum est, quod non; quia in matrimonio animus debet gaudere plena libertate." The edition consulted is *Decretum Gratiani emendatum et notationibus illustratum una cum glossis* (Venice, 1584).

152. Johannes Teutonicus, *Glossa Ordinaria*, C. 32, q. 2, c. 12, v. *legitima*.

153. See Peter of Poitiers, *Sententiarum Libri Quinque*, bk. V. 14, PL 211: 1257.

154. Bk. V. 14, PL 211: 1257.

155. Bk. V. 14, PL 211: 1259. Peter stressed as well that as a result of this consent each party subjected himself or herself to the "law" (*legi*) of the other, at least insofar as the rendering of the conjugal debt was concerned.

156. On the attribution of this work, see Noonan, *Contraception: A History of Its Treatment by the Catholic Theologians and Canonists*, enlarged ed. (Cambridge, MA: Harvard University Press, 1986), p. 175, note 9 and the source therein cited.

157. See *Summa Sententiarum*, bk. VII.6, PL 176: 158.

158. Bk. VII.6, PL 176: 159.

159. Bk. VII.6, PL 176: 159: "Ex hac auctoritate intelligitur conjugium fieri inter consentientes et spontaneos, et non inter renuentes et invitos."

160. See Peter Lombard, *Sententiarum Libri Quattuor* (Paris: Vivés, 1892), bk. IV, dist. 29, p. 668.

161. Lombard, *Sententiae,* p. 668. Cf. above, pp. 38-40.

162. Lombard, *Sententiae,* p. 668: "Ex his apparet, conjugium fieri inter consentientes et spontaneos, non inter renitentes et invitos."

163. Lombard, *Sententia,* p. 668: ". . . facultate discedendi vel reclamandi habita. . . ."

164. Lombard, *Sententia,* p. 668.

165. See Charles Donahue, Jr., "The Policy of Alexander the Third's Consent Theory of Marriage," *Proceedings of the Fourth International Congress of Medieval Canon Law* (Vatican City: Biblioteca Apostolica Vaticana, 1976): 251-81; and Charles Donahue, "The Dating of Alexander the Third's Marriage Decretals," *Zeitschrift der Savigny-Stiftung für Rechtsgeschichte (kan. Abt.)* 68 (1982): 70-124.

166. X.4.1.14.

167. X.4.1.14. "Cum locum non habeat consensus ubi metus vel coactio intercedit, necesse est, ubi assensus cuiusdam requiritur, coactionis materia repellitur."

168. X.4.1.15.

169. X.4.1.15.

170. See John T. Noonan, Jr., "The Steady Man: Process and Policy in the Courts of the Roman Curia," *California Law Review* 58 (1970): 628, 654.

171. X.4.1.29.

172. X.4.1.29.

173. How much practical effect *Gemma* had is difficult to determine. One can certainly identify situations in the Middle Ages where parents exerted financial pressures on their offspring in order to marry in accord with parental wishes. Parents could and did, for instance, disinherit children who resisted parental marriage plans. See Juliette Turlan, "Recherches sur le mariage dans la pratique coutumière, xii-xiv. siècles," *Revue d'histoire de droit français et étranger* 35 (1957): 477, 487-89. At the same time, a writer such as Pierre de la Palude cautioned fathers that they would commit a wrong by disinheriting children who married clandestinely. See Brundage, *Law, Sex, and Christian Society,* p. 443.

174. See Tancred, *Summa de Matrimonio,* ed. Agathon Wunderlich (Göttingen: Vandenhoeck and Ruprecht, 1841), p. 46.

175. Tancred, *Summa de Matrimonio,* p. 46. "Nam ubi metus vel coactio intercedit, non potest consensus locum habere [citation omitted]."

176. Tancred, *Summa de Matrimonio,* p. 46. "Ergo si consensus non locum habet, nec matrimonium aliquod est, quod solo consensu contrahitur."

177. Tancred, *Summa de Matrimonio,* p. 46.

178. Tancred, *Summa de Matrimonio,* p. 47.

179. See *Glossa Ordinaria,* X.4.1.15, v. *in virum constantem.*

180. *Glossa Ordinaria,* X.4.1.15, v. *ut uxorem.*

181. *Glossa Ordinaria,* X.4.1.29, *casus.*

182. Innocent IV, *Apparatus in V Libros Decretalium* (Frankfurt, 1570; repr. 1841), X.4.1.14, v. *coactio*.

183. See Hostiensis, *Lectura* (Turin: Bottega d'Erasmo, 1965), X.4.1.15, v. *in constantem*. On Hostiensis's analysis of force and fear in the case of women, see p. 56.

184. See Raymond de Peñafort, *Summa de Penitentia*, ed. Xavier Ochoa and Aloisio Diez (Rome: Commentarium pro religiosis, 1978), col. 370.

185. Raymond de Peñafort, *Summa de Penitentia*, cols. 370-71.

186. Raymond de Peñafort, *Summa de Penitentia*, col. 371.

187. Raymond de Peñafort, *Summa de Penitentia*, col. 371. Cf. *Digest* 4.2.1.

188. Raymond de Peñafort, *Summa de Penitentia*, ed. Xavier Ochoa and Aloisio Diez (Rome: Commentarium pro religiosis, 1978), col. 372; *Summa de Matrimonio*, cols. 955-57.

189. See Raymond de Peñafort, *Summa de Matrimonio*, col. 955.

190. *Summa de Matrimonio*, col. 956.

191. *Summa de Matrimonio*, cols. 956-57.

192. *Summa de Matrimonio*, col. 957.

193. *Summa de Matrimonio*, col. 957. "[E]t sic iudex secundum diversitatem personarum et locorum iudicabit qualis sit metus, et iudicabit matrimonium aliquod, vel nullum."

194. See, for example, X.4.15.2 and X.4.15.3.

195. See Richard Flathman, *The Practice of Rights* (Cambridge, UK: Cambridge University Press, 1976), p. 154.

196. See *infra*, Chapter Two, on paternal power.

197. See Brundage, *Law, Sex, and Christian Society*, p. 438. Cf. Diane Owen Hughes, "Urban Growth and Family Structure in Medieval Genoa," *Past and Present* 66 (1975): 3-28 (documenting familial constraints that limited free choice of marriage partners among urban elites).

198. See Reid, "The Canonistic Contribution to the Western Rights Tradition: An Historical Inquiry," *Boston College Law Review* 33 (1991): 78.

199. See Hostiensis, *Summa* (Lyon, 1537; repr. Aalen: Scientia Verlag, 1962), bk. I, *de postulando*, sec. 2.

200. See X.4.1.23; X.4.1.25.

201. X.4.8.2.

202. X.4.9.1. Hadrian's decretal and the commentary it generated is the subject of Peter Landau's study, "Hadrians IV Dekretale 'Dignum Est' (X.4.9.1.) und die Eheschliessung Unfreier in der Diskussion von Kanonisten und Theologen des 12. und 13. Jahrhunderts," *Studia Gratiana* 12 (Collectanea Stephan Kuttner, 1967): 511-53. See also below, Chapter Three, pp. 122-26 (on the conjugal rights of the servile).

203. Sicard wrote: "Then it is asked whether a marriage may take place between a serf and a servant girl when their lords do not know, or know and refuse permission. It should happen in this manner. All persons are by natural law free, even them. Whence they are able to do all those things permitted by the natural law. But the conjunction of man and woman is a part of the natural law. Therefore even they are able to contract marriage." ["Deinde queritur utrum nescientibus dominis vel etiam scientibus et contradicentibus matrimonium sit inter servum et ancillam. Quod fit in hunc modum. Omnes homines de naturali iure sunt liberi, quia isti. Unde et ea que sunt iuris naturalis

possunt facere. Set coniunctio maris et femine est de iure naturali, ergo et isti possunt contrahere matrimonium."] Quoted in Landau, "Dignum Est," p. 532, note 99, quoting Sicard at C. 29, q. 2, c. 8.

204. See Bernard of Pavia, *Summa de Matrimonio* in Bernard of Pavia, *Summa decretalium* (Graz: Akademische -u. Verlagsanstalt, 1956), pp. 294-95.

205. See Hostiensis, *Lectura*, X.4.1.23, v. *surdus*. Hostiensis explained that persons laboring under such handicaps were still able to understand sexuality and could still make use of natural reason, even if unable to express himself or herself: "[Q]uia talis cognoscere potest mulierem, et naturali utitur ratione, licet illam non possit exprimere."

206. See Raymond de Peñafort, *Summa de Matrimonio*, col. 916.

207. *Summa de Matrimonio*, col. 928.

208. *Glossa Ordinaria*, X.4.9.1., v. *inter servos*.

209. See *Glossa Ordinaria*, X.4.1.24, v. *furore*. The decretalists also seem to have been untroubled by interracial marriages. Legislation in the crusading kingdom was directed at marriages between those of different faiths, not those of different ethnic backgrounds. See James A. Brundage, "Prostitution, Miscegenation, and Sexual Purity in the First Crusade," in P. W. Edbury, ed., *Crusade and Settlement: Papers Read at the First Conference of the Society for the Study of the Crusades and Presented to R. C. Small* (Cardiff, Wales: University Press, 1985), pp. 57-65.

210. See Brundage, *Law, Sex, and Christian Society*, p. 431.

211. Regarding the relationship of freedom to the sacrament of marriage, Hugh of St. Victor wrote: "Married persons have a sacrament, who by equal consent have mutually agreed to keep an indivisible society, which society God has instituted between a man and a woman." [Sacramentum autem coniugii habent, qui pari consensu ad eam quae a Deo inter masculum et feminam instituta est societatem indivise ad invicem conservandam convenerunt."] *De sacramentis*, PL 176: 498. Cf. Seamus P. Heaney, *The Development of the Sacramentality of Marriage from Anselm of Laon to Thomas Aquinas* (Washington, DC: Catholic University of America Press, 1963), p. 88 (quoting and analyzing Hugh of St. Victor).

212. See above, p. 36.

213. C. 30, q. 5, c. 1. On pseudo-Evaristus, see above, pp. 35-36.

214. C. 30, q. 5, c. 1.

215. C. 30, q. 5, c. 3.

216. C. 30, q. 5, d.p.c. 6.

217. C. 30, q. 5, c. 7.

218. C. 30, q. 5, c. 8. Cf. Genesis 24:63-67.

219. C. 30, q. 5, d.p.c. 8.

220. C. 30, q. 5, d.p.c. 8.

221. C. 30, q. 5, d.p.c. 8.

222. The abruptness and the inconsistencies found in this part of the *Decretum* may be the result of the problems identified in the received text by Anders Winroth. See above, pp. 12-13.

223. See Raymond G. Decker, "Institutional Authority Versus Personal Responsibility in the Marriage Sections of Gratian's *A Concordance of Discordant Canons*," *The Jurist* 32 (1972): 51, 57.

224. See Paucapalea, *Summa*, C. 30, q. 5, p. 123. Cf. C. 30, q. 5, d.p.c. 9.

225. *The Summa Parisiensis on the Decretum Gratiani*, ed. Terence P. McLaughlin (Toronto: Pontifical Institute of Medieval Studies, 1952), C. 30, q. 5, p. 237.

226. *Summa Parisiensis*, ed. McLaughlin, p. 237.

227. See Rufinus, *Summa*, C. 30, q. 5, p. 468.

228. Rufinus, *Summa*, C. 30, q. 5, p. 468.

229. Rufinus, *Summa*, C. 30, q. 5, p. 468.

230. X.4.3.1.

231. X.4.3.2.

232. X.4.3.3.

233. X.4.3.3.

234. X.4.16.1.

235. X.4.16.1.

236. See Innocent IV, *Apparatus*, X.4.3.3., v. *proponantur.*

237. Hostiensis, *Summa*, bk. IV, *De Matrimoniis*, sec. 10.

238. Hostiensis, *Summa*, bk. IV, *De Matrimoniis*, sec. 10.

239. See Hostiensis, *Summa*, bk. IV, *De Clandestina Desponsatione*.

240. *De Clandestina Desponsatione*, sec. 1.

241. *De Clandestina Desponsatione*, sec. 1.

242. *De Clandestina Desponsatione*, sec. 1.

243. *De Clandestina Desponsatione*, sec. 1.

244. *De Clandestina Desponsatione*, sec. 1. Hostiensis provides a slightly different list in his *Lectura*. See *Lectura*, X.4.3.1. See also Brundage, *Law, Sex, and Christian Society*, pp. 440-41.

245. Hostiensis, *Summa*, bk. IV, *De Clandestina Desponsatione*, sec. 1.

246. Surveying the records of English ecclesiastical courts, Richard Helmholz has noted the extreme imaginativeness parties exercised in their choice of where and how to marry: "[W]e hear of marriages contracted under an ash tree, in a bed, in a garden, in a small storehouse, in a field. There were marriages contracted in a blacksmith's shop, near a hedge, in a kitchen, by an oak tree, at a tavern. Even the King's Highway was the scene of one alleged marriage." See Richard H. Helmholz, *Marriage Litigation in Medieval England* (Cambridge, UK: Cambridge University Press, 1974), p. 29.

247. Raymond of Peñafort, for instance, distinguished between two types of marriage: "legitimate" (*legitimum*) and "clandestine" (*clandestinum*). Legitimate marriage occurs where a spouse is properly sought from her parents, a dowry given, the priest pronounces his blessing, and the husband solemnly accepts her as wife. Clandestine marriage, according to Raymond, should, on the contrary be viewed not as presumptively valid, but as presumptively adulterous and should be called a form of fornication. See *Summa de Matrimonio*, col. 921.

248. See Panormitanus, *Commentaria* (Lyons, 1578), X.4.3.1, no. 2: "Nota quod clandestinitas non vitiat matrimonium solus ergo contrahentium consensus sufficit matrimonium licet clam sit praestitum quamquam peccent sic contrahentes."

249. Panormitanus, *Commentaria*, no. 3: "Nota secundo quod super contractu matrimonium debet credi simplici verbo ipsorum contrahentium ac si ab initio in conspectu ecclesiae fuisset contractum."

250. Panormitanus, *Commentaria*, no. 4: "Ex quo inferunt Doctores quod proles nata ante publicationem est censenda legitima."

251. See Brundage, *Law, Sex, and Christian Society*, p. 501. Richard Helmholz has found even more extreme examples in fifteenth-century England. Thus he notes that "of the forty-one marriages contracted by words of present consent and found in the Canterbury deposition book of 1411-1420, fully thirty-eight took place at home or in some other private place. Only three were made in church." See Helmholz, *Marriage Litigation in Medieval England* p. 28.

252. X.4.1.28.

253. X.4.1.28.

254. *Glossa Ordinaria*, X.4.1.28, v. *in constantem*. "Sic supra eodem veniens. . . ." On *Veniens*, see above, p. 45.

255. *Glossa Ordinaria*, X.4.1.28, v. *in constantem*. Innocent IV entirely omits discussion of force and fear at this point. See *Apparatus*, X.4.1.28.

256. See Hostiensis, *Summa*, bk. IV, *De Matrimoniis*, sec. 27.

257. Hostiensis, *De Matrimoniis*, sec. 27. Hostiensis was not the only canonist who proposed that the analysis of force and fear cases had to take account of the particular circumstances of the parties. Raymond of Peñafort, for instance, stressed that "such fear is not said to fall upon one as upon another." A man of great dignity living in a city, or a king faced with some "small knight" will respond to fear in ways different than others might. The good judge must take account of these differences, Raymond argued. See Raymond de Peñafort, *Summa de Matrimonio*, col. 957. See also supra p. 47, on Raymond's psychology of force and fear.

258. See Hostiensis, *Summa*, bk. IV, *De Matrimoniis*, sec. 27.

259. *De Matrimoniis*, sec. 27.

260. *De Matrimoniis*, sec. 27.

261. See Shannon MacSheffrey, "'I Will Never Have Ayenst My Fader's Will': Consent and the Making of Marriage in the Late Medieval Diocese of London," in Constance M. Rousseau and Joel T. Rosenthal, eds., *Women, Marriage, and Family in Medieval Christendom: Essays in Memory of Michael M. Sheehan* (Kalamazoo, MI: Medieval Institute, 1998), pp. 153-74.

262. MacSheffrey, "Consent," pp. 160-62.

263. MacSheffrey, "Consent," p. 164. MacSheffrey goes on to give examples, pp. 164-65.

264. See Michael M. Sheehan, "Choice of Marriage Partners in the Middle Ages: Development and Mode of Application of a Theory of Marriage," reprinted in James K. Farge, ed., *Marriage, Family, and Law in Medieval Europe: Collected Studies* (Toronto: University of Toronto Press, 1996), pp. 113-17.

265. Sheehan, "Choice of Marriage Partners," p. 113.

266. See Jacqueline Murray, "Individualism and Consensual Marriage: Some Evidence from Medieval England," in Rousseau and Rosenthal, eds., *Women, Marriage, and Family*, pp. 121-51.

267. Regarding Wetheringsett, Murray notes: "There is little information available . . . and his manual remains unedited." P. 134, note 38.

268. Murray, "Individualism," p. 135.

269. Thomas hailed from obscure origins and was probably of illegitimate birth. He was trained in theology in Paris and returned to England between 1189 and 1192. He served in various capacities in the Church at London and Salisbury, and composed the

bulk of his *Summa* prior to the year 1216. See F. Broomfield, ed., *Thomae de Chobham Summa Confessorum* (Louvain: Éditions Nauwelaerts, 1963), pp. xxviii-xxxviii (providing biographical details); and pp. xl-lxii (establishing date of composition).

270. "Notandum tamen quod aliquis metus est magnus uni persone qui est parvus alteri persone. Unde legitur in quadam decretali, quod puellela que erat sub potestate parentum suorum compellebatur ab eis per quasdam minas et per quosdam terrores quod consentiret in quemdam iuvenem ad ostium ecclesie, et cum quereretur ab ea: 'vis tu habere istum in virum?' flendo respondit: 'volo.' Flebat etiam ducebatur ad ecclesiam, et postea dixit quod nunquam haberet eum in virum, nec unquam voluit intrare lectum eius. Et dixit dominus papa in illa decretali quod lacrime ille sufficiebant ad probandum violentiam. Modicum enim metus potuit compellere iuvenculam puellam ut confiteretur se illum velle habere in quem tamen animo non consensit." Broomfield, ed., p. 182. Cf. note 132, indicating that the decretal cited by Thomas is not extant.

The dissemination and acceptance of Gratian's marital ideal can be further illustrated by the emergence, in the popular literature of the later Middle Ages, of literary plots that centered on themes implicating the freedom of the individual to contract marriage. See Leah Otis-Cour, "'Gratian's Revenge': Le mariage dans les 'romans de couple' médiévaux," in Bertrand Durand and Laurent Mayali, eds., *Excerptiones iuris: Studies in Honor of André Gouron* (Berkeley, CA: The Robbins Collection, 2000), pp. 469-82.

271. The story of the Paston family is told by many historians. See classically H. S. Bennett, *The Pastons and Their England* (Cambridge: Cambridge University Press, 1968) (originally published in 1921); and more recently Frances and Joseph Gies, *A Medieval Family: The Pastons of Fifteenth-Century England* (New York: Harper Collins, 1998).

272. On the letters, see Frances and Joseph Gies, *A Medieval Family,* pp. 1-6. The letters have been published in edited form. See Norman Davis, ed., *Paston Letters and Papers of the Fifteenth Century,* 2 vols. (Oxford: At the Clarendon Press, 1971-1976).

273. See Frances and Joseph Gies, *A Medieval Family,* p. 17.

274. See Ann S. Haskell, "The Paston Women on Marriage in Fifteenth-Century England," *Viator* 4 (1973): 459-61.

275. See Frances and Joseph Gies, *A Medieval Family,* p. 39.

276. See Haskell, p. 460.

277. See Ffiona Swabey, *Medieval Gentlewoman: Life in a Gentry Household in the Later Middle Ages* (New York: Routledge, 1999), p. 37.

278. Swabey, *Medieval Gentlewoman,* p. 37.

279. See letter from Sir John Fastolf to John Paston, no. 509, in Davis, ed., *Paston Letters,* vol. II, pp. 104-5; cf. Frances and Joseph Gies, p. 106.

280. See Davis, ed., *Paston Letters,* vol. I, no. 85, pp. 156-57.

281. See letter no. 174, Margaret Paston to John Paston, in Davis, vol. I, pp. 286-87.

282. See letter of John Paston III to John Paston II, no. 332, Davis, ed., *Paston Letters,* vol. I, pp. 541-43.

283. See Frances and Joseph Gies, p. 209.

284. See Haskell, p. 467.

285. Davis, ed., *Paston Letters,* no. 861, vol. II, p. 498.

286. See Frances and Joseph Gies, p. 219.

287. See letter of Margaret Paston to John Paston II, no. 203, Davis, ed., *Paston Letters,* vol. I, pp. 341-44.

288. *Paston Letters,* vol. I, p. 342.

289. *Paston Letters,* vol. I, p. 342.

290. *Paston Letters,* vol. I, p. 342.

291. *Paston Letters,* vol. I, pp. 342-43.

292. See Haskell, p. 468.

293. Haskell, p. 468.

294. See Davis, ed., *Paston Letters,* no. 230, vol. I, p. 388.

295. *Paston Letters,* vol. I, p. 383.

296. See Bennett, *Pastons and Their England,* p. 30; see also Frances and Joseph Gies, p. 72 (on Scrope's smallpox).

297. See letter of Elizabeth Clere to John Paston, no. 445, Davis, ed., *Paston Letters,* vol. II, p. 32.

298. See Haskell, p. 467.

299. See Karl P. Wentersdorf, "The Clandestine Marriages of the Fair Maid of Kent," *Journal of Medieval History* 5 (1979): 203.

300. Wentersdorf, "Fair Maid," p. 203.

301. Wentersdorf, pp. 204-5.

302. Wentersdorf, p. 205.

303. Wentersdorf, pp. 205-7.

304. Wentersdorf, p. 207.

305. Wentersdorf, pp. 207-8.

306. Wentersdorf, p. 229, note 11.

307. See Appendix A, pp. 219-20.

308. Wentersdorf, p. 220.

309. Wentersdorf, p. 220.

310. Wentersdorf, p. 220. "Thomas . . . urgente eum conscientia ius suum prosequi apud sedem apostolicam intendebat. . . ."

311. Wentersdorf, pp. 215-16.

312. See Appendix B, p. 222 ("inter Thomam et Johannem predictos vere fuisse et esse contractum . . .").

313. ("sibi invicem obsequia coniugalia exhibendum . . .").

314. Wentersdorf, p. 222. On the nuances involved in translating the word *obsequia,* see below, p. 168.

315. Wentersdorf, p. 216.

316. Wentersdorf, pp. 216-17. Thomas's knightly career was distinguished. He was among the founding members of the Order of the Garter, established by King Edward III as the highest recognition bestowed on knights for their martial accomplishments.

317. Wentersdorf, p. 217.

318. Wentersdorf, p. 217.

319. Wentersdorf, pp. 217-18.

320. See Appendices C-G, pp. 222-27.

321. Petition to Pope Innocent VI, September 7, 1361, Appendix C, p. 223.

322. Wentersdorf, p. 223.

323. See Appendices D and E, Bull of Pope Innocent VI, dated September 7, 1361, and Private Brief of Pope Innocent VI, dated September 7, 1361, pp. 223-24.

324. Wentersdorf, p. 219.

325. Wentersdorf, p. 219.

326. In an important book, Eric Josef Carlson questions the vitality of this right, particularly as it pertained to England, in light of a variety of common-law rules that restricted the property and inheritance rights of those who married without the proper consent — either of parents, guardians, or overlords. See Eric Josef Carlson, *Marriage and the English Reformation* (Oxford: Blackwell, 1994), pp. 9-33. Carlson is certainly correct to call attention to these restrictions, which had the effect of making defiance of those who had power over the couple a costly proposition. But as the examples of Margery Paston and the Fair Maid of Kent make clear, there were always a few young people ready to challenge the strictures of society and risk the loss of worldly goods all in the name of love. And in so acting, they could call upon the legal backing of the Church.

327. See above, p. 60, and note 285.

328. See Desiderius Erasmus, *Epistola Pauli Apostoli ad Ephesios,* cap. IV, in *Opera Omnia* (Leiden: Peter Van der Aa, 1705), vol. 6, col. 855, note 37.

329. Erasmus, *Opera Omnia,* vol. 6, col. 855, note 37.

330. Erasmus, *Opera Omnia,* vol. 6, col. 855, note 37 ("quae longe absunt a natura Sacramentorum").

331. See John Witte, *From Sacrament to Contract: Marriage, Religion, and Law in the Western Tradition* (Louisville, KY: John Knox Press, 1997), p. 57.

332. Witte, *From Sacrament to Contract,* p. 57.

333. See John Witte, "The Reformation of Marriage Law in Martin Luther's Germany: Its Significance Then and Now," *Journal of Law and Religion* 4 (1986): 293, 326.

334. See Martin Bucer, *De Regno Christi Libri Duo,* ed. François Wendel (Paris: Presses Universitaires de France, 1955) (*Martini Buceri opera latina,* vol. 15; originally published 1550), p. 157.

335. Bucer, vol. 15, p. 157.

336. Bucer, vol. 15, p. 157.

337. Bucer, vol. 15, p. 158.

338. Bucer, vol. 15, pp. 160-61.

339. Summarizing Bucer's teaching, Steven Ozment has written: "For Bucer, what was at stake . . . was not a child's freedom to follow his heart's desire, but a child's sense of responsibility to family and society. A secret marriage showed 'immeasurable levity' in a matter of utmost seriousness, as if a valid contract affecting not only the body, temporal goods, and property, but also one's very soul, could be made without advice and counsel and off the public record." See Steven Ozment, *When Fathers Ruled: Family Life in Reformation Europe* (Cambridge, MA: Harvard University Press, 1983), p. 29.

340. See John W. O'Malley, *Trent and All That: Renaming Catholicism in the Early Modern Era* (Cambridge, MA: Harvard University Press, 2000), pp. 8-11; cf. John W. O'Malley, "Was Ignatius of Loyola a Church Reformer? How to Look at Early Modern Catholicism," *Catholic Historical Review* 77 (1991): 177-93 (originally proposing the term "early modern Catholicism").

341. See Robert Bireley, *The Refashioning of Catholicism, 1450-1700: A Reassess-*

ment of the Counter Reformation (Washington, DC: Catholic University of America Press, 1999), pp. 1-30. Cf. Carter Lindberg, *The European Reformations* (Cambridge, MA: Blackwell Publishers, 1996), pp. 335-38.

342. See Bireley, *Refashioning,* pp. 45-69. See also H. Outram Evennett, *The Spirit of the Counter-Reformation* (Cambridge: Cambridge University Press, 1968), pp. 1-23.

343. See the important collection and evaluation of the sources found in Reinhard Lettmann, *Die Diskussion über die klandestinen Ehen und die Einführung einer zur Gültigkeit verpflichtenden Eheschliessungsform auf dem Konzil von Trient. Eine kanonistische Untersuchung* (Münster: Aschendorffsche Verlagsbuchhandlung, 1967).

344. The decree was not approved unanimously. The final vote on *Tametsi,* in November 1563, was "126 votes for, 47 against, 7 abstentions." Those who opposed the decree tended to support retention of the old system. See R. Po-Chia Hsia, *The World of Catholic Renewal: 1540-1770* (Cambridge, UK: Cambridge University Press, 1998), p. 23.

345. See *Tametsi,* quoted in *Canones et Decreta Sacrosancti Oecumenici Concilii Tridentini* (Rome: Propaganda Fide, 1862), p. 173 ("quinque falso affirmant, matrimonia a filiis familias sine consensu parentum contracta, irrita esse . . .").

346. *Canones et Decreta,* p. 173. It is not to be doubted, the Council declared, that marriages are "made by the free consent of the parties" ("libero contrahentium consensu facta").

347. *Canones et Decreta,* p. 173.

348. *Canones et Decreta,* p. 173.

349. *Canones et Decreta,* p. 173. Notably missing from the Council's listing of abuses was the concerns of parents. It might be permissible to limit matrimonial freedom in order to curb sinful behavior, but not to ensure that parental objections were met.

350. *Canones et Decreta,* p. 174.

351. *Canones et Decreta,* p. 174.

352. The decree *Tametsi* was only gradually received as binding by the Catholic states of Europe. Brundage thus notes that "[i]n Normandy, for example, *Tametsi* was not published until the seventeenth century. . . ." See Brundage, *Law, Sex, and Christian Society,* p. 565.

353. See R. B. Outhwaite, *Clandestine Marriage in England: 1500-1800* (London: Hambledon Press, 1995), p. 54.

354. Outhwaite, *Clandestine Marriage,* pp. 75-97; see also Christopher Lasch, "The Suppression of Clandestine Marriage in England: The Marriage Act of 1753," *Salmagundi* 26 (1974): 91-109.

355. See generally Otto E. Koegel, *Common Law Marriage and Its Development in the United States* (Washington, DC: John Byrne and Company, 1922); and Robert E. Dillon, *Common Law Marriage* (Washington, DC: Catholic University of America Press, 1942) (Canon Law Studies, no. 153), especially pp. 35-93. An important judicial history of the migration of this legal concept, particularly as it pertained to territories of the United States formerly in the possession of Spain, is *Hallett v. Collins,* 51 U.S. 174, 180-182 (1850).

356. See Tomás Sánchez, *De Sancti Matrimonii Sacramento* (Lyon, 1637).

357. See Brundage, *Law, Sex, and Christian Society,* p. 564.

358. See John T. Noonan, Jr., *Power to Dissolve: Lawyers and Marriages in the Courts of the Roman Curia* (Cambridge, MA: Harvard University Press, 1972), p. 31.

359. Noonan, *Power to Dissolve*, p. 31.

360. Noonan, *Power to Dissolve*, pp. 31-32.

361. Sánchez's arguments are carefully examined by David Sereno, *Whether the Norm Expressed in Canon 1103 Is of Natural Law or of Positive Church Law* (Rome: Editrice Pontificia Università Gregoriana, 1997), pp. 77-92.

362. Sereno, *Norm in Canon 1103*, p. 78. Cf. Sánchez, bk. IV, disp. 14, no. 1: "[Q]uia coactio est contra principalem matrimonium finem, qui est procreatio sobolis, et mutuum conjugium obsequium: quae requirunt animos voluntarie conjunctos, mutuumque amorem. Ergo repugnat naturae matrimonii." (Quoted in Sereno, p. 79, note 95.)

363. See Sereno, *Norm in Canon 1103*, p. 79.

364. Sánchez, bk. IV, disp. 14, no. 1: "Omnis traditio, per quam transfertur dominium, debet esse plene libera, donatio enim dicit dationem liberalem, et metu extorta obligat ad restitutionem. . . ." (Quoted in Sereno, p. 79, note 96.)

365. See bk. IV, disp. 14, no. 4. (Quoted in Sereno, p. 89, note 119.)

366. See bk. IV, disp. 14, no 4: "Et donatio importat donationem liberalem, id est, nullo pretio recepto, non tamen quod omnino libera sit." (Quoted in Sereno, p. 90, note 120.)

367. Bk. IV, disp. 14, no. 1. Cf. Sereno, p. 77, note 89.

368. Bk. IV, disp. 14, no. 2. Cf. Sereno, p. 77, note 90.

369. See Sereno, pp. 9-31. Sereno himself raises doubts about the natural-law origin of the invalidating effect of coerced consent to marriage.

370. See Sánchez, bk. IV, disp. VI, no. 4, *summarium:* "metus reverentiae quo inferior reverentia superioris, uxor viri, filius patris, etc. . . .").

371. Sánchez, bk. IV, disp. VI, no. 4.

372. Sánchez, bk. IV, disp. VI, no. 7: "Ultima sententia (quam multo veriorem reputo) docet, solum metum reverentialem, nisi minae aut verbera, aut alius metus gravis adiungatur, non cadere in virum constantem . . .").

373. Bk. IV, disp. VI, no. 8: "Unus tamen . . . hanc sententiam limitat, dicens ad matrimonium irritandum non sat esse metum reverentialem patris cum minis nisi simul adsint verbera, in filio masculo adultae aetatis, secus in filia puella et filio impubere."

374. Bk. IV, disp. VI, no. 14: "Infertur si filia matrimonium contrahat non praecedentibus minis, solum eo timore ne patris indignationem incurrat, esse validum; non enim is metus censetur cadens in virum constantem."

375. Bk. IV, disp. VI, no. 14: "Hoc tamen moderarer, ut intelligatur quando indignatio illa patris vel viri non diu permanebit, sed spes est futurae reconciliationis; si enim teneret probabiliter diuturnam fore indignationem et semper se habiturum patrem aut virum valde infestum et indignatum, obiecturumque passim illam inobedientiam crediderim timorem cadentem in virum constantem."

Notes to Chapter 2

1. On the family as a "spiritual womb" *(spirituali utero)*, see Thomas Aquinas,

Summa Theologiae, 2a 2ae, q. 10, art. 12, reply. On marital affection and the canonists, see John T. Noonan, Jr., "Marital Affection in the Canonists," *Studia Gratiana* 12 *(Collectanea Stephan Kuttner)* (1967): 481-509.

2. See Antti Arjava, *Women and Law in Late Antiquity* (Oxford: Clarendon Press, 1996), p. 41.

3. Arjava, *Women and Law,* p. 41.

4. See Richard P. Saller, "Patria Potestas and the Stereotype of the Roman Family," *Continuity and Change* 1 (1986): 7-22; and Richard P. Saller, "Men's Age at Marriage and Its Consequences in the Roman Family," *Classical Philology* 82 (1987): 21-34.

5. See R. Yaron, "Vitae Necisque Potestas," *Tijdschrift voor Rechtsgeschiedenis* 30 (1962): 243-45.

6. See Susan Treggiari, *Roman Marriage: Iusti Coniuges from the Time of Cicero to the Time of Ulpian* (Oxford: Clarendon Press, 1991), pp. 282-83.

7. See *Digest* 48.5.24 pr. Cf. Treggiari, *Roman Marriage,* p. 283.

8. See Max Radin, "The Exposure of Infants in Roman Law and Practice," *Classical Journal* 20 (1925): 337-43.

9. See John Boswell, *The Kindness of Strangers: The Abandonment of Children in Western Europe from Late Antiquity to the Renaissance* (New York: Pantheon Books, 1988), pp. 39-49. On the Greek evidence, see also Cynthia Patterson, "'Not Worth the Rearing': The Causes of Infant Exposure in Ancient Greece," *Transactions of the American Philological Association* 115 (1985): 103-23 (examining exposure of infants in the light of physical handicap, illegitimate birth, economic necessity, and other factors that contributed to the decision to expose).

10. See Suzanne Dixon, *The Roman Family* (Baltimore: Johns Hopkins University Press, 1992), p. 122, and the sources cited therein. One occasionally finds concern voiced for the children exposed in the legal sources. Thus Paulus declared that they are held to commit homicide *(necare)* who suffocate their children, or cast them out, deny them nourishment, or abandon them in a public place to arouse the sympathy of strangers. See *Digest* 25.3.4.

11. See Boswell, *Kindness of Strangers,* pp. 62-63.

12. See Beryl Rawson, "Adult-Child Relationships in Roman Society," in Beryl Rawson, ed., *Marriage, Divorce, and Children in Ancient Rome* (Oxford: Clarendon Press, 1991), pp. 7, 27.

13. Rawson, "Adult-Child Relationships," pp. 7, 27. See also Boswell, *Kindness of Strangers,* pp. 62-63.

14. See Boswell, *Kindness of Strangers,* pp. 65-68.

15. See the decree of Diocletian and Maximian, *Codex* 4.43.1. Cf. Boswell, *Kindness of Strangers,* p. 67.

16. Boswell, *Kindness of Strangers,* p. 67.

17. See Gaius, *Institutes,* bk. I, sec. 55, Francis de Zulueta, ed. (Oxford: Clarendon Press, 1946), vol. I, pp. 16-17.

18. Justinian, *Institutes,* 1.9.

19. Justinian, *Institutes,* 1.9.

20. For a careful review of the classical terminology of *familia* and its kindred term *domus,* see Richard P. Saller, "*Familia, Domus,* and the Roman Concept of the Family," *Phoenix* 38 (1984): 336-55.

21. See *Digest* 50.16.195.2. Justinian's *Institutes* taught that upon the death of a father, the offspring were immediately freed from *patria potestas*. See *Institutes*, 1.12. Maternal power conferred on women the right to manage their own estates, but where the management of surviving minor children's estates was concerned a male guardian was required, at least until late in the fourth century. See Arjava, *Women and Law*, pp. 89-94.

22. *Digest* 50.16.195.2 and 3. Cf. Jane F. Gardner, *Family and Familia in Roman Law and Life* (Oxford: Clarendon Press, 1998), pp. 1-5.

23. See David Herlihy, *Medieval Households* (Cambridge, MA: Harvard University Press, 1985), pp. 2-3.

24. See *Digest* 50.16.195.2.

25. See Percy Ellwood Corbett, *The Roman Law of Marriage* (Oxford: Clarendon Press, 1930), pp. 71-90.

26. Corbett, *Roman Law of Marriage*, pp. 91-95.

27. See Herlihy, *Medieval Households*, pp. 8-10.

28. See Treggiari, *Roman Marriage*, pp. 442-46.

29. Treggiari, *Roman Marriage*, pp. 442-44.

30. See Arjava, *Women and Law*, pp. 123-24. Cf. Otto Seeck, ed., Symmachus, *Epistle* 6.3, *Monumenta Germaniae Historica, Auctorum Antiquissimorum*, VI (Berlin: Weidmanns, 1883), p. 153.

31. See Herlihy, *Medieval Households*, pp. 9-10.

32. Herlihy, *Medieval Households*, p. 10.

33. Herlihy, *Medieval Households*.

34. See Eva Marie Lassen, "The Roman Family: Ideal and Metaphor," in Halvor Moxnes, ed., *Constructing Early Christian Families: Family as Social Reality and Metaphor* (London: Routledge, 1997), pp. 103, 114-15.

35. Galatians 3:28.

36. Ephesians 5:22-23.

37. *Digest* 48.9.5.

38. Although the exact words and deeds are subject to continuing debate, scholars agree that a ritual of some sort was employed by Romans to signify the admission of newborn children to the household. Mirielle Corbier, "Child Exposure and Abandonment," in Suzanne Dixon, ed., *Childhood, Class, and Kin in the Roman World* (London: Routledge, 2001), pp. 52, 54-55. Exposure in the ancient world was a much more likely alternative than abortion, because of the risks posed by the medical practices of the time. Konstantinos Kapparis, *Abortion in the Ancient World* (London: Duckworth, 2002), pp. 154-62.

39. Athenagoras, *Legatio* 35; see Athenagoras, *Legatio and De Resurrectione*, ed. and trans. William R. Schoedel (Oxford: Clarendon Press, 1972), pp. 82-85.

40. Clement of Alexandria, *Les Stromates*, 2.18, in C. Mondésert, ed., Sources chrétiennes, no. 38 (Paris: Éditions du Cerf, 1954), p. 105.

41. See Saint Justin, *Apologies*, I.27, André Wartelle, ed. (Paris: Études Augustiniennes, 1987), pp. 134-35.

42. Justin, *Apologies*, pp. 134-35.

43. See Minucius Felix, *Octavius*, 31.4, Josefus Martin, ed. (Bonn: Petri Hanstein, 1930), pp. 71-72.

44. Tertullian, *Apologeticus*, 9.6-7, PL 1: 318-19.

45. Tertullian, *Apologeticus,* 9.17, PL 1: 325-27.

46. *Codex Theodosianus* 5.9.1.

47. Boswell, *Kindness of Strangers,* p. 71.

48. Boswell, *Kindness of Strangers,* p. 71.

49. *Codex,* 8.47.10 (". . . ut patribus quibus ius vitae in liberos necisque potestas olim erat permissa . . .").

50. See Boswell, *Kindness of Strangers,* p. 71.

51. *Codex Theodosianus* 9.14.1.

52. See Tertullian, *Ad Uxorem,* 2.8.7–2.8.8, Charles Munier, ed., Sources chretiennes, no. 273 (Paris: Les Éditions du Cerf, 1980), p. 148. Cf. Matthew 19:6.

53. Tertullian, *Ad Uxorem,* 2.8.7–2.8.8.

54. Tertullian, *Ad Uxorem,* 2.8.7–2.8.8.

55. See St. Augustine, *De Genesi ad Litteram, Corpus Scriptorum Ecclesiasticorum Latinorum,* vol. 28, p. 271. Cf. Kari Elisabeth Borresen, *Subordination and Equivalence: The Nature and Role of Woman in Augustine and Thomas Aquinas* (Kampen, The Netherlands: Kok Pharos Publishing, 1995), p. 17.

56. See St. Ambrose, *De paradiso* IV.2, *Corpus Scriptorum Ecclesiasticorum Latinorum,* vol. 32, pp. 280-81. The man's position was elevated after the Fall *(in meliore loco),* while the woman was placed in a worse position *(in inferiore loco). Id.,* p. 280.

57. See Borresen, *Subordination and Equivalence,* p. 30.

58. St. Jerome, *Ad Jovinianum,* PL 23: 221-52.

59. See generally the summary of this argument in Philippe Delhaye, "Les dossier anti-matrimonial de l'*Adversus Jovinianum* et son influence sur quelques écrits latins du XIIe siècle," *Mediaeval Studies* 13 (1951): 65, 66-70.

60. See Jane Barr, "The Influence of Saint Jerome on Medieval Attitudes to Women," in Jane Martin Soskice, ed., *After Eve: Women, Theology, and the Christian Tradition* (London: Marshall, Pickering, 1990), pp. 89, 94.

61. See Patricia Ranft, *Women and Spiritual Equality in Christian Tradition* (New York: St. Martin's Press, 1998), p. xi.

62. See Dyan Elliott, *Spiritual Marriage: Sexual Abstinence in Medieval Wedlock* (Princeton, NJ: Princeton University Press, 1993), especially pp. 178-79.

63. A passage of Peter Lombard might be taken as an allusion to this aspect of Mary's marriage with Joseph. Mary, Peter wrote, consented to marital society *(coniugalem societatem)* with Joseph, but carnal copulation was reserved to a special judgment of God. See *Libri IV Sententiarum,* bk. IV, dist. 30, c. 2, p. 670. By the fourteenth and fifteenth centuries, Catholic theologians had come to exalt the position of St. Joseph. See Marina Werner, *Alone of All Her Sex: The Myth and the Cult of the Virgin Mary* (New York: Knopf, 1976), pp. 188-90. Elliott notes that this effort to exalt Joseph entailed Mary's submission to his earthly authority. See Elliott, *Spiritual Marriage,* pp. 179-80.

64. See the important reconstruction of this legislation by John T. Noonan, Jr., *Contraception: A History of Its Treatment by the Catholic Theologians and Canonists,* enl. ed. (Cambridge, MA: Harvard University Press, 1986), pp. 20-23.

65. See Majorian, *Novellae* 6.9. Cf. Philip Lyndon Reynolds, *Marriage in the Western Church: The Christianization of Marriage during the Patristic and Early Medieval Periods* (Leiden: E. J. Brill, 1994), p. 15 and note 40.

66. Justinian, *Institutes*, 1.2.pr. This text, in turn, is a close adaptation of Ulpian, *Digest* 1.1.1.3.

67. *Digest* 23.2.1.

68. See St. Augustine, *De Bono Coniugali*, 17.19, in P. G. Walsh, ed. and trans. (Oxford: Clarendon Press, 2001), pp. 36-37.

69. *De Bono Coniugali*, 1.1, pp. 2-3.

70. *De Bono Coniugali*, 3.3, pp. 6-7.

71. *De Bono Coniugali*, 7.7, pp. 16-17.

72. See *Contra Faustum*, 22.31, *Corpus Scriptorum Ecclesiasticorum Latinorum*, vol. 25, p. 625. Augustine asserts rhetorically: "Who does not know that a wife ought to serve her husband as if he were a lord? . . . In all other actions [save the sexual relationship] pertaining to human tranquillity, the woman ought to be subservient to her husband. . . ." ["Quis enim nescit uxorem marito tamquam domino debere servire. . . . [S]ed mulier, ut cum in ceteris actibus ad humanam pacem pertinentibus mulier viro debeat servitutem. . . ."]

73. *Contra Faustum*, 22.31. Cf. *De Bono Coniugali*, 4.4, pp. 8-9. On the conjugal debt as a source of equality between the parties, see below, pp. 103-5.

74. D. 1.7.

75. See Stephanus Tornacensis, *Die Summa über das Decretum Gratiani*, Johann Friedrich von Schulte, ed. (Aalen: Scientia Verlag, 1965), D. 1, pp. 7-8.

76. See Rufinus von Bologna, *Summa Decretorum*, D. 1, c. 7, v. *Ius autem naturale*, vol. 1, p. 8. On Rufinus's blending of scriptural and Romanist sources, see Jeremy Cohen, *"Be Fertile and Increase, Fill the Earth and Master It": The Ancient and Medieval Career of a Biblical Text* (Ithaca, NY: Cornell University Press, 1989), p. 277.

77. See *Glossa Ordinaria*, D.1, c. 7, v. *Ius naturale*: "[D]icitur natura quidam stimulus seu instinctus naturae ex sensualitate proveniens. . . ."

78. See Hostiensis, *Summa*, bk. IV, *De Matrimoniis*, sec. 2.

79. *De Matrimoniis*, sec. 2.

80. *De Matrimoniis*, sec. 1.

81. *De Matrimoniis*, sec. 2.

82. See William of Auxerre, *Summa Aurea*, ed. Jean Ribaillier (Paris: Centre National de la Recherche Scientifique, 1985), vol. 4, p. 395. "Universal" natural law was that which nature taught all animals, such as carnal coupling, while "most universal" natural law (*quoddam universalissimum*) was the "harmony of all things" (*concordia omnium rerum*).

83. William of Auxerre, Ribaillier ed., pp. 395-97.

84. See Thomas Aquinas, *Summa Theologiae, Supplementum*, q. 41, art. 1.

85. Aquinas, *Summa, Supplementum*, q. 41, art. 1.

86. C. 33, q. 5, c. 11: "Manifestum est, ita voluisse legem feminam sub viro esse. . . ."

87. See C. 33, q. 5, c. 12: "Est ordo naturalis . . . ut feminae serviant viris, et filii parentibus, quia in illis hec iusticia est, ut maiori serviat minor."

88. C. 33, q. 5, c. 13.

89. C. 33, q. 5, c. 15: "Cum caput mulieris vir sit, caput autem viri Christus, quecumque uxor non subicitur viro hoc est capiti suo, eiusdem criminis rea est, cuius et vir, si non subiciatur capiti suo."

90. C. 33, q. 5, c. 17: "Mulierem constat, subiectam dominio viri esse et nullam auctoritatem habere; nec docere potest, nec testis esse, neque fidem dare, nec iudicare."

91. See C. 33, q. 5, c. 14; C. 33, q. 5, c. 18; and C. 33, q. 5, c. 19. Gratian balanced these misogynistic passages with a text of St. Ambrose declaring that at creation man and woman were made of the same material, shared the same human nature, and arose from the same common font of humanity. Hence, male and female complement one another and have done so from the time of creation. See C. 33, q. 5, c. 20.

92. See C. 33, q. 5, d.p.c. 20: "Evidentissime itaque apparet, ita virum esse caput mulieris. . . ."

93. See C. 33, q. 5, c. 12 (= Ivo, *Decretum*, VIII, 94); C. 33, q. 5, c. 13 (= Ivo, *Decretum*, VIII, 95); C. 33, q. 5, c. 14 (= Ivo, *Decretum*, VIII, 96); C. 33, q. 5, c. 17 (= Ivo, *Decretum*, VIII, 85); and C. 33, q. 5, c. 18 (Ivo, *Decretum*, VIII, c. 91).

94. *Summa Magistri Rolandi*, ed. Friedrich Thaner (Aalen: Scientia Verlag, 1962), C. 33, q. 5, c. 11, v. *manifestum est*, p. 199. Rolandus recognized a major exception to this rule with respect to the conjugal debt. See also below, Chapter Three.

95. C. 33, q. 5, c. 15, v. *cum caput*, p. 506. Cf. Genesis 3:16.

96. *Summa Parisiensis*, C. 33, q. 5, c. 11, v. *manifestum est*, p. 254.

97. See *Glossa Ordinaria*, C. 33, q. 5, c. 12, v. *est ordo naturalis*.

98. *Glossa Ordinaria*, C. 33, q. 5, c. 17, v. *auctoritatem*.

99. *Glossa Ordinaria*, C. 33, q. 5, c. 17, v. *auctoritatem*. See also C. 33, q. 5, c. 17, v. *mulierem*.

100. See Albert the Great, *Commentarii in Octo Libros Politicorum Aristotelis*, bk. I, c. 9. See Albert the Great, *Opera Omnia* (Paris: Vivès, 1891), vol. 8, pp. 74-75.

101. See William of Auxerre, vol. 4, p. 396.

102. See Kristin Mary Popik, *The Philosophy of Woman of St. Thomas Aquinas* (Rome: Extract from Faith and Reason, 1978), p. 53.

103. See *Summa Theologiae*, 2a 2ae, Q. 50, art. 3, ad 3.

104. See Popik, *Philosophy of Woman*, p. 63.

105. Popik, *Philosophy of Woman*, p. 57.

106. Popik, *Philosophy of Woman*, pp. 4-6. Thomas did argue that while in essence men and women were alike in the way in which they were created in God's image and likeness, secondarily, or accidentally, men resembled God more closely because of their "intellectual nature . . ." (p. 4).

107. See *Lectura*, X.1.33.12, v. *suae iurisdictioni*.

108. See *Summa*, bk. I, *De Maioritate et Obedientia*, sec. 7.

109. *Id.* "[R]espondeo deo obedit dum in hoc viro obedit quia in hoc facit iuris auctoritate."

110. See *Lectura*, X.1.14.3, v. *gubernare*.

111. See Innocent IV, *Apparatus*, X.3.34.8, v. *pro defensione*.

112. Thus Thomas Aquinas criticized the practice of forcibly baptizing Jewish children on the basis of the right of Jewish fathers (*ius patria potestatis*) to direct the upbringing of their children. See *Summa Theologiae*, 2a, 2ae, q. 10, art. 12, reply.

113. See above, p. 71.

114. Placentinus, *Summa Codicis* (Turin: Bottega D'Erasmo, 1962), bk. VIII, tit. 50, p. 411.

115. Placentinus, *Summa Codicis*, p. 411.

116. Placentinus, *Summa Codicis,* p. 411.

117. Azo, *Summa Aurea Super Codice et Institutis cum additionibus* (Lyon, 1557; repr. Frankfurt am Main: Minerva, 1968), in octavum librum Codicis, 222 vb.

118. "[N]ulli enim sunt tales homines qui tale ius habeant . . . ."

119. See Placentinus, *Summa Institutionum* (Turin: Ex Officina Erasmiana, 1973), bk. I, tit. 7, *De Patria Potestate,* p. 9; cf. *Summa Codicis,* bk. VIII, tit. 50, p. 411.

120. *Summa Institutionum,* bk. I, tit. VII, p. 9.

121. For an extended discussion of this theme, see Peter Riesenberg, *Citizenship in the Western Tradition: Plato to Rousseau* (Chapel Hill, NC: University of North Carolina Press, 1992), pp. 85-186 ("Citizenship in the Medieval Italian City").

122. See Phillipe Ariès, *Centuries of Childhood: A Social History of Family Life,* trans. Robert Baldick (New York: Random House, 1962), p. 353. English translation of *L'Enfant et la vie familiale sous l'ancient régime* (Paris: Librairie Plon, 1960).

123. Ariès, *Centuries of Childhood,* p. 353.

124. See Danièle Alexandre-Bidon and Didier Lett, *Children in the Middle Ages: Fifth through Fifteenth Centuries,* trans. Jody Gladding (Notre Dame, IN: Notre Dame University Press, 1999), pp. 53-56 and 58-59.

125. See Nicholas Orme, *Medieval Children* (New Haven, CT: Yale University Press, 2001), p. 6.

126. See Shulamith Shahar, *Childhood in the Middle Ages,* trans. Chaya Galai (London: Routledge, 1990), p. 2. Shahar adds: "There were prevailing norms as to the duties of parents toward their children; there was a tradition of childcare practices, and parents invested both materially and emotionally in their children" (p. 3).

127. See Peter Fleming, *Family and Household in Medieval England* (Houndsmill, UK: Palgrave, 2001), pp. 59-65 (on medieval England); and James A. Schultz, *The Knowledge of Childhood in the German Middle Ages: 1100-1350* (Philadelphia: University of Pennsylvania Press, 1995), *passim* (on Germany). An important summary of scholarly criticism of Ariès's thesis is found in Colin Heywood, *A History of Childhood: Children and Childhood in the West from Medieval to Modern Times* (Cambridge, UK: Blackwell, 2001), pp. 12-15; 20-23.

128. See Daniel T. Kline, ed., *Medieval Literature for Children* (Routledge: New York, 2003).

129. See Ricardus Pisanus, *Lo Codi,* Hermann Fitting, ed. (Aalen: Scientia Verlag, 1968), pp. 171-72.

130. *Codex* 5.25.1.

131. See *Novella* 89.15, pr. Spurious children were those born outside either wedlock or concubinage. See Adolf Berger, *Encyclopedic Dictionary of Roman Law* (Philadelphia: American Philosophical Association, 1983), p. 717, v. *spurius;* p. 771, v. *vulgo conceptus.*

132. See *Institutes,* bk. I.9.1.

133. The mothers of such children were nevertheless obliged to furnish support. See *Digest* 25.3.5.4.

134. See *Lo Codi,* p. 172: "[S]ed pater non cogitur nutrire filios, si ipsi non sunt legitimi." ("But a father is not compelled to nourish his sons, if they are not legitimate.")

135. See Azo, *Summa Aurea Super Codice,* bk. V, sec. *De Alendis Liberis a*

Parentibus, p. 133va. Classical Roman law had also taught that a mother was responsible for the illegitimate children she brought into the world. See *Digest* 25.3.5.4.

136. See Odofredus, *Summa super Codice* (Bologna: Forni, 1968), vol. I, p. 268ra: "[F]ilii concepti ex nefario coitu filii non sunt, nec a patre alendi."

137. See Bernard of Parma, *Glossa Ordinaria,* X.4.7.5, v. *secundum facultates.*

138. See Mansi, Council of Gangra, c. 15, in *Sacrorum Conciliorum Decreta,* vol. 2: 1103: "Si quis liberos relinquit, nec eos alit, nec quantum in se est ad convenientem, pietatem religionemque adducit, sed exercitationis praetextu negligit, sit anathema."

139. *Glossa Ordinaria,* X.4.7.5, v. *secundum facultates.* Cf. *dist.* 1, c. 7.

140. *Glossa Ordinaria,* X.4.7.5, v. *secundum facultates.*

141. *Glossa Ordinaria,* X.4.7.5, v. *secundum facultates:* ". . . inductum in detestationem criminis."

142. *Glossa Ordinaria,* X.4.7.5, v. *secundum facultates.*

143. *Glossa Ordinaria,* X.4.7.5, v. *secundum facultates:* "[N]am educatio filiorum de iure naturali est . . . et instinctu naturae precedit. [U]nde ius istud praeferter civili . . . ."

144. See Hostiensis, *Lectura,* X.4.7.5, v. *secundum facultates.*

145. Hostiensis, *Lectura,* X.4.7.5, v.

146. "[N]am secundum benignitatem et aequitatem iuris canonici semper alendi sunt, considerato iure naturali . . . ."

147. "[N]aturale nempe ius inter omnia iura primatum tenet et tempore et dignitate. . . ." Hostiensis closed by noting that truth should always prevail over juristic subtlety: "[E]t magis insistit veritati, quam subtilitati. . . ."

148. See Richard H. Helmholz, "Support Orders, Church Courts, and the Rule of *Filius Nullius:* A Reassessment of the Common Law," *Virginia Law Review* 63 (1977): 431-48, reprinted in Richard H. Helmholz, *Canon Law and the Law of England* (London: Hambledon Press, 1987), pp. 169-86.

149. Helmholz, *Canon Law and the Law of England,* p. 177.

150. Helmholz, *Canon Law and the Law of England,* p. 178. By the twelfth century, the term *fama,* or *publica fama* ("common fame") had acquired a juridic meaning as the common opinion or judgment of a community. See Peter Landau, *Die Entstehung des kanonischen Infamiebegriffs von Gratian bis zur Glossa Ordinaria* (Köln: Böhlau Verlag, 1966), p. 3. Also writing of the twelfth century, Chris Wickham observed:

> *Fama,* most often *publica fama* (public fame), sometimes *vulgaris et frequens fama* (common and frequent fame), *communis fama* (common fame), or *consentiens fama* (accepted fame), was one form of knowledge in twelfth-century Tuscany. It was contrasted with knowledge *per visum* (eyewitness knowledge), which was more reliable; it was also, however, distinct from *per auditum* (hearsay), which was not reliable at all.

See Chris Wickham, "*Fama* and the Law in Twelfth-Century Tuscany," in Thelma Fenster and Daniel Lord Smail, eds., *Fama: The Politics of Talk and Reputation in Medieval Europe* (Ithaca: Cornell University Press, 2003), pp. 15, 16.

Writing in the same collection of essays, about the late Middle Ages, Thomas Kuehn has observed: "In the late medieval *ius commune* and the statutes of Italian city-states, *fama* was more than gossip, reputation, or common knowledge. *Fama* could also refer to the legal condition or status of a person or even a group. . . . It qualified people as witnesses, notaries, family members or citizens — all positions of trust in some manner." See Thomas Kuehn, "*Fama* as a Legal Status in Renaissance Florence," in Fenster and Smail, eds., *Fama,* p. 27.

151. See Helmholz, *Canon Law and the Law of England,* pp. 175-84.

152. See Orme, *Medieval Children,* p. 57 (reviewing other English records on support proceedings).

153. See above, p. 74.

154. X.5.11.1.

155. X.5.11.1.

156. X.5.11.1.

157. See also pp. 187-88 below, on adoption.

158. See Bernard of Parma, *Glossa Ordinaria,* X.5.11.1, v. *liberatus.*

159. *Glossa Ordinaria,* X.5.11.1, v. *languidis*

160. *Glossa Ordinaria,* X.5.11.1, v. *languidis.*

161. *Glossa Ordinaria,* X.5.11.1, v. *vendicare.*

162. See Hostiensis, *Lectura,* X.5.11.1, v. *liberatus.*

163. *Lectura,* X.5.11.1, v. *extiterit.*

164. *Lectura,* X.5.11.1, v. *eorum.*

165. See Johannes Andreae, *In quinque decretalium libros novella commentaria,* X.5.11.1, v. *liberatus.*

166. Johannes Andreae, *In quinque decretalium,* X.5.11.1, v. *vel alicui eorum.*

167. Johannes Andreae, *In quinque decretalium,* X.5.11.1, v. *vel alicui eorum..*

168. See Odofredus, *Lectura super Infortiato* (Bologna: Forni, 1968), p. 22ra. (*Digest* 25.3.4.) Odofredus here was explicating and echoing the sentiment of an excerpt from Paulus that began with the words *necare videtur* and declared that those who deny a child nourishment are understood to kill that child. Paulus's text was apparently intended as a criticism of the practice of exposure. See Radin, "Exposure of Infants," pp. 339-40. Although Odofredus did not use the term *pater,* he made use variously of the terms *parens* and *mulieres,* suggesting that he means to cover more than simply mothers exposing their young.

169. See Accursius, *Glossa in Codicem,* 8.46.9, v. *consulta* (Turin: Ex Officina Erasmiana, 1968), p. 263va.

170. Accursius, *Glossa in Codicem,* 8.46.9.

171. Accursius, *Glossa in Codicem,* 8.51.3.

172. Accursius, *Glossa Digestum Infortiatum, Digest* 25.3.4, v. *publicis locis* (Turin: Ex Officina Erasmiana, 1968), p. 13rb.

173. See Richard H. Helmholz, "Infanticide in the Province of Canterbury during the Fifteenth Century," *History of Childhood Quarterly* 2 (1975): 379-90, reprinted in *Canon Law and the Law of England,* pp. 157-68.

174. Helmholz, *Canon Law and the Law of England,* p. 159.

175. Helmholz, *Canon Law and the Law of England,* p. 161. On infanticide, exposure, and official efforts, ecclesiastical and secular, to forbid such practice, see also Shahar, *Childhood in the Middle Ages,* pp. 126-32; and Orme, *Medieval Children,* pp. 95-96.

In her study of English coroner records, Barbara Hanawalt has documented some of the ways infants might be accidentally killed. Thirty-three percent of accidental deaths of children under the age of one were the result of fire, whether because cribs were left too close to the fire place, or because animals like chickens had caught fire and spread the flames throughout the house. Barbara Hanawalt, *The Ties That Bound: Peasant Families in Medieval England* (New York: Oxford University Press, 1986), pp. 175-76.

According to Hanawalt, 47 percent of all accidental deaths occurred during the months of May through August, apparently because parents would leave their children "in less than optimal circumstances" while they performed agricultural chores (p. 176). Another 5 percent of deaths resulted from animal bites or attacks, usually by livestock kept by the parents (p. 177).

176. See Gandulf of Bologna, *Sententiarum Libri Quattuor,* ed. Johannes de Walter (Vienna: Aemilius Haim, 1924), p. 533.

177. Thomas Aquinas, *Supplementum,* Q. 49, art. 2, reply.

178. 2 Corinthians 12:13-14.

179. 2 Corinthians 12:14-15.

180. Thomas's Latin also echoed phrases found in the Vulgate version of this passage. The Vulgate in relevant part reads: "nec enim debent filii parentibus thesaurizare, sed parentes filiis." 1 Corinthians 12:14 ("For offspring ought not to endow their parents, but parents their offspring").

181. St. Bonaventure, *De Perfectione Evangelica,* q. 3, art. 2, conc., in St. Bonaventure, *Opera Omnia* (Quarrachi: Typographia Collegii S. Bonaventurae, 1896), vol. V, p. 162.

182. St. Bonaventure, *De Perfectione Evangelica,* in *Opera Omnia,* vol. V, p. 162.

183. St. Bonaventure, *Commentaria in Quattuor Libros Sententiarum Magistri Petri Lombardi,* dist. 33, art. 1, q. 1, *Opera Omnia,* vol. 4, p. 747.

184. Vol. 4, p. 747. See also Matthew M. De Benedictis, *The Social Thought of St. Bonaventure: A Study in Social Philosophy* (Westport, CT: Greeenwood Press, 1972), pp. 148-50.

185. Frederick J. Roensch, *Early Thomistic School* (Dubuque, IA: Priory Press, 1964), p. 117 (quoting Martin Grabmann). On Hervaeus's career, see also pp. 106-10 (reviewing details of Hervaeus's biography). See also Brian Tierney's important account of Hervaeus's rights thought, in *The Idea of Natural Rights: Studies in Natural Rights, Natural Law, and Church Law, 1150-1625* (Atlanta: Scholars Press, 1997), pp. 104-8.

186. See Tierney, *Idea of Natural Rights,* pp. 94-95.

187. Tierney, *Idea of Natural Rights,* p. 95.

188. J. G. Sikes, ed., "Hervaeus Natalis: De Paupertate Christi et Apostolorum," *Archives d'histoire doctrinale et littéraire du moyen âge* 12-13 (1937/1938): 209-97.

189. Tierney, *Idea of Natural Rights,* pp. 106-7. On possible translations of *servus,* see below, p. 123.

190. Michel Villey, "Du sens de l'expression *jus in re* en droit romain classique," *Revue internationale des droits d'antiquité (Fernand de Visscher II)* 3 (1949): 417-36. This essay was written early in Villey's career, before he posited a fourteenth-century break between a classical worldview that emphasized objective order and a post-fourteenth-, post-William-Ockham worldview that emphasized individual claims and the clash of egoistic interests dressed up in rights language. The essay contains helpful examples of

the term *ius in re* signifying a right. For criticism of Villey's later historiography, see Tierney, *Idea of Natural Rights,* pp. 130-42.

191. *De Paupertate Christi,* p. 236: "Sic ergo ius, dominium, et proprietas important posse licite uti rebus venientibus in usum vitae humanae. . . ."

192. *De Paupertate Christi,* p. 238: "Alio modo potest aliquis habere ius in aliquo re non nomine suo, tamen pro se, sicut si aliquis concederet alicui domum suam ad inhabitandum vel bladum vel vinum ad comedendum et bibendum quamdio placeret sibi."

193. *De Paupertate Christi,* p. 238: "Et consimile etiam ius habet filiusfamilias et servus in necessariis vitae sibi ministrandis a patre et a domino qui sunt principales domini rerum."

194. *De Paupertate Christi,* p. 242.

195. *De Paupertate Christi.* On the diminished status of the monk, see Paulin M. Blecker, "The Civil Rights of the Monk in Roman and Canon Law: The Monk as *Servus,*" *American Benedictine Review* 17 (1966): 185-98.

196. Juan Lopez, *Tractatus vere Catholicus de Matrimonio et Legitimatione,* in *Tractatus Universi Iuris* (Venice, 1584), vol. 9, pp. 39b-46b. Lopez was a well-placed ecclesiastical official who served as an advisor to Cardinal Aeneas Silvius Piccolomini, the future Pope Pius III, during his tenure as archbishop of Siena. His treatise on marriage bears the date of November 1478. See Ernest Nys, "Introduction," to Francisco de Victoria, *De Indis et de Iure Belli Relectiones* (Washington, DC: Carnegie Institution, 1917), p. 64.

197. Juan Lopez, *Tractatus,* Sec. 15, p. 40b.

198. Sec. 15, p. 40b.

199. Secs. 15-16, p. 40b.

200. Sec. 13, p. 40b ("In prole, ut matre suscipiatur et religiose educetur, cum proles non dicitur bonum matrimonii solum inquantum per matrimonium generatur, sed inquantum in matrimonio suscipitur et educatur").

201. Sec. 20, p. 40b.

202. Thus the Gloss to Gratian's *Decretum* known as *Ordinaturus Magister* stated regarding the dispensation given to the patriarchs: "Per legem aliquam super hoc specialiter latam; erat tamen quodam modo interdictum in paradiso cum dominus ait, 'erunt duo in carne una,' et etiam lege naturali, quia cuique naturaliter erat insitum quod tibi non vis, etc. . . ." ("Concerning this [Abraham's polygamous relationship with his handmaiden], it was specially laid down by law; nevertheless, this was forbidden in another respect in Paradise, when the Lord said, 'you will be two in one flesh,' and also by the natural law situated in every person, that, 'what you do not wish for yourself, etc.'"). Quoted in Rudolf Weigand, *Die Naturrechtslehre der Legisten und Dekretisten von Irnerius bis Accursius und von Gratian bis Johannes Teutonicus* (Munich: Max Hueber Verlag, 1967), p. 416. Peter Lombard made similar arguments. See *Sententiarum Libri Quattuor,* bk. IV, dist. 33, pp. 681-82.

203. Lopez, *Tractatus vere Catholicus,* sec. 21, p. 40b ("causa multiplicandi fideles et prolem ad cultum divinum").

204. Sec. 21, p. 41a ("Nam, ut dixi, non solum est de bonis matrimonii procreatio prolis, sed educatio; quia educatio seu alimentatio perturbaretur, quando mulier habere plures viros propter confusionem et incertitudinem patris . . .").

205. Sec. 21, p. 41a ("[E]t sic proles a nullo homine alimentaretur, ut filius et confunderetur matrimonium, et finis matrimonii, in his quae sunt de iure naturali . . .").

206. Sec. 22, p. 41a. ("[S]icut natura speciei, quae convenit homini sub ratione, qua est homo, ut ne ex aliqua dispensatione posset perturbari inter homines educatio, seu alimentatio prolis, et sic de iure naturali est, ut unus tantum unam habeat in matrimonium").

207. Domingo de Soto, *De Justitia et Jure libri decem* (Venice, 1589), bk. IV, q. 1, art. 1, p. 283.

208. Domingo de Soto, bk. IV, q. 1, art. 1, p. 283.

209. Domingo de Soto, bk. IV, q. 1, art. 1, p. 283.

210. Domingo de Soto, bk. IV, q. 1, art. 1, p. 283.

211. Domingo de Soto, bk. IV, q. 1, art. 1, p. 283.

212. Domingo de Soto, bk. IV, q. 1, art. 1, p. 283. This letter and its legal consequences are discussed below, p. 103.

213. Domingo de Soto, bk. IV, q. 1, art. 1, p. 283 ("Et filius in parente, qui curam suorum habere tenentur").

214. Domingo de Soto, bk. IV, q. 1, art. 1, p. 283.

215. Domingo de Soto, bk. IV, q. 1, art. 1, p. 283. "Enimvero pater ius habet in filios; dominium autem si proprie fandum est, non item. Est inquam aequum et iustum atque adeo ius, ut pater filiis imperet ob suum ipsorum bonum, quos propter ipsos diligit, instituit, et educat. Dominium autem non quodcunque ius et potestas significat, sed certe illam, quae est in rem, qua uti pro libito nostro possumus in nostram propriam utilitatem, quamque ob nosipsos diligimus."

Elsewhere, Soto incorporated this distinction into his general definition of *dominium:* "Adiectum tamen est definitioni, quod dominium sit facultas ad proprium utentis commodum, quo differat ab aliis iuris speciebus, quibus superior inferiores ob suum ipsorum bonum gubernat." ("It is added to the definition that *dominium* is a faculty of seeking one's own advantage, in which it differs from other types of rights, by which a superior governs inferiors for the sake of the good.")

216. See *Codex* 9.15.

217. See Richard Saller, "Corporal Punishment, Authority, and Obedience in the Roman Household," in Rawson, ed., *Marriage, Divorce, and Children,* pp. 144, 162. Not so, however, with the Roman schoolmaster. According to Stanley F. Bonner: "Throughout antiquity, from the time of Socrates to that of St. Augustine and beyond, across the whole Mediterranean world, from Egypt to Bordeaux and from Carthage to Antioch, corporal punishment was a constant feature of school life. Even though prominent individuals from time to time protested against it in the strongest terms, it was never widely condemned by public opinion." See Stanley F. Bonner, *Education in Ancient Rome: From the Elder Cato to the Younger Pliny* (Berkeley: University of California Press, 1977), p. 143.

218. At least one medieval Romanist writer maintained a similar silence. Placentinus wrote simply that an elder may correct the younger members of the family by paternal right, but did not specify how much or how little force might permissibly be used. See *Summa Codicis,* sec. *De Emendatione Propinquorum,* p. 433.

219. X.5.12.12.

220. *Glossa Ordinaria,* X.5.12.12.

221. See *Glossa Ordinaria*, X.5.12.12, v. *corrigere quendam de familia.*

222. See Hostiensis, *Lectura*, at X.5.12.12, v. *corrigere*. ". . . ne immoderate iure suo utatur." [Citation omitted.]

223. See Barbara Hanawalt, *The Ties That Bound*, p. 183. See also Fleming, *Family and Household*, p. 64; and Shahar, *Childhood in the Middle Ages*, pp. 109-11.

224. Under Roman law, one's paternal rights might also be severed where the emperor imposed the penalty of banishment with loss of citizenship for some grave crime. See *Institutes*, 1.12.1. A penal reduction to slave status also resulted in termination of paternal rights. See *Institutes*, 1.12.3. Placentinus observed that some of the crimes that qualified for loss of paternal rights included: exposure of one's children, treason, and incest. See *Summa Institutionum* (Turin: Ex Officina Erasmiana, 1973), bk. 1, title 10, p. 11.

225. See *Institutes*, 1.12.6-8.

226. See *Institutes*, 1.12.4.

227. *Institutes*, 1.12.4.

228. See Thomas Kuehn, *Emancipation in Late Medieval Florence* (New Brunswick, NJ: Rutgers University Press, 1982), p. 1.

229. Kuehn, *Emancipation*, pp. 28-32.

230. See C. 20, q. 2, c. 1.

231. See C. 20, q. 2, c. 2.

232. See Paucapalea, *Summa über das Decretum Gratiani*, ed. Johann Friedrich von Schulte (Aalen: Scientia Verlag, 1965), C. 20, qq. 1 and 2, pp. 94-95; and Johannes Teutonicus, *Glossa Ordinaria*, C. 20, q. 2, c. 1, v. *de his.*

233. Johannes Teutonicus did ask whether a mother, equally with a father, might recall a child from a monastery. C. 20, q. 2, c. 1, v. *aut unus*. It seemed she had such power, Johannes began, "because what touches all . . ." *(quia quod omnes tangit, etc)*. But where the father consents, Johannes continued, the mother may not usually revoke consent.

234. Goffredus Tranensis, for instance, repeated the *Decretum*, indicating that where a child was under the age of discretion the parents might invalidate the entry into monastic life within a year, but added that the time began to run from the time the parents actually learned of their child's actions. Goffredus further qualified the rule by noting that a slightly longer period might be tolerated where the monastery was in a remote location. When, however, a child reached the age of sixteen and ratified his or her admission to the monastery, the presumption shifted in favor of the child's free choice and parents were precluded from raising objections. See *Summa super titulis decretalium* (Aalen: Scientia Verlag, 1992), bk. III, *De Regularibus*, sec. 4, p. 150rb. Hostiensis largely echoed Goffredus's analysis. See *Summa*, bk. III, *De Regularibus et Transeuntibus ad Religionem*, sec. 9.

235. See *Summa*, bk. III, *De Voto et Voti Redemptione*, sec. 7.

236. Bk. III, *De Voto et Voti Redemptione*, sec. 7.

237. Bk. III, *De Voto et Voti Redemptione*, sec. 7.

238. Bk. III, *De Voto et Voti Redemptione*, sec. 7.

239. The practice of oblation arose in the eighth and ninth centuries. See Boswell, *Kindness of Strangers*, pp. 238-45. It was an expectation of this period that children would ratify their vocations when of the age to do so, but the point was not without con-

troversy. Rabanus Maurus authored a treatise asserting that children, once handed over, were to remain irrevocably attached to the monastery. See pp. 244-46.

Did oblation still occur in the thirteenth century? Examples might be drawn from the lives of a pair of well-known historical personages. St. Gertrude of Helfta, sometimes also called "St. Gertrude the Great," was born probably in 1256. Virtually nothing is known of her parents or her family circumstances. She was given to the monastery at Helfta probably in her fifth year, where she flourished as an intellectual and as a spiritual writer. See Sister Maximilan Marnau, "Introduction," Gertrude of Helfta, *The Herald of Divine Love* (New York: Paulist Press, 1993), pp. 5-10. See also "Gertrude the Great," in Shawn Madigan, ed., *Mystics, Visionaries, and Prophets: A Historical Anthology of Women's Spiritual Writings* (Minneapolis: Fortress Press, 1998), pp. 148-51.

And, of course, the example of Thomas Aquinas provides a second vivid example of the continued vitality of oblation. In his biography of St. Thomas, Jacques Maritain reports: "At the age of five he was placed as an oblate in the abbey of Monte Cassino; he persistently interrogated the monks, had only one question upon his lips: 'What is God?' was his constant inquiry.

"The silent child had no thought of anything but study and devotion; his desire was to consecrate himself to God. Could anything be simpler? They would make him a Benedictine." Jacques Maritain, *The Angelic Doctor: The Life and Thought of Saint Thomas Aquinas*, trans. J. F. Scanlan (New York: Dial Press, 1931), p. 25. As is well known, Thomas eventually repudiated his childhood calling to the Benedictines and became a member of the Dominicans.

René Metz has noted that "the practice of oblation was perpetual through the medieval period. . . . It was only abolished officially in the fifteenth century, by Pope Martin V, in 1430." René Metz, "L'enfant dans le droit canonique médiéval. Orientations de recherche," *Recueils de la Société Jean Bodin* 36 (1976): 9, 51.

240. Innocent IV, *Apparatus*, X.1.14.3, v. *Noverunt.*

241. *Apparatus*, X.1.14.3. Paternal power might continue to be asserted, Innocent stated, with respect to paternal goods *(in rebus paternis).*

242. *Apparatus*, X.1.14.3.

243. *Apparatus*, X.1.14.3.

244. See *Lectura*, X.1.14.3, v. *gubernare.*

245. *Lectura*, X.1.14.3.

246. *Lectura*, X.1.14.3.

247. *Lectura*, X.1.14.3. "[U]nde dicas quod quantum ad patrimonialia profectitia omnino remanent in patria potestate. . . ."

248. *Lectura*, X.1.14.3. This rule remained intact through the end of the Middle Ages. An *additio* to the text of Panormitanus taught that "spiritual dignities" — such as the episcopacy or an abbacy, or other similar ecclesiastical status — "liberated" one from paternal power. Lesser dignities, it seems, at least by implication, did not. See Panormitanus, *Commentaria*, X.1.14.3, *additio:* "Sub patria potestate. Dic quod dignitas spiritualis vel episcopalis abbatialis et reliquiae id genus liberant quem a patria potestate."

249. See Hostiensis, *Summa*, bk. III, *De Contrahenda Emptione et Venditione*, sec. 2: "[P]otest tamen pater vendere filium necessitate famis ingruente. . . ." Cf. *Codex* 4.43.2 (recognizing the possibility a child might be sold).

250. See Hostiensis, *Summa,* bk. III, *De Contrahenda et Venditione,* sec. 2: "Sed nunquid mater potest filium vendere non puto [citation omitted]. Et quia nec l. [lex] reperitur concessum nec filium habet in potestate sicut pater. . . ."

Notes to Chapter 3

1. On the significance of fault, *culpa,* for the loss of rights, see above, p. 94.

2. See especially pp. 88-93 above.

3. See Luke 8:2, and Mark 16:9.

4. John 19:25.

5. See Luke 24:10; and John 20:1-2; and 11-18. See also Mary Anne Getty-Sullivan, *Women in the New Testament* (Collegeville, MN: Liturgical Press, 2001), pp. 182-91.

6. See Luke 1:36-37; and 39-65.

7. The scholarship on Mary is, of course, enormous. A recent, helpful study is Sally Cunneen, *In Search of Mary: The Woman and the Symbol* (New York: Ballantine Books, 1996).

8. See Elizabeth Castelli, "Paul on Women and Gender," in Ross Shepard Kraemer and Mary Rose D'Angelo, eds., *Women and Christian Origins* (New York: Oxford University Press, 1999), pp. 221, 224. Cf. Romans 16:1-2. Castelli proposes that the term *diakonos,* used by Paul in its masculine and not its feminine form, should probably be understood as signifying an important position of leadership, and that the term *prostatis,* the "feminine form of the noun *prostates*[,] suggests a public role of patronage and protection."

9. See Romans 16:3. See also Acts 18:2.

10. See 1 Corinthians 1:11.

11. See Acts 1:13-14.

12. See Ekkehard W. Stegemann and Wolfgang Stegemann, *The Jesus Movement: A Social History of the First Century,* trans. O. C. Dean, Jr. (Minneapolis: Fortress Press, 1999), p. 395.

13. Stegemann and Stegemann, *The Jesus Movement,* p. 395. For a review of the scholarship identifying Junia as a woman, see Ute E. Eisen, *Women Officeholders in Early Christianity: Epigraphical and Literary Studies* (Collegeville, MN: Michael Glazier Books, 2000), pp. 47-49.

14. Stegemann and Stegemann, *The Jesus Movement,* p. 397; and Roger Gryson, *The Ministry of Women in the Early Church,* trans. Jean Laporte and Mary Louise Hall (Collegeville, MN: Liturgical Press, 1976), pp. 5-6. Cf. 1 Corinthians 11:5.

15. 1 Timothy 2:12. Cf. Gryson, *Ministry of Women,* pp. 7-8.

16. 1 Timothy 2:11.

17. 1 Timothy 2:13-14.

18. This is Jezebel, who has seduced others to fornication and to commit other sins. See Revelation 2:20-23.

19. On the earliest mention of virgins as a rank or order, see Jean La Porte, *The Role of Women in Early Christianity* (New York: Edwin Mellen Press, 1982), p. 70; on widows, see Bonnie Bowman Thurston, *The Widows: A Women's Ministry in the Early*

Church (Minneapolis: Fortress Press, 1989), pp. 36-75; and Gryson, *Ministry of Women*, pp. 8-14.

20. See the text and notes provided by J. K. Elliott, *The Apocryphal New Testament* (Oxford: Oxford University Press, 1993), pp. 48-67. Scholars now date this work, "or at least the bulk of [its] first draft," to the second half of the second century.

21. *Apocryphal New Testament*, p. 50.

22. Over 100 Greek manuscripts survive, as well as translations into languages such as Syriac, Old Church Slavonic, Armenian, and Ethiopic. *Apocryphal New Testament*, p. 48.

23. Jerome criticized the *Protoevangelion* for asserting that Joseph was previously married with children. He argued that the scriptural and other references to Jesus' siblings should rather be understood as referring to cousins. *Apocryphal New Testament*, pp. 50-51.

24. See Jerome, *Letter* 108, *Corpus Scriptorum Ecclesiasticorum Latinorum* 55: 306-51 (*Epitaphiam Sanctae Paulae*).

25. See Jerome, *Letter* 127, *Corpus Scriptorum Ecclesiasticorum Latinorum* 56: 145-56 (*Ad Principiam Virginem De Vita Sanctae Marcellae*).

26. *Contra Faustum*, XXIV.2 (quoted in T. J. van Bavel, "Augustine's Views on Women," *Augustiniana* 39 [1989]: 5, 19, note 55).

27. See van Bavel, "Augustine's Views on Women," p. 19, note 54.

28. *De beata vita*, 2.10, *Corpus Christianorum Series Latina* 29: 70-71 ("Ipsam, inquam, prorsus, mater, arcem philosophiae tenuisti"). Cf. van Bavel, "Augustine's Views on Women," p. 8 and note 10 (quoting St. Augustine).

29. See van Bavel, "Augustine's Views on Women," pp. 15-18. "[Men] feel themselves superior and think that they can do with impunity all that they want, whereas they are unreasonably exacting vis à vis their wives. They excuse themselves by saying that their body makes conjugal fidelity impossible. . . . Nevertheless, women show a greater self-control and fidelity" (pp. 16-17).

30. See Peter Lombard, *Sententiarum Libri Quatuor* (Paris: Louis Vives, 1892), bk. II, dist. 18, p. 291.

31. See Hostiensis, *Lectura*, X.3.26.18, v. *masculis* ("Sic erit deterioris conditionis ius mulierum quod et in multis casibus est reperire").

32. See Frederic William Maitland, ed., *Select Passages from the Works of Bracton and Azo* (London: Selden Society, 1895), p. 60.

33. Maitland, ed., *Bracton and Azo*, p. 60.

34. *Digest* 1.5.9 (Papinian, *Quaestionum* 31) ("In multis iuris nostri articulis deterior est condicio feminarum quam masculorum").

35. 1 Corinthians 7:3-6 (Saint Joseph New Catholic Edition).

36. See Henry G. Liddell and Rupert Scott, *A Greek-English Lexicon* (Oxford: Clarendon Press, 1940), p. 1277.

37. For this translation of *opheile*, see John T. Noonan, Jr., *Contraception: A History of Its Treatment by the Catholic Theologians and Canonists*, enlarged edition (Cambridge, MA: Harvard University Press, 1986), p. 42.

Jeffrey Ford has recently stressed the importance of Paul's duty-based treatment of the conjugal relationship: "By reminding husbands and wives that they have a *duty* to serve rather than by teaching that the married have the *right* to sexual satisfaction, the apostle reminds believers that charity and self-sacrifice, not self-indulgence or even self-fulfillment, are the aims of piety." See Jeffrey E. Ford, *Love, Marriage, and Sex in the Christian Tradition from Antiquity to Today* (San Francisco: International Scholars Publications, 1999), p. 143.

The canonists, of course, were no modern-day liberals who associated rights-talk with ideas of an autonomous self seeking self-gratification at the expense of a larger set of duties toward others. What is significant about the canonists' use of rights language is not the idea of self-fulfillment, but the idea that the requirement to preserve the rights of innocent parties is itself a moral obligation of the highest order. This principle led the canonists into using rights language as a way of calling spouses to heroic conduct (such as preserving the rights of spouses with leprosy, see below), but also led them to harsh conclusions (such as on the role of self-help in addressing the question of the bride reluctant to consummate the union, see below).

38. See Glenn W. Olsen, "Progeny, Faithfulness, Sacred Bond: Marriage in the Age of Augustine," in Glenn W. Olsen, ed., *Christian Marriage: An Historical Study* (New York: Seabury, 2001), p. 121.

39. Olsen, "Progeny, Faithfulness, Sacred Bond," pp. 121-22.

40. In a thoughtful essay, David Hunter calls particular attention to Augustine's reliance on the standard Roman marriage-contract to assert that "sex beyond the need of procreation is a violation of [the contractual term which stipulates intercourse *liberorum procreandorum causa* — 'For the sake of procreation of children']." David G. Hunter, "Augustine and the Making of Marriage in Roman North Africa," *Journal of Early Christian Studies* 11 (2003): 63, 78-79, and note 49.

41. See St. Augustine, *De Nuptiis et Concupiscentia*, 1.14.15, in *Corpus Scriptorum Ecclesiasticorum Latinorum* 42, pp. 228-29; and St. Augustine, *De Bono Coniugali*, in *Corpus Scriptorum Ecclesiasticorum Latinorum* 41, pp. 193-96.

42. See St. Augustine, *De Bono Coniugali*, sec. 5.5., at *CSEL*, vol. 42, p. 194 (". . . ardore concupiscentiae ipso suo iure intemperanter utentes . . .").

43. See St. Augustine, *Epistle* 262 (to Ecdicia), *CSEL*, vol. 57, pp. 621-31. On Ecdicia, see also Dyan Elliott, *Spiritual Marriage: Sexual Abstinence in Medieval Wedlock* (Princeton, NJ: Princeton University Press, 1993), pp. 57-58.

44. See Elliott, *Spiritual Marriage*, pp. 57-58.

45. See *Epistle* 262, *CSEL*, 57, pp. 621-623.

46. *CSEL*, 57, p. 622.

47. See Tertullian, *Exhortation à la chastité*, 9.4, Sources chrétiennes, no. 319, p. 100: ". . . et ideo virginis principalis est sanctitas, quia caret stupri affinitate." ("And so the principal sanctity is virginity, because it lacks the affinity to fornication.")

48. Tertullian, *Exhortation*, 10.1, p. 102 ("Desisti esse debitor: o te felicem!").

49. Tertullian, *Exhortation*: "Rape occasionem, etsi non exoptatissimam, attamen opportunam, non habere cui debitum solveres et a quo exsolveris" ("Seize the occasion, even if it is not ideal, nevertheless it is opportune, not to have to pay the debt or have it demanded from you"). Tertullian here is addressing widows and widowers on the death of their spouses.

50. See Hincmar, *Epistle* 22, PL: 126, 132, 139.

51. Hincmar, *Epistle* 22.

52. Aside from Augustine's single usage of the word *ius* in *De Bono Coniugali* (see

above, note 42), at least one other patristic document makes use of this term in describing the conjugal relationship. Again, it is a vague, almost *pro forma* usage. In a letter attributed, probably wrongly, to Paulinus of Nola, the woman Celancia is criticized for taking a vow of chastity "as if forgetful of the marriage covenant and mindless of the pact of right" (". . . quasi oblita foederis nuptialis pactique huius ac iuris immemor . . ."). See *Epistle* II, *Ad Celanciam*, in *CSEL*, vol. 29, pp. 455-56.

53. See Elizabeth M. Makowski, "The Conjugal Debt and Medieval Canon Law," *Journal of Medieval History* 3 (1977): 99, 100-101.

54. See C. 32, q. 2, d.p.c. 2.

55. C. 32, q. 2, d.p.c. 2. See also C. 32, q. 2, d.p.c. 5.

56. C. 33, q. 5, pr.

57. C. 33, q. 5, c. 1.

58. C. 33, q. 5, cc. 4 and 5.

59. C. 33, q. 5, d.p.c. 11.

60. C. 33, q. 5, d.p.c. 11.

61. See Paucapalea, *Summa über das Decretum Gratiani*, C. 33, q. 5, pp. 133-34.

62. See Rufinus, *Summa Decretorum*, C. 33, q. 5, v. *quod autem sine consensu*, pp. 504-5. Rufinus extended this obligation to obtain spousal consent to other actions that had the same practical effect as a vow of continence, such as the decision to take a long pilgrimage, say, to the tomb of St. James in Spain.

63. See *Summa Parisiensis on the Decretum Gratiani*, Terence P. McLaughlin, ed. (Toronto: Pontifical Institute, 1952), C. 33, q. 11, and d.p.c. 11, p. 254.

64. See *Glossa Ordinaria*, C. 33, q. 5, c. 11, v. *nisi auctor.*

65. See *Summa, 'Induent Sancti,'* C. 33, q. 5, c. 11, p. 650: "Votum vero viri quo ius leditur uxoris ipsa revocare potest iudicis auctoritate interveniente. . . ."

66. C. 28, q. 1, pr. Cf. Romans 14:23.

67. C. 28, q. 1, pr.

68. C. 28, q. 1, pr.

69. C. 28, q. 1, pr.

70. C. 28, q. 1, pr. Cf. Luke 12:52-53 (Jesus comes to divide families, meaning, presumably, that they nevertheless remained valid families before the law); Luke 14:26 ("If anyone comes to me and does not hate his father and mother, and wife and children, and brothers and sisters . . ."); Matthew 19:29 ("And everyone who has left house, or brothers, or sisters, or father, or mother, or wife, or children, or lands, for my name's sake, shall receive a hundredfold").

71. 1 Corinthians 7:12-14.

72. C. 28, q. 1, pr. Cf. 1 Corinthians 7:12-14. Gratian did not mean to approve the marriages of Christians with non-believers. Rather, the sort of Christian/infidel marriage he had in mind involved an unbeliever who converted to Christianity and chose to remain with her or his spouse.

73. C. 28, q. 1, cc. 10-17.

74. C. 28, q. 1, d.p.c. 17.

75. C. 28, q. 1, d.p.c. 17.

76. C. 28, q. 1, d.p.c. 17.

77. See Rufinus, C. 28, q. 1, *Quod autem inter fideles*, pp. 453-54. A *ratum* marriage can only be effected by "taking up the faith" (*per fidei susceptionem*).

78. *Summa Magistri Rolandi,* C. 28, q. 1, p. 133.

79. See Rufinus, *Summa Decretorum,* C. 28, q. 1, c. 5, v. *idolatria.*

80. Rufinus, *Summa Decretorum,* C. 28, q. 1, c. 5, v. *idolatria.*

81. See Hugh of St. Victor, *De Sacramentis Fidei Christianae,* PL 176: 504-10, col. 504.

82. Hugh of St. Victor, *De Sacramentis,* col. 506 ("Et ego dico quod quando infidelis uxorem propter propagationem filiorum ducit, fidem toro conjugali servat, sociam diligit et custodit, et illa vivente ad alienam societatem non transit: quamvis in alio infidelis sit, quia scilicet non credit, in hoc tamen neque contra fidem neque contra divinam institutionem facit"). Hugh would even make the case that it was possible, in some sense, to call these marriages sacramental. For an understanding of Hugh's sacramental theology, consult Teresa Olsen Pierre, "Marriage, Body, and Sacrament in the Age of Hugh of St. Victor," in Glenn Olsen, ed., *Christian Marriage: A Historical Study* (New York: Crossroad, 2001), pp. 213, 217-20, 223-27, and 236-37.

83. Hugh of St. Victor, *De Sacramentis,* col. 506.

84. *De Sacramentis,* col. 506.

85. *De Sacramentis,* col. 507.

86. *De Sacramentis,* col. 505. ("Dicit tibi uxor tua: 'Christianus factus es, ego te non sequar; quia idola non colis, quia parentum tuorum ritum et consuetudinem abjecisti, eo ad alium, vel si ad alium non eo, tecum jam non eo, non te cognosco maritum nisi Christum neges.' Hic tibi intende: 'Injuria Creatoris jus solvit matrimonii.'")

87. It must be stressed also that the canonists did not contemplate the possibility of Christians marrying non-Christians. A statement by Laurentius Hispanus on the impossibility of a Christian marrying a Jew according to Jewish ritual is typical. Such a union, Laurentius declared, was "against the nature of marriage," and so should be disregarded. See Brendan J. McManus, "The Ecclesiology of Laurentius Hispanus (c. 1180-1248) and His Contribution to the Romanization of Canon Law Jurisprudence: With an Edition of the Apparatus Glossarum Laurentii Hispani in Compilationem Tertiam" (Ph.D. dissertation, Syracuse University, 1991), Comp. III, 4.10.1, pp. 548-49. It has been noted that the canon law, Roman law, Spanish and German law all prohibited intermarriage between Jews and Christians and imposed harsh penalties on offenders. Walter Pakter, *Medieval Canon Law and the Jews* (Ebelsbach: Verlag Rolf Gremer, 1988), pp. 271-77.

The situation the canonists had in mind chiefly was that of a marriage in which one partner, but not the other, converted to Christianity. Where it became impossible for the new Christian to remain in such a union because of the threats posed to his or her faith, it was possible to separate so as to remarry within the Christian faith. This practice was known as the "Pauline privilege." For a history of this doctrine, see John T. Noonan, Jr., *Power to Dissolve: Lawyers and Marriages in the Courts of the Roman Curia* (Cambridge, MA: Harvard University Press, 1972), pp. 342-59.

88. Peter Lombard wrote: "The efficient cause of marriage is consent, not any [consent], but that expressed through words not of future, but of present tense." ("Efficiens autem causa matrimonii est consensus, non quilibet, sed per verba expressus, nec de futuro sed de praesenti.") *Libri IV Sententiarum,* bk. IV, dist. 27, p. 659.

89. See James A. Brundage, "Implied Consent to Intercourse," in Angeliki E.

Laiou, ed., *Marriage in Ancient and Medieval Societies* (Washington, DC: Dumbarton Oaks Research Library, 1993), pp. 246-48.

90. See Penny S. Gold, "The Marriage of Mary and Joseph in the Twelfth-Century Ideology of Marriage," in Vern L. Bullough and James A. Brundage, eds., *Sexual Practices and the Medieval Church* (Buffalo, NY: Prometheus Books, 1982), p. 102. The decretist Rolandus argued that even though Joseph and Mary refrained from sexual intercourse, they nevertheless satisfied all three goods of marriage: fidelity, children, and sacramental unity. See Rolandus, *Summa, C.* 27, q. 2, c. 10, p. 128.

91. On Rolandus, who probably should not be associated with Pope Alexander III, see John T. Noonan, Jr., "Who Was Rolandus?" in Kenneth Pennington and Robert Somerville, eds., *Law, Church, and Society: Essays in Honor of Stephan Kuttner* (Philadelphia: University of Pennsylvania Press, 1977), pp. 21-48. See also Rudolf Weigand, "Magister Rolandus und Papst Alexander III," *Archiv für katholisches Kirchenrecht* 149 (1980): 3-44.

92. See Rolandus, *Summa, C.* 27, q. 2, cc. 6 and 7, pp. 127-28. See also James A. Coriden, *The Indissolubility Added to Christian Marriage by Consummation* (Rome: Catholic Book Agency, 1961), pp. 7-9.

93. See Benno Grimm, ed., *Die Ehelehre des Magister Honorius. Ein Beitrag zur Ehelehre der anglo-normanisschen Schule* (Rome: Studia Gratiana, 1989), p. 264.

94. Grimm, ed., *Die Ehelehre des Magister Honorius*, p. 264.

95. Grimm, ed., *Die Ehelehre des Magister Honorius*, pp. 264-66.

96. Grimm, ed., *Die Ehelehre des Magister Honorius*, pp. 269-70.

97. Grimm, ed., *Die Ehelehre des Magister Honorius*, pp. 269-70. The husband, according to Honorius, had the "power of demanding" the debt (*potestatem exigendi*). The wife, however, was under no obligation to accede to his wishes: "Illa tamen non habet necessitatem reddendi, quia vinculum illud nondum habet secundum effectum . . ." (p. 270).

98. See "Summa d'Huguccio sur le Décret de Gratien," ed. J. Roman, *Nouvelle revue historique de droit français et étranger* 27 (1903): 745, 755-56.

99. "Summa d'Huguccio," p. 756. As Huguccio put it: "Mihi videtur jus exigendi est ipsum conjugium, vel oritur ex eo, et statim competit ex quo est conjugium, sed non statim competit illius executio, id est, actus exequendi illud jus. . . . Potest dici quod a tempore traductionis vel traditionis vel benedictionis sacerdotalis." *Traductio* and *traditio* referred to the act of handing over the bride at the time of the wedding ceremony. See Coriden, '*Indissolubility*,' p. 3; and James Brundage, *Law, Sex, and Christian Society* (Chicago: University of Chicago Press, 1987), p. 262.

100. "Summa d'Huguccio," p. 779.

101. "Summa d'Huguccio," p. 756.

102. "Summa d'Huguccio," p. 756.

103. "Summa d'Huguccio," p. 756.

104. See Bernard of Pavia, *Summa de Matrimonio*, contained in *Summa Decretalium*, ed. E. A. T. Laspeyres (Graz: Akademische Druck-und Verlaganstalt, 1956), pp. 287-306.

105. See *Summa de Matrimonio*, p. 299.

106. *Summa de Matrimonio*, p. 299.

107. *Summa de Matrimonio*, p. 299.

108. See *Summa, 'Induent Sancti,'* C. 27, q. 2, c. 6, pp. 602-3.

109. *Summa, 'Induent Sancti,'* pp. 603-4.

110. *Summa, 'Induent Sancti,'* pp. 603-4. Cf. X.3.32.7 (giving the text of *Ex Publico*).

111. *Summa, 'Induent Sancti,'* p. 604.

112. *Summa, 'Induent Sancti,'* p. 604.

113. *Summa, 'Induent Sancti,'* p. 604: "[E]t vis ista sine dolo fuit, et vis iusta dici potest, sicut vis a magistratu. . . ."

114. *Summa, 'Induent Sancti,'* p. 605.

115. *Summa, 'Induent Sancti,'* p. 605: "Interim tamen nihilominus potest vir eam cognoscere suo iure, etiam ea repugnante."

116. *Summa, 'Induent Sancti,'* p. 605: "Petenti autem illa negare sine mortali peccato non potest nisi parata sit statim monasterium intrare. . . ." The author compared the obedience the wife owed to her husband to that owed by a cleric to his bishop: if the cleric was not prepared to obey his bishop, he was required immediately to enter a monastery. The woman was under the same obligation.

117. See Hostiensis, *Lectura,* X.3.32.7, v. *vel ad virum.*

118. *Lectura,* X.3.32.7, v. *vel ad virum.*

119. *Lectura,* X.3.32.7, v. *vel ad virum.* The decretals Hostiensis cites include: X.4.1.10, which permits a party to compel consummation by means of ecclesiastical censure; X.4.1.9, which stands for the proposition that present-tense consent makes a marriage; and X.4.1.22, which again recognized the Church's power to enforce a marriage contract by ecclesiastical censure.

120. Alexander of Hales, *Glossa in Quatuor Libros Sententiarum Petri Lombardi* (Quaracchi: Ex Typographia Collegii S. Bonaventurae, 1957), vol. IV, p. 469.

121. Vol. IV, p. 469.

122. Vol. IV, p. 469: "Ergo videtur talis usus fuisse iure suo et Matrimonium consummasse."

123. Vol. IV, p. 469. The term Alexander uses, *animae delectatio,* carries rich subjective coloration: where there had been no "delighting," or "pleasure" of the soul, on this choice of words, there was no true consummation.

124. See Thomas Aquinas, *Summa Theologiae,* 2a 2ae, q. 154, art. 7.

125. *Summa,* 2a 2ae, q. 154, art. 7, resp: "Dicendum quod raptus. . . . quando aliquis violentiam infert ad virginem illicite deflorandam."

126. *Summa,* 2a 2ae, q. 154, art. 7, resp. 4.

127. *Summa:* "[E]t ideo quamvis peccet violentiam inferendo, excusatur tamen a crimine raptus."

128. See Panormitanus, *Commentaria,* X.3.32.7, notes 1 and 2.

129. See Jill Elaine Hasday, "Contest and Consent: A Legal History of Marital Rape," *California Law Review* 88 (2000): 1373, 1382.

130. Hasday, "Contest and Consent," p. 1397, note 68.

131. See James A. Brundage, "Sexual Equality in Medieval Canon Law," in Joel T. Rosenthal, ed., *Medieval Women and the Sources of Medieval History* (Athens, GA: University of Georgia Press, 1990), p. 66.

132. See Peter Lombard, *IV Libri Sententiarum,* bk. IV, dist. 32, p. 678: "Sciendum est etiam, quia, cum in omnibus aliis vir praesit mulieri, ut caput corpori, est enim 'vir

caput mulieris,' in solvendo tamen carnis debito pares sunt" (quoting 1 Corinthians 11:3).

133. See Gandulf of Bologna, *Sententiarum Libri Quatuor,* ed. Johannes de Walter (Vienna: Aemilius Haim, 1924), lib. 4, sec. 227, p. 515.

134. Gandulf of Bologna, *Sententiarum Libri Quatuor,* p. 515: "Sunt autem pares in carnali debito reddendo coniugati. . . . In aliis vero praeest vir."

135. See Hostiensis, *Summa,* bk. IV, *De Matrimonio,* sec. 21: "Et etiam est tantus effectus matrimonii consummati quod mulier non habet potestatem sui corporis, sed vir, et econtra."

136. Bk. IV, *De Matrimonio,* sec. 21: "Unde nec alter altero invito potest vitam mutare nec ad religionem convolare."

137. Bk. IV, *De Matrimonio,* sec. 20.

138. See Agathon Wunderlich, ed., *Tancredi Summa de Matrimonio* (Göttingen: Vandenhoeck und Ruprecht, 1841), tit. 15, "Quis sit effectus matrimonii," pp. 15-16.

139. See David Lyons, "The Correlativity of Rights and Duties," *Nous* 4 (1970): 45, 46-49.

140. Lyons, "Correlativity," p. 48.

141. See Richard H. Helmholz, *Marriage Litigation in Medieval England* (Cambridge: Cambridge University Press, 1974), pp. 1-5.

142. See Pierre J. Payer, *The Bridling of Desire: Views of Sex in the Later Middle Ages* (Toronto: University of Toronto Press, 1993), pp. 89-92.

143. See below, especially the discussion of conjugal rights and leprosy, pp. 119-22. From an early stage, however, the canonists agreed that the marital right could, indeed must, be forfeited where a party was at fault. Thus in a decretal dateable to the years 1168-1181, Alexander III dealt with a particularly egregious case of adultery: a woman, apparently a widow, married a man, who promptly had sexual relations with her daughter. The pope urged the bishop who wrote him to impose an appropriate penance on the husband, and also declared that the man should no longer seek sexual relations with his new wife. But, Alexander admonished the bishop, should the wife seek relations with her spouse, he must not refuse her, lest by this deprivation she be led into sin. The husband lost his right through his misconduct, but his wife, who was blameless, was not thereby to be deprived of her right. Stanley Chodorow and Charles Duggan, eds., *Decretales ineditae saeculi XII* (Vatican City: Biblioteca Apostolica Vaticana, 1982), p. 29.

144. On Gregory's teaching, see Regine Birkmeyer, *Ehetrennung und monastische Konversion im Hochmittelalter* (Berlin: Akademie Verlag, 1998), pp. 76-77.

145. See X.3.32.16.

146. Leaving nothing to the imagination, Hostiensis noted that L. meant by this threat self-castration. See Hostiensis, *Lectura,* X.3.32.16, v. *inutilem.*

147. X.3.32.16.

148. X.3.32.16.

149. X.3.32.16.

150. See Bernard of Parma, *Glossa Ordinaria,* X.3.32.16, *casus.*

151. *Glossa Ordinaria,* X.3.32.16, v. *captiose asseruit.*

152. See Hostiensis, *Lectura,* X.3.32.16, v. *audienda.*

153. X.3.32.16. Cf. Hostiensis, *Lectura,* X.3.32.9, v. *uxorem.*

154. X.3.32.17.

155. X.3.32.17.

156. X.3.32.17.

157. See Bernard of Parma, *Glossa Ordinaria*, X.3.32.17, v. *processu vero temporis.*

158. See Hostiensis, *Lectura*, X.3.32.17, v. *exhibeat.* As Hostiensis laconically put it: "exactus, ipse tamen non debet exigere. . . ."

159. See Adhémar Esmein, *Le mariage en droit canonique* (Paris: Sirey, 1895), vol. II, pp. 25-29.

160. See Hostiensis, *Lectura*, X.3.32.1, v. *servare.*

161. See Peter Richards, *The Medieval Leper and His Northern Heirs* (Cambridge, UK: D. S. Brewer, 1977), pp. 3-12; and Ann G. Carmichael, "Leprosy," in Kenneth F. Kiple, *The Cambridge History of Human Diseases* (Cambridge, UK: Cambridge University Press, 1993), p. 834.

162. See Saul N. Brody, *The Disease of the Soul: Leprosy in Medieval Literature* (Ithaca, NY: Cornell University Press, 1974), pp. 60-86; and Katherine Park, "Medicine and Society in Medieval Europe, 500-1500," in Andrew Wear, ed., *Medicine in Society: Historical Essays* (Cambridge, UK: Cambridge University Press, 1992), pp. 59, 86-89.

163. See François-Olivier Touati, *Maladie et société au Moyen âge. La lèpre, les lèpreux, et les lèprosaries dans la province ecclésiastique de Sens jusqu'au milieu du XIV siècle* (Brussels: De Boeck Université, 1998), pp. 51, 247-307.

164. See Brody, *Disease of the Soul*, pp. 65-66; see also Peter Lewis Allen, *The Wages of Sin: Sex and Disease, Past and Present* (Chicago: University of Chicago Press, 2000), pp. 35-37. Some medieval sources associated leprosy with uncontrolled sexual appetites, although it was also the case that "leprosy was sometimes seen as a mark of divine favour. . . ." See David Marcombe, *Leper Knights: The Order of St. Lazarus of Jerusalem in England, c. 1150-1544* (Woodbridge, UK: Boydell Press, 2003), p. 140. Jesus set the model by showing special solicitude for lepers, and through his example it was agreed that one might achieve some measure of sanctification in this world through acts of charity on behalf of lepers (pp. 140-41).

165. See Édouard Jeanselme, "Comment l'Europe, au Moyen Âge, se protége contre la lèpre," *Bulletin de la société française d'histoire de la médecine* 25 (1931): 1.

166. See Brody, *Disease of the Soul*, p. 69.

167. Brody, *Disease of the Soul*, pp. 67-68.

168. X.4.8.1.

169. X.4.8.1.

170. X.4.8.2.

171. X.4.8.2.

172. Matthew 19:9.

173. See Allen, *Wages of Sin*, pp. 33-35.

174. See Goffredus of Trani, *Summa*, bk. IV, *De Coniugio Leprosorum*, p. 179vb.

175. *De Coniugio Leprosorum*, p. 179vb. Goffredus cited Alexander's decretal *Quoniam* on the conjugal debt.

176. See Bernard of Parma, *Glossa Ordinaria*, X.4.8.1, v. *ministrent.*

177. *Glossa Ordinaria*, X.4.8.1, v. *ministrent.*

178. *Glossa Ordinaria*, X.4.8.1, v. *ministrent.*

179. Innocent IV, *Apparatus*, X.4.8.1, v. *et viri.*

180. *Apparatus*, X.4.8.1, v. *potuerunt.*

181. See Hostiensis, *Lectura,* X.4.8.1, v. *una caro.*

182. *Lectura,* X.4.8.1, v. *ministrent.*

183. *Lectura,* X.4.8.1, v. *ministrent.* The response of the scholastic theologian Alexander of Hales bore some similarities to Hostiensis's solution. He cited the book of Leviticus (13: 46), which required that lepers be separated from the community, but maintained that the harshness of the Old Law had been abrogated by Christ's teaching on the indissolubility of the marital bond and St. Paul's teaching that parties to a marriage no longer enjoyed power over their bodies. See *Summa,* vol. IV, p. 505. Alexander then asked whether the parties were obliged to "have each other" (i.e., be sexually intimate with one another), but responded that because of the danger of contracting the disease, this was not necessary. Nevertheless, Alexander went on, the parties should remain close by *(prope sint),* so that the leprous party not be defrauded of the debt by reason of distance. Here, Alexander's invocation of the conjugal debt must embrace something more than mere sexual relations. Alexander must have included within this term some larger conception of marital affection.

184. Hostiensis, *Lectura,* X.4.8.2, v. *praecepto apostoli.*

185. *Lectura,* X.4.8.2, v. *praecepto apostoli.*

186. See Panormitanus, *Commentaria* X.4.8.1, note 1: "Lepra superveniens non dissolvit matrimonium nec matrimonii effectum ideo adinvicem maritali affectione coniuncti se tractare debet. Aut ad perpetuam continentiam vovendam induci."

187. On "marital affection" as a canonistic term of art, see John T. Noonan Jr., "Marital Affection in the Canonists," *Studia Gratiana* 12 *(Collectanea Stephan Kuttner)* (1967): 481-509.

188. Panormitanus, *Commentaria* X.4.8.2, note 5.

189. See "Statuts de la lèproserie de Meaux," pars. 2-4, in Léon le Grand, ed., *Statuts d'Hotels-Dieu et de léproseries* (Paris: Alphonse Picard et fils, 1901), pp. 184-85.

190. See "Statuts de la léproserie de Lille," para. 4, in Le Grand, *Statuts,* p. 200. See also para. 9, p. 201, prohibiting contact between the residents and any "outside woman" *(mulier foranea).*

191. See "Statuts de la léproserie de Brives," para. 9, in Le Grand, *Statuts,* p. 208.

192. While avoiding any mention of leprosy, Peter Lombard established as a principle that one is not allowed to dismiss one's spouse on account of physical disability. Under the rubric "A Wife is not to be Dismissed for any Defect or Deformity of the Body," Peter wrote that neither party was free to abandon the other merely because of physical imperfection: One might not leave a wife, he wrote, because "she was sterile, or defective in her body, or weak in her limbs, or blind, or deaf, or mute, or for anything else, whether she is made ill or is laboring under sadness." See Peter Lombard, *Sententiae,* bk. IV, dist. 34, p. 688.

193. See Frederick Pollock and F. W. Maitland, *The History of English Law before the Time of Edward I,* 2d ed. (Cambridge, UK: Cambridge University Press, 1968), vol. I, p. 415. Maitland adds: "[A]s regards other persons, [the serf] has all or nearly all the rights of a free man. It is nothing to them that he is a serf." Paul Vinogradoff, on the other hand, recognized that a serf could assert a limited class of rights even against his lord. See Paul Vinogradoff, *Villainage in England: Essays in English Medieval History* (London: Oxford University Press, 1927), pp. 67-78. Neither Maitland nor Vinogradoff, it seems, ever considered canon law as a possible source of rights in the feudal context.

194. See Paul Freedman, *Images of the Medieval Peasant* (Stanford, CA: Stanford University Press, 1999), p. 242.

195. Freedman, *Images,* p. 242.

196. See Michael M. Sheehan, "Theory and Practice: Marriage of the Unfree and Poor in Medieval Society," *Mediaeval Studies* 50 (1988): 457, 463 (reprinted in Michael M. Sheehan, *Marriage, Family, and Law in Medieval Europe: Collected Studies,* ed. James K. Farge [Toronto: University of Toronto Press, 1996], pp. 211, 218).

197. See Keechang Kim, *Aliens in Medieval Law: The Origins of Modern Citizenship* (Cambridge: Cambridge University Press, 2000), p. 3, note 9. See also Iris Origo, "The Domestic Enemy: The Eastern Slaves in Tuscany in the Fourteenth and Fifteenth Centuries," *Speculum* 30 (1955): 321-66. Origo notes that many of the Tuscan slaves of the later Middle Ages were ethnically different from their masters: "[M]ost of them [were] Tartars, but some also Russian, Circassian or Greek, Moorish, or Ethiopian" (p. 321). William D. Phillips documents the extent of the slave trade in southern Europe, and the economic motives for its survival, in *Slavery from Roman Times to the Early Transatlantic Trade* (Minneapolis: University of Minnesota Press, 1985), pp. 88-113.

198. See Paul R. Hyams, *King, Lords, and Peasants in Medieval England: The Common Law of Villeinage in the Twelfth and Thirteenth Centuries* (Oxford: Clarendon Press, 1980), pp. 98-124.

199. *Servi,* for instance, were not to be ordained, and restitution was to be made to their lords if they were ordained without their masters' knowledge or permission. See X.1.18.2. Raymond de Peñafort noted that in these circumstances the lord enjoyed the right of recalling his serf to his servile condition — *habet ius revocandi.* See *Summa de Paenitentia,* col. 620.

200. See Freedman, *Images of the Medieval Peasant,* p. 240.

201. See Hostiensis, *Lectura,* X.4.9.1, v. *sacramentis.* The balance to be struck between the master's right in the serf and the serf's right to marriage and the conjugal debt was a recurrent one in both the decretist and decretalist literature. See Peter Landau, "Hadrians IV Dekretale, 'Dignum est' (X.4.9.1) und die Eheschliessung Unfreier in der Diskussion von Kanonisten und Theologen des. 12. und 13. Jahrhunderts," in *Studia Gratiana* 12 (*Collectanea Stephan Kuttner*) (1967), pp. 513, 535-46. See also Antonina Sahaydachny Bocarius, "The Marriage of Unfree Persons: Twelfth Century Decretals and Letters," *Studia Gratiana* 27 (1996), pp. 482-506.

202. See Bernard of Parma, *Glossa Ordinaria,* X.4.9.1, v. *servitia.*

203. *Glossa Ordinaria,* X.4.9.1, v. *servitia.*

204. *Glossa Ordinaria,* X.4.9.1, v. *servitia.*

205. Innocent IV, *Apparatus,* X.4.9.1, v. *servitia.*

206. Innocent IV, *Apparatus,* X.4.9.1, v. *servitia.*

207. See Hostiensis, *Summa,* bk. IV, *De Coniugio Servorum,* sec. 4.

208. *Summa,* Bk. IV, *De Coniugio Servorum,* sec. 4.

209. Hostiensis, *Lectura,* X.4.9.1, v. *exhiberi.*

210. Hostiensis, *Lectura,* X.4.9.1, *exhiberi.*

211. Hostiensis, *Lectura,* X.4.9.1, v. *a sacramentis.* The letter, as excerpted in the *Liber Extra,* began by noting St. Paul's observation that there was "neither free nor slave in Christ Jesus."

212. Hostiensis, *Lectura,* X.4.9.1, v. *inter servos.*

213. X.4.9.1.

214. See Raymond de Peñafort, *Summa de Matrimonio,* col. 928.

215. Col. 928.

216. Col. 928.

217. X.3.34.9. Cf. James A. Brundage, "The Crusader's Wife: A Canonistic Quandary," *Studia Gratiana* 12 (1967) (*Collectanea Stephan Kuttner*), pp. 425-41.

218. See Hostiensis, *Lectura,* X.3.34.9, v. *assensum.* For earlier canonistic criticism, see Brundage, "Crusading Wife," pp. 435-37.

219. See the sources collected in Bruce Gordon and Peter Marshall, "Introduction: Placing the Dead in Late Medieval and Early Modern Europe," in Bruce Gordon and Peter Marshall, eds., *The Place of the Dead: Death and Remembrance in Late Medieval and Early Modern Europe* (Cambridge: Cambridge University Press, 2000), pp. 1-9.

220. See Patrick J. Geary, *Living with the Dead in the Middle Ages* (Ithaca, NY: Cornell University Press, 1994), pp. 1-3; and Natalie Zeman Davis, "Some Tasks and Themes in the Study of Popular Religion," in Charles Trinkaus and Heiko Obermann, eds., *The Pursuit of Holiness in Late Medieval and Renaissance Religion* (Leiden: Brill, 1974), pp. 307, 327-28.

221. On pagan attitudes toward resurrection, see the sources collected in Charles J. Reid, Jr., "'So It Will Be Found That the Right of Women in Many Cases Is of Diminished Condition': Rights and the Legal Equality of Men and Women in Twelfth- and Thirteenth-Century Canon Law," *Loyola (Los Angeles) Law Review* 35 (2002): 471, 478. Cf. Alfred C. Rush, *Death and Burial in Christian Antiquity* (Washington, DC: Catholic University of America Press, 1941), pp. 7-10.

222. See Reid, "'So It Will Be Found,'" p. 478.

223. See C. F. Evans, *Resurrection and the New Testament* (London: SCM Press, 1970), p. 1.

224. See generally Joanne E. McWilliam Dewart, *Death and Resurrection* (Wilmington, DE: Michael Glazier, 1986), exploring early Christian writing on the dead and the life of the world to come.

225. A good account of this gradual process of transformation, with a focus on the burial practices of the Christian community of the eastern Mediterranean, is Byron R. McCane, *Roll Back the Stone: Death and Burial in the World of Jesus* (Harrisburg, PA: Trinity Press, 2003), especially pp. 109-40.

226. See Frederick Paxton, *Christianizing Death: The Creation of a Ritual Process in Early Medieval Europe* (Ithaca, NY: Cornell University Press, 1990), pp. 21-27.

227. See Donald Bullough, "Burial, Community, and Belief in the Early Medieval West," in Patrick Wormald, ed., *Ideal and Reality in Frankish and Anglo-Saxon Society: Studies Presented to J. M. Wallace-Hadrill* (Oxford: Blackwell, 1983), p. 179.

228. See Lawrence Butler, "The Churchyard in Eastern England, AD 900-1100: Some Lines of Development," in Philip Rahtz, Tania Dickinson, and Lorna Watts, eds., *Anglo-Saxon Cemeteries, 1979: The Fourth Anglo-Saxon Symposium at Oxford* (Oxford: British Archaeological Reports, 1980), p. 383.

229. See John Witte, *From Sacrament to Contract: Marriage, Religion, and Law in the Western Tradition* (Louisville, KY: John Knox Press, 1997), pp. 19-22.

230. See Matthew 19:5-6.

231. See Philip Lyndon Reynolds, *Marriage in the Western Church: The*

Christianization of Marriage during the Patristic and Early Medieval Periods (Leiden: E. J. Brill, 1994), pp. 331-37.

232. Luke 20:34-38.

233. See Michel Parisse, "Des veuves au monastère," in Michel Parisse, ed., *Veuves et veuvage dans le Haut Moyen Âge* (Paris: Picard, 1993), pp. 255-74; and Joceylyn Wogan-Browne, *Saints' Lives and Women's Literary Culture: Virginity and Its Authorizations* (Oxford: Oxford University Press, 2001), pp. 46-48.

234. See Burchard of Worms, *Decretorum Libri XX* (Aalen: Scientia Verlag, 1992), bk. III, c. 160, p. 72ra-rb. The text is a paraphrase of a passage of St. Jerome's *Liber de Situ et Nominibus Locorum Hebraicorum*, PL 23: 903, 906.

235. Bk. III, c. 160, p. 72ra-rb. Cf. *Tobit* 4:5. This part of the quotation apparently no longer survives in the corpus of Jerome's works, although it is preserved in the legal tradition. See vol. I of Friedberg's edition of the *Corpus Iuris Canonici*, at p. 721, note 23, C. 13, q. 2, c. 2.

236. See Burchard, *Decretorum Libri XX*, bk. III, c. 161, p. 72rb. This passage also appears no longer to be extant in Jerome's work, but it is also preserved in the legal tradition. See vol. I, *Corpus Iuris Canonici*, p. 721, note 23.

237. Bk. III, c. 162, 72rb: "Unaquaque mulier sequatur virum suum, sive in vita, sive in morte."

238. Bk. III, c. 163, p. 72rb. Cf. Gregory the Great, *Dialogues*, bk. I, c. 34.

239. See Hermann Wasserschleben, ed., *Die Irische Kanonensammlung* (Leipzig: Bernhard Tauchnitz, 1885), bk. XVII, c. 1, pp. 55-56. On the dating of this work, see now Lotte Kéry, *Canonical Collections of the Early Middle Ages (ca. 400-1140): A Bibliographic Guide to the Manuscripts and Literature* (Washington, DC: Catholic University of America Press, 1999), p. 73.

240. See *Historia Francorum*, bk. I, c. 47, *Monumenta Germaniae Historica, Scriptores Rerum Merovingicarum* (Hanover, 1885), vol. I, part 1, pp. 54-55.

241. Vol. I, part 1, p. 54.

242. Vol. I, part 1, p. 55: "[U]t quos tenet socios caelum, sepultorum hic corporum non separet monumentum" ("So that those whom heaven judges to be companions might not have a monument separate their bodies").

243. See *Gloria Confessorum*, sec. 74. *Monumenta Germaniae Historica, Scriptores Rerum Merovingicarum*, vol. I, part 1, pp. 791-92.

244. *Gloria Confessorum*, pp. 791-92. Cf. Elliott, *Spiritual Marriage*, pp. 70-71 (reviewing the stories of Iniuriosus and Scholastica and of Bishop Reticius).

245. See "Vita Sanctae Ydae," in II *Acta Sanctorum Septembris* (Antwerp, 1748) (September 4), cols. 260-269. Cf. Jean Leclercq, *Monks on Marriage: A Twelfth-Century View* (New York: Seabury Press, 1982), pp. 48-50.

246. "Quod super hoc convenientius profertur, quam duobus in carne una unam inesse Spiritus Sancti indiscissam operationem, quae illos deforis connubiali jure connexos ardentiori caelestium intus inflammavit amore" ("What could be more appropriately proposed, than that through a single indivisible operation of the Holy Spirit the two became one flesh, joined outwardly by connubial right, inflamed inwardly by a brighter love of heaven"). *Vitae Sanctae Ydae*, above, p. 262.

247. See *Vita Sanctae Ydae*, col. 261; Leclercq, *Monks*, pp. 48-49.

248. *Vita Sanctae Ydae*, col. 262; Leclercq, *Monks*, pp. 49-50.

249. See *Vita Sanctae Ydae*, col. 262.

250. See Leclercq, *Monks*, p. 50.

251. See Valerie I. J. Flint, *The Rise of Magic in Early Medieval Europe* (Princeton, NJ: Princeton University Press, 1990), pp. 213-16; and Stephen Wilson, *The Magical Universe: Everyday Ritual in Pre-Modern Europe* (London: Hambledon Press, 2000), pp. 297-302.

252. See Flint, *Rise of Magic*, pp. 101-8, and 146-72. Cf. Peter M. De Wilde, "Between Life and Death: The Journey in the Otherworld," in Edelgard DuBruck and Barbara Gusick, eds., *Death and Dying in the Middle Ages* (New York: Peter Lang, 1999), pp. 175-82 (documenting visions and other experiences of the spirit world).

253. An important new biography of Peter Abelard reviews these many facets of his intellectual career. See M. T. Clanchy, *Abelard: A Medieval Life* (Oxford: Blackwell, 1999).

254. Étienne Gilson's *Heloise and Abelard* (Chicago: Henry Regnery Company, 1951) remains a powerful retelling of this story.

255. Peter Abelard wrote in his *Historia Calamitatum* that he and Heloise were careful to observe the legal forms of marriage. The marriage took place following the birth of their son. The ceremony occurred in the early morning hours, preceded by a vigil that lasted the entire night. It was witnessed by a few friends. Peter Abélard, *Historia Calamitatum*, ed. J. Monfrin (Paris: J. Vrin, 1978), p. 79.

Regarding marriage, Peter Abelard would reflect on its demands at a much later date in a sermon to monks: "For what is a greater bond than conjugal coupling? What greater servitude than that a man not have power over his own body? What, finally, more burdensome life than to be crucified daily by the aggravation of caring as much for one's wife as for one's children?" ("Quod enim vinculum majus quam copulae conjugalis? Quae gravior servitus, quam ut homo proprii corporis potestatem non habeat? Quae denique vita onerosior, quam molestiis quotidianae sollicitudinis tam pro uxore quam pro filiis cruciari?")

Peter Abelard, *Sermo* 33, in PL 178: 582. Abelard reveals much of his own personality in this statement, of course, but it also demonstrates a common mind-set, particularly in monastic communities, that took St. Paul's teaching on the obligations of married life as a literal and burdensome truth.

256. *Historia Calamitatum*, pp. 79-80.

257. Abelard records that he sent Heloise to the convent of Argenteuil while he remained teaching in Paris, a decision Clanchy criticizes as a violation of the canon law, which required a mutual and voluntary decision by *both* parties to enter monastic life. Clanchy, *Abelard: A Medieval Life*, p. 192. Abelard did not pursue a monastic life until after his castration.

258. Clanchy, *Abelard: A Medieval Life*, p. 196 (quoting a letter of Abelard to Heloise).

259. A recent historian has noted that Peter the Venerable, in his effort to engage in real intellectual disputation with Islam, as opposed to vitriolic name-calling, represented "without a doubt a qualitative leap forward, even if its limits and blind alleys ought not to be glossed over." Dominique Iogna-Prat, *Order and Exclusion: Cluny and Christendom Face Heresy, Judaism, and Islam (1000-1150)*, trans. Graham Robert Edwards (Ithaca, NY: Cornell University Press, 2002), p. 338. See also generally James Kritzeck,

Peter the Venerable and Islam (Princeton, NJ: Princeton University Press, 1964), reproducing Peter's writings on Islam.

260. Clanchy, *Abelard: A Medieval Life*, pp. 262-63; Gilson, *Heloise and Abelard*,
pp. 118-23.

261. Peter the Venerable, Letter 115, in Giles Constable, ed., *The Letters of Peter
the Venerable* (Cambridge, MA: Harvard University Press, 1967), vol. I, p. 308 ("cui post
carnalem copulam tanto validiore, quanto meliore divinae caritatis vinculo
adhesisti . . .").

262. Gilson, *Heloise and Abelard*, p. 123.

263. Clanchy, *Abelard: A Medieval Life*, p. 328.

264. Clanchy, *Abelard: A Medieval Life*, p. 328.

265. See Ivo of Chartres, *Decretum* III, c. 223 (= Burchard of Worms, III, c. 160);
Decretum III, c. 224 (= Burchard of Worms, III, c. 161); *Decretum* III, c. 225 (= Burchard
of Worms, III, c. 162); and *Decretum* III, c. 226 (= Burchard of Worms, III, c. 163). All of
these provisions are found at PL 161: 252.

266. See C. 13, q. 2, c. 2 (= Ivo, *Decretum*, III, cc. 223-224); and C. 13, q. 2, c. 3
(= Ivo, *Decretum*, cc. 225-226).

267. See C. 13, q. 2, pr.

268. C. 13, q. 2, d.a.c. 2. The problem of burial fees remained a significant issue
throughout the Middle Ages. Such fees were a principal means by which local pastors
and parishes were supported. A decree of Pope Boniface VIII known as *Super cathedram*,
reissued by Pope Clement V, laid down detailed rules for the distribution of fees. See
Clem. 3.7.2. See also Thomas Izbicki, "The Problem of Canonical Portion in the Later
Middle Ages: The Application of 'Super cathedram,'" in Peter Linehan, ed., *Proceedings
of the Seventh International Congress of Medieval Canon Law* (Vatican City, 1988), pp.
459-73. See also Richard H. Helmholz, *The Ius Commune in England: Four Studies* (Oxford: Oxford University Press, 2001), pp. 135-86 (examining burial fees in English law).

By the time one arrives at the period just before and just after the promulgation of
the 1917 Code of Canon Law, one finds canonists distinguishing between a *jus funeris*,
which embraced the church's claim to fees pertaining to burial, the *jus tumuli*, which included the believing Christian's right to burial assertable generally against civil society,
and the *jus sepulturae electivae*, the right of selecting one's place of burial. See Amleto
Tondini, *De Ecclesia Funerante ad Normam Novi Codicis* (Forli: Valbonesi, 1927), pp.
20-24.

269. C. 13, q. 2, d.a.c. 2. "Sicut Ieronimus scribit, coniugati in uno sepulcro
videntur esse ponendi."

270. C. 13, q. 2, d.p.c. 3.

271. C. 13, q. 2, d.p.c. 3.

272. C. 13, q. 2, d.p.c. 3.

273. C. 13, q. 2, d.p.c. 3.

274. C. 13, q. 2, d.p.c. 3.

275. C. 13, q. 2, d.p.c. 3.

276. C. 13, q. 2, c. 4.

277. C. 13, q. 2, c. 6.

278. C. 13, q. 2, d.p.c. 7: "Sed aliud est, ex temeritatis superbia, usum antiquorum
parentum non sequi, atque aliud rationabili occasione novam sibi sepulturam. . . ."

279. C. 13, q. 2, d.p.c. 7. "Secundum Gregorium autem liberam habet ultimam voluntatem qui certae rationis causa novum suo corpori querit hospitium." Gratian acknowledged that the expression "last will" might have a double meaning. While he used the expression to specify one's final determinations regarding burial, "certain others" (*quidam*) use the term to describe the *testamentum*, the property arrangements one makes in contemplation of death.

280. See *Summa Parisiensis*, C. 13, q. 2, d.a.c. 3, p. 166.

281. See Stephen of Tournai, *Summa*, C. 13, q. 2, c. 2, v. *Ebron*, p. 219.

282. See Rufinus, *Summa*, C. 13, q. 2, c. 4, v. *ultima voluntas*, p. 335.

283. See above, Introduction, p. 18.

284. X.3.28.7.

285. X.3.28.7.

286. See above, p. 20.

287. See Goffredus Tranensis, *Summa*, bk. III, tit. *De sepulturis*, sec. 3. "Mihi autem videtur ut quis possit sibi eligere sepulturam ubicunque velit. . . ."

288. See Bernard of Parma, *Glossa Ordinaria*, X.3.28.7, v. *casus:* "Sicut liberum est viro eligere sepulturam, ita liberum est mulieri; nulla est in hoc casu inter eos differentia, cum a lege viri soluta esse intelligatur."

289. Bernard of Parma, X.3.28.7, v. *casus.*

290. Bernard of Parma, X.3.28.7, v. *aequalem.*

291. Bernard of Parma, X.3.28.7, v. *aequalem.*

292. Innocent IV, *Apparatus*, X.3.28.7, v. *liberam.*

293. *Apparatus*, X.3.28.7, v. *liberam.*

294. Innocent IV, *Apparatus*, at X.3.28.1, v. *sepulturam.* On Innocent's borrowing from Vincentius Hispanus, see Antoine Bernard, *Le sépulture en droit canonique* (Paris: Les éditions domat-montchrestien, 1933), p. 85.

295. *Apparatus*, X.3.28.7, v. *liberam.*

296. See *Summa de Paenitentia*, col. 435: "[D]ico . . . quod quilibet adultus et discretus vivens potest eligere sepulturam ubicumque. . . ."

297. Col. 436: "De uxore, dico, cuius maritus defunctus est, quod potest eligere sepulturam, etiam alibi quam in sepulcro viri. Si tamen moriatur, non electa sepultura, credo quod debeat sepeliri cum viro."

298. Hostiensis, *Lectura*, X.3.28.7, v. *aequalem.*

299. *Lectura*, X.3.28.7, v. *aequalem.* Cf. *Novella* 22:20 ("Deinceps autem matrimoniorum terminum quae omne similiter solvit expectat mors"). ("And so death, which dissolves all things, awaits the end of marriages.")

300. *Lectura*, X.3.28.7, v. *aequalem.* Cf. *Codex* 9.32.4.

301. *Lectura*, X.3.28.7, v. *aequalem.*

302. *Lectura*, X.3.28.7, v. *aequalem.*

303. *Lectura*, X.3.28.7, v. *aequalem.*

304. *Lectura*, X.3.28.7, v. *aequalem.* Hostiensis cited *Codex* 12.1.13, a decree of Valentinian, Theodosius, and Arcadius, ordering that women share the same social status as their husbands; and *Digest* 50.1.22.1, teaching that a widow retains the same domicile as her deceased husband. By analogy, Hostiensis reasoned, where a wife has not elected otherwise, her domicile should remain the same in death as in life.

305. *Lectura*, X.3.28.7, v. *aequalem.*

306. *Lectura*, X.3.28.7, v. *Aequalem*.

307. *Lectura*, at X.3.28.7, v. *facultatem*.

308. *Lectura*, X.3.28.7, v. *facultatem*.

309. See F. J. Moulart, *De Sepultura et Coemeteriis* (Paris: P. Letheeilleux, 1862), pp. 146-48.

310. Johannes Andreae, *In quinque Decretalium*, X.3.28.7, *casus*.

311. Panormitanus, *Commentaria*, X.3.28.7, note 6 *additio*.

312. See Luis de Molina, *De Iustitia et Iure* (Mainz: Balthazar Lippius, 1602), bk. I, disp. 214, cols. 904-8.

313. Bk. I, disp. 214, cols. 904-8. By "less holy," Molina meant places where the sacrifice of the Mass and the divine office were said less frequently.

314. Bk. I, disp. 214, col. 907.

315. Bk. I, disp. 214, col. 907.

316. See Johannes Paulus Lancellotti, *Institutiones Juris Canonici* (Mantua, 1695), bk. II, tit. 24, col. 82.

317. Bk. II, tit. 24, col. 82.

318. See Peter de Murga, *Disquisitiones Morales et Canonicae* (1666).

319. Peter de Murga, *Disquisitiones*, p. 300.

320. Peter de Murga, *Disquisitiones*, p. 300. "Sicut liberum est viro eligere Sepulturam, ita liberum est mulieri. Nulla est differentia inter eos in hoc casu, cum a lege viri soluta esse intelligatur."

321. See Reid, "'So It Will Be Found,'" pp. 490-91.

322. See Louis M. Epstein, *The Jewish Marriage Contract: A Study in the Status of the Woman in Jewish Law* (New York: Arno Press, 1973) pp. 193-206.

323. Epstein, *Jewish Marriage Contract*, pp. 194-95. Epstein here is paraphrasing the teaching of Philo and Josephus on the husband's legal capacity to divorce. He is also following the Scripture. See Deuteronomy 24:1.

324. Thus one finds in Malachi 2:14-16 a condemnation of divorce ("For I hate divorce, says the Lord God of Israel," v. 16), coupled with an exhortation to men to remain faithful to the wives of their youth.

325. The *Mishnah* records the following: "The School of Shammai says: A man may not divorce his wife unless he has found unchastity in her, for it is written, 'Because he hath found in her indecency in anything.' And the School of Hillel say: [He may divorce her] even if she spoiled a dish for him, for it is written, 'Because he hath found in her indecency in' anything. R. Akiba says: Even if he found another fairer than she, for it is written, 'And it shall be if she find no favour in his eyes.'" Herbert Danby, ed. and trans., *The Mishnah*, Gittin 9.10 (Oxford: Oxford University Press, 1933), p. 321.

Brundage, *Law, Sex, and Christian Society*, p. 53, notes that rabbinic courts retained the power to allocate the distribution of property following divorce, which probably served to check some of the worst arbitrariness. Cf. David Werner Amram, *The Jewish Law of Divorce according to Bible and Talmud* (New York: Sepher-Hermon Press, 1975), pp. 32-37 (restating and analyzing the views of Hillel and Shammai and their followers, including among them the New Testament writers).

326. See Percy Ellwood Corbett, *The Roman Law of Marriage* (Oxford: Clarendon Press, 1930), p. 222. As a social phenomenon, prior to the third century BC, it seems that

any type of divorce was extremely rare. See Alan Watson, "The Divorce of Carvilius Ruga," *Tijdschrift voor Rechtsgeschiedenis* 33 (1965): 38-50.

327. See Corbett, *Roman Law of Marriage*, p. 222.

328. See Matthew 19:9. On the possible translations of *porneia*, see Bruce Malina, "Does *Porneia* Mean Fornication?" *Novum Testamentum* 14 (1972): 10-17; and Joseph Jensen, "Does *Porneia* Mean Fornication? A Critique of Bruce Malina," *Novum Testamentum* 20 (1978): 161-84.

329. Matthew 19:3-9. Cf. Matthew 5:31-32 (recapitulating the teaching on divorce).

330. See Mark 10:4-9.

331. Luke 16:18.

332. 1 Corinthians 7:10-11.

333. 1 Corinthians 7:12-16.

334. On the importance of this work to second- and third-century Christian writers, see Carolyn Osiek, *Shepherd of Hermas: A Commentary* (Minneapolis, MN: Fortress Press, 1999), pp. 4-7.

335. See *Shepherd of Hermas*, Mandate IV. 1, in Kirsopp Lake, ed. and trans., *The Apostolic Fathers*, vol. II (London: William Heinemann, 1930), pp. 78-79.

336. Lake, ed. and trans., *Apostolic Fathers*, pp. 80-81. The male genitive pronoun *autou* is used twice by the *Shepherd* in referring to the relapsed party.

337. See *De Virginitate*, 6.31. PL 16: 273. ("[C]onjugium . . . non esse solvendum, nisi ex causa fornicationis.") Theodore Mackin notes that the word *solvendum* is borrowed from the vocabulary of Roman law and signifies an actual dissolution of the marriage, not a separation. See Theodore Mackin, *Divorce and Remarriage* (New York: Paulist Press, 1989), p. 157.

338. See *Expositio Evangelii Secundum Lucam*, 8.2. PL 15: 1765. On the significance of the distinction between valid and invalid marriages, see Mackin, *Divorce and Remarriage*, p. 158.

339. See *Expositio Evangelii Secundum Lucam*, PL 15: 1765. "[N]on a Deo omne conjugium; neque enim Christianae gentilibus Dei judicio copulantur; cum Lex prohibeat." ("Not every marriage is from God; nor may Christian women copulate in accord with the judgment of God with gentiles; since this the law prohibits.")

340. PL 15: 1765.

341. See Augustine, *De Bono Coniugali*, sec. 7.7, pp. 14-15, Walsh edition (= *CSEL* 41: 196-97).

342. *De Bono Coniugali*, sec. 7.7, pp. 14-15.

343. See *De Sermone Domini in Monte, Corpus Christianorum Series Latina*, vol. 35 (1967), line 1084, p. 51: "fornicatio est etiam ipsa infidelitas."

344. *De Bono Coniugali*, sec. 7.7, pp. 16-17 (Walsh ed.) (= *CSEL* 41: 196-197).

345. Pp. 14-15. Theodore Mackin emphasizes: "Augustine is perhaps for the first time in the Christian writing on the subject clear and decisive that, whatever the reason for it, the divorce action allowed by civil law leaves the spouses still married to one another, and that the apparent dissolution effected by the divorce is no more than the 'separation from bed and board.'" See Mackin, *Divorce and Remarriage*, p. 202.

346. See Judith Evans Grubbs, *Law and Family in Late Antiquity: The Emperor Constantine's Marriage Legislation* (Oxford: Clarendon Press, 1995), p. 253. Grubbs re-

views the scholarship, pro and con, regarding the possible Christian influence on this legislation at pp. 253-55.

347. See *Codex Theodosianus* 3.16.1.

348. *Codex Theodosianus* 3.16.1.

349. On the importance of this document, see John Noonan's study, "Novel 22," in William W. Bassett, ed., *The Bond of Marriage* (Notre Dame, IN: University of Notre Dame Press, 1968), pp. 41-96.

350. See *Novella* 22.4.

351. See *Novella* 22.15.

352. *Novella* 22.15.

353. See Brundage, *Law, Sex, and Christian Society,* p. 235.

354. C. 27, q. 2, pr.

355. C. 27, q. 2, pr. "matrimonium viri mulierisque coniunctio, individuam vitae consuetudinem retinens." Cf. *Institutes,* 1.9.1.

356. See C. 27, q. 2, c. 1 (attributed to Chrysostom); and C. 27, q. 2, c. 2 (Nicholas I). John Alesandro makes the point that the text attributed to Chrysostom is probably not his work, but "pertains to [an] uncompleted homily . . . by an unknown author." See John A. Alesandro, *Gratian's Notion of Consummation* (Rome: Officium Libri Catholici, 1971), p. 3, note 7.

357. C. 27, q. 2, d.p.c. 2.

358. C. 27, q. 2, c. 5.

359. See C. 27, q. 2, c. 6 (Isidore); and c. 9 (St. Augustine).

360. C. 27, q. 2, d.p.c. 10. Cf. Deuteronomy 22:25.

361. See C. 27, q. 2, c. 10 and c. 12.

362. C. 27, q. 2, d.p.c. 15: "His auctoritatibus probantur isti coniuges esse."

363. C. 27, q. 2, c. 16.

364. C. 27, q. 2, c. 17. Alesandro notes that Gratian was here working with a variant textual tradition that differed from Leo's actual language, which did not make consummation the central defining feature Gratian wished it to be. On the history of this variant reading, see Alesandro, *Gratian's Notion,* pp. 18-21.

365. C. 27, q. 2, d.p.c. 18.

366. These texts are reviewed above, pp. 103-8.

367. See C. 27, q. 2, cc. 31-39.

368. C. 27, q. 2, d.p.c. 39.

369. C. 27, q. 2, d.p.c. 39.

370. C. 27, q. 2, cc. 27-28, and C. 27, q. 2, d.p.c. 28.

371. C. 27, q. 2, d.p.c. 39.

372. See Brundage, *Law, Sex, and Christian Society,* pp. 242-45.

373. See, among other texts, C. 35, q. 5, cc. 1-2.

374. Brundage, *Law, Sex, and Christian Society,* pp. 193-95, 238.

375. See C. 30, q. 3, cc. 1 and 2.

376. C. 32, q. 7, c. 26 and d.p.c. 26.

377. C. 28, q. 1, cc. 15-16.

378. See especially D. 27, c. 8, which declared that priests, deacons, subdeacons, and monks may not marry and, should they do so, they must be separated from their wives.

379. See C. 29, q. 1, and q. 2, d.p.c. 6.

380. See, among other texts, C. 31, q. 2, c. 3.

381. C. 33, q. 1, d.p.c. 3.

382. See Brundage, *Law, Sex, and Christian Society*, pp. 199-200.

383. Brundage, *Law, Sex, and Christian Society*, pp. 242-43.

384. Brundage, *Law, Sex, and Christian Society*, p. 243, and note 62.

385. C. 33, q. 5, d.p.c. 11 and d.p.c. 20.

386. C. 33, q. 1, d.p.c. 3. "[Q]uod impossibilitas reddendi debitum vinculum solvit coniugii."

387. C. 33, q. 1, d.p.c. 3.

388. See Brundage, *Law, Sex, and Christian Society*, p. 243.

389. C. 35, q. 8, pr. and c. 1.

390. C. 35, q. 8, c. 2.

391. See Brundage, *Law, Sex, and Christian Society*, p. 243.

392. Brundage, *Law, Sex, and Christian Society*, pp. 243-44.

393. See C. 28, q. 1, cc. 10-14; and c. 17.

394. See C. 28, q. 1, cc. 3-6.

395. C. 28, q. 1, c. 3.

396. C. 28, q. 2, c. 1.

397. C. 28, q. 2, c. 2.

398. C. 28, q. 2, d.p.c. 2.

399. C. 32, q. 5, c. 19.

400. C. 32, q. 5, c. 22.

401. C. 32, q. 5, c. 23.

402. C. 32, q. 6, c. 5.

403. C. 32, q. 7, c. 8.

404. Reid, "The Augustinian Goods of Marriage," pp. 456-59.

405. Canon 1152 sec. 1 of the 1983 Code of Canon Law recognizes that the innocent spouse possesses the "right to dissolve their conjugal way of living" *(ius ipsi est solvendi coniugalem convictum)* where the other partner committed adultery. The innocent party must not have "tacitly condoned" the act in order to obtain an ecclesiastical separation (c. 1152, sec. 2). Ecclesiastical separation on the ground of adultery does not carry the right of remarriage. Adequate provision must be made for the support and training of children (c. 1154). Reconciliation in such circumstances is encouraged, in which case the innocent party renounces his or her right of separation (c. 1155) *(quo in casu iuri separatione renuntiat)*.

406. See Peter Lombard, *Libri IV Sententiarum*, bk. IV, dist. 35, c. 1, p. 688.

407. Bk. IV, dist. 35, c. 1, p. 688.

408. Bk. IV, dist. 35, c. 1, p. 688.

409. Gandulf of Bologna, *Sententiarum Libri Quatuor*, pp. 575-79.

410. *Sententiarum Libri Quatuor*, p. 575.

411. *Sententiarum Libri Quatuor*, pp. 575-77.

412. *Sententiarum Libri Quatuor*, p. 579: "Si uterque istorum, scilicet adulteri viri et adulterae uxoris, privatus est potestate debitum exigendi, neuter ergo ab altero potest exigere debitum. Uterque ergo eorum alterum dimittere proptre fornicationem potest."

413. *Sententiarum*, pp. 579-80.

414. Rolandus, *Summa Magistri Rolandus,* C. 33, q. 2, p. 189. Rolandus's choice of language — "probatur uxorem a viro non discedere posse absque iudiciario ordine" ("it is established that a wife is unable to leave her husband absent judicial process") — makes it clear that a wife, as well as husband, enjoyed the right to seek a separation in appropriate circumstances.

415. See Rufinus, *Summa Decretorum,* C. 33, q. 2, p. 498.

416. See *Glossa Ordinaria,* C. 33, q. 2, c. 4, v. *reddita.*

417. See Bernard of Pavia, *Summa Decretalium,* ed. E. A. T. Laspeyres (Graz: Akademische Druck-u. Verlagsanstalt, 1956), bk. IV, tit. 19, p. 183.

418. *Summa Decretalium,* p. 184.

419. *Summa Decretalium,* p. 184. "[V]el vir uxorem vel econtra, quia in talibus non ad imparia iudicantur. . . ."

420. *Summa Decretalium,* p. 184. Cf. C. 32, q. 1, c 4; and C. 32, q. 5, cc. 19 and 23.

421. *Summa Decretalium,* p. 184.

422. *Summa Decretalium,* pp. 184-85.

423. See Tancred, *Summa de Matrimonio,* p. 79.

424. Hostiensis, *Summa,* bk. IV, *De Divortiis,* secs. 6-7.

425. Raymond de Peñafort, *Summa de Matrimonio,* cols. 979-80. "Ad quod sciendum est quod quilibet potest accusare matrimonium ad plenum divortium celebrandum, qui non prohibetur."

426. *Summa de Matrimonio,* col. 986.

427. See Tancred, *Ordo Iudiciarius,* in Pilius, Tancredus, Gratia, *Libri De Iudiciorum Ordine,* ed. Friedrich Christian Bergmann (Aalen: Scientia Verlag, 1965), p. 283.

428. See William Durantis, *Speculum Iudiciale* (Aalen: Scientia Verlag, 1975), bk. IV, partic. IV, vol. II, p. 467.

429. Durantis, *Speculum Iudiciale,* bk. IV, partic. IV, vol. II, p. 467: "[E]xtraneorum enim non interest."

430. Bk. IV, partic. IV, vol. II, p. 467.

431. See the thought-provoking essay by Knut Wolfgang Nörr, "Ehe und Eheschiedung aus der Sicht des Rechtsbegriffs: ein historischer Exkurs," in Peter Linehan, ed., *Life, Law, and Letters: Historical Studies in Honour of Antonio García y García* (Rome: LAS, 1998) (*Studia Gratiana* 29), pp. 671-84.

432. See X.4.19.7.

433. X.4.19.7.

434. See Bernard of Parma, *Glossa Ordinaria,* X.4.19.7, *casus.*

435. *Glossa Ordinaria,* X.4.19.7, v. *qui relinquitur.*

436. See Innocent IV, *Apparatus,* X.4.19.7, v. *infidelium.*

437. *Apparatus,* X.4.19.7, v. *infidelium.* See also, *Apparatus,* X.4.19.7, v. *per hanc.*

438. See Raymond de Peñafort, *Summa de Matrimonio,* cols. 951-52. *Verum matrimonium,* in Raymond's words.

439. *Summa de Matrimonio,* col. 952.

440. See Hostiensis, *Lectura,* X.4.19.7, v. *qui relinquitur:* "Notabis etiam, quod hic solvitur matrimonium, non per sententiam sed ipso iure propter contumeliam Creatoris, vel quia non vult cohabitare, vel cohabitans blasphemat, vel trahit ad mortale peccatum."

441. *Lectura,* X.4.19.7, v. *qui relinquitur.*

442. See J. Marquardt, *The Loss of Right to Accuse a Marriage* (Rome: Officium Libri Catholici, 1951), pp. 15-22.

443. See Raymond of Peñafort, *Summa de Matrimonio,* col. 987.

444. *Summo de Matrimonio,* col. 987.

445. *Summo de Matrimonio,* col. 987.

446. *Summo de Matrimonio,* col. 987.

447. See Charles J. Reid, Jr., "The Canonistic Contribution to the Western Rights Tradition: An Historical Inquiry," *Boston College Law Review* 33 (1991): 37, 85-86.

448. See Rufinus, *Summa Decretorum, C.* 28, q. 1, c. 5, v. *idolatria.*

449. See the introduction by Gerard Fransen and Stephan Kuttner, *Summa, 'Elegantius in Iure Divino,'* vol. I, p. xi.

450. See Gérard Fransen and Stephen Kuttner, eds., *Summa, 'Elegantius in Iure Divino'* (Vatican City: Biblioteca Apostolica Vaticana, 1969-90), vol. IV, pp. 50-51.

451. Vol. IV, p. 52.

452. Vol. IV, p. 52.

453. X.4.19.7. See Jean Dauvillier, *Le mariage dans le droit classique de l'Église: Depuis le Décret de Gratien (1140) jusqu'a la mort de Clément V (1314)* (Paris: Sirey, 1933), pp. 335-36 (on the early history of the term "spiritual fornication").

454. X.4.19.7.

455. X.4.19.7.

456. X.4.19.7.

457. Bernard of Parma, *Glossa Ordinaria,* X.4.19.7, v. *sine culpa.*

458. Innocent IV, *Apparatus,* X.4.19.7, v. *infidelium.*

459. Hostiensis, *Lectura,* X.4.19.7, v. *verum et ratum.*

460. *Lectura,* X.4.19.7, v. *perduret.*

461. *Lectura,* X.4.19.7, v. *perduret.*

462. *Lectura,* X.4.19.7, v. *perduret:* ("iure infidelium omnino censetur").

463. See Raymond de Peñafort, *Summa de Matrimonio,* cols. 986-87.

464. See X.2.13.8 (Alexander III); and X.2.13.13 (Innocent III).

465. See X.2.13.13.

466. See Bernard of Parma, *Glossa Ordinaria,* X.2.13.8, *casus;* and X.2.13.13, *casus.*

467. See Hostiensis, *Lectura,* X.2.13.13, v. *ab eo, etc.* See also Helmholz, *Marriage Litigation,* pp. 100-101, 105.

468. See Raymond de Penafort, *Summa de Matrimonio,* col. 977.

469. See Johannes Andreae, *In Quinque Decretalium Libros Novella Commentaria,* X.5.10.2, *casus* (husband may not separate from wife); and v. *abiurare* (wife has committed a crime and should be held *in odium*).

470. See Panormitanus, *Commentaria,* X.2.13.13, note 7.

471. See *Summa, 'Elegantius in Iure Divino,'* vol. IV, p. 68 ("in quo prelatior et in quo par sit uxori maritus").

472. Vol. IV, p. 68.

473. Vol. IV, p. 68.

474. The sturdiness of Peter Lombard's exegesis of the Genesis account is illus-

trated by the teaching of an English Protestant writer active at the end of the sixteenth century. Robert Cleaver, in his treatise on household governance, wrote:

> The husband is also to understand, that as God created the woman, not the head, and so equall in authoritie with her husband; so also he created her not of *Adams* foote, that she should be troden downe and despised, but he tooke out of the rib, that she might walke joyntly with him, under the conduct and government of her head.
>
> And in that respect, the husband is not to command his wife, in the manner, as the Maister his servant, but as the soule doth the bodie, as being conjoyned in like affection and good will.

Robert Cleaver, *A Godlie Forme of Householde Government* (London: Barnard's, 1612) (originally published 1598). The compromises between headship and equality first developed by the canonists are illustrated in Cleaver's treatise.

Notes to Chapter 4

1. An important article exploring the power and the limitations of this catch phrase in American jurisprudence is Melanie B. Leslie, "The Myth of Testamentary Freedom," *Arizona Law Review* 38 (1996): 235-90. Little contends that evocation of the phrase "testamentary freedom," without regard to recognition of corresponding duties toward others, has led to confusion in American law. In calling for reform, she has asserted: "Analysis must start with an exploration of whether and to what extent testamentary freedom is to be valued above all other principles" (p. 290).

2. There are exceptions to this rule. One exception is the State of Wisconsin, where the Supreme Court "[has] frequently held that . . . a right to make a will is a sacred and constitutional right. . . ." See *Will of Wright*, 12 Wis. 2d 375, 380, 107 N.W. 2d 146, 149 (1961). Another exception is an opinion of the Supreme Court of Idaho that has spoken of children's "natural rights of inheritance." *Bedal v. Johnson*, 37 Idaho 359, 384, 218 P. 2d 641, 648 (1923).

3. Echoing the traditional view, the Supreme Court has written: "Rights of succession to property of a deceased, whether by will or by intestacy, are of statutory creation, and the dead hand rules succession only by sufferance. Nothing in the Federal Constitution forbids the legislature of a state to limit, or even abolish the power of testamentary disposition over property within its jurisdiction." See *Irving Trust Company v. Day*, 314 U.S. 556, 562 (1942).

This prevailing doctrine was questioned in *Hodel v. Irving*, 481 U.S. 704 (1987), which held a federal statutory scheme to abrogate inheritance rights on Indian tribal lands violated the constitutional prohibition on the taking of property without compensation. One scholarly commentator has seen in the *Hodel* case the triumph of a "natural rights" view of testamentary freedom. See Ronald Chester, "Inheritance in American Legal Thought," in Robert K. Miller, Jr., and Stephen J. McNamee, eds., *Inheritance and Wealth in America* (New York: Plenum Press, 1998), pp. 23, 32-34. Cf. Jesse Dukeminier and Stanley M. Johanson, *Wills, Trusts, and Estates,* 6th ed. (New York: Aspen Publishers, 2000), pp. 10-11 (criticizing this turn to natural-rights conceptions of testamentary freedom). Elsewhere, Chester has written, concerning the state of the question following *Hodel v. Irving:* "The view expressed by *Irving Trust* can be called the legal positivist view of inheritance. Although this has long been the dominant conception, there has also been a competing view — that inheritance, either in its transmission, receipt, or both, is a natural property right." Ronald Chester, "Is the Right to Devise Property Constitutionally Protected? The Strange Case of *Hodel v. Irving,*" *Southwestern University Law Review* 24 (1995): 1195, 1196.

4. The exception is Louisiana, which was more directly influenced by the Roman and canon law systems of Continental Europe than the other states of the Union. See Ralph C. Brashier, "Protecting the Child from Disinheritance: Must Louisiana Stand Alone?" *Louisiana Law Review* 57 (1996): 1-26 (arguing that Louisiana's experience should become a national model). Cf. Deborah A. Batts, "'I Didn't Ask to Be Born': The American Law of Disinheritance and a Proposal for Change to a System of Protected Inheritance," *Hastings Law Journal* 41 (1990): 1197-1270 (considering inconsistencies in American law and proposing reforms that resemble the forced-share provisions of those European systems derived from the *ius commune* of the medieval and early modern worlds).

5. One such doctrine is the rule of "unjust" or "unnatural wills," which allows courts to scrutinize a testator's mental state carefully where offspring seem to be treated unfairly, particularly with respect to more generous provisions made on behalf of familial strangers. See, for instance, *Abel v. Dickinson,* 250 Ark. 648, 467 S.W. 2d 154 (1971) ("[w]e have held . . . that the courts may consider that the provisions of a will are unjust, unnatural, and unreasonable as a circumstance in determining the mental capacity of the testator"). 250 Ark. at 652, 467 S.W. 2d at 156. On the other hand, "[a] testator of sound mind has a perfect right to make an unjust and unnatural will." See *Hamilton v. Morgan,* 93 Fla. 311, 316, 112 So. 80, 82 (1927).

6. See Dukeminier and Johanson, *Wills, Trusts, and Estates,* p. 536.

7. See Dukeminier and Johanson, *Wills, Trusts, and Estates,* p. 480.

8. See William M. McGovern and Sheldon F. Kurtz, *Wills, Trusts, and Estates,* 2d ed. (St. Paul, MN: West Publishing, 2001), p. 113.

9. See Dukeminier and Johanson, *Wills, Trusts, and Estates,* p. 480.

10. The starting point for analyzing the canon law of spousal inheritance is Innocent III's decretal *Nuper a nobis,* X.4.20.6, which recognized that where the law of the land did not make provision for a wife's inheritance she was to rely on the *donatio propter nuptias* made by the husband at the time of the wedding. See also Brian Edwin Ferme, *Canon Law in Late Medieval England: A Study of William Lyndwood's Provinciale with Particular Reference to Testamentary Law* (Rome: LAS, 1996), p. 132. Roman practice, which canon law generally retained, was that spouses were to look to their wedding gifts for support following the death of their partner (p. 122).

11. See *Digest* 28.1.6; *Digest* 28.1.8. See also Gaius, *Institutes,* bk. I.115.a (discussing the limited circumstances in which a woman had the right of making a will — "feminae testamenti faciendi ius habebant . . .").

12. See *Digest* 28.1.16; *Digest* 28.1.18.

13. See *Digest* 28.1.19.

14. *Codex* 1.3.33.

15. See, for example, *Codex* 1.7.4; *Codex* 5.5.6.4; *Codex* 5.9.3; and *Codex* 6.23.13.

16. See Alan Watson, *The Law of Succession in the Later Roman Republic* (Oxford: Clarendon Press, 1971), p. 22.

17. Watson, *Law of Succession,* p. 24.

18. See Watson, *Law of Succession,* pp. 22-23; W. W. Buckland, *A Text-Book of Roman Law from Augustus to Justinian,* 3d ed., rev. by Peter Stein (Cambridge: Cambridge University Press, 1963), p. 288; Gaius, *Institutes,* bk. 1, 115a. Essentially, in the late Roman Republic, a woman had to undergo a formal process, known as *capitis diminutio,* which allowed her to seek the protection of a guardian independent of her family — a so-called *tutor fiduciarius* — who might look after her interests and approve the will.

19. See *Institutes,* bk. II.12.

20. *Institutes,* bk. II.12.

21. See *Institutes,* bk. II.11.

22. *Institutes,* bk. II.12.1.

23. *Institutes,* bk. II.12.1.

24. *Institutes,* bk. II.12.2.

25. *Institutes,* bk. II.12.3.

26. *Institutes,* bk. II.12.4.

27. *Institutes,* bk. II.12.5.

28. *Digest* 28.1.3 ("Testamenti factio non privati, sed publici iuris est").

29. *Digest* 28.1.1.

30. *Digest* 28.1.2.

31. *Digest* 28.1.4.

32. *Digest* 28.1.5.

33. See *Digest* 28.1.6.1 (denying the right to make a will even to children given permission to do so by their father); *Digest* 28.1.6.2 (denying perpetual deaf-mutes the right to make a will); *Digest* 28.1.8 (denying captives the right to make wills while in captivity). The jurists added further categories, such as prisoners who have been condemned. See *Digest* 28.1.8.1.

34. *Digest* 28.1.16.

35. See *Codex* 6.22.3.

36. *Codex* 6.22.2.

37. See above, Chapter Two, pp. 71-72.

38. See Caesarius of Arles, Sermon 60, in G. Morin, ed., *Sancti Caesarii episcopi Arelatensis Sermones,* Part I (Turnholt: Brepols, 1953), *Corpus Christianorum Series Latina, sermo* 60, p. 252.

39. *Sermo* 60, p. 252.

40. *Sermo* 60, p. 254.

41. *Sermo* 60, p. 254.

42. *Sermo* 60, p. 254. Cf. Michael M. Sheehan, *The Will in Medieval England: From the Conversion of the Anglo-Saxons to the End of the Thirteenth Century* (Toronto: Pontifical Institute of Mediaeval Studies, 1963), p. 12 and note 29.

43. See *Sermo de Disciplina Christiana,* PL 40: 673.

44. *Sermo de Disciplina Christiana,* col. 673.

45. *Sermo de Disciplina Christiana,* col. 674. Cf. Matthew 25:40, 45.

46. *Sermo de Disciplina Christiana,* col. 674: "Ecce quis eget, et filios tuos numeras? Postremo numera filios tuas, adde unum inter illos, Dominum tuum. Unum

habes, sit ille secundus; duos habes, sit ille tertius; tres habes, sit ille quartus." PL 40: 674. Cf. Eberhard Friedrich Bruck, *Kirchenväter und soziales Erbrecht* (Berlin: Springer Verlag, 1956), pp. 86-87.

47. St. Augustine, *Sermo* 86, PL 38: 529. "Fac locum Christo cum filiis tuis, accedat familiae tuae Dominus tuus, accedat ad prolem Creator tuus, accedat ad numerum filiorum tuorum frater tuus. . . . Duos filios habes, tertium illum computa; tres habes, quartus numeratur; quintum habes, sextus dicatur; decem habes, undecima sit. Nolo amplius dicere: unius filii tui serva locum Domino tuo. Quod enim dabis Domino tuo, et tibi proderit et filiis tuis. . . . Dabis autem portionem unam, quam unius filiis deputasti." Cf. Bruck, p. 87.

48. On Salvian, see Bruck, pp. 105-6 (and the sources cited therein).

49. See *Timothei ad Ecclesiam libri IV,* bk. III. 17-19, in Georges LaGarrigue, ed., Sources chrétiennes no. 176 (Paris: Les Éditions du Cerf, 1971), pp. 250-53.

50. *Timothei ad Ecclesiam libri IV,* bk. III. 17, p. 250. "[H]oc specialiter dico et peculiari admonitione commoneo. . . ."

51. "[N]e ullum omnino aliquis quamvis carissimum pignus animae suae praeferat. Neque enim iniquum est ut quilibet Christianorum etiam legitimis heredibus in hoc saeculo minus congerat, dummodo sibimet in aeternitate succurrat multis modis, quia et facilius est hic deesse filiis quippiam quam parentibus in futuro, et multo levior praesens tenuitas quam aeterna paupertas . . ." (bk. III. 17, pp. 250-52).

52. Bk. III. 18, p. 252.

53. Bk. III, 18, p. 252.

54. See Mario Falco, *Le Disposizioni 'pro Animo': Fondamenti dottrinali e forme giuridiche* (Turin, 1911), cited in Bruck, *Kirchenväter,* p. 108, note 17.

55. See Bruck, *Kirchenväter,* p. 111. Salvian himself wrote: "I honor all who are not other than imitators of Christ, I revere them as not other than the images of Christ, I uplift them as not other than members of Christ. . . ." ["Hos enim ego omnes non aliter quam imitatores Christi honoro, non aliter quam Christi imagines colo, non aliter quam Christi membra suspicio . . ."]. *Timothei ad Ecclesiam libri IV,* Sources chrétiennes, vol. 176, p. 194. Salvian's preceding remarks, which stressed the extreme demands of the Christian message, makes clear his asceticism.

56. See Regino of Prüm, *Libri duo de Synodalibus Causis et Discipinis Ecclesiasticis,* bk. I, c. 105, PL 132: 212.

57. Regino of Prüm, PL 132: 212.

58. Regino of Prüm, PL 132: 212.

59. See Burchard of Worms, *Decretorum Libri XX* (Aalen: Scientia Verlag, 1992), bk. XVIII, *argumentum,* p. 181 ra.

60. Bk. XVIII, *argumentum,* p. 181 ra.

61. See Hermann Wasserschleben, *Die irische Kanonensammlung* (Aalen: Scientia Verlag, 1966); on the dating, see Lotte Kéry, *Canonical Collections of the Early Middle Ages (ca. 400-1140): A Bibliographic Guide to the Manuscripts and Literature* (Washington, DC: Catholic University of America Press, 1999), p. 73.

62. See *Die irische Kanonensammlung,* bk. XXXII, c. 13, p. 113.

63. Bk. XXXII, c. 13, p. 113. Cf. bk. XXXII, c. 22, p. 117 (admonishing a testator to divide his moveable goods among the minister who has tended to his needs; his children; and the church where he was to be buried).

64. On the dating, see Dorothy Whitelock, ed., *Anglo-Saxon Wills* (Holmes Beach, FL: William W. Gaunt and Sons, 1986), p. 179.

65. See "The Will of Thurketel of Palgrave," in Whitelock, ed., *Anglo-Saxon Wills,* p. 69.

66. "The Will of Thurketel," p. 69.

67. "The Will of Thurketel," p. 69.

68. Thus, for instance, a certain Wulfgyth, in a will dated to around 1046, granted the estate Stisted to the monks of Christchurch, with a life interest in her sons; she "grant[s] to my sons Ulfketel and Ketel the estates at Walsingham and at Carleton and at Harling; and I grant to my two daughters, Gode and Bote, Saxlingham and Somerleyton. And to the church at Somerleyton sixteen acres of land and one acre of meadow. And to my daughter Ealdgyth, I grant the estates at Chadacre and at Ashford, and the wood which I attached to the latter. And I grant Fritton to Earl Godwine and Earl Harold." See "The Will of Wulfgyth," in *Anglo-Saxon Wills,* p. 85. On dating, see p. 197. The will goes on to make other smaller bequests. It should be noted that Wulfgyth was a female, not a male, testator.

69. See C. 13, q. 2, cc. 4, 6-7.

70. C. 13, q. 2, c. 4. On this text, see also Chapter Three, above, p. 131.

71. C. 13, q. 2, c. 6. On this text, see also Chapter Three, above, p. 131.

72. C. 13, q. 2, c. 7.

73. C. 13, q. 2, d.p.c. 7.

74. C. 13, q. 2, d.p.c. 7.

75. C. 13, q. 2, d.p.c. 7.

76. C. 13, q. 2, d.p.c. 7. On St. Augustine's teaching, see above, p. 158.

77. See C. 16, q. 1, c. 14 (Gregory the Great on pious wishes); C. 16, q. 1, c. 15 (Gelasius I on just disposition).

78. See C. 13, q. 2, cc. 9, 11.

79. C. 19, q. 3, d.a.c. 7.

80. C. 19, q. 3, cc. 7-8.

81. C. 19, q. 3, d.p.c. 8. On monastic inheritance rights, see also Paulin M. Blecker, "The Civil Rights of the Monk in Roman and Canon Law: The Monk as *Servus,*" *American Benedictine Review* 17 (1966): 185, 190-91.

82. See Henri Auffroy, *Evolution du testament en France des origines aux XIIIe siècle* (Paris: Arthur Rousseau, 1899), pp. 388-89.

83. Auffroy, *Evolution du testament en France,* pp. 388-89.

84. See Rufinus, *Summa,* C. 13, q. 2, pp. 335-36.

85. Rufinus, *Summa,* C. 13, q. 2, c. 4, v. *ultima voluntas,* p. 335.

86. Rufinus, *Summa,* C. 13, q. 2, d.a.c. 8, pp. 335-36.

87. Rufinus, *Summa,* C. 13, q. 2, d.a.c. 8, pp. 335-36.

88. C. 19, q. 3, cc. 8-9.

89. Rufinus, *Summa,* C. 13, q. 2, d.a.c. 9, p. 336.

90. C. 13, q. 2, c. 8.

91. Rufinus, *Summa,* C. 13, q. 2, c. 8, *Si quis irascitur,* p. 336.

92. See I Comp. 3.22. Found at Emil Friedberg, *Quinque Compilationes Antiquae* (Graz: Akademische Druck-und-Verlagsanstalt, 1956), p. 32.

93. See X.3.26.2 (= I Comp. 3.22.1) (testamentary freedom of bishops); X.3.26.9 (= I Comp. 3.22.6) (testamentary capacity of clerics).

94. C. 3.26.11 (= I Comp. 3.22.10).

95. X.3.26.4 (I Comp. 3.22.13).

96. X.3.26.13.

97. X.3.26.19.

98. See Bernard of Pavia, *Summa Decretalium,* bk. III. 22, p. 96.

99. Bk. III. 22, p. 96.

100. Bk. III. 22, p. 96: "Testamentum est dispositio, qua quis disponit, quid de rebus suis post mortem suam fieri velit, et dicitur testamentum quasi testatio mentis, i.e., manifestatio voluntatis."

101. Bk. III. 22, p. 97. Bernard agreed with the Roman-law rule that a son in his father's power who was also a soldier might be allowed to make a will.

102. Bk. III. 22, p. 97. Bernard's use of the modifier *omnino* suggests that he would agree with the Roman law's acknowledgement that the conditions of deafness and muteness truly had to disable one from expressing his or her will; presumably, they had to be permanent conditions, and not simply the result of age or illness. Compare this treatment of deaf-mutes with the canonists' insistence on their capacity for marriage. See above, Chapter One.

103. Bk. III. 22, p. 97.

104. Bk. III. 22, pp. 97-98 ("Reliqui testamentum facere possunt, quia quicunque non prohibetur testamentum facere valet, quia cuncta licent, nisi decreto vel lege vetentur").

105. See Goffredus Tranensis, *Summa super Titulis Decretalium,* bk. III, *De Testamentis,* p. 143 rb.

106. *De Testamentis,* p. 143va.

107. *De Testamentis,* p. 144rb ("Unde voluntas testatoris est lex").

108. Bernard of Parma, *Glossa Ordinaria,* X.3.27.2, v. *morientium.*

109. Hostiensis, *Summa,* bk. III, *De Testamentis et Ultimis Voluntatibus,* sec. 7.

110. Hostiensis, *Summa,* bk. III, *De Donationibus,* sec. 4.

111. See Hostiensis, *Lectura,* X.3.24.1, v. *sponte.*

112. Hostiensis, *Summa,* bk. III, *De Testamentis et Ultimis Voluntatibus,* sec. 1 ("just expression of our will") and sec. 2 (derived from *testatio mentis*).

113. Bk. III, *De Testamentis et Ultimis Voluntatibus,* sec. 10.

114. Bk. III, sec. 10.

115. There were, furthermore, two types of illegitimate children. Constance Rousseau explains the difference:

> Natural illegitimate children were those born of unmarried parents who were still free to marry at their children's conception, pregnancy and birth. Spurious illegitimate children were those born of parents who were unable to marry validly at these designated times because of a canonical impediment. This second category, considered more deplorable than the first, included children born from incest, adultery, and those with parents in sacred orders or bound by a solemn religious vow.

> Constance M. Rousseau, "Innocent III, Defender of the Innocents and the Law: Children and Papal Policy (1198-1216)," *Archivum Historiae Pontificiae* 32 (1994): 31, 32.

116. On the promulgation of the *lex Falcidia,* see Alan Watson, *The Law of Succession in the Later Roman Republic* (Oxford: Clarendon Press, 1971), pp. 170-71.

117. The Twelve Tables, Gaius recorded, provided: "Whatever a man arranges by will concerning his property, let it be ratified with these words: So has he bequeathed his goods, so let the law/right *(ius)* be." See Gaius, *Institutes,* bk. II. 224.

118. Bk. II. 224.

119. Bk. II. 226. "Nam in multas legatariorum personas distributo patrimonio poterat [testator] adeo heredi minimum relinquere, ut non expediret heredi huius lucri gratia totius hereditatis onera sustinere."

120. Sec. 227.

121. Sec. 227.

122. See *Digest* 35.2.1 pr.

123. *Digest* 35.2.1 pr.

124. Justinian, *Institutes,* 2.13.pr. and 1. An edited and reconstructed version of the *Lex Falcidia* can be found in M. H. Crawford, ed., *Roman Statutes* (London: Institute of Classical Studies, 1996), vol. II, pp. 779-80.

125. Justinian, *Institutes,* 2.13.pr.

126. Gaius, *Institutes,* bk. II.127-28.

127. Justinian, *Institutes,* 2.13.1.

128. Justinian, *Institutes,* 2.18.pr.

129. Justinian, *Institutes,* 2.18.pr.

130. Justinian, *Institutes,* 2.18.pr.

131. On this reconciling function of legal fictions, see Lon L. Fuller, *Legal Fictions* (Stanford, CA: Stanford University Press, 1967), pp. 51-53.

132. See Cicero, *De Inventione,* II.22.66 ("pietatem, quae erga patriam aut parentes aut alios sanguine coniunctos officium conservare moneat"). See also Hendrik Wagenvoort, *Pietas: Selected Studies in Roman Religion* (Leiden: E. J. Brill, 1980), p. 7, analyzing Cicero's definition of *pietas.*

133. See *De Inventione,* II.22.66. See also Wagenvoort, above, pp. 7-14.

134. See Richard P. Saller, "*Pietas,* Obligation, and Authority in the Roman Family," in Peter Kneissl and Volker Losemann, eds., *Alte Geschichte und Wissenschaftsgeschichte. Festschrift für Karl Christ zum 65. Geburtstag* (Darmstadt: Wissenschaftliche Buchgesellschaft, 1988), pp. 393, 399.

135. Saller notes, with respect to Justinian's *Digest:* "By my count, there are actually more references to *pietas paterna* and *materna* (16) than to filial *pietas* (12) . . ." (*Pietas,* p. 402, note 39). It has been maintained that this concept of mutual duty has deep roots in Greco-Roman philosophical thought. See E. Renier, *Étude sur l'histoire de la Querela Inofficiosi en droit romain* (Liége: Vaillant-Carmanne, 1942), pp. 54-76.

136. See Saller, *Pietas,* pp. 401-2; see also Renier, *La Querela Inofficiosi,* pp. 65-74.

137. *Institutes,* 2.18.3.

138. *Institutes,* 2.18.3.

139. See *Digest* 5.2.8.16.

140. See Christoph G. Paulus, "Changes in the Power Structure within the Family in the Late Roman Republic," *Chicago-Kent Law Review* 70 (1995): 1503, 1506. Paulus adds: "If the dispute between the *paterfamilias* and his son now came to the point where the father threatened his son with disinheritance, the son could relax and lean back. The

possibility of disinheritance was drastically reduced, with the law requiring good cause for it."

141. *Digest* 5.2.2.

142. *Digest* 5.2.15.

143. *Codex* 3.28.28.

144. See *Codex Theodosianus* 2.19.2 (interpretation).

145. See *Digest* 35.2.1.17 ("Id quod natura hereditati debetur . . .").

146. *Codex* 3.28.36.2.

147. See *Novella* 1.1.2.

148. See *Novella* 115.3.1 (treating parents with violence); 115.3.5 (attempt on parents' lives); 115.3.4 (habitual criminal).

149. See *Novella* 115.3.6.

150. *Novella* 115.3.13.

151. *Novella* 115.3.14.

152. *Novella* 115.3.14.

153. Edward Champlin has noted that disinheritance might sometimes be part of a larger, more complex testamentary plan involving the giving of trusts or other gifts to children in lieu of their share of the estate. See Edward Champlin, *Final Judgments: Duty and Emotion in Roman Wills, 200 B.C.–A.D. 250* (Berkeley, CA: University of California Press, 1991), pp. 107-20.

154. See, for example, *Codex* 3.28.30 (holding that a will which did not specify the payment of the "legitimate portion" due the heirs was facially valid but subject to legal challenge as inofficious; and *Codex* 3.28.31 (permitting the estate in certain circumstances where less than the Falcidian fourth was set aside to supplement the "legitimate portion").

155. *Digest* 36.1.1. On the dating of this decree, see Buckland, *A Text-Book of Roman Law*, p. 355.

156. See *Institutes*, 2.23.7.

157. *Institutes*, 2.23.7.

158. *Institutes*, 2.23.7.

159. X.3.26.16.

160. X.3.26.18.

161. X.3.26.16.

162. X.3.26.16.

163. X.3.26.16.

164. X.3.26.16.

165. X.3.26.16.

166. X.3.26.16.

167. X.3.26.16.

168. X.3.26.18.

169. X.3.26.18.

170. X.3.26.18 ("et salvo nihilominus ei ex iure institutionis beneficio legis Facidiae . . .").

171. Goffredus Tranensis, *Summa Super Titulis Decretalium*, p. 144 rb ("testamentorum defensio ad ecclesiam pertinet").

172. See Hostiensis, *Summa,* bk. III, *De Testamentis et Ultimis Voluntatibus,* secs. 11-12.

173. Bk. III, sec. 11.

174. Bk. III, sec. 11.

175. Bk. III, sec. 11. Cf. *Digest* 5.2.2.

176. Hostiensis, *Summa,* bk. III, sec. 11.

177. One sees the expansion of the notion of *pietas* in the work of a writer like Philippe the Chancellor, a Parisian scholastic writer of the early thirteenth century, possibly also trained in canon law. *Pietas,* Philippe wrote, was in the first instance the fear and reverence God's creatures feel for their Creator. In the earthly realm, it is the feeling of devotion one has toward one's parents, namely, those who brought us into being. This devotion, Philippe observed, is in keeping with the *ius nature,* the natural law. To support this understanding of *pietas,* Philippe cited, among others, Cicero. Philippe le Chancelier, *Summa de Bono,* Nikolaus Wicki, ed. (Bern: Editiones Francke, 1985), vol. II, p. 989. On Philippe's life and training, see Wicki's introduction, "Vie de Philippe le Chancelier," pp. 11-28.

Thomas Aquinas also wrote that the name of piety *(nomen pietatis)* embraced the worship of God, who is "the Father of all," in addition to the "reverence owed to father and nation." *Summa Theologiae,* 1a, 2ae, q. 68, art. 4, ad 2.

178. Hostiensis, *Summa,* bk. III, sec. 11.

179. Bk. III, sec. 11.

180. Bk. III, sec. 11. ("[U]t dicatur quod homo debet homini ex natura. . . .") The Romanist writer Placentinus, in his *Summa* on Justinian's *Codex,* provided instructions on how *pietas* as a legal category might look in practice.

A son, Placentinus wrote, owed his father "reverence in speaking and acting, and similarly a wealthy son ought to assist a father without resources." But this kind of filial devotion was not one-sided. It did not mean that children were at the mercy of their parents when it came to determining who might take as an heir. Where children had satisfied the demands of *pietas* — and they were presumed to act piously toward their parents unless otherwise proven — they acquired a claim, derived from natural law, that could be enforced through the assertion of a right of action as part of the judicial process. Placentinus, *Summa Codicis,* p. 411.

The claim to succeed to an estate, furthermore, was typically defined as a right. The mid-fourteenth-century lawyer Albericus de Rosate, for instance, wrote of the *ius succedendi* in his legal dictionary. See *Vocabularium Utriusque Iuris* (Venice, 1546), p. 129vb, v. *ius succedendi.*

181. See Hostiensis, *Summa,* bk. III, *De Testamentis et Ultimis Voluntatibus,* sec. 12.

182. Bk. III, *De Testamentis,* sec. 12

183. Bk. III, *De Testamentis,* sec. 12.

184. Bk. III, *De Testamentis,* sec. 13.

185. Hostiensis, *Lectura,* X.3.26.16, sec. 1 *(casus).*

186. *Lectura,* X.3.26.16, sec. 1.

187. *Lectura,* X.3.26.16, secs. 63-69.

188. See, e.g., *Glossa Ordinaria,* X.3.26.16, v. *legitimam ipsam.* Bernard noted here that because this claim was based on natural *ius,* a father might not defraud his son of

this right and could only disinherit because of the "just cause of ingratitude." Cf. *Glossa Ordinaria*, X.3.26.18, v. *licet ipsas non expresserit* (also discussing the claim *iure naturae*).

189. See Innocent IV, *Apparatus*, X.3.26.18, v. *uni*.

190. See VI. 3.11.1 *(portione iure naturae debita)*. Boniface's concern is with giving effect to a provision in the will allowing the testator's possessions to pass to the "poor of Christ" *(Christi pauperes)* under the circumstance of the decretal.

191. Johannes Andreae, *In Quinque Decretalium*, X.3.26.16, sec. 2.

192. X.3.26.16.

193. Johannes Andreae, *In Quinque Decretalium*, X.3.26.16, sec. 9.

194. See Antonio de Butrio, *Super prima primi . . . Decretalium Commentarii* (Venice: Iuntas, 1578).

195. *Super prima primi*, X.3.26.16, pr.

196. *Super prima primi*, X.3.26.16, sec. 1.

197. *Super prima primi*, X.3.26.16, sec. 1: "Sunt iure naturae debita filio. . . ."

198. *Super prima primi*, X.3.26.16, sec. 2: "[I]d est, iure gentium, ideo iura civilia necessitarunt patrem ad relinquendum filio legitimam, quae est triens, vel semis, secundum numerum liberorum. . . ."

199. *Super prima primi*, X.3.26.16, sec. 23.

200. *Super prima primi*, X.3.26.16, sec. 23.

201. *Super prima primi*, X.3.26.16, sec. 23.

202. *Super prima primi*, X.3.26.16, sec. 23.

203. *Super prima primi*, Sec. 23: "[Q]uod statutum vel consuetudo tenendaex toto ad tollendam legitimam militantis contra naturalem aequitatem et pietatem, nam ex naturali iure astringitur parens aliquid relinquere filio pro alimentis. . . ."

This rhetoric of natural rights persisted through the end of the Middle Ages. Panormitanus in his *Commentaria* began his analysis of *Raynutius* by writing: "In the goods of one's father, mother, and grandparent, one has a certain claim owing by nature, which cannot be encumbered." ("In bonis patris, matris, et aviae habet quis debitam iure naturae, in qua gravari nequit.") X.3.26.16, note 1.

204. See Stephen P. Bensch, *Barcelona and Its Rulers, 1096-1291* (Cambridge, UK: Cambridge University Press, 1995), pp. 244-46.

205. See K. Zeumer, ed., *Leges Visigothorum* IV.5.1., *Monumenta Germaniae Historica* (Hanover: Hahn, 1902), vol. I, p. 195.

206. Zeumer, ed., *Leges Visigothorum*, p. 197.

207. See *Lex Visigothorum*, IV.5.1, pp. 195-98; cf. Bensch, *Barcelona and Its Rulers*, p. 245.

208. Stephen P. Bensch, *Barcelona and Its Rulers*, p. 246.

209. See Robert I. Burns, S.J., "The *Partidas*: An Introduction," in *Las Siete Partidas*, trans. Samuel Parsons Scott, and ed. Robert I. Burns (Philadelphia, PA: University of Pennsylvania Press, 2001), vol. I, p. xi.

210. For a summary of Alfonso's legislative program, see Jerry R. Craddock, "The Legislative Works of Alfonso de Sabio," in Robert I. Burns, ed., *Emperor of Culture: Alfonso X the Learned of Castile and His Thirteenth-Century Renaissance* (Philadelphia: University of Pennsylvania Press, 1990), pp. 182-97; and Joseph F. O'Callaghan, *The Learned King: The Reign of Alfonso X of Castile* (Philadelphia: University of Pennsylvania Press, 1993), pp. 36-37.

211. See *Las Siete Partidas del Rey don Alfonso el Sabio,* 3 vols. (Madrid: Real Academia de la Historia, 1807). It has been noted that the *Siete Partidas* "went through stages — not always even — of growth and modification" before its definitive promulgation by King Alfonso XI in 1348. See Robert A. MacDonald, "Law and Politics: Alfonso's Program of Political Reform," in Robert I. Burns, S.J., ed., *The Worlds of Alfonso the Learned and James the Conqueror: Intellect and Force in the Middle Ages* (Princeton, NJ: Princeton University Press, 1985), pp. 150, 182.

212. See Craddock, "Legislative Works of Alfonso de Sabio," p. 190.

213. *Las Siete Partidas,* bk. VI.1.17 ("et á esta parte legitima dicen en latin 'pars debita iure naturae'"), vol. III, p. 368.

214. Bk. VI.1.17, vol. III, pp. 368-69.

215. Bk. VI.1.17, vol. III, pp. 368-69.

216. Bk. VI.7.1, vol. III, p. 424.

217. Bk. VI.7.5.

218. Bk. VI.7.5.

219. Bk. VI.7.6.

220. Bk. VI.7.7.

221. Bk. VI.7.7.

222. See Craddock, "Legislative Works of Alfonso de Sabio," p. 184.

223. Craddock, "Legislative Works of Alfonso de Sabio," p. 184.

224. See Joseph W. McKnight, "Spanish *Legitim* in the United States: Its Survival and Decline," *American Journal of Comparative Law* 44 (1996): 75, 79-98. For an important defense of the natural-law foundations of Louisiana's system of forced shares, see Ralph C. Brashier, "Protecting the Child from Disinheritance: Must Louisiana Stand Alone?" *Louisiana Law Review* 57 (1996): 1, 4-7, 19-24.

225. See William S. Holdsworth, *A History of English Law* (Boston: Little, Brown, 1923), vol. III, pp. 74-75.

226. See G. D. G. Hall, ed. and trans, *The Treatise on the Laws and Customs of England Commonly Called Glanvill* (Oxford: Clarendon Press, 1993), p. 75 ("tunc secundum ius regni Anglie primogenitus filius patri succedit in totum").

227. See A. W. B. Simpson, *A History of the Land Law,* 2d ed. (Oxford: Clarendon Press, 1986), p. 62.

228. See Hall, *Glanvill,* p. 80. The testator was said to have "the free faculty of disposing" of one-third of the estate *(liberam disponendi facultatem).* See also Ferme, *Canon Law in Late Medieval England,* pp. 122-23.

229. See *Magna Carta,* c. 26, in Appendix IV, J. C. Holt, *Magna Carta* (Cambridge: Cambridge University Press, 1965), p. 324 ("salvis uxori ipsius et pueris racionabilibus partibus suis"). On the relationship of this provision to the European *ius commune,* see Richard H. Helmholz, "*Magna Carta* and the *Ius Commune,*" *University of Chicago Law Review* 66 (1999): 297, 331-33.

230. See George E. Woodbine, ed., and Samuel E. Thorne, trans. and rev., Henry Bracton, *De Legibus et Consuetudinibus Angliae* (Cambridge, MA: Harvard University Press, 1968), vol. 2, p. 180.

231. Woodbine and Thorne, *De Legibus,* vol. 2, p. 180.

232. See Richard H. Helmholz, "*Legitim* in English Legal History," *University of Il-*

linois Law Review (1984): 659-74 (reprinted in Richard H. Helmholz, *Canon Law and the Law of England* (London: Hambledon Press, 1987), p. 253.

233. Helmholz, *Canon Law and the Law of England*, p. 254.

234. Helmholz, *Canon Law and the Law of England*, pp. 253-55.

235. Helmholz, *Canon Law and the Law of England*, p. 255.

236. For Lyndwood's biography, see Ferme, *Canon Law in Late Medieval England*, pp. 19-41.

237. Christopher R. Cheney, "William Lyndwood's *Provinciale*," *The Jurist* 21 (1961): 405-34.

238. Frederic William Maitland, *Roman Canon Law in the Church of England: Six Essays* (New York, NY: Burt Franklin, 1968) (reprint of 1898 edition), pp. 1-50.

239. See William Lyndwood, *Provinciale seu Constitutiones Angliae* (Oxford: H. Hall, 1679), p. 178a, v. *defunctum*.

240. Lyndwood, *Provinciale*, p. 178a.

241. Lyndwood, *Provinciale*, p. 178a, v. *consuetum*. What was meant by common law in this passage was not the royal law of England but the law common to the entire Church.

242. See George W. Keeton and L. C. B. Gower, "Freedom of Testation in English Law," *Iowa Law Review* 20 (1934/35): 326, 337-40.

243. Keeton and Gower, "Freedom of Testation," p. 338.

244. Keeton and Gower, "Freedom of Testation," p. 328.

245. Azo, *Summa Aurea Super Codice*, pp. 175va-177rb.

246. Azo, *Summa Aurea Super Codice*, p. 177ra.

247. Azo, *Summa Aurea Super Codice*, pp. 175va-177rb.

248. See Accursius, *Glossa in Codicem*, 3.28, p. 76ra.

249. See Bartolus, *Ad Librum Tertium Codicem* (Venice, 1590), 3.28.Auth., 103vb, v. *unde si parens*.

250. Bartolus, *Ad Librum Tertium Codicem*, v. *unde si parens*.

251. Bartolus, *Unde si parens*, *Codex* 3.28.28, p. 104rb. ("Liberi exhaeredati praesumantur ingrati, nisi probent se gratus, et parentes praesumantur grati, nisi probentur ingrati. . . . Et est hodie lex correcta, quia quilibet praesumitur gratus, nisi probetur ingratus.")

252. Bartolus, *Unde si parens*, *Codex* 3.28.30, pp. 104vb-105ra.

253. Jack Goody, *The Development of the Family and Marriage in Europe* (Cambridge, UK: Cambridge University Press, 1983), especially pp. 99-101. James A. Brundage has challenged Goody's contribution in an important essay. See "Adoption in the Medieval *Ius Commune*," *Proceedings of the Tenth International Congress of Medieval Canon Law* (Vatican City: Biblioteca Apostolica Vaticana, 2001): 889-905.

254. See Gaius, *Institutes*, bk. I, secs. 97-99, Francis de Zulueta, ed., vol. I, p. 32.

255. Bk. I, sec. 99, p. 32.

256. Bk. I, secs. 99-100, p. 32.

257. Bk. I, secs. 99-100, p. 32.

258. Bk. I, sec. 100, p. 32.

259. Bk. I, sec. 101, p. 32.

260. Bk. I, sec. 102, p. 32.

261. *Institutes*, 1.11.1.

262. *Institutes,* 1.11.1.

263. See Gaius, *Institutes,* bk. I, sec. 104, de Zulueta, p. 32.

264. *Codex* 8.47.5.

265. *Codex* 8.47.5.

266. *Institutes,* bk. I. 11.10.

267. *Digest* 1.7.1.

268. *Digest* 1.7.16. And, again, it should be stressed that by the time one arrives at Justinian's compilation, the adoption of daughters was also permitted.

269. See *Digest* 1.7.9.

270. *Digest* 1.7.30.

271. Thus, for instance, if a *paterfamilias* adopted someone as a grandson, without the consent of his natural son, the adopted grandson did not come within the control of the son upon the death of the grandfather. See *Digest* 1.7.11.

272. *Codex* 8.47.10.

273. *Codex* 8.47.10.

274. *Codex* 8.47.10.

275. *Codex* 8.47.10.

276. *Codex* 8.47.10.1.

277. *Codex* 8.47.10.1.

278. *Codex* 8.47.10.1.

279. *Codex* 8.47.10.1.

280. *Codex* 8.47.10.5.

281. *Codex* 8.47.10.5.

282. *Institutes,* bk. I.11.3.

283. See, for example, Suetonius, bk. III, "Life of Tiberius" II.4 (Publius Clodius, a member of the senatorial Claudian dynasty, is adopted as a plebeian to gain political advantage over Cicero); bk. V, "The Deified Claudius," II.1 (Claudius's older brother adopted into Julian clan); bk. VII, "Life of Galba," IV.1 (Galba adopted by his stepmother Livia, even though women were not ordinarily allowed to adopt). Other examples might also be given. Thus the emperor Hadrian was adopted by his predecessor Trajan shortly before the older man's death. See Marco Barbati, *La Rilevanza del Consensus dell'adottando nell'adrogatio e nell'adoptio* (Rome: Pontificia Università Lateranense, 2000), p. 9.

284. See Deuteronomy 24:19-22 (decreeing that surplus food should be set aside for widows and orphans); Proverbs 23:10-11 (do not "invade the fields of orphans; for their redeemer is strong; he will defend their cause against you"); Jeremiah 22:3 ("Do not wrong or oppress the resident alien, or the orphan, or the widow"); Acts 6:1-2 (establishment of the order of deacon to meet the needs, *inter alia,* of widows and orphans).

285. Galatians 4:5.

286. Ephesians 1:5.

287. Romans 8:14-15.

288. See above, Chapter Two.

289. See James Brundage, *Law, Sex, and Christian Society* (Chicago: University of Chicago, 1987), p. 152.

290. Brundage, *Law, Sex, and Christian Society,* p. 153.

291. See *Canones Gregorii*, cc. 102-103, in F. W. H. Wasserschleben, ed., *Die Bussordnungen der abendländischen Kirche* (Halle: Verlag von Ch. Graeger, 1851), p. 172.
292. See Theodorus, *Penitentiale*, cc. 25-26, in *Bussordnungen*, p. 200.
293. See *Poenitentiale Vallicellanum*, c. 13, *Bussordnungen*, p. 558.
294. See *Libri Duo de Synodalibus Causis*, PL 132: 298, bk. II, c. 57.
295. Bk. II, c. 58.
296. See *Lex Visigothorum*, VI.3.7, in *Monumenta Germaniae Historica, Legum Sectio* I, vol. I (Hanover: Hahn, 1902), p. 262 ("Nihil est eorum pravitate deterius, qui, pietatis immemores, filiorum suorum necatores existunt").
297. See Karl August Eckhardt and Albrecht Eckhardt, eds., *Lex Frisionum* (Hanover: MGH Fontes Iuris Germani Antiqui, 1982), p. 46. On this law, see John Boswell, *The Kindness of Strangers: The Abandonment of Children in Western Europe from Late Antiquity to the Renaissance* (New York: Pantheon, 1988), p. 211, note 108.
298. See Letter of Boniface and Five German Bishops to Ethelbald, King of Mercia, ca. 744-747, in Arthur West Haddan and William Stubbs, eds., *Councils and Ecclesiastical Documents Relating to Great Britain and Ireland* (Oxford: At the Clarendon Press, 1871), vol. III, p. 354 (". . . [N]on implentes Christi ecclesias filiis adoptivis, sed tumulos corporibus et inferos miseris animabus satiantes"). See also Boswell, *Kindness of Strangers*, pp. 210-11 (analyzing and translating this text).
299. See *Concilium Vasense Primum*, c. 9, PL 84: 262-263.
300. See c. 9, PL, cols. 262-63. Boswell notes that the purpose of this legislation was to "encourag[e] people to pick up and rear abandoned children without fear of unpleasant consequences or of losing the child in whom they invest time and money." *Kindness of Strangers*, p. 173.
301. On the misidentification, see Boswell, *Kindness of Strangers*, p. 223, and note 152.
302. See *Libri Duo de Synodalibus Causis*, bk. II, c. 99, PL 132: 298.
303. Bk. II, c. 99, PL 132.
304. Bk. II, c. 99, PL 132.
305. See *Lex Visigothorum*, IV.1.1, in *Monumenta Germaniae Historica, Legum* 1.1, p. 193.
306. *Legum* 1.1, p. 193.
307. The text closes by praising the "piety of strangers" (*pietas aliena*), who take in such a child and raise it as their own. *Legum* 1.1, p. 194.
308. See *Historia Francorum*, V. 17, in *Monumenta Germaniae Historica, Scriptorum Rerum Merovingicarum*, vol. I, p. 208.
309. *Scriptorum Rerum Merovingicarum*, vol. I, p. 208 ("[U]t hic nepus meus mihi sit filius").
310. See Danièle Alexandre-Bidon and Didier Lett, *Children in the Middle Ages: Fifth through Fifteenth Centuries*, trans. Jody Gladding (South Bend, IN: Notre Dame University Press, 1999), p. 19.
311. See *Historia Francorum*, IX.20, *Monumenta Germaniae Historica, Scriptorum Rerum Merovingicarum*, vol. 1, p. 379.
312. Alexandre-Bidon and Lett, *Children in the Middle Ages*, p. 19.
313. See *Formulae Marculfi* II, 13, quoted in Karl August Eckhardt, *Studia Merovingia* (Aalen: Scientia Verlag, 1975), p. 241.

314. On Peter's importance to the law reform that commenced in the mid-eleventh century, see John Joseph Ryan, *Saint Peter Damian and His Canonical Sources: A Preliminary Study in the Antecedents of the Gregorian Reform* (Toronto: Pontifical Institute for Mediaeval Studies, 1956).

315. See *Acta Sanctorum*, February, vol. III (February 23) (vol. VI of *Acta Sanctorum*), p. 423.

316. *Acta Sanctorum*, p. 423.

317. *Acta Sanctorum*, p. 423.

318. *Acta Sanctorum*, p. 423.

319. *Acta Sanctorum*, p. 423.

320. *Acta Sanctorum*, p. 423. ("[U]t ipsis suis Doctoribus mirabilis haberetur"). See also Shulamith Shahir, *Childhood in the Middle Ages*, trans. Chaya Galai (London: Routledge, 1990), p. 156 (reviewing Peter's life and adoption against the background of the treatment of abandoned and orphaned children in eleventh-century Europe).

321. See D. 87, c. 9.

322. D. 87, c. 9.

323. D. 87, c. 9.

324. See Stephen of Tournai, *Die Summa über das Decretum Gratiani* (Aalen: Scientia Verlag, 1965), D. 87, v. *contestationis epistola*, p. 109.

325. Stephen of Tournai, *Die Summa*, D. 87, v. *securus habeatur.*

326. See *The Summa Parisiensis on the Decretum Gratiani*, ed. Terence P. McLaughlin (Toronto: Pontifical Institute of Mediaeval Studies, 1952), D. 87, c. 9, v. *si expositus*, p. 69.

327. See Rufinus, *Summa Decretorum*, ed. Heinrich Singer (Aalen: Scientia Verlag, 1963), D. 87, c. 9, v. *securus habeat*, p. 179.

328. See *Summa*, 'Induent Sancti,' D. 87, c. 9, v. *expositus*, p. 267.

329. *Summa*, 'Induent Sancti,' v. *expositus*, p. 267.

330. See Johannes Teutonicus, *Glossa Ordinaria*, D. 87, c. 9, v. *expositus*.

331. Johannes Teutonicus, v. *expositus*.

332. On Guido's career, see Brundage, *Medieval Canon Law*, pp. 212-13.

333. See Guido de Baysio, *Rosarium*, D. 87, c. 9, Lyon, 1549. By the late Middle Ages, one could discern a network of *hospitalia* spread over much of Europe, providing for the needs of foundlings. Pope Innocent III himself took the initiative to establish a foundling home, the Hospital of the Holy Spirit, to look after abandoned children in the heart of Rome. Rousseau, "Innocent III, Children and Papal Policy," p. 31. These homes for foundlings sometimes placed children with families. Thus medieval Spanish hospitals would seek out new homes for infants from among willing friends and neighbors of the parents who sought to abandon their children. James William Brodman, *Charity and Welfare: Hospitals and the Poor in Medieval Catalonia* (Philadelphia: University of Pennsylvania Press, 1998), pp. 115-16. In Florence, in the fifteenth century, "boys were put up for adoption, usually as apprentices." Philip Gavitt, *Charity and Children in Renaissance Florence: The Ospedale degli Innocenti, 1410-1536* (Ann Arbor, MI: University of Michigan Press, 1990), p. 189. Efforts were also made to place girls with families, although children who were not so placed continued to reside at the hospital where they worked during the day in apprenticeships or "as household or domestic servants."

334. X.5.11.1. Cf. above, p. 85.

335. C. 30, q. 3, c. 1.

336. C. 30, q. 3, c. 1 ("gratuita et sancta communio").

337. C. 30, q. 3, c. 1.

338. See Rufinus, *Summa Decretorum,* C. 30, q. 3, c. 1, v. *Quod autem spirituales vel adoptivi, etc.,* p. 462.

339. Rufinus, *Summa Decretorum,* pp. 462-63.

340. Rufinus, *Summa Decretorum,* p. 463 ("in potestate parentum naturalium").

341. See *Summa, 'Induent Sancti,'* C. 31, q. 3, p. 620.

342. Huguccio, *Summa,* C. 30, q. 3, d.a.c. 1, v. *Quod autem:* "Nota quod filius hic dicitur legitimus scilicet de carne patris et matris ad differentiam spiritualis vel adoptivi . . ." (Paris, Bibl. nat. mss, lat. 15367, quoted in Franck Roumy, *L'Adoption dans le droit savant du xiie au xvie siècle* [Paris: L. G. D.J., 1998], p. 109, note 96).

343. See Raymond de Peñafort, *Summa de Matrimonio,* col. 945.

344. Raymond de Peñafort, *Summa de Matrimonio,* col. 946.

345. Raymond de Peñafort, *Summa de Matrimonio,* col. 946.

346. See *Summa de Matrimonio,* ed. Agathon Wunderlich (Göttingen: Vandenhoeck und Ruprecht, 1841), pp. 39-40.

347. *Summa de Matrimonio,* p. 40 ("Effectus adoptionis est . . . per omnia quasi adoptantis filius habeatur, ita ut etiam ab intestato succedat . . .").

348. *Summa de Matrimonio,* p. 40.

349. *Summa de Matrimonio,* p. 40.

350. See Raymond de Peñafort, *Summa de Matrimonio,* col. 945.

351. Cols. 945-46.

352. Col. 946. Raymond proposed a set of verses to explain the distinction:

> "Arrogo, qui suus est, et habet meus esse necesse.
> "Patris adopto suum, nec patris desinit esse."

Roughly translated, the verse means: "I arrogate who is his own, and he is held as mine [and made] a necessary [heir]. I adopt one who has another father, and he does not lose his father."

353. Cols. 946-47.

354. Placentinus, *Summa Codicis,* p. 411.

355. Placentinus, *Summa Codicis,* p. 412.

356. Placentinus, *Summa Codicia,* p. 412.

357. See Azo, *Summa Aurea* (Frankfurt am Main: Minerva, 1968), bk. VIII, tit. *De adoptionibus,* sec. 1, p. 223 ra.

358. Azo, *De adoptionibus,* sec. 1, p. 223 ra.

359. *De adoptionibus,* sec. 7, at p. 223 rb.

360. *De adoptionibus,* sec. 7, p. 223 rb.

361. See Odofredus, *Lectura Super Codice* (Bologna: Forni Editore, 1968) (reprint of Lyon edition of 1552), vol. II, p. 174 vb.

362. Odofredus, *Lectura Super Codice,* vol. II, p. 174 vb.

363. Vol. II, p. 175 rb.

364. Vol. II, p. 175 rb.

365. Vol. II, p. 175 rb.

366. Vol. II, p. 175 rb ("concurrunt in unum iura naturalia et civilia . . .").

367. Vol. II, p. 175 rb.

368. Cino da Pistoia, *In Codicem et aliquot titulos primi Pandectorum tomi, id est Digesti veteris, doctissima commentaria,* 2 vols. (Turin: Bottega d'Erasmo, 1964), 8.48, p. 517A.

369. *In Codicem Commentaria,* 8.48, p. 517A.

370. Roumy, *L'Adoption dans le droit savant du xiie au xvi siècle, supra,* pp. 168-71.

371. See Goody, *Development of the Family,* pp. 99-101.

372. Goody, *Developmnet of the Family,* pp. 99-101.

373. Goody, *Development of the Family,* pp. 99-101. See also above, pp. 158-59 (quoting and analyzing Salvian).

374. See Goody, *Development of the Family,* p. 100.

375. Goody, *Development of the Family,* p. 99.

376. "[A]doptivus filius non succedit." *Libri Feudorum,* bk. II, tit. 26, quoted in Kristin Elizabeth Gager, *Blood Ties and Fictive Ties: Adoption and Family Life in Early Modern France* (Princeton, NJ: Princeton University Press, 1996), pp. 47-48. Franck Roumy has demonstrated that commentators on the feudal law steadily created exceptions to this seemingly ironclad rule. Roumy, *L'Adoption dans le droit savant du xiie au xvi siècle, supra,* pp. 284-92.

377. Brundage, "Adoption in the Medieval *Ius Commune,*" pp. 896-97.

378. Brundage, "Adoption in the Medievel *Ius Commune,*" p. 896. See also William Durandus, *Speculum iudiciale,* lib. IV, partic. IV, pp. 454-55.

379. *Speculum iudiciale,* lib. IV, partic. IV, p. 455.

380. *Speculum iudiciale,* lib. IV, partic. IV, p. 455 ("omni iure naturali sibi et in se in integrum reservato . . .").

381. Brundage, "Adoption in the *Ius Commune,*" p. 896. Cf. Geoffrey Barraclough, *Papal Notaries and the Roman Curia: A Calendar and a Study of a formularium notariorum curie from the Early Years of the Fourteenth Century* (London: Macmillan, 1934), pp. 244-45.

382. See René Aubenas, "L'adoption en Provence au Moyen Âge," *Revue historique de droit français et étranger* 13 (1934): 700-726.

383. Aubenas, "L'adoption en Provence," p. 704.

384. Aubenas, "L'adoption en Provence," p. 705 ("établissent le lien fictif de paternité lien définitif et perpétuel").

385. Aubenas, "L'adoption en Provence," pp. 712-26.

386. Aubenas's findings are given further support by the recent study of Andrée Courtemanche, "Lutter contre la solitude: Adoption et affiliation à Manosque au xv siècle," *Médiévales* 19 (1990): 37-42.

387. See Gager, *Blood Ties and Fictive Ties,* pp. 47-50.

388. Gager, *Blood Ties and Fictive Ties,* p. 48, note 48.

389. Gager, *Blood Ties and Fictive Ties,* pp. 49-50.

390. Gager, *Blood Ties and Fictive Ties,* p. 50.

391. Roumy, *L'Adoption dans le droit savant,* pp. 301-9. Benoit (1455-1516) attributed this legal disability to the *ius naturale.* Citing Maseur, Benoit asserted that "marriage, consummated by carnal and natural copulation . . . both produces sons and blood descendants able to succeed by the right/law of nature" ("[M]atrimonium carnali et naturali copula consummaturm, quae ambo filios producunt et consanguineos iure

naturae ad succedendum habiles"). Quoted in Roumy, p. 308, note 240. Benoit noted further that: "By testament, however, they [adopted children] may succeed them [their adoptive parents], just as any outsider can" ("Ex testamento autem, bene succedere possent et eis succedi, sicut posset quilibet extraneus"). Roumy adds that this doctrine was "affirmed and extended during the first half of the sixteenth century" (p. 309).

392. Gager, *Blood Ties and Fictive Ties,* p. 47.

393. Gager, *Blood Ties and Fictive Ties,* p. 47.

394. Brundage has written: "I have . . . been unable to discover any evidence that Salvian ever became a recognized source of canon law in the Middle Ages." "Adoption in the Medieval *Ius Commune,*" p. 893.

395. See Sánchez, *De Sancto Matrimonio* (Lyon, 1637), bk. VII, disp. 63, vol. II, p. 212.

396. Sánchez, *De Sancto Matrimonio,* bk. VII, disp. 63, vol. II, p. 212 ("extraneae personae").

397. Bk. VII, disp. 63, vol. II, p. 212.

398. In classical Roman law, the term "necessary heir" *(necessarius haeres)* was one required to take the estate in the event of insolvency. Buckland explains: "*Necessarii heredes:* These are slaves of the testator freed and instituted by his will, *heredes* with no power of refusal. The name applied to all such slaves freed and instituted, but its most important application was in insolvency. An insolvent might name a slave as one of his *heredes,* so that, if the others refused, the slave would be *heres,* and the disgrace of insolvency would fall on him and not on the deceased." Buckland, *A Text-Book of Roman Law,* p. 304.

399. Sánchez, *De Sancto Matrimonio,* bk. VII, disp. 63, vol. II, p. 212.

400. Sánchez, *De Sancto Matrimonio,* bk. VII, disp. 63, vol. II, p. 212.

401. Bk. VII, disp. 63, vol. II, p. 212.

402. Bk. VII, disp. 63, vol. II, p. 212.

403. See Susan Treggiari, *Roman Marriage: Iusti Coniuges from the Time of Cicero to the Time of Ulpian* (Oxford: Clarendon, 1991), p. 52.

404. See Beryl Rawson, "Roman Concubinage and Other De Facto Marriages," *Transactions of the American Philological Association* 104 (1974): 279-305.

405. See *Digest* 25.7.1.1-2.

406. *Digest* 25.7.3.

407. *Digest* 25.7.3.

408. *Digest* 25.7.3.

409. *Digest* 25.7.3.

410. *Digest* 25.7.3.1.

411. Buckland, *Text-Book of Roman Law,* pp. 128-29. Buckland notes that gifts to such children were "subject to the claims of the *legitimi*" (p. 129).

412. *Digest* 38.8.2.

413. *Digest* 38.8.4. Buckland notes that *cognatio* might entitle "even illegitimate children [to claim] in succession to the mother or her cognates, or *vice versa,* or to each other." Buckland, *Text-Book of Roman Law,* p. 371.

414. *Digest* 38.8.4. Cf. *Digest* 38.8.8 (Modestinus declaring that such children might also inherit through their maternal grandmother).

415. Buckland, *Text-Book of Roman Law*, p. 105, note 2 and sources therein discussed. See also Treggiari, *Roman Marriage*, pp. 317-18.

416. See Hippolytus, *The Treatise on the Apostolic Tradition*, Gregory Dix, ed. and trans. (London: Society for Promoting Christian Knowledge, 1968), pp. 27-28.

417. Hippolytus, *Treatise*, p. 28.

418. See Leo the Great, Letter 167 (to Rusticus), PL 54: 1204-5.

419. Col. 1204.

420. See First Council of Toledo, c. 17, in Vives, ed., *Concilios Visigóticos*, p. 24. See also Brundage, *Law, Sex, and Christian Society*, p. 101.

421. See *Codex Theodosianus* 4.6.3.

422. See *Codex Theodosianus* 4.6.4.

423. *Codex Theodosianus* 4.6.4.

424. See *Codex Theodosianus* 4.6.5.

425. *Codex Theodosianus* 4.6.6 ("ex quolibet susceperint contubernio").

426. See *Codex* 5.27.3.

427. See *Codex* 5.27.4.

428. See *Codex* 5.27.5. Cf. Brundage, *Law, Sex, and Christian Society*, p. 103.

429. *Novella* 89, pr.

430. *Novella* 89.3.

431. *Novella* 89.3.

432. *Novella* 89.9.

433. *Novella* 89.10.

434. *Novella* 89.1.

435. *Novella* 89.1.

436. *Novella* 89.1.

437. See St. Augustine, *De Bono Coniugali and De Sancta Virginitate*, ed. and trans. P. G. Walsh (Oxford: Clarendon Press, 2001), sec. 5.5, p. 10 ("ut nec ille cum altera nec illa cum altero id faciat").

438. Sec. 5.5, p. 10.

439. Sec. 5.5, pp. 10-12.

440. Sec. 5.5, p. 12.

441. D. 34, c. 4.

442. D. 34, c. 5.

443. C. 32, q. 2, c. 12.

444. See Brundage, *Law, Sex, and Christian Society*, p. 245.

445. See D. 34, d.p.c. 3.

446. See Brundage, *Law, Sex, and Christian Society*, p. 245.

447. D. 34, c. 6.

448. See Paucapalea, *Summa über das Decretum Gratiani*, D. 34, p. 27 ("[a]ffectus hanc coniugem facit, lex concubinam vocat").

449. Paucapalea, *Summa*, D. 34, p. 28.

450. Rufinus, *Summa Decretorum*, D. 34, d.a.c. 4, p. 80.

451. Rufinus, *Summa Decretorum*, D. 34, d.a.c. 4, p. 80.

452. See *Summa Parisiensis*, D. 34, c. 4, p. 33.

453. See Stephen of Tournai, *Die Summa über das Decretum Gratiani*, C. 32, q. 2. c. 12, v. *non omnis . . . nec omnis filius*, p. 244.

454. See Bernard of Pavia, *Summa Decretalium*, bk. IV, title 18, p. 182.

455. Bk. IV, title 18, p. 182.

456. Bk. IV, title 18, p. 182.

457. Bk. IV, title 18, p. 182.

458. Bk. IV, title 18, p. 182. Cf. *Institutes* 1.10.13.

459. Bernard of Pavia, *Summa Decretalium*, bk. IV, title 18, pp. 182-83.

460. Bk. IV, title 18, pp. 182-83.

461. Bk. IV, title 18, p. 183.

462. See Tancred, *Summa ad Compilationem Primam*, 4.18.6, v. *hereditate*, quoted in Brundage, *Law, Sex, and Christian Society*, p. 408, note 436.

463. Tancred, *Summa ad Compilationem Primam*, 4.18.6, v. *hereditate*.

464. X.4.17.1.

465. X.4.17.2.

466. X.4.17.9.

467. X.4.17.13.

468. See especially Brian Tierney, *"Tria quippe distinguit iudicia:* A Note on Innocent III's *Per venerabilem,"* *Speculum* 37 (1962): 48-59; and Kenneth Pennington, "Pope Innocent III's Views on Church and State: A Gloss to *Per venerabilem,"* in Kenneth Pennington and Robert Somerville, eds., *Law, Church, and Society: Essays in Honor of Stephan Kuttner* (Philadelphia: University of Pennsylvania Press, 1977), pp. 49-67.

469. X.4.17.13.

470. X.4.17.13.

471. X.4.17.13.

472. X.4.17.13.

473. X.4.17.13 ("Videretur siquidem monstruosum ut, qui legitimus ad spirituales fieret actiones, circa saeculares actus illegitimus remaneret").

474. X.4.17.13.

475. X.4.17.13. On Philip's marital difficulties and the political machinations that led to Pope Innocent III's decision to legitimate Philip's children, see John W. Baldwin, *The Government of Philip Augustus: Foundations of French Royal Power in the Middle Ages* (Berkeley: University of California Press, 1986), pp. 84-87. The older narrative by William Holden Hutton, *Philip Augustus* (London: Macmillan and Company, 1896), pp. 159-76, retains some value.

476. X.4.17.13.

477. X.4.17.13 ("Insuper cum rex ipse superiorem in temporalibus minime recognascat, sine iuris alterius laesione in eo se iurisdictioni nostrae subiicere potuit et subiecit").

478. X.4.17.13 ("non quod alieno iuri praeiudicare velimus").

479. X.4.17.13.

480. See Pennington, "Pope Innocent III's Views on Church and State," pp. 55, 65, and note 41. Both Vincentius and Johannes, Pennington notes, wrote: "Tamen per hoc non probatur quod papa habeat iurisdictionem in temporalibus, nam legitimare spectat ad voluntariam iurisdictionem" ("Nevertheless, it is not proven through this that the pope has jurisdiction in temporalities, for legitimation belongs to voluntary jurisdiction"). (Quoted p. 65, note 41.)

481. See Bernard of Parma, *Glossa Ordinaria*, X.4.17.13, v. *habeat potestatem*

("[N]on probatur, quod habeat iurisdictionem in temporalibus. [L]egitimare enim pertinet ad voluntariam iurisdictionem").

482. Bernard of Parma, *Glossa Ordinaria*, X.4.17.113, v. *habeat potestatem* ("[S]ed contrarium credo, scilicet quod dominus Papa non possit legitimare aliquem quantum ad hoc, ut succedat in haereditate tamquam legitimus haeres, qui non sit").

483. See Innocent IV, *Apparatus*, X.4.17.13, v. *evaderet*.

484. *Apparatus*, X.4.17.13, v. *evaderet*.

485. *Apparatus*, X.4.17.13, v. *evaderet*.

486. See John A. Watt, *The Theory of Papal Monarchy in the Thirteenth Century: The Contribution of the Canonists* (London: Burns and Oates, 1965), p. 111.

487. Hostiensis, *Summa*, bk. IV, *Qui Filii sint Legitimi*, sec. 11 ("Salva reverentia aliorum mihi videtur dominum papam habere potestatem legitimandi quo ad spiritualia et temporalia, et ipsum solum, ut innuitur *i. eo., per venerabilem . . .*").

488. *Summa*, bk. IV, *Qui Filii sint Legitimi*, sec. 11 ("[C]um enim causa matrimonialis spiritualiter pertineat ad ecclesiam adeo quod secularis iudex de ipsa cognoscere non potest etiam si inciderit").

489. *Summa*, bk. IV, *Qui Filii sint Legitimi*, sec. 11 ("[N]ec de legitima filiatione").

490. Hostiensis, *Lectura*, X.4.17.13, v. *casualiter.*

491. *Lectura*, X.4.17.13, v. *testamento*.

492. *Lectura*, X.4.17.13, v. *testamento*.

493. F. M. Powicke, *King Henry III and the Lord Edward: The Community of the Realm in the Thirteenth Century* (Oxford: Clarendon Press, 1947), vol. I, p. 151.

494. Johannes Andreae, *In Quinque*, X.4.17.13, sec. 3 ("Scias et est arg. quod papa non debet dispensare sine causa; quia homo est, et peccare potest, sicut alius licet in isto mundo a nemine iudicetur" [citation omitted]).

495. Johannes Andreae, *In Quinque*, X.4.17.13, sec. 30.

496. X.4.17.13, sec. 30.

497. X.4.17.13, sec. 30.

498. X.4.17.13, sec. 30.

499. See Panormitanus, *Commentaria*, X.4.17.13, notes 1, 4, and 21.

500. See Richard H. Helmholz, *The Spirit of the Classical Canon Law* (Athens, GA: University of Georgia Press, 1996), p. 127 and note 21; p. 425.

501. Benedict declared: "Potiori iure ad tribunalia ecclesiastica provocare permittuntur viduae, orphani, pupilli, aliaeque miserabiles personae . . ." ("By a more powerful right are widows, orphans, wards, and other vulnerable persons permitted to beseech ecclesiastical tribunals"). See Benedict XIV, *De Synodo Dioecesana*, bk. IX, ch. X, in *Opera Omnia* 11 (Prato: Aldina, 1844), p. 320. Elsewhere Benedict added: "Nam in primis tuitio, et defensio, ne sit inefficax, debet esse conjuncta cum jurisdictione . . ." ("For in the first place, safeguarding and defense, lest it be ineffectual, must be joined to jurisdiction").

502. A sixteenth-century work, Johannes Brunellus's *Tractatus Insignis de Sponsalibus et Matrimoniis*, illustrates the kind of fine distinctions that lawyers continued to draw among types of children even into the early-modern era. There were six types of children, according to Brunellus: (1) Spiritual children, who were all the "sons of the Lord Pope, who is the father of fathers" (Brunellus might have been referring obliquely to the offspring of papal concubines, but his context suggests that he had di-

rectly in mind the whole of Christendom); (2) spiritual and legitimate children, who have been born in legitimate marriage and received the sacraments; (3) legitimate children, who may lack the sacraments, but have been born of legitimate marriage; (4) natural children born of a concubine, who may inherit two-twelfths of their father's estate where their father dies intestate, provided there are no legitimate offspring; (5) natural children born of a spurious relationship, who were not entitled to inherit; and (6) natural and legitimate children, those born of irregular unions legitimized in accord with the law. The *Tractatus* is found in the *Tractatus Universi Iuris,* vol. IX, pp. 6a, 6b-7a.

Notes to the Conclusion

1. This is a criticism voiced by Hadley Arkes, "The New Jural Mind: Rights Without Grounds, Without Truths, and Without Things That Are Truly Rightful," in Austin Sarat and Thomas R. Kearns, eds., *Legal Rights: Historical and Philosophical Perspectives* (Ann Arbor, MI: University of Michigan Press, 1996), pp. 177, 192. Arkes sees this failure to acknowledge the proper ground of rights as a feature of both the contemporary left and the contemporary right. "For the liberals, it may be a recoil from the claim to know moral truths. For the conservatives, it may be a dubiety about the claims of reason or a recoil from people, swollen with conceit and moralism, who have been all too cavalier in annexing the claims of reason to their partisan agendas." *Id.,* pp. 202-203.

2. See John Stuart Mill, *On Liberty and Other Essays,* John Gray ed. (Oxford: Oxford University Press, 1991), especially pp. 83-103.

3. John Rawls thus celebrates the process of choosing from a behind a "veil of ignorance" the norms by which we are to be governed: "Among the essential features of [the original position] is that no one knows his place in society, his class position or social status, nor does any one know his fortune in the distribution of natural assets and abilities, his intelligence, strength, and the like. I shall even assume that the parties do not know their conceptions of the good or their special psychological propensities. The principles of justice are chosen behind a veil of ignorance." John Rawls, *A Theory of Justice* (Cambridge, MA: Harvard University Press, 1971), p. 12.

Bibliography

Abelard, Peter. *Historia Calamitatum*. Edited by J. Monfrin. Paris: J. Vrin, 1978.

Accursius. *Glossa Digestum Infortiatum, Digest*. Turin: Ex Officina Erasmiana, 1968.

————. *Glossa in Codicem*. Turin: Ex Officina Erasmiana, 1968.

Ackerman, Bruce. *Social Justice in the Liberal State*. New Haven: Yale University Press, 1980.

Albericus de Rosate. *Vocabularium Utriusque Iuris*. Venice, 1546.

Albertus Magnus. *Opera Omnia, Ex Editione Lugdunensi Religiose Castigata*. Edited by Auguste Borgnet. 38 vols. Parisiis: Vives, 1890-1899.

Alesandro, John A. *Gratian's Notion of Consummation*. Rome: Officium Libri Catholici, 1971.

Alexander of Hales. *Glossa in Quatuor Libros Sententiarum Petri Lombardi*. Quaracchi: Ex Typographia Collegii S. Bonaventurae, 1957.

Alexandre-Bidon, Danièle, and Didier Lett. *Children in the Middle Ages: Fifth Through Fifteenth Centuries*. Translated by Jody Gladding. Notre Dame: Notre Dame University Press, 1999.

Allen, Peter Lewis. *The Wages of Sin: Sex and Disease, Past and Present*. Chicago: University of Chicago Press, 2000.

Ambrose. *Qua Continentur Libri Exameron, De Paradiso, De Cain et Abel, De Noe, De Abraham, De Isaac, De Bono Mortis*. Edited by Karl Schenkl. Corpus Scriptorum Ecclesiasticorum Latinorum 32 [pars 1]. Vindobonae: F. Tempsky, 1897.

Amram, David Werner. *The Jewish Law of Divorce According to Bible and Talmud*. New York: Sepher-Hermon Press, 1975.

Arcanum Divinae Sapientiae. In *De Matrimonio Christiano*. Rome: Pontificia Universitas Gregoriana, 1942.

Ariès, Phillipe. *Centuries of Childhood: A Social History of Family Life*. Translated by Robert Baldick. New York: Random House, 1962.

Arjava, Antti. *Women and Law in Late Antiquity*. Oxford: Clarendon Press, 1996.

Arkes, Hadley. "The New Jural Mind: Rights Without Grounds, Without Truths, and Without Things That Are Truly Rightful." In *Legal Rights: Historical and Philosophical Perspectives,* edited by Austin Sarat and Thomas R. Kearns, pp. 177-203. Ann Arbor, MI: University of Michigan Press, 1996.

Asci, Donald P. *The Conjugal Act as a Personal Act: A Study of the Catholic Concept of the Conjugal Act in Light of Christian Anthropology.* San Francisco, CA: Ignatius Press, 2002.

Athenagoras. *Legatio and De Resurrectione.* Edited and translated by William R. Schoedel. Oxford: Clarendon Press, 1972.

Aubenas, René. "L'adoption en Provence au Moyen Âge." *Revue historique de droit français et étranger* 13 (1934): 700-726.

Auffroy, Henri. *Evolution du testament en France des origins aux XIIIe siècle.* Paris: Arthur Rousseau, 1899.

Augustine. *De Bono Coniugali; De Sancta Uirginitate.* Edited and translated by P. G. Walsh. Oxford Early Christian Texts. Oxford: Clarendon Press, 2001.

———. *De Genesi Ad Litteram Libri Dvodecim; Eivsdem Libri Capitvla. De Genesi Ad Litteram Inperfectvs Liber.* Edited by Joseph Zycha. Corpus Scriptorum Ecclesiasticorum Latinorum, 28 [pars 1]. Vindobonae: F. Tempsky, 1894.

———. *De Perfectione Ivstitiae Hominis, De Gestis Pelagii, De Gratia Christi et De Peccato Originali Libri Dvo.* Edited by Karl Franz Urba and Joseph Zycha. Corpus Scriptorum Ecclesiasticorum Latinorum 42. Vindobonae: F. Tempsky, 1902.

Azo. *Azonis Summa: Aurea Recens Pristinae Suae Fidei Restituta, Ac Archetypo Collata.* Frankfurt/Main: Minerva, 1968.

Baldwin, John W. *The Government of Philip Augustus: Foundations of French Royal Power in the Middle Ages.* Berkeley: University of California Press, 1986.

Barbati, Marco. *La Rilevanza del Consensus dell'adottando nell'adrogatio e nell'adoptio.* Rome: Pontificia Università Lateranense, 2000.

Barr, Jane. "The Influence of St. Jerome on Medieval Attitudes to Women." In *After Eve: Women, Theology, and the Christian Tradition,* edited by Jane Martin Soskice, pp. 89-102. London: Marshall, Pickering, 1990.

Barraclough, Geoffrey. *Papal Notaries and the Roman Curia: A Calendar and a Study of a formularium notariorum curie from the Early Years of the Fourteenth Century.* London: Macmillan, 1934.

Batts, Deborah A. "'I Didn't Ask to Be Born': The American Law of Disinheritance and a Proposal for Change to a System of Protected Inheritance." *Hastings Law Journal* 41 (1990): 1197-1270.

Bavel, Tarcisius J. van. "Augustine's Views on Women." *Augustiniana* 39 (1989): 5-53.

Beal, John P., James A. Coriden, and Thomas J. Greene, eds. *New Commentary on the Code of Canon Law.* New York, NY: Paulist Press, 2000.

Bellomo, Manlio. *The Common Legal Past of Europe, 1000-1800.* Washington, D.C.: The Catholic University of America Press, 1995.

Benedict XIV. *De Synodo Dioecesana.* In *Opera Omnia II.* Prato: Aldina, 1844.

Bennett, H. S. *The Pastons and Their England.* Cambridge: Cambridge University Press, 1968.

Bensch, Stephen P. *Barcelona and Its Rulers, 1096-1291.* Cambridge: Cambridge University Press, 1995.

Berger, Adolf. *Encyclopedic Dictionary of Roman Law.* Philadelphia: American Philosophical Association, 1983.

Berman, Harold J. *Law and Revolution: The Formation of the Western Legal Tradition.* Cambridge, MA: Harvard University Press, 1983.

Berman, Harold J., and Charles J. Reid, Jr. "Roman Law in Europe and the *Ius Commune*: A Historical Overview with Emphasis on the New Legal Science of the Sixteenth Century." *Syracuse Journal of International Law and Commerce* 20 (1994): 1-31.

Bernard, Antoine. *Le sépulture en droit canonique.* Paris: Les éditions domat-montchrestien, 1933.

Bernard of Pavia. *Summa de Matrimonio.* In *Summa Decretalium,* edited by E. A. T. Laspeyres, 287-306. Graz: Akademische Druck- u. Verlagsanstalt, 1956.

————. *Summa Decretalium: Ad Librorum Manuscriptorum Fidem Cum Aliis Eiusdem Scriptoris Anecdotis.* Edited by Ernst Adolph Theodor Laspeyres. Graz: Akademische Druck- u. Verlagsanstalt, 1956.

Bireley, Robert. *The Refashioning of Catholicism, 1450-1700: A Reassessment of the Counter Revolution.* Washington, D.C.: The Catholic University of America Press, 1999.

Birkmeyer, Regine. *Ehetrennung und monastiche Konversion im Hochmittelalter.* Berlin: Akademie Verlag, 1998.

Bishop, Joel Prentiss. *Commentaries on the Law of Marriage and Divorce.* 4th ed. Boston, MA: Little, Brown, and Company, 1864.

Blackstone, William. *Commentaries on the Laws of England.* Chicago, IL: University of Chicago Press, 1979.

Blecker, Paulin M. "The Civil Rights of the Monk in Roman and Canon Law: The Monk as *Servus.*" *The American Benedictine Review* 17 (1966): 185-198.

Bocarius, Sahaydachny. "The Marriage of Unfree Persons: Twelfth Century Decretals and Letters." *Studia Gratiana* 27 (1996): 482-506.

Bonaventure. *Opera Omnia.* Quarrachi: Typographia Collegii S. Bonaventurae, 1882-1902.

Bonner, Stanley F. *Education in Ancient Rome: From the Elder Cato to the Younger Pliny.* Berkeley, CA: University of California Press, 1977.

Borresen, Kari Elisabeth. *Subordination and Equivalence: The Nature and Role of Women in Augustine and Thomas Aquinas.* Kampen, The Netherlands: Kok Pharos Publishing, 1995.

Boswell, John. *The Kindness of Strangers: The Abandonment of Children in Western Europe from Late Antiquity to the Renaissance.* New York: Pantheon Books, 1988.

Bourleau, Alain. "Droit et théologie au XIII siècle." *Annales ESC* 47 (1992): 1113-1125.

Brashier, Ralph C. "Protecting the Child from Disinheritance: Must Louisiana Stand Alone?" *Louisiana Law Review* 57 (1996): 1-26.

Brett, Annabel. *Liberty, Right, and Nature: Individual Rights in Later Scholastic Thought.* Cambridge: Cambridge University Press, 1997.

Brodman, James William. *Charity and Welfare: Hospitals and the Poor in Medieval Catalonia.* Philadelphia: University of Pennsylvania Press, 1998.

Brody, Saul N. *"The Disease of the Soul": Leprosy in Medieval Literature.* Ithaca, NY: Cornell University Press, 1974.

Broomfield, F., ed. *Thomae de Chobham Summa Confessorum.* Louvain: Éditions Nauwelaerts, 1963.

Bruck, Eberhard Friedrich. *Kirchenväter und soziales Erbrecht.* Berlin: Springer Verlag, 1956.

Brundage, James A. "Adoption in the Medieval *Ius Commune*." In *Proceedings of the Tenth International Congress of Medieval Canon Law,* pp. 889-905. Vatican City: Biblioteca Apostolica Vaticana, 2001.

———. "The Crusader's Wife: A Canonistic Quandary." In *Studia Gratiana.* Collectanea Stephan Kuttner 12 (1967): 425-441.

———. "Implied Consent to Intercourse." In *Marriage in Ancient and Medieval Societies,* edited by Angeliki E. Laiou, pp. 245-256. Washington, D.C.: Dumbarton Oaks Research Library, 1993.

———. *Law, Sex, and Christian Society in Medieval Europe.* Chicago, IL: University of Chicago Press, 1987.

———. *Medieval Canon Law.* London: Longmans, 1995.

———. "Prostitution, Miscegenation, and Sexual Purity in the First Crusade." In *Crusade and Settlement: Papers Read at the First Conference of the Society for the Study of the Crusades and Presented to R. C. Small,* edited by P. W. Edbury, pp. 57-65. Cardiff, Wales: University Press, 1985.

———. "Sexual Equality in Medieval Canon Law." In *Medieval Women and the Sources of Medieval History,* edited by Joel T. Rosenthal, pp. 66-79. Athens, GA: University of Georgia Press, 1990.

Brunellus, Johannes. "Tractatus Insignis de Sponsalibus et Matrimoniis." In *Tractatus Universi Iuris, Duce, & Auspice Gregorio XIII Pontifice Maximo in Unum Congesti.* Venetiis: [s.n.], 1584-1586.

Bucer, Martin. *De Regno Christi. Libri Duo,* 1550. Edited by François Wendel. In *Opera Latina,* vol. 15. Paris: Presses Universitaires de France, 1955.

Buckland, W. W. *A Text-Book of Roman Law from Augustus to Justinian.* 3d ed. Revised by Peter Stein. Cambridge: Cambridge University Press, 1963.

Bullough, Donald. "Burial, Community, and Belief in the Early Medieval West." In *Ideal and Reality in Frankish and Anglo-Saxon Society: Studies Presented to J. M. Wallace-Hadrill*, edited by Patrick Wormald, pp. 177-201. Oxford: Blackwell, 1983.

Burchard of Worms. *Decretorum Libri XX*. Aalen: Scientia Verlag, 1992.

Burke, Cormac. *Covenanted Happiness: Love and Commitment in Marriage*. San Francisco, CA: Ignatius Press, 1990.

Burns, Robert I., S.J. "The *Partidas:* An Introduction." In *Las Siete Partidas*, translated by Samuel Parsons Scott and edited by Robert I. Burns, vol. I, pp. xi-xxix. Philadelphia, PA: University of Pennsylvania Press, 2001.

Butler, Lawrence. "The Churchyard in Eastern England, AD 900-1100: Some Lines of Development." In *Anglo-Saxon Cemeteries, 1979: The Fourth Anglo-Saxon Symposium at Oxford*, edited by Philip Rahtz, Tania Dickinson, and Lorna Watts, pp. 383-389. Oxford: British Archaeological Reports, 1980.

Bynum, Carolyn Walker. "Did the Twelfth Century Discover the Individual?" *Journal of Ecclesiastical History* 31 (1980): pp. 1-17.

Caesarius of Arles. "Sermon 60." In *Sancti Caesarii episcopi Arelatensis Sermones, Part I*. Corpus Christianorum Series Latina. Turnholt: Brepols, 1953.

Canones et Decreta Sacrosancti Oecumenici Concilii Tridentini. Rome: Propaganda Fide, 1862.

Capello, Felix. *Tractatus Canonico-Moralis De Sacramentis*. Turin: Marietti, 1950.

Carlson, Eric Josef. *Marriage and the English Reformation*. Oxford: Blackwell, 1994.

Carmichael, Ann G. "Leprosy." In *The Cambridge World History of Human Diseases*, edited by Kenneth F. Kiple, pp. 834-839. Cambridge: Cambridge University Press, 1993.

Castelli, Elizabeth. "Paul on Women and Gender." In *Women and Christian Origins*, edited by Ross Shepard Kraemer and Mary Rose D'Angelo, pp. 221-235. New York: Oxford University Press, 1999.

Catholic Church. *Codex Iuris Canonici*. [Romae]: Typis Polyglottis Vaticanus, 1931.

———. *Codex Iuris Canonici*. Vatican City: Libreria Editrice Vaticana, 1983.

———. *Corpus Iuris Canonici*. Editio Lipsiensis Secunda. Edited by Emil Friedberg. Lipsiae, Ex Officina Bernhardi Tauchnitz, 1879-1881.

———. *Decretales D. Gregorii Papae IX: Svae Integritati Vna Cvm Glossis Restitvtae*. (Bernard of Parma, Glossa Ordinaria). Canon law 154. Romae: In Aedibus Populi Romani, 1582.

Champlin, Edward. *Final Judgments: Duty and Emotion in Roman Wills, 200 B.C.–A.D. 250*. Berkeley, CA: University of California Press, 1991.

Cheney, Christopher R. "William Lyndwood's *Provinciale*." *The Jurist* 21 (1961): 405-434.

Chester, Ronald. "Inheritance in American Legal Thought." In *Inheritance and Wealth in America*, edited by Robert K. Miller, Jr., and Stephen J. McNamee. pp. 23-43. New York: Plenum Press, 1998.

————. "Is the Right to Devise Property Constitutionally Protected? The Strange Case of *Hodel v. Irving.*" *Southwestern University Law Review* 24 (1995): 1195-1213.

Chodorow, Stanley. *Christian Political Theory and Church Politics in the Mid-Twelfth Century: The Ecclesiology of Gratian's Decretum.* Berkeley, CA: University of California Press, 1972.

————, and Charles Duggan, eds. *Decretales ineditae saeculi XII.* Vatican City: Biblioteca Apostolica Vaticana, 1982.

Cicognani, Amleto G. *Canon Law.* Philadelphia, PA: The Dolphin Press, 1935.

Clanchy, M. T. *Abelard: A Medieval Life.* Oxford: Blackwell, 1999.

Cleaver, Robert. *A Godlie Forme of Householde Government.* London: Barnard's, 1612.

Clement of Alexandria. "Les Stromates." In *Sources chrétiennes,* no. 38, edited by C. Mondesert, pp. 96-108. Paris: Editions du Cerf, 1954.

Codex Theodosianus. Hildesheim: Weidmann, 2000-2002.

Cohen, Jeremy. *'Be Fertile and Increase, Fill the Earth and Master It': The Ancient and Medieval Career of a Biblical Text.* Ithaca, NY: Cornell University Press, 1989.

"Concilium Aurelianiense." In *Monumenta Germaniae Historica. Legum Sectio III, Concilia,* vol. 1. Concilia Aevi Merovingici. Hanover: Hahn, 1893.

"Concilium Baiuwaricum." In *Monumenta Germaniae Historica. Legum Sectio III, Concilia,* vol. II, part 1. Concilia Aevi Karolini. Hanover: Hahn, 1896.

Constable, Giles, ed. *The Letters of Peter the Venerable.* Cambridge, MA: Harvard University Press, 1967.

Corbett, Percy Ellwood. *The Roman Law of Marriage.* Oxford: Clarendon Press, 1930.

Corbier, Mirielle. "Child Exposure and Abandonment." In *Childhood, Class, and Kin in the Roman World,* edited by Suzanne Dixon, pp. 52-73. London: Routledge, 2001.

Coriden, James A. *The Indissoulubility Added to Christian Marriage by Consummation.* Rome: Catholic Book Agency, 1961.

Cott, Nancy F. *Public Vows: A History of Marriage and the Nation.* Cambridge, MA: Harvard University Press, 2000.

Coughlin, John J. "Natural Law, Marriage, and the Thought of Karol Wojtyla." *Fordham Urban Law Journal* 28 (2001): 1771-1786.

Courtemanche, André. "Lutter contre la solitude: Adoption et affiliation à Manosque au xv siècle." *Médiévales* 19 (1990): 37-42.

Craddock, Jerry R. "The Legislative Works of Alfonso de Sabio." In *Emperor of Culture: Alfonso X the Learned of Castile and His Thirteenth-Century Renaissance,* edited by Robert I. Burns, pp. 182-197. Philadelphia: University of Pennsylvania Press, 1990.

Crawford, M. H., ed. *Roman Statutes.* London: Institute of Classical Studies, 1996.

Cunneen, Sally. *In Search of Mary: The Woman and the Symbol*. New York: Ballantine Books, 1996.

Danby, Herbert, ed. and trans. *The Mishnah*. Oxford: Oxford University Press, 1933.

Dauvillier, Jean. *Le marriage dans le droit classique de l'Église: Depuis le Décret de Gratien (1140) jusqu'a la mort de Clément V (1314)*. Paris: Sirey, 1933.

Davis, Natalie Zeman. "Some Tasks and Themes in the Study of Popular Religion." In *The Pursuit of Holiness in Late Medieval and Renaissance Religion,* edited by Charles Trinkaus and Heiko Oberman, pp. 307-336. Leiden: Brill, 1974.

Davis, Norman, ed. *Paston Letters and Papers of the Fifteenth Century.* 2 vols. Oxford: At the Clarendon Press, 1971-1976.

De Benedictis, Matthew M. *The Social Thought of St. Bonaventure: A Study in Social Philosophy*. Westport, CT: Greenwood Press, 1972.

De Wilde, Peter M. "Between Life and Death: The Journey in the Otherworld." In *Death and Dying in the Middle Ages,* edited by Edelgard Du Bruck and Barbara Gusick, pp. 175-187. New York: Peter Lang, 1999.

Decker, Raymond G. "Institutional Authority Versus Personal Responsibility in the Marriage Sections of Gratian's *A Concordance of Discordant Canons.*" *The Jurist* 32 (1972): 51-65.

Delhaye, Philippe. "Les dossier anti-matrimonial de *l'Adversus Jovinianum* et son influence sur quelques écrits latins du XIIe siècle." *Medieval Studies* 13 (1951): 65-86.

Dewart, Joanne E. McWilliam. *Death and Resurrection*. Wilmington, DE: Michael Glazier, 1986.

Dictionary of Moral Theology. Westminster, MD: The Newman Press, 1962.

Didier, Noel. "Henri de Suse, évêque de Sisteron (1244-1250)." *Revue historique de droit français et étranger* 31 (4th ser., 1953): 244-270.

———. "Henri de Suse in Angleterre (1236?-1244)." In *Studi in onore de Vincenzo Arangio-Ruiz nel XLV anno del suo insegnamento,* pp. 333-352. Naples: Jovene, 1953.

———. "Henri de Suse, prévôt de Grasse (1235-1244)." *Studia Gratiana* 2 (1954): 595-617.

Dillon, Robert E. *Common Law Marriage*. Canon Law Studies, no. 153. Washington, D.C.: The Catholic University of America Press, 1942.

Dixon, Suzanne. *The Roman Family*. Baltimore: Johns Hopkins University Press, 1992.

Donahue, Charles, Jr. "'The Case of the Man Who Fell Into the Tiber': The Roman Law of Marriage at the Time of the Glossators." *American Journal of Legal History* 22 (1978): 1-53.

———. "The Dating of Alexander the Third's Marriage Decretals." *Zeitschrift der Savigny-Stiftung für Rechtsgeschichte (kan. Abt.)* 68 (1982): 70-124.

———. "The Policy of Alexander the Third's Consent Theory of Marriage." In *Pro-*

ceedings of the Fourth International Congress of Medieval Canon Law, pp. 251-281. Vatican City: Biblioteca Apostolica Vaticana, 1976.

———. "Roman Canon Law in the Medieval English Church: Stubbs vs. Maitland Re-examined After 75 Years in the Light of Some Records from the Church Courts." *Michigan Law Review* 72 (1974): 647-716.

Dukeminier, Jesse, and Stanley M. Johanson. *Wills, Trusts, and Estates.* 6th ed. New York: Aspen Publishers, 2000.

Eckhardt, Karl August, and Albrecht Eckhardt, eds. *Lex Frisionum.* Hanover: MGH Fontes Iuris Germani Antiqui, 1982.

Eisen, Ute E. *Women Officeholders in Early Christianity: Epigraphical and Literary Studies.* Collegeville, MN: Michael Glazier Books, 2000.

Elliott, Dyan. *Spiritual Marriage: Sexual Abstinence in Medieval Wedlock.* Princeton, NJ: Princeton University Press, 1993.

Elliott, J. K., ed. *The Apocryphal New Testament.* Oxford: Oxford University Press, 1993.

Epstein, Louis M. *The Jewish Marriage Contract: A Study in the Status of the Woman in Jewish Law.* New York: Arno Press, 1973.

Erasmus, Desiderius. *Opera Omnia* . . . Lugduni Batavorum: P. Vander, 1703-1706.

Evans, C. F. *Resurrection and the New Testament.* London: SCM Press, 1970.

Evennett, H. Outram. *The Spirit of the Counter-Reformation.* Cambridge: Cambridge University Press, 1968.

Falco, Mario. *Le Disposizioni 'pro Animo' Fondamenti dottrinali e forme giuridiche.* Turin, 1911.

Fellhauer, David E. "The *Consortium omnis vitae* as a Juridical Element of Marriage." *Studia Canonica* 13 (1979): 3-171.

Ferme, Brian Edwin. *Canon Law in Late Medieval England: A Study of William Lyndwood's Provinciale with Particular Reference to Testamentary Law.* Rome: LAS, 1996.

Fitzgibbon, Scott. "Marriage and the Good of Obligation." *American Journal of Jurisprudence* 47 (2002): 41-69.

Flathman, Richard. *The Practice of Rights.* Cambridge: Cambridge University Press, 1976.

Fleming, Peter. *Family and Household in Medieval England.* Houndsmill, UK: Palgrave, 2001.

Flint, Valerie I. J. *The Rise of Magic in Early Medieval Europe.* Princeton, NJ: Princeton University Press, 1990.

Ford, Jeffrey E. *Love, Marriage, and Sex in the Christian Tradition from Antiquity to Today.* San Francisco: International Scholars Publications, 1999.

Fortin, Ernest L. "Sacred and Inviolable: *Rerum Novarum* and Natural Rights." *Theological Studies* 53 (1992): 203-233.

Fraher, Richard. "Summa, 'Induent Sancti': A Critical Edition of a Twelfth-Century Canonical Treatise." Diss., Cornell University, 1978.

Francisco de Victoria. *De Indis et de Iure Belli Relectiones*. Washington, D.C.: The Carnegie Institution, 1917.

Freedman, Paul. *Images of the Medieval Peasant*. Stanford, CA: Stanford University Press, 1999.

Friedberg, Emil. *Die Canones-Sammlungen Zwischen Gratian und Bernhard von Pavia*. Canon law 137. Graz: Akademische Druck- und Verlagsanstalt, 1958.

————. *Quinque Compilationes Antiquae*. Graz: Akademische Druck- und Verlagsanstalt, 1956.

Fuller, Lon L. *Legal Fictions*. Stanford, CA: Stanford University Press, 1967.

Gager, Kristin Elizabeth. *Blood Ties and Fictive Ties: Adoption and Family Life in Early Modern France*. Princeton, NJ: Princeton University Press, 1996.

Gaius. *Institutes*. Edited by Francis de Zulueta. Oxford: Clarendon Press, 1946.

Gandulf of Bologna. *Sententiarum Libri Quattuor*. Edited by Johannes de Walter. Vienna: Aemilius Haim, 1924.

Gardner, Jane F. *Family and Familia in Roman Law and Life*. Oxford: Clarendon Press, 1998.

Garrison, Marsha. "Toward a Contractarian Account of Family Governance." *Utah Law Review* (1998): 241-269.

Gasparri, Pietro. *Tractatus Canonicus de Matrimonio*. 3d ed. Paris: Beauchesne, 1904.

Gauthier, Albert. *Roman Law and Its Contribution to the Development of Canon Law*. Ottawa: Saint Paul University Press, 1996.

Gavitt, Philip. *Charity and Children in Renaissance Florence: The Ospedale degli Innocenti, 1410-1536*. Ann Arbor, MI: University of Michigan Press, 1990.

Geary, Patrick J. *Living with the Dead in the Middle Ages*. Ithaca, NY: Cornell University Press, 1994.

Getty-Sullivan, Mary Anne. *Women in the New Testament*. Collegeville, MN: Liturgical Press, 2001.

Gies, Frances, and Joseph Gies. *A Medieval Family: The Pastons of Fifteenth-Century England*. New York, NY: Harper Collins, 1998.

Gilles, Stephen G. "On Educating Children: A Parentalist Manifesto." *University of Chicago Law Review* 63 (1996): 937-1034.

Gilson, Étienne. *Heloise and Abelard*. Chicago: Henry Regnery Company, 1951.

Glendon, Mary Ann. "Marriage and the State: The Withering Away of Marriage." *Virginia Law Review* 62 (1976): 663-720.

Gold, Penny S. "The Marriage of Mary and Joseph in the Twelfth-Century Ideology of Marriage." In *Sexual Practices and the Medieval Church*, edited by Vern L Bullough and James A. Brundage, pp. 102-117. Buffalo, NY: Prometheus Books, 1982.

Goody, Jack. *The Development of the Family and Marriage in Europe*. Cambridge, UK: Cambridge University Press, 1983.

Gordon, Bruce, and Peter Marshall. "Introduction: Placing the Dead in Late Medieval and Early Modern Europe." In *The Place of the Dead: Death and Remembrance in Late Medieval and Early Modern Europe,* edited by Bruce Gordon and Peter Marshall, pp. 1-16. Cambridge: Cambridge University Press, 2000.

Gratian. *Decretvm Gratiani Emendatvm et Annotationibvs: Illvstratum Vna Cum Glossis: Gregorii XIII. pont. max. ivssv editvm: Ad Exemplar Romanvm Diligenter Recognitum.* (Johannes Teutonicus, Glossa Ordinaria.) Canon law 35. Parisiis, 1601.

Grimm, Benno, ed. *Die Ehelehre des Magister Honorius. Ein Beitrag zur Ehelehre der anglo-normanisschen Schule.* Rome: Studia Gratiana, 1989.

Grubbs, Judith Evans. *Law and Family in Late Antiquity: The Emperor Constantine's Marriage Legislation.* Oxford: Clarendon Press, 1995.

Gryson, Roger. *The Ministry of Women in the Early Church.* Translated by Jean Laporte and Mary Louise Hall. Collegeville, MN: Liturgical Press, 1976.

Guido de Baysio. *Enarrationes Super Decreto, Autor Ipse Rosarium Appellari Maluit.* Lyon, 1549.

Haddan, Arthur West, and William Stubbs, eds. *Councils and Ecclesiastical Documents Relating to Great Britain and Ireland.* Oxford: At the Clarendon Press, 1871.

Hall, G. D. G., ed. *Treatise on the Laws and Customs of England Commonly Called Glanvill.* Oxford: Clarendon Press, 1993.

Hanawalt, Barbara. *The Ties That Bound: Peasant Families in Medieval England.* New York: Oxford University Press, 1986.

Hasday, Jill Elaine. "Contest and Consent: A Legal History of Marital Rape." *California Law Review* 88 (2000): 1373-1506.

Haskell, Ann S. "The Paston Women on Marriage in Fifteenth-Century England." *Viator* 4 (1973): 459-471.

Heaney, Seamus P. *The Development of the Sacramentality of Marriage from Anselm of Laon to Thomas Aquinas.* Washington, D.C.: The Catholic University of America Press, 1963.

Helmholz, Richard H. *Canon Law and the Law of England.* London: The Hambledon Press, 1987.

———. "Infanticide in the Province of Canterbury During the Fifteenth Century." *History of Childhood Quarterly* 2 (1975): 379-390.

———. *The Ius Commune in England: Four Studies.* Oxford: Oxford University Press, 2001.

———. "*Legitim* in English Legal History." *University of Illinois Law Review* (1984): 659-674.

———. "*Magna Charta* and the *Ius Commune*." *University of Chicago Law Review* 66 (1999): 297-372.

———. *Marriage Litigation in Medieval England.* Cambridge, UK: Cambridge University Press, 1974.

————. *Roman Canon Law in Reformation England.* Cambridge, UK: Cambridge University Press, 1990.

————. *The Spirit of the Classical Canon Law.* Athens, GA: University of Georgia Press, 1996.

————. "Support Orders, Church Courts, and the Rule of *Filius Nullius*: A Reassessment of the Common Law." *Virginia Law Review* 63 (1977): 431-448.

Henricus de Segusio. *Henrici de Segusio cardinalis Hostiensis . . . In Primum [-Sextum] Decretalium Librum Commentaria: Doctissimorvm Virorvm Quampluribus Adnotationibus Illustrata: Hac Nouissima Editione Summo Fludio, Ac Diligentia Ab Innumeris Erroribus Expurgata, Suoque Pristino Typo Restituta: Recens Accesserunt Svmmaria, & Index Locupletissimus.* Venetiis: Apud Ivntas, 1581.

————. *Summa.* Aalen: Scientia, 1962.

Herlihy, David. *Medieval Households.* Cambridge, MA: Harvard University Press, 1985.

Heywood, Colin. *A History of Childhood: Children and Childhood in the West from Medieval to Modern Times.* Cambridge, UK: Blackwell, 2001.

Hincmar of Rheims. *De Divortio Lotharii Regis et Theutbergae Reginae,* edited by Letha Bohringer. Germaniae Historica, Concilia, vol. 4, supp. 1 (= PL 125: 619-772). Hannover: Hahnsche Buchhandlung, 1992.

Hinschius, Paulus, ed. *Decretales Pseudo-Isidorianae et Capitula Angilramni.* Aalen: Scientia Verlag, 1963.

Hippolytus. *The Treatise on the Apostolic Tradition.* Edited and translated by Gregory Dix. London: Society for Promoting Christian Knowledge, 1968.

Hohfeld, Wesley N. *Fundamental Legal Conceptions as Applied in Judicial Reasoning.* New Haven, CT: Yale University Press, 1923.

Holdsworth, Christopher J. "Christina of Markyate." In *Medieval Women,* edited by Derek Baker, pp. 185-204. Oxford, UK: Basil Blackwell, 1978.

Holdsworth, William S. *A History of English Law.* Boston: Little, Brown, 1923.

Holt, John. *Escape From Childhood.* New York: E. P. Dutton, 1974.

Hsia, R. Po-Chia. *The World of Catholic Renewal: 1540-1770.* Cambridge, UK: Cambridge University Press, 1998.

Hughes, Diane Owen. "Urban Growth and Family Structure in Medieval Genoa." *Past and Present* 66 (1975): 3-28.

Hunter, David G. "Augustine and the Making of Marriage in Roman North Africa." *Journal of Early Christian Studies* 11 (2003): 63-85.

Hutton, William Holden. *Philip Augustus.* London: Macmillan and Company, 1896.

Hyams, Paul R. *King, Lords, and Peasants in Medieval England: The Common Law of Villeinage in the Twelfth and Thirteenth Centuries.* Oxford: Clarendon Press, 1980.

Innocent IV. *Commentaria, apparatus in V Libros Decretalium.* Frankfurt/Main: Minerva, 1968.

Iogna-Prat, Dominique. *Order and Exclusion: Cluny and Christendom Face Heresy, Judaism, and Islam (1000-1150)*. Translated by Graham Robert Edwards. Ithaca, NY: Cornell University Press, 2002.

Izbicki, Thomas. "The Problem of Canonical Portion in the Later Middle Ages: The Application of 'Super cathedram.'" In *Proceedings of the Seventh International Congress of Medieval Canon Law*, edited by Peter Linehan, pp. 459-473. Vatican City, 1988.

Jeanselme, Édouard. *Comment l'Europe, au moyen âge, se protége contre la lèpre: rapport présenté au VIIIe Congrès international d'histoire de la médecine à Rome (22-27 septembre 1930)*. 2e tirage, rev. et corr. Paris: Société d'histoire de la médecine, 1931.

Jensen, Joseph. "Does *Porneia* Mean Fornication? A Critique of Bruce Malina." *Novum Testamentum* 20 (1978): 161-184.

Johannes Andreae. *In Primum [-Quintum] Decretalium Librum Nouella Commentaria: Ab Exemplaribvs Per Petrvm Vendramaenvm in Pontificio Venetiarum foro Aduocatum Mendis, Quibus Referta Erant, Diligenter, Expurgatis, Nunc Impressa: His Accesserunt Doctissimorum Virorum Annotationes: Cum Summis Eiusdem Nouis, & Indice Locupletissimo*. Canon law 106. Venetiis: Apud Franciscum Franciscium, Senensem, 1581.

John XXIII. *Pacem in Terris, Acta Apostolicae Sedis 55*. 1963.

Justin. *Apologies*. Paris: Etudes Augustiniennes, 1987.

Kalb, Herbert. "Bermerkungen zum Verhältnis von Theologie und Kanonistik am Beispiel Rufins und Stephans von Tournai." *Zeitschrift der Savigny-Stiftung für Rechtsgeschichte (kan. Abt.)* 76 (1986): 338-348.

Kapparis, Konstantinos. *Abortion in the Ancient World*. London: Duckworth, 2002.

Keeton, George W., and L. C. B. Gower. "Freedom of Testation in English Law." *Iowa Law Review* 20 (1934/35): 326-340.

Kéry, Lotte. *Canonical Collections of the Early Middle Ages (ca. 400-1140): A Bibliographic Guide to the Manuscripts and Literature*. Washington, DC: The Catholic University of America Press, 1999.

Kim, Keechang. *Aliens in Medieval Law: The Origins of Modern Citizenship*. Cambridge: Cambridge University Press, 2000.

Kippley, John. *Sex and the Marriage Covenant: A Basis for Morality*. Cincinnati, OH: Couple to Couple League, 1991.

Kline, Daniel T., ed. *Medieval Literature for Children*. New York: Routledge, 2003.

Koegel, Otto E. *Common Law Marriage and Its Development in the United States*. Washington, D.C.: John Byrne and Company, 1922.

Kritzeck, James. *Peter the Venerable and Islam*. Princeton, NJ: Princeton University Press, 1964.

Kuehn, Thomas. *Emancipation in Late Medieval Florence*. New Brunswick, NJ: Rutgers University Press, 1982.

———. "Fama as a Legal Status in Renaissance Florence." In *Fama: The Politics of*

Talk and Reputation in Medieval Europe, edited by Thelma Fenster and Daniel Lord Smail, pp. 27-46. Ithaca, NY: Cornell University Press, 2003.

Kunkel, Wolfgang. *An Introduction to Roman Legal and Constitutional History.* Translated by J. M. Kelly. Oxford: Clarendon Press, 1973.

Kuttner, Stephan. "The Father of the Science of Canon Law." *The Jurist* 1 (1941): 2-19.

————, and Beryl Smalley. "The *Glossa Ordinaria* to the Gregorian Decretals." *English Historical Review* 60 (1945): 97-105.

————. "Notes on the *Glossa Ordinaria* of Bernard of Parma." *Bulletin of Medieval Canon Law* 11 (1981): 86-93.

————. "Raymond of Peñafort as Editor: The 'decretales' and 'constitutiones' of Gregory IX." *Bulletin of Medieval Canon Law* 12 (1982): 65-80.

————. "Research on Gratian: Acta and Agenda." In *Proceedings of the Seventh International Congress of Medieval Canon Law.* Edited by Peter Linehan, pp. 3-26. Vatican City: Biblioteca Apostolica Vaticana, 1988.

Lake, Kirsopp, ed. *Shepherd of Hermas.* In *The Apostolic Fathers,* vol. II. London: William Heinemann, 1930.

Lancellotti, Johannes Paulus. *Institutiones Juris Canonici.* Mantua, 1695.

Landau, Peter. *Die Entstehung des kanonischen Infamiebegriffs von Gratian bis zur Glossa Ordinaria.* Köln: Böhlau Verlag, 1966.

————. "Hadrians IV Dekretale 'Dignum Est' (X.4.9.1.) und die Eheschliessung Unfreier in der Diskussion von Kanonisten und Theologen des 12. und 13. Jahrhunderts." *Studia Gratiana* 12 (1967): 511-553.

Laporte, Jean. *The Role of Women in Early Christianity.* New York: The Edwin Mellen Press, 1982.

Larrainzar, Carlos. "El Borrador de la Concordia de Graciano: Sankt Gallen, Stiftsbibliothek MS. 673 (= Sg)." *Ius Ecclesiae* 11 (1999): 593-666.

————. "El Decreto de Graciano del Códice Fd (= Firenze, Biblioteca Nazionale Centrale, *Conventi Soppressi* A.I. 402)." In *Ius Ecclesiae* 10 (1998): 421-489.

Lasch, Christopher. "The Suppression of Clandestine Marriage in England: The Marriage Act of 1753." *Salmagundi* 26 (1974): 90-109.

Lassen, Eva Marie. "The Roman Family: Ideal and Metaphor." In *Constructing Early Christian Families: Family as Social Reality and Metaphor,* edited by Halvor Moxnes, pp. 103-120. London: Routledge, 1997.

Leclercq, Jean. *Monks on Marriage: A Twelfth-Century View.* New York: Seabury Press, 1982.

Lefebvre, Charles. "Hostiensis." In *Dictionnaire de droit canonique.* vol. 5. Paris: Letouzey et Ané, 1953.

————. "Sinibalde dei Fieschi (Innocent IV)." In *Dictionnaire de droit canonique.* vol. 7. Paris: Letouzey et Ané, 1965.

Lesage, Germain. "The *Consortium vitae coniugalis*: Nature and Applications." *Studia Canonica* 6 (1972): 99-113.

Leslie, Melanie B. "The Myth of Testamentary Freedom." *Arizona Law Review* 38 (1996): 235-290.

Lettmann, Reinhard. *Die Diskussion über die klandestinen Ehen und die Einführung einer zur Gültigkeit verpflichtenden Eheschliessungsform auf dem Konzil von Trient. Eine kanonistische Untersuchung.* Münster: Aschendorffsche Verlagsbuchhandlung, 1967.

Levy, Ernst. *West Roman Vulgar Law: The Law of Property.* Philadelphia, PA: American Philosophical Society, 1951.

Liddell, Henry G., and Rupert Scott. *A Greek-English Lexicon.* Oxford: Clarendon Press, 1940.

Lindberg, Carter. *The European Reformations.* Cambridge, MA: Blackwell Publishers, 1996.

Lombard, Peter. *Sententiarum Libri Quatuor.* Paris: Louis Vives, 1892.

Lopez, Juan. "Tractatus vere Catholicus de Matrimonio et Legitimatione." In *Tractatus Universi Iuris*, vol. 9. Venice, 1584.

Lyndwood, William. *Provinciale seu Constitutiones Angliae.* Oxford: H. Hall, 1679.

Lyons, David. "The Correlativity of Rights and Duties." *Nous* 4 (1970): 45-57.

MacDonald, Robert A. "Law and Politics: Alfonso's Program of Political Reform." In *The Worlds of Alfonso the Learned and James the Conqueror: Intellect and Force in the Middle Ages*, edited by Robert I. Burns, pp. 150-202. Princeton, NJ: Princeton University Press, 1985.

Mackin, Theodore. *Divorce and Remarriage.* New York: Paulist Press, 1989.

MacPherson, C. B. *The Political Theory of Possessive Individualism: Hobbes to Locke.* Oxford, UK: Clarendon Press, 1962.

MacSheffrey, Shannon. "'I Will Never Have Ayenst My Fader's Will': Consent and the Making of Marriage in the Late Medieval Diocese of London." In *Women, Marriage, and Family in Medieval Christendom: Essays in Memory of Michael M. Sheehan*, edited by Constance M. Rousseau and Joel T. Rosenthal, pp. 153-174. Kalamazoo, MI: Medieval Institute, 1998.

Madigan, Shawn. *Mystics, Visionaries, and Prophets: A Historical Anthology of Women's Spiritual Writings.* Minneapolis: Fortress Press, 1998.

Maitland, Frederic William. *Roman Canon Law in the Church of England: Six Essays.* New York, NY: Burt Franklin, 1968.

———, ed. *Select Passages from the Works of Bracton and Azo.* London: Selden Society, 1895.

Makowski, Elizabeth M. "The Conjugal Debt and Medieval Canon Law." *Journal of Medieval History* 3 (1977): 99-114.

Malina, Bruce. "Does *Porneia* Mean Fornication?" *Novum Testamentum* 14 (1972): 10-17.

Marcombe, David. *Leper Knights: The Order of St. Lazarus of Jerusalem in England, c. 1150-1544.* Woodbridge, UK: The Boydell Press, 2003.

Maritain, Jacques. *The Angelic Doctor: The Life and Thought of Saint Thomas Aquinas.* Translated by J. F. Scanlan. New York: The Dial Press, 1931.

Marnau, Sister Maximilian. Introduction to "Gertrude of Helfta." In *The Herald of Divine Love,* translated and edited by Margaret Winkworth, pp. 5-44. New York: Paulist Press, 1993.

Marquardt, J. *The Loss of Right to Accuse a Marriage.* Rome: Officium Libri Catholici, 1951.

McCane, Byron R. *Roll Back the Stone: Death and Burial in the World of Jesus.* Harrisburg, PA: Trinity Press, 2003.

McGovern, William M., and Sheldon F. Kurtz. *Wills, Trusts, and Estates.* 2d ed. St. Paul, MN: West Publishing, 2001.

McKnight, Joseph W. "Spanish *Legitim* in the United States: Its Survival and Decline." *American Journal of Comparative Law* 44 (1996): 75-107.

McLaughlin, Terence P., ed. *Summa Parisiensis on the Decretum Gratiani.* Toronto: Pontifical Institute of Medieval Studies, 1952.

McManus, Brendan J. "The Ecclesiology of Laurentius Hispanus (c. 1180-1248) and His Contribution to the Romanization of Canon Law Jurisprudence: With an Edition of the Apparatus Glossarum Laurentii Hispani in Compilationem Tertiam." Diss., Syracuse University, 1991.

Melloni, Alberto. *Innocenzo IV: La concezione e l'esperienza della cristianità come regimen unius personae.* Genoa: Marietti, 1990.

Metz, Rene. "L'enfant dans le droit canonique médiéval. Orientations de recherche." *Recueils de la Société Jean Bodin* 36 (1976): 9-96.

Migne, J.-P. *Patrologiae cursus completus . . . scriptorumque ecclesiasticorum latinorum.* Parisiis: Migne, 1844-1902.

Mill, John Stuart, *On Liberty and Other Essays.* Edited by John Gray. Oxford: Oxford University Press, 1991.

Miller, Fred D. "Legal and Political Rights in Demosthenes and Aristotle." In *Law and Rights in the Ancient Greek Tradition,* edited by George Anagnostopoulos. Berkeley, CA: University of California Press, forthcoming.

————. *Nature, Justice, and Rights in Aristotle's Politics.* Oxford, UK: Clarendon Press, 1995.

Minucius Felix. *Octavius.* Edited by Josefus Martin. Bonn: Petri Hanstein, 1930.

Molina, Luis de. *De Iustitia et Iure.* Mainz: Balthazar Lippius, 1602.

Morris, Colin. *The Discovery of the Individual, 1050-1200.* New York, NY: Harper and Row, 1972.

————. "Individualism in Twelfth-Century Religion: Some Further Reflections." *Journal of Ecclesiastical History* 31 (1980): 195-206.

Moses, Diana C. "Livy's Lucretia and the Validity of Coerced Consent in Roman Law." In *Consent and Coercion to Sex and Marriage in Ancient and Medieval Societies,* edited by Angeliki E. Laiou, pp. 39-81. Washington, D.C.: Dumbarton Oaks Research Library, 1993.

Moulart, F. J. *De Sepultura et Coemeteriis*. Paris: P. Letheeilleux, 1862.

Müller, Wolfgang. "The Recovery of Justinian's Digest in the Middle Ages." *Bulletin of Medieval Canon Law* 29 (1990): 1-29.

Murga, Peter de. *Disquisitiones Morales et Canonicae*. Lyon, 1666.

Murray, Jacqueline. "Individualism and Consensual Marriage: Some Evidence from Medieval England." In *Women, Marriage, and Family in Medieval Christendom: Essays in Memory of Michael M. Sheehan*, edited by Constance M. Rousseau and Joel T. Rosenthal, pp. 121-151. Kalamazoo, MI: Medieval Institute, 1998.

Navarette, Urbano. "De Iure ad vitae communionem: Observationes ad Nova Schema Canonis 1086 sec. 2." *Periodica de re morali, canonica, liturgica* 66 (1977): 249-270.

Naz, R. "Décrétistes." In *Dictionnaire de droit canonique*, vol. 4. Paris: Letouzey et Ané, 1949.

Panormitanus (Niccol de' Tudeschi). *In Qvinqve Decretalivm Epistolarvm Libros, Commentaria, Sev Lectvrae. Lam Olim Andr. Barb., S. Sapi, Ant. Francisci, & Berth. de Bellentzinis & Ailorum Doctissimorum Iurisconsultorum Annotationibus Perquam Vtilibus Illustrata*. Lvgdvni: Sumptibvs Philippi Tinghi, 1578.

Noonan, John T., Jr. *Contraception: A History of Its Treatment by the Catholic Theologians and Canonists*. Enlarged ed. Cambridge, MA: Harvard University Press, 1986.

———. "The Family and the Supreme Court." *Catholic University of America Law Review* 23 (1973): 255-274.

———. "Gratian Slept Here: The Changing Identity of the Father of the Systematic Study of Canon Law." *Traditio* 35 (1979): 145-172.

———. "Marital Affection in the Canonists." *Studia Gratiana* 12 (1967): 481-509.

———. "Novel 22." In *The Bond of Marriage*, edited by William W. Bassett, pp. 41-96. Notre Dame, IN: University of Notre Dame Press, 1968.

———. "Power to Choose." *Viator* 4 (1973): 419-434.

———. *Power to Dissolve: Lawyers and Marriages in the Courts of the Roman Curia*. Cambridge, MA: Harvard University Press, 1972.

———. "The True Paucapalea?" *Proceedings of the Fifth International Congress of Medieval Canon Law* (1980): 157-186.

———. "The Steady Man: Process and Policy in the Courts of the Roman Curia." *California Law Review* 58 (1970): 628-700.

———. "Who Was Rolandus?" In *Law, Church, and Society: Essays in Honor of Stephan Kuttner*, edited by Kenneth Pennington and Robert Somerville, pp. 21-48. Philadelphia: University of Pennsylvania Press, 1977.

Nörr, Knut Wolfgang. "Ehe und Eheschiedung aus der Sicht des Rechtsbegriffs: ein historischer Exkurs." In *Life, Law, and Letters: Historical Studies in Honour of*

Antonio Garcia y Garcia, edited by Peter Linehan, pp. 671-684. Studia Gratiana 29. Rome: LAS, 1998.

Nys, Ernest. "Introduction." *Francisco de Victoria, De Indis et de Iure Belli Relectiones*, pp. 1-100. Washington, DC: The Carnegie Institution, 1917.

O'Callaghan, Joseph F. *The Learned King: The Reign of Alfonso X of Castile*. Philadelphia: University of Pennsylvania Press, 1993.

Odofredus. *Lectura Super Codice*. Bologna: Forni Editore, 1968.

———. *Lectura super Infortiato*. Bologna: Forni, 1968.

———. *Summa super Codice*. Bologna: Forni, 1968.

Olsen, Glenn W. "Progeny, Faithfulness, Sacred Bond: Marriage in the Age of Augustine." In *Christian Marriage: An Historical Study*, edited by Glenn W. Olsen, pp. 101-145. New York: Seabury, 2001.

O'Malley, John W. *Trent and All That: Renaming Catholicism in the Early Modern Era*. Cambridge, MA: Harvard University Press, 2000.

———. "Was Ignatius of Loyola a Church Reformer? How to Look at Early Modern Catholicism." *Catholic Historical Review* 77 (1991): 177-193.

Origo, Iris. "The Domestic Enemy: The Eastern Slaves in Tuscany in the Fourteenth and Fifteenth Centuries." *Speculum* 30 (1955): 321-366.

Orme, Nicholas. *Medieval Children*. New Haven, CT: Yale University Press, 2001.

Osiek, Carolyn. *Shepherd of Hermas: A Commentary*. Minneapolis, MN: Fortress Press, 1999.

Otis-Cour, Leah. "'Gratian's Revenge': Le mariage dans les 'romans de couple' médiévaux." In *Excerptiones iuris: Studies in Honor of André Gouron*, edited by Bertrand Durand and Laurent Mayali, pp. 469-482. Berkeley, CA: The Robbins Collection, 2000.

Outhwaite, R. B. *Clandestine Marriage in England: 1500-1800*. London: Hambledon Press, 1995.

Ozment, Steven. *When Fathers Ruled: Family Life in Reformation Europe*. Cambridge, MA: Harvard University Press, 1983.

Pakter, Walter. *Medieval Canon Law and the Jews*. Ebelsbach: Verlag Rolf Gremer, 1988.

Parisse, Michel. "Des veuves au monastère." In *Veuves et veuvage dans le Haut Moyen Âge*, edited by Michel Parisse, pp. 255-274. Paris: Picard, 1993.

Park, Katherine. "Medicine and Society in Medieval Europe, 500-1500." In *Medicine in Society: Historical Essays*, edited by Andrew Wear, pp. 59-90. Cambridge, UK: Cambridge University Press, 1992.

Patterson, Cynthia. "'Not Worth the Rearing': The Causes of Infant Exposure in Ancient Greece." *Transactions of the American Philological Association* 115 (1985): 103-123.

Paucapalea. *Summa über das Decretum Gratiani*, edited by Johann Friedrich von Schulte. Aalen: Scientia Verlag, 1965.

Paulus, Christoph G. "Changes in the Power Structure Within the Family in the Late Roman Republic." *Chicago-Kent Law Review* 70 (1995): 1503-1513.

Paxton, Frederick. *Christianizing Death: The Creation of a Ritual Process in Early Medieval Europe.* Ithaca, NY: Cornell University Press, 1990.

Payer, Pierre J. *The Bridling of Desire: Views of Sex in the Later Middle Ages.* Toronto: University of Toronto Press, 1993.

Pennington, Kenneth. "Henricus de Segusio (Hostiensis)." In *Popes, Canonists, and Texts, 1150-1550,* ch. 16, pp. 1-12. Aldershot, UK: Variorum, 1993.

———. "Pope Innocent III's Views on Church and State: A Gloss to *Per venerabilem.*" In *Law, Church, and Society: Essays in Honor of Stephan Kuttner,* edited by Kenneth Pennington and Robert Somerville, pp. 49-67. Philadelphia: University of Pennsylvania Press, 1977.

———. *The Prince and the Law, 1200-1600: Sovereignty and Rights in the Western Legal Tradition.* Berkeley, CA: University of California Press, 1993.

Peter of Blois. *Speculum Iuris Canonici,* edited by T. A. Reimarus. Berlin: G. Reimeri, 1837.

Philippe le Chancelier. *Summa de Bono,* edited by Nikolaus Wicki. Bern: Editiones Francke, 1985.

Phillips, William D. *Slavery from Roman Times to the Early Transatlantic Trade.* Minneapolis: University of Minnesota Press, 1985.

Pierre, Teresa Olsen. "Marriage, Body, and Sacrament in the Age of Hugh of St. Victor." In *Christian Marriage: A Historical Study,* edited by Glenn Olsen, pp. 213-268. New York: Crossroad, 2001.

Placentinus. *Placentini Summa Codicis: Accessit Proemium Quod in Moguntina Editioine Desiderabatur.* Turin: Bottega D'Erasmo, 1962.

———. *Summa Institutionum.* Turin: Ex Officina Erasmiana, 1973.

Pollock, Frederick, and F. W. Maitland. *The History of English Law Before the Time of Edward I.* 2d ed. Cambridge, UK: Cambridge University Press, 1968.

Popcak, Gregory K. *For Better . . . Forever! A Catholic Guide to Lifelong Marriage.* Huntington, IN: Our Sunday Visitor, 1999.

Popik, Kristin Mary. *The Philosophy of Woman of St. Thomas Aquinas.* Rome: Extract from Faith and Reason, 1978.

Powicke, F. M. *King Henry III and the Lord Edward: The Community of the Realm in the Thirteenth Century.* Oxford: Clarendon Press, 1947.

Radin, Max. "The Exposure of Infants in Roman Law and Practice." *Classical Journal* 20 (1925): 337-343.

Ranft, Patricia. *Women and Spiritual Equality in Christian Tradition.* New York : St. Martin's Press, 1998.

Rawls, John. *A Theory of Justice.* Cambridge, MA: Harvard University Press, 1971.

Rawson, Beryl. "Adult-Child Relationships in Roman Society." In *Marriage, Divorce, and Children in Ancient Rome,* edited by Beryl Rawson, pp. 7-30. Oxford: Clarendon Press, 1991.

————. "Roman Concubinage and Other De Facto Marriages." *Transactions of the American Philological Association* 104 (1974): 279-305.

Raymond of Peñafort. *[Opera]*. Universa Bibliotheca Iuris 1. Roma: Commentarium Pro Religiosis, 1975-1978.

Reid, Charles J., Jr. "The Augustinian Goods of Marriage: The Disappearing Cornerstone of the American Law of Marriage." *BYU Journal of Public Law* 18 (2004): 449-478.

————. "The Canonistic Contribution to the Western Rights Tradition: An Historical Inquiry." *Boston College Law Review* 33 (1991): 37-92.

————. "The Medieval Origins of the Western Natural Rights Tradition: The Achievement of Brian Tierney." *Cornell Law Review* 83 (1998): 437-463.

————. "Rights in Thirteenth-Century Canon Law: An Historical Investigation." Diss., Cornell University, 1995.

————. "'So It Will Be Found That the Right of Women in Many Cases Is of Diminished Condition': Rights and the Legal Equality of Men and Women in Twelfth- and Thirteenth-Century Canon Law." *Loyola (Los Angeles) Law Review* 35 (2002): 471-512.

————. "Thirteenth-Century Canon Law and Rights: The Word *ius* and Its Range of Subjective Meanings." *Studia Canonica* 30 (1996): 295-342.

Renier, E. *Étude sur l'histoire de la Querela Inofficiosi en droit romain.* Liége: Vaillant-Carmanne, 1942.

Rerum Novarum. In *Two Basic Social Encyclicals on the Condition of Workers,* pp. 2-81. Washington, D.C.: The Catholic University of America Press, 1943.

Reynolds, Philip Lyndon. *Marriage in the Western Church: The Christianization of Marriage During the Patristic and Early Medieval Periods.* Leiden: E. J. Brill, 1994.

Ricardus Pisanus. *Lo Codi.* Edited by Hermann Fitting. Aalen: Scientia Verlag, 1968.

Richards, Peter. *The Medieval Leper and His Northern Heirs.* Cambridge, UK: D. S. Brewer, 1977.

Riesenberg, Peter. *Citizenship in the Western Tradition: Plato to Rousseau.* Citizenship in the Medieval Italian City. Chapel Hill, NC: University of North Carolina Press, 1992.

Roensch, Frederick J. *Early Thomistic School.* Dubuque, IA: Priory Press, 1964.

Roman, J., ed. "Summa d'Huguccio sur le Décret de Gratien." *Nouvelle revue historique de droit français et étranger* 27 (1903): 745-805.

Roumy, Franck. *L'Adoption dans le droit savant du xiie au xvie siècle.* Paris: L.G.D.J., 1998.

Rousseau, Constance M. "Innocent III, Defender of the Innocents and the Law: Children and Papal Policy (1198-1216)." *Archivum Historiae Pontificiae* 32 (1994): 31-42.

Rufinus. *Summa Decretorum.* Edited by Heinrich Singer. Aalen: Scientia Verlag, 1963.

Rush, Alfred C. *Death and Burial in Christian Antiquity.* Washington, DC: The Catholic University of America Press, 1941.

Ryan, John Joseph. *Saint Peter Damian and His Canonical Sources: A Preliminary Study in the Antecedents of the Gregorian Reform.* Toronto: Pontifical Institute for Mediaeval Studies, 1956.

"Sacrae Romanae Rotae Decisiones, coram Serrano, May 9, 1980." *Studia Canonica* 15 (1981): 285-309.

Saller, Richard. "Corporal Punishment, Authority, and Obedience in the Roman Household." In *Marriage, Divorce, and Children in Ancient Rome*, edited by Beryl Rawson, pp. 144-165. New York: Oxford University Press, 1991.

―――. "*Familia, Domus*, and the Roman Concept of the Family." *Phoenix* 38 (1984): 336-355.

―――. "Men's Age at Marriage and Its Consequences in the Roman Family." *Classical Philology* 82 (1987): 21-34.

―――. "*Patria Potestas* and the Stereotype of the Roman Family," *Continuity and Change* 1 (1986): 7-22.

―――. "Pietas, Obligation, and Authority in the Roman Family." In *Alte Geschichte und Wissenschaftsgeschichte. Festschrift für Karl Christ zum 65. Geburtstag*, edited by Peter Kneissl and Volker Losemann, pp. 393-410. Darmstadt: Wissenschaftliche Buchgesellschaft, 1988.

―――. "The Social Dynamics of Consent to Marriage and Sexual Relations: The Evidence of Roman Comedies." In *Consent and Coercion to Sex and Marriage in Ancient and Medieval Societies*, edited by Angeliki E. Laiou, pp. 83-104. Washington, D.C.: Dumbarton Oaks Research Library, 1993.

Salvian. "Timothei ad Ecclesiam libri IV." In *Oeuvres*. Sources chrétiennes, 176. Paris: Les Éditions du Cerf, 1971-1975.

Sánchez, Tomás. *De Sancto Matrimonii Sacramento Disputationum Tomi Tres.* Lyon: Sumptibus societatis typographorum, 1637.

Schouler, James. *A Treatise on the Law of Marriage, Divorce, Separation, and Domestic Relations.* 6th ed. Albany, NY: Matthew Bender & Company, 1921.

Schultz, James A. *The Knowledge of Childhood in the German Middle Ages: 1100-1350.* Philadelphia: University of Pennsylvania Press, 1995.

Sereno, David. *Whether the Norm Expressed in Canon 1103 Is of Natural Law or of Positive Church Law.* Rome: Editrice Pontificia Università Gregoriana, 1997.

Serrano Ruiz, Jose Maria. "Le droit à la communauté de vie et d'amour conjugal comme objet de consentement matrimonial." *Studia Canonica* 10 (1976): 271-301.

Shahar, Shulamith. *Childhood in the Middle Ages.* Translated by Chaya Galai. London: Routledge, 1990.

Sheehan, Michael M. "Choice of Marriage Partner in the Middle Ages: Development and Theory of Marriage." In Michael M. Sheehan's *Marriage, Family, and Law* in *Medieval Europe: Collected Studies*, edited by James K. Farge, pp. 87-117. Toronto: University of Toronto Press, 1996.

———. "Theory and Practice: Marriage of the Unfree and Poor in Medieval Society." *Mediaeval Studies* 50 (1988): 457-487.

———. *The Will in Medieval England: From the Conversion of the Anglo-Saxons to the End of the Thirteenth Century*. Toronto: Pontifical Institute of Mediaeval Studies, 1963.

Siegel, Stephen A. "Joel Bishop's Orthodoxy." *Law and History Review* 13 (1995): 215-259.

Las Siete Partidas del Rey don Alfonso el Sabio. 3 vols. Madrid: Real Academia de la Historia, 1807.

Sikes, J. G., ed. "Hervaeus Natalis: De Paupertate Christi et Apostolorum." *Archives d'histoire doctrinale et littéraire du moyen âge* 12-13 (1937/1938): 209-297.

Simpson, A. W. B. *A History of the Land Law*. 2d ed. Oxford: Clarendon Press, 1986.

Smith, J. A. Clarence. *Medieval Law Teachers and Writers*. Ottawa: University of Ottawa Press, 1975.

Soto, Domingo de. *De Justitia et Jure libri decem*. Venice, 1589.

Statuts d'Hotels-Dieu et de léproseries. Paris: Alphonse Picard et fils, 1901.

Stegemann, Ekkehard W., and Wolfgang Stegemann. *The Jesus Movement: A Social History of the First Century*. Edited by O. C. Dean, Jr. Minneapolis, MN: Fortress Press, 1999.

Stein, Peter. *Roman Law in European History*. Cambridge, UK: Cambridge University Press, 1999.

Stephen of Tournai. *Die Summa über das Decretum Gratiani*. Aalen: Scientia Verlag, 1965.

Story, Joseph. *Commentaries on the Conflicts of Law*. Boston, MA: Hilliard, Gray, and Company, 1834.

Strauss, Leo. *Natural Right and History*. Chicago, IL: University of Chicago Press, 1953.

Swabey, Ffiona. *Medieval Gentlewoman: Life in a Gentry Household in the Later Middle Ages*. New York: Routledge, 1999.

Symmachus. *Q. Aurelii Symmachi Quae Supersunt*, edited by Otto Seeck. *Monumenta Germaniae Historica, Auctorum Antiquissimorum*, vol. 6. Berlin: Weidmanns, 1883.

Talbot, C. H. *The Life of Christina of Markyate: A Twelfth Century Recluse*. Toronto: University of Toronto Press, 1998.

Tancred. *Ordo Iudiciarius*. In *Pilius, Tancredus, Gratia, Libri De Iudiciorum Ordine*, edited by Friedrich Christian Bergmann. Aalen: Scientia Verlag, 1965.

———. *Tancredi Summa de Matrimonio*. Edited by Agathon Wunderlich. Gottingae: Apud Vandenhoeck et Ruprecht, 1841.

Tertullian. "Ad Uxorem." In *Sources Chretiennes*, no. 273, pp. 92-151. Paris: Les Éditions du Cerf, 1980.

Thaner, Friedrich, ed. *Summa Magistri Rolandi*. Aalen: Scientia Verlag, 1962.

Thomas Aquinas. *Summa Theologiae*. Alba (& Roma): Editiones Paulinae, [1962].

Thurston, Bonnie Bowman. *The Widows: A Women's Ministry in the Early Church*. Minneapolis: Fortress Press, 1989.

Tierney, Brian. *The Idea of Natural Rights: Studies on Natural Rights, Natural Law, and Church Law, 1150-1625*. Atlanta, GA: Scholars Press, 1997.

——. "*Ius* and Metonymy in Rufinus." In *Studia in Honorem Eminentissimi Cardinalis Alphonsi Stickler*, edited by Rosalio Castillo Lara, ed., pp. 549-558. Rome: LAS, 1992.

——. "Origins of Natural Rights Language: Texts and Contexts, 1150-1250." *History of Political Thought* 10 (1989): 615-646.

——. "*Tria quippe distinguit iudicia:* A Note on Innocent III's *Per venerabilem.*" *Speculum* 37 (1962): 48-59.

——. "Villey, Ockham, and the Origin of Individual Rights." In *The Weightier Matters of the Law: Essays on Law and Religion (A Tribute to Harold J. Berman)*, edited by John Witte, Jr. and Frank S. Alexander, pp. 1-31. Atlanta, GA: Scholars Press, 1988.

Tondini, Amleto. *De Ecclesia Funerante ad Normam Novi Codicis*. Forli: Valbonesi, 1927.

Touati, François-Olivier. *Maladie et société au Moyen âge. La lèpre, les lèpreux, et les lèprosaries dans la province ecclésiastique de Sens jusqu'a milieu du XIV siècle*. Brussels: De Boeck Université, 1998.

Treggiari, Susan. *Roman Marriage: Iusti Coniuges from the Time of Cicero to the Time of Ulpian*. Oxford: Clarendon Press, 1991.

Turlan, Juliette. "Recherches sur le mariage dans la pratique coutumière, xii-xiv siècles." *Revue d'histoire de droit français et étranger* 35 (1957): 477-528.

Valdes, Rodolfo, and Maria Valdes. "The Christian Family at the Service of Reconciliation." In *The Pontifical Council for the Family: Marriage and Family*, pp. 165-172. San Francisco, CA: Ignatius Press, 1989.

Van Engen, John. "From Practical Theology to Divine Law: The Work and Mind of Medieval Canonists." In *Proceedings of the Ninth International Congress of Medieval Canon Law*, pp. 873-896. Vatican City: Biblioteca Apostolica Vaticana, 1997.

Viejo-Ximenez, Jose M. "'Concordia' y 'Decretum' del maestro Graciano." *Ius Canonicum* 39 (1999): 333-347.

——. "La Redacción Original de C. 29 Del Decreto de Graciano." *Ius Ecclesiae* 10 (1998): 148-185.

Villey, Michel. "Du sens de l'expression jus in re en droit romain classique." *Revue internationale des droits d'antiquité (Fernand de Visscher II)* 3 (1949): 417-436.

——. *Le Droit et les droits de l'homme*. Paris: Presses universitaires de France, 1983.

Vinogradoff, Paul. *Villainage in England: Essays in English Medieval History.* London: Oxford University Press, 1927.

Wagenvoort, Hendrik. *Pietas: Selected Studies in Roman Religion.* Leiden: E. J. Brill, 1980.

Wasserschleben, F. W. H., ed. "Canones Gregorii." In *Die Bussordnungen der abendländischen Kirche,* pp. 160-180. Halle: Verlag von Ch. Graeger, 1851.

———, ed. *Die Irische Kanonensammlung.* Leipzig: Bernhard Tauchnitz, 1885.

Watson, Alan. *The Law of Succession in the Later Roman Republic.* Oxford: Clarendon Press, 1971.

Watt, John A. *The Theory of Papal Monarchy in the Thirteenth Century: The Contribution of the Canonists.* London: Burns and Oates, 1965.

Weber, Edouard-Henri. *La personne humaine au XIIe siècle: L'avènement chez mâitres parisiens de l'acception moderne de l'homme.* Paris: J. Vrin, 1991.

Weigand, Rudolf. "Chancen und Probleme einer baldigen kritischen Edition der ersten Redaktions de Dekrets Gratians." *Bulletin of Medieval Canon Law* 22 (1998): 53-75.

———. "Magister Rolandus und Papst Alexander III." *Archiv für katholisches Kirchenrecht* 149 (1980): 3-44.

———. *Die Naturrechtslehre der Legisten und Dekretisten von Irnerius bis Accursius und von Gratian bis Johannes Teutonicus.* Munich: Max Hueber Verlag, 1967.

———. "Paucapale und die frühe Kanonistik." *Archiv für Katholisches Kirchenrecht* 150 (1981): 137-157.

Weitzman, Lenore J. *The Marriage Contract: Spouses, Lovers, and the Law.* New York: The Free Press, 1981.

Wemple, Suzanne Fonay. *Women in Frankish Society: Marriage and the Cloister, 500-900.* Philadelphia, PA: University of Pennsylvania Press, 1981.

Wentersdorf, Karl P. "The Clandestine Marriages of the Fair Maid of Kent." *Journal of Medieval History* 5 (1979): 203-231.

Werner, Marina. *Alone of All Her Sex: The Myth and the Cult of the Virgin Mary.* New York: Knopf, 1976.

Wernz, F. X., and P. Vidal. "Ius Matrimoniale." In *Ius Canonicum,* vol. 5. Rome: Gregorianum, 1925.

White, Patricia. *Beyond Domination: An Essay in the Political Philosophy of Education.* London: Routledge & Kegan Paul, 1983.

Whitelock, Dorothy, ed. *Anglo-Saxon Wills.* Holmes Beach, FL: William W. Gaunt and Sons, 1986.

Wickham, Chris. "Fama and the Law in Twelfth-Century Tuscany." In *Fama: The Politics of Talk and Reputation in Medieval Europe,* edited by Thelma Fenster and Daniel Lord Smail. Ithaca, NY: Cornell University Press, 2003.

William of Auxerre. *Summa Aurea,* edited by Jean Ribaillier. Paris: Centre National de la Recherche Scientifique, 1985.

Wilson, Stephen. *The Magical Universe: Everyday Ritual in Pre-Modern Europe.* London: Hambledon Press, 2000.

Winroth, Anders. *The Making of Gratian's Decretum.* Cambridge: Cambridge University Press, 2000.

———. "Le manuscrit florentin du Décret de Gratien." *Revue de droit canonique* 51 (2001): 211-231.

Witte, John, Jr. *From Sacrament to Contract: Marriage, Religion, and Law in the Western Tradition.* Louisville, KY: John Knox Press, 1997.

———. *Law and Protestantism: The Legal Teachings of the Lutheran Reformation.* Cambridge: Cambridge University Press, 2002.

———. "The Reformation of Marriage Law in Martin Luther's Germany: Its Significance Then and Now." *Journal of Law and Religion* 4 (1986): 293-351.

Wogan-Browne, Joceyln. *Saints' Lives and Women's Literary Culture: Virginity and Its Authorizations.* Oxford: Oxford University Press, 2001.

Woodbine, George E., ed. *Bracton De Legibus et Consuetudinibus Angliae.* Translated and revised by Samuel E. Thorne. Cambridge, MA: Harvard University Press, 1968.

Yaron, Reuven. *"Vitae Necisque Potestas." Tijdschrift voor Rechtsgeschiedenis* 30 (1962): 243-251.

Younger, Judith T. "Responsible Parents and Good Children." *Journal of Law and Inequality* 14 (1996): 489-520.

Zeumer, K., ed. *"Leges Visigothorum."* In *Monumenta Germaniae Historica, Leges Nationum Germanicarum,* vol. 1. Hanover: Hahn, 1902.

Appendix: Table of Cases

Abel v. Dickinson, 250 Ark. 648, 467 S.W.2d 154 (1971), 153, 277 n5

Baehr v. Lewin, 852 P.2d 44 (1993), 2, 215 n4

Bedal v. Johnson, 37 Idaho 359, 218 P.2d 641 (1923), 153, 276 n2

Biggs v. State, 29 Ga. 723 (1860), 10, 219 n69

Browning v. Jones, 52 Ill. 597 (1894), 10, 219 n64

Campbell's Administrators and Heirs v. Gullatt, 43 Ala. 57 (1869), 8-9, 218 n55

Davis v. Beason, 133 U.S. 333 (1890), 8, 218 n51

Deane v. Aveling, 1 Robertson's Eccl. Rep. 279 (1845), 9, 219 n59

Ditson v. Ditson, 4 R.I. 87 (1856), 10, 219 n62

Eisenstadt v. Baird, 405 U.S. 438 (1972), 1-2, 215 n2

Foot v. Card, 58 Conn. 1, 18 A. 1027 (1889), 10, 219 n67

Gussin v. Gussin, 73 Haw. 470, 836 P.2d 484 (1992), 215 n4

Hallett v. Collins, 51 U.S. 174 (1850), 66, 239 n355

Hamilton v. Morgan, 93 Fla. 311, 112 So. 80 (1927), 153, 277 n5

Hardin v. Hardin, 17 Ala. 250 (1850), 10, 219 nn65-66

Henningsen v. Bloomfield Motors, 161 A.2d 69 (N.J., 1960), 14, 221 n88

Hodel v. Irving, 481 U.S. 704 (1987), 153, 276 n3

Hunt v. Hayes, 64 Vt. 89, 23 A. 920 (1892), 10, 219 n68

In re Bruce R. 234 Conn. 194, 662 A.2d 107 (1995), 11, 219 n74

Irving Trust Company v. Day, 314 U.S. 556 (1942), 153, 276 n3

Lewis v. Lewis, 174 Cal. 336 (1917), 11, 220 n75

Lewis v. Tapman, 90 Md. 294, 45 A. 459 (1900), 8, 218 nn53-54

Loving v. Virginia, 388 U.S. 1 (1967), 29, 226 nn29-31

Maynard v. Hill, 125 U.S. 190 (1888), 8, 218 n52

Miranda v. Arizona, 384 U.S. 436 (1966), 14, 221 n88

Index

abandoned children, 74, 86, 187-88, 289n.300, 290n.333

abductions in marriage formation, 35, 41

Abelard, Peter, 129-30, 267n.255

abortion, 215n.2, 242n.38

abusive marriage, 149

Accursius, 15, 17, 86, 178

Ackerman, Bruce, 2

Adam and Eve, 75, 79-80, 100, 102, 127, 245n.91, 275n.474

Adiecta, 170

ad majorem cautelam, 52

adoption: abandoned children, 289n.300, 290n.333; adrogatio, 180-82, 189, 195; daughters, 288n.268; grandchildren, 288n.271; in high society, 186, 288n.283; inheritance rights, 179-95, 292n.391; marriage impediment, 140, 188-89; murder, 184-85; right to adopt, 181; simple, 180-82, 195

adultery, 135-38, 142-45, 147, 201, 234n.247, 273n.405

Aeneas, 167

Alabama Supreme Court, 8-9

Albericus de Rosate, 284n.180

Albert the Great, 79

Alexander III, Pope: abusive marriages, 149; adultery, 261n.143; coerced marriages, 45; consent to marriage, 49; consummation of marriage, 112; decretals, 14; illegitimate children, 203; leprosy, 49, 119-20; marital freedom, 45-46; steady man test, 45-46

Alexander of Hales, 113, 260n.123, 263n.183

Alexander VI, Pope, 65

Alexandre-Bidon, Danièle, 82

Alfonso, the Learned, King, 179, 210

Alfonso X, King, 175-76

Alfonso XI, King, 286n.211

alienation of marital affection, 10, 219n.67

Alterocha, 170

Amandus, 33

Ambrose, Saint: divorce, 136-37; equality of the sexes, 75; infidel marriage, 107; remarriage, 142; women, 51, 78

Ambrosiaster. *See* Isaac (first Latin commentator on Paul)

Anchises, 167

Andreae, Johannes: background, 16; burial sites, 134; exposure of children, 86; legitimation of children, 207-8; marital abuse, 149; right to inherit, 173

Anne, Saint, 101

annulment of marriage, 140-43

Anthemius, Emperor, 198

anti-miscegenation, 29

Antoninus Pius, 83

- 325 -

Celsus, 32

Champlin, Edward, 283n.153

chastity, 104-5, 111

Childebert, 186

children: abuse, 5; accidental death, 248n.175; blindness, 49-50; concubines, 195-204; discipline, 92-93, 251n.217; education, 2, 5, 87, 216n.10; exposure, 70-71, 73-74, 85-86, 183-85, 240n.9, 248n.175; free will, 95; illegitimacy, 83-85, 195-208, 246n.135, 281n.115; inheritance rights, 154, 165-208, 277n.4, 282n.140, 284n.180, 296n.502; rights, 90-92; right to make a will, 155-56; safety, 87; selling of, 71, 96; spiritual, 189, 296n.502; support, 11, 82-85, 89, 93, 246n.133, 246n.135; vows, 94-95

children's literature, 83

children's rights. *See* children — rights

child support. *See* children — support

Chloe, 100

Chobham, Thomas, 57-58, 235n.269

Christina of Markyate, 25-28

Cicero, 167, 288n.283

Cino da Pistoia, 192

citizenship, Roman. *See* Roman law — citizenship

civilians, 80-82

civil right, 81

clandestine marriage, 50-55, 58-64, 66, 202, 231n.173, 234n.247, 238n.339

Claudius, 288n.283

Cleaver, Robert, 276n.474

Clemens, Terentius, 32

Clement III, Pope, 92

Clement of Alexandria, 73

Clement VI, Pope, 62

Clera, 170

Cley, John, 59

coercion to marry: betrothals, 45-46; case studies, 59-63; consummation, 260n.119; evidence, 43; financial, 46; generally, 55-56, 118, 226n.32, 229n.129, 231n.173, 235n.257,

240n.369; invalidation of marriage, 67-68; Visigothic law, 35. *See also* consent to marriage

common-law marriage, 66

community formation role, 3, 5

community of life, 7

concubinage, 195-204

conjugal debt: adultery, 261n.143; desertion, 10; duty, 6-7, 255n.37; equality of the sexes, 99-102; feudal authority, 122-26; leprosy, 119-22, 263n.183; renunciation, 106, 117-19; right to claim, 218n.39, 259n.97; Roman law, 11-12; vows of continence, 256n.52, 257n.62; women, 103-4, 106

consanguinity, 140-41, 145

consent to marriage: daughters, 31, 40; guardians, 31-32; parents, 29-43, 50, 64-66, 229n.137, 231n.173, 238n.326; by the parties involved, 28-29, 39-40, 42-43; sons, 31-32, 40; women, 55-58. *See also* coercion to marry

consortium omnis vitae, 7, 218n.46

Constantine I, Emperor: concubinage, 197-98; divorce, 138; exposure of children, 74; inheritance, 168; soldiers, 34

consuetudo vitae, 6

consummation of marriage, 110-15, 140, 260n.119

contraception, 215n.2

coram Serrano, 7

Corbett, Percy, 135

corporal punishment. *See* children — discipline

Council of Elvira, 40, 143

Council of Gangra, 84

Council of Toledo (1st), 197, 200

Council of Toledo (4th), 187, 201

Council of Toledo (10th), 95

Council of Trent, 65-66, 239n.344, 239n.349

Council of Tribur, 95, 131, 161

Council of Vaisons, 184-85

daughters, 166, 176, 288n.268